The Causes of War
and the
Consequences of Peacekeeping
in Africa

Edited by Ricardo René Laremont

Foreword by Ali A. Mazrui

HEINEMANN
PORTSMOUTH, NH

Heinemann
A division of Reed Elsevier Inc.
361 Hanover Street
Portsmouth, NH 03801–3912
www.heinemann.com

ISBN 0–325–07062–8 (Heinemann cloth)
ISBN 0–325–07061–X (Heinemann paper)

Library of Congress Cataloging-in-Publication Data

The causes of war and the consequences of peacekeeping in Africa / [edited by] Ricardo René Laremont ; foreword by Ali A. Mazrui.
    p. cm.
    Includes bibliographical references and index.
    ISBN 0–325–07062–8 (alk. paper)—ISBN 0–325–07061–X (pbk. : alk.paper)
    1. Africa—Politics and government—1960– 2. Low-intensity conflicts (Military science)—Africa—Prevention. 3. Peacekeeping forces—Africa. 4. Democratization—Africa. 5. Democracy—Africa. I. Laremont, Ricardo René.
DT30.5.C38   2002
341.5'84—dc21   2001039190

British Library Cataloguing in Publication Data is available.

Printed in the United States of America on acid-free paper.

05 04 03 02 01 SB 1 2 3 4 5 6 7 8 9

Copyright Acknowledgments

The editor and publisher gratefully acknowledge permission to use the following material:

"Mozambique: What Nexus among Peacemaking, Peacekeeping, and Development?" by João Honwana, based on The Instituto de Estudos Estrategicos e Internacionais (IEEI) Lumiar Paper no. 7, "The UN and Mozambique: A Sustainable Peace?" December 1996.

To

Li Shen Yun

Contents

III. POLITICAL ISSUES

List of Tables

Foreword

Ali A. Mazrui

Most studies of regional peacekeeping and peacemaking view them simply as alternatives to international peacekeeping or peacemaking. The pursuit of Africa's peace by Africans themselves, however, is not just an extension of international peacekeeping, but rather is a process of *Pax Africana*. As such, the implications of this process extend well beyond international politics, but to domestic politics as well. To this end, two questions must be addressed. First, to what extent does participation of African countries in peacekeeping in their region contribute to national demilitarization domestically? Second, to what extent is such regional peacemaking a contribution to the regional and national development of countries involved? This book is partly about areas of intersection between development, pacification, and democratization.

When the old colonial order ended, one question arose: Who was going to keep the peace? That question has had four answers at various times. For awhile, the answer was still, "The old colonial master will keep the peace when the chips are down." Such was the case in 1964 when troops mutinied, in separate incidents, in Tanganyika, Kenya, and Uganda. The postcolonial governments of all three countries invited the British troops back to disarm their soldiers and to restore order. British weapons (but not British troops) also were called in to help end the Biafran civil war in Nigeria (1967–1970). In other examples, the French have repeatedly intervened to restore order or to change governments in their former colonies, as well as in Belgium's former colonial possessions.

A second answer to the question "Who will keep the peace?" came from the United Nations (UN). The UN made efforts in peacekeeping and peacemaking in several of Africa's extended conflicts. In the Congo during 1960–1961, the United Nations intervened in an attempt to stabilize the country and to support the fledgling government of Patrice Lumumba. The UN has also played varying roles in trying to quell unrest and civil war in Mozambique, Angola, and Liberia. Thirty years after its failed intervention in the Congo, the UN Secretary-General Boutrous Boutrous-Ghali sent peacekeeping troops into Somalia in order to alleviate civil war induced famine. That mission also failed to quell the unrest and eventually led to a pullout of UN troops and US troops to the embarrassment of the leading country in that peacekeeping contingent, the United States.

The Somalia operation itself was representative of the third answer to the question of who will keep the peace in Africa—the United States. The United States' involvement in peacekeeping has been sporadic over the post–World War Two period, though in recent years, its activity has increased dramatically since the collapse of the Cold War. United States international peacekeeping and peacemaking—*Pax Americana*—played an influential role in ending the rule of Mengistu Haile Mariam in Ethiopia and the creation of the new Eritrea of the 1990s. It has also more recently attempted some peacemaking in the war between Eritrea and Ethiopia. Under the leadership of former Assistant Secretary of State Chester Crocker, the United States also was influential in gaining independence for Namibia using a strategy of "constructive engagement" with South Africa.

Attempts by all three of these parties, the former colonial powers, the United Nations, and the United States, all met with little to moderate success. The collapse of the Cold War also meant that few had any interest in becoming involved in the internal affairs of Africa; the battle lines were no longer drawn along old ideological divisions. Africans themselves began to deal with questions of peacekeeping and peacemaking through a variety of methods, including

- enforced regional integration;
- international vigilantism;
- regional force or acting on behalf of regional organizations;
- transnational ethnic solidarity; and
- various rapid-deployment forces.

ENFORCED REGIONAL INTEGRATION

When I started the debate about inter-African colonization early in the 1990s, few people took me seriously. In 1994, while Africa was still in its downward spiral, which led to the successive collapse of several states, I suggested that a once-unthinkable solution be attempted: recolonization. The system of colonization, of course, would look much different than it did under the Europeans. One option that I had proposed was that a truly international trusteeship system—like that of the United Nations over the Congo in 1960—could be established. Administration of the trusteeship would be done by Africans or Asians, as well as from the rest of the United Nations membership. The other option I proposed was recolonization of weaker African states by stronger ones for benevolent reasons. Critics internationally have argued that my thesis was either evil or unreal, the most outspoken of them being Archie Mafeje of the American University, Cairo.

Although the idea was new, the practice was not. The union of Tanganyika and revolutionary Zanzibar was a prime example of de facto inter-African colonization. At the time of the Hutu-Tutsi conflict in Rwanda, I had proposed a federation of Rwanda and Burundi with Tanzania to solved the Hutu-Tutsi divide. By the second half of the decade it was evident that history was indeed turning in my direction. Africans were beginning to assert control over their unruly neighbors, though sometimes bungling the worthy mission, and sometimes getting in each other's way.

INTERNATIONAL VIGILANTISM

International vigilantism occurs when one country occupies another to restore and maintain order. In 1971, Idi Amin Dada overthrew the government of Milton Obote of Uganda. One of those most deeply shattered by the event was President Julius K. Nyerere of Tanzania. He roundly condemned the coup, and personally refused to have any dealings with Idi Amin Dada. But was anybody prepared to use force to try and reverse the coup? At that time not even Nyerere was. *Pax Africana* was indeed sensitive, but not yet forceful.

Eight years later Julius Nyerere was indeed prepared to use force against Idi Amin's persistent national and regional destabilization. In 1979, after Idi Amin's Ugandan forces invaded Tanzania, Nyerere was at last ready to order Tanzania's army to march all the way to Kampala to overthrow Idi Amin. Nyerere was successful in ousting the Ugandan dictator and in establishing a temporary Tanzanian protectorate in Uganda before multiparty elections could be held. Nyerere made two mistakes in his protectorate over Uganda. He made his *Pax Africana* too brief, and he tried too hard to ensure the return of Milton Obote to power. Both decisions were catastrophic for Uganda. The interlude of *Pax Africana* was good but not well focused. The second Obote administration in Uganda turned out to be a tragedy, only to be ended by Yoweri Museveni's triumph in 1986. By 1999 Julius K. Nyerere was asking in a speech in Abuja, Nigeria, that no delegation be recognized at the Organization of African Unity (OAU) if it represented a new military coup. This recommendation was accepted by the OAU at its summit meeting in Algiers later that year.

REGIONAL FORCE

Regional forces have been a relatively new phenomenon in Africa. A different kind of successful *Pax Africana* is the story of Liberia and the role of ECOMOG (Economic Community Monitoring Group) in ending its civil war and leading Liberia towards a relatively peaceful election in July 1997. Once again, this was a case of neighboring African countries's accepting responsibility for a malfunctioning brotherly state, and going into the weaker state to attempt a solution.

ECOMOG's lack of experience, along with disarray in Lagos, initially resulted in many disastrous false starts in peacekeeping in Liberia. But in the end, the mission was relatively successful, and Liberians had their say at the ballot box. While the overwhelming choice of Charles Taylor (the architect of the civil war) by Liberians puzzled many observers, it was a free and democratic choice. Behind the choice was the fumbling but historic role of ECOMOG in pioneering *Pax Africana*.

TRANSNATIONAL ETHNIC SOLIDARITIES

The most dramatic of these transethnic events was Uganda's role in helping the Tutsi to reassert control over Rwanda in 1994. This was a kind of "Bay of Pigs" operation, African style. More than thirty years after the original 1961 Bay of Pigs operation, exiled Rwandans, trained in Uganda, invaded Rwanda in order to overthrow the Hutu regime there and end the genocide against the Tutsi. The aim of the Rwanda Patriotic Front from Uganda was not counter-genocide but conquest and control. This particular "Bay of Pigs" operation—African style—was completely successful in 1994. The genocide was ended not by French troops, but by the Rwanda Patriotic Front, aided by Uganda. It was an impressive case of transnational ethnic solidarity working toward *Pax Africana*, at least for a while.

Then came the problems of 1996 and early 1997 in what was then Zaire. The Mobutu regime had overreached itself when it tried to empower remnants of the Hutu *Umtirahamwa* in refugee camps in Zaire, and strip indigenous Zairean Tutsi of their Zairean citizenship. The Zairean Tutsi—helped by Rwanda—decided to resist the intimidation of the Zairean armed forces. To the astonishment of everybody, the then Zairean armed forces proved to be a paper monkey, even less than a paper tiger. They were easily defeated by the Tutsi resisters. The ouster of Mobutu Sese Seko was also a triumph for *Pax Africana*, though we still did not know how much of an improvement over Mobutu Laurent Kabila would become.

Mobutu was ousted by a combination of trans-Tutsi forces and other regional and ethnic forces involving not only Rwanda but also Uganda, Angola, Congo (Brazzaville) and others.

RAPID DEPLOYMENT FORCES

This is at a stage of a plant in a nursery, a process in formation since former US Secretary of State Warren Christopher's tour of Africa in 1996. Members of the United States military and African militaries have been working to build the African Crisis Response Initiative. The Clinton administration has committed more than $8 million since 1993 to the OAU's Conflict Management Center to support African efforts to resolve disputes. The idea for both these initiatives is to be able to respond to military crises in African countries before they reach catastrophic levels. Additional programs have been set up at the African Center for Strategic Studies, Arlington, Virginia, which has held various sessions aimed at senior Africans (both civilian and military leaders) in civil-military relations, national security strategies, and defense economics through various rotating seminars.

My own disagreement with the Clinton paradigm concerns the *accountability* of any African rapid deployment force. The Clinton Administration would like to trace accountability ultimately to the Security Council of the United Nations, which is itself controlled by Western powers. I believe that the Pan African Emergency force should be accountable to Africa itself, through such revised institutions of the OAU as Africa may be able to devise. Alternatively, accountability should be towards relevant subregional organizations in Africa—to ECOWAS (Economic Community of West African States) in West Africa, to SADC (Southern African Development Community) in Southern Africa, and to a newly evolving Eastern African Economic Community. Only such an Afro-centered accountability would save *Pax Africana* from becoming a mere extension of *Pax Americana*.

The idea of a Pan African emergency force was gathering momentum in the 1990s. The Blue Eagle Project in southern Africa involved training the troops of at least eight African countries to be in readiness for special responsibilities in situations of political crisis. Much of the training occurred initially in Zimbabwe. The Blue Eagle could develop into the ECOMOG of Southern Africa, but with more appropriate training for a peacekeeping role. Here again is a potential arm of *Pax Africana*.

Also relevant to the unfolding saga of self-colonization in Africa is the hesitant hegemonic role of the Republic of South Africa. Within the wider picture of Pan-Africanism is an emerging subtheme of *Pax Pretoriana,* the muscle of Pretoria, in sorting out political crises in neighboring countries. Sorting out Lusotho's problems with its military is one case in point, though South Africa bungled badly in Maseru in 1998. In fact, the Republic of South Africa is under pressure to be more active in other African crises— from helping reconstruction in the Democratic Republic of Congo to pressuring UNITA (National Union for the Total Independence of Angola) to stop fighting and join the democratic process in Angola. *Pax Pretoriana* at its best can be a branch of *Pax Africana*.

DOMESTIC CONSEQUENCES

What are the consequences of inter-African interventions for a) the intervening state b) the target state? One of the crises for the military in postcolonial Africa has been a *crisis of purpose*—a crisis of reason for existence *(raison d'être)*. What is the military for? Most postcolonial African governments did not have any external enemies against whom their armies could be employed. In fact, most of the postcolonial wars in Africa have been *internal to a country*, not external. Who was the military "Other"? This was the void. In the absence of an external "Other," African armed forces developed domestic "others"—either ethnic, or regional (internal north-south in Obote's and Amin's Uganda), or sectarian (Muslim, non-Muslim as in Sudan), or all three (regional, ethnic and sectarian) as in Nigeria.

How do we discourage African armies from staging military coups against democratically elected governments? The dilemma arose in 1963 with the first Black African military coup against Sylvanus Olympio in Togo, who was also postcolonial Africa's first assassinated president. The initial Pan-African response was in boycotting the successor regime in Togo. The newly formed OAU's Charter explicitly included a clause "condemning political assassination in all its forms." At the inaugural meeting of the Organization of African Unity (OAU) in 1963, there was one vacant seat. It was Togo's—originally intended for the assassinated Sylvanus Olympio. Julius K. Nyerere of Tanzania wept publicly for Olympio. But was anybody prepared to use force to oust the regime which had assassinated Sylvanus Olympio? At that time no one was.

But *Pax Africana* a quarter of a century later took a wholly unexpected turn in Sierra Leone. In 1997, the military overthrew the elected government of Ahmad Tejan Kabbah. In this case of *Pax Africana*, a military government in Nigeria decided to defend, and attempt to reinstate, a democratically elected government in Sierra Leone. This case of the military in defense of democracy was certainly an improvement on the older story of Western democracies propping up military regimes like that of Mobutu Sese Seko— which was twice saved *militarily* by the West in the face of a domestic challenge from its own Shaba province.

I personally would rather see a military regime like that of Nigeria in 1998 defending democracy in Sierra Leone, than see a democracy like that of France or the United States propping up military dictatorships in Less Developed Countries. Yet for the time being the story of Sierra Leone seems to be a stalemate. *Pax Africana* has not yet fully triumphed, though the whole of Africa has condemned the coup in Freetown.

Patriotism among the military in postcolonial Africa has needed a worthier sense of mission than ethnic, regional, and sectarian strife. Is regional involvement and sense of identity one of the answers? Would regional peacekeeping give African armies the *beginnings* of a high sense of mission? If the purpose of a military intervention is to end tyranny or reverse a military coup, is that mission democratizing for both the target state (Sierra Leone in 1998 or Uganda in 1979) and the intervening state (Nigeria going into Sierra Leone and Tanzania going into Uganda)? Is such intervention potentially democratizing for both states—intervener and intervenee?

And what is *demilitarization* in this sense? The two sides of the coin are as follows:

1. The demilitarization of the political system (reducing the role of the military).
2. The depoliticization of the military (withdrawing the military from overt political roles).

Does regional peacekeeping help to demilitarize the countries participating in it? We need to place this whole issue within a wider framework about Africa. We must start from the premise that some African countries are *coup-prone* (sociologically susceptible to military intervention in politics, perhaps repeatedly) while other African countries have so far been relatively *coup-proof* (sociologically safeguarding civilian supremacy for as long as possible).

Examples of *coup-prone* countries in the first forty years or so of Africa's independence have included Nigeria, Uganda, Sudan, Burkina Faso, the two Congos and perhaps Ghana. Examples of relatively *coup-proof* countries in approximately the first forty years of their independence have included Senegal, Morocco, Tanzania, Zambia, Malawi, Kenya, as well as South Africa.

Where does regional peacekeeping fit in? Can countries which are *endogenously coup-prone* be made *exogenously coup-proof?* If *internal* factors within a country favor coups, can *regional* factors *externally* discourage those coups? Can endogenous coup-proneness be neutralized by exogenous coup-proofness?

This is one of the central questions of demilitarization *within* countries arising out of regional military initiatives external to those countries. Until the military coup in the Ivory Coast in December 1999, ECOMOG as a regional organization seemed to be making progress in making military coups in West Africa illegitimate. The strong response by Nigeria and ECOMOG against the military coup in Sierra Leone seemed to illegitimize all future military coups in West Africa against elected governments. Such a gain would have amounted to substantial regional demilitarization. Exogenous forces of demilitarization in the region seemed to be checking and arresting the endogenous forces of domestic militarization.

The neutralization of the Sierra Leonean coup by Nigeria and ECOMOG was not strong enough to avert a military coup in the Ivory Coast. Nor was the OAU's commitment against coups in Algiers in 1999 enough to save a thoroughly unpleasant and increasingly undemocratic civilian regime in Abidjan, Ivory Coast, from being overthrown by widely cheered soldiers in the country. The struggle for both endogenous and exogenous demilitarization suffered a setback in Abidjan in the final days of the twentieth century, yet the struggle has to continue. At this time of writing (October 2000), military ruler Robert Guei was overthrown in a show of "people power"—but clashes followed leading to questions about its democratic stability.

Democratic trends in Africa are real, but still very fragile. The remaining military regimes are under pressure to democratize; single-party systems have been giving way to multiparty systems; authoritarian systems like that in Kenya are facing angry demands for constitutional reform. Africa is taking hesitant steps towards democracy. But are these regional activities of peacekeeping themselves part of the democratizing process?

Democratization within individual African countries is only part of the process of resuming control over Africa's destiny. *Pax Africana* is the continental face of this self-determination—provided the motives, goals and means are in tune with Africa's ultimate well being.

Acknowledgments

This book has been made possible by financial assistance from both the United States Institute of Peace and the Rockefeller Foundation. The United States Institute of Peace and David Smock, one of the officers there, supported this project from the beginning. At the Rockefeller Foundation, Susan Garfield and the other staff at the Bellagio Conference Center managed all logistical details of our conference on peacekeeping, making our discussions and deliberations on this project much easier. Dr. Margaret Vogt, formerly of the International Peace Academy and presently with the United Nations Department of Political Affairs, assisted substantially in planning the research for this volume.

At the Institute of Global Cultural Studies here at the State University of New York at Binghamton, Tracia Leacock Seghatolislami, Fouad Kalouche, and Michael Toler, our graduate students, provided editing and proofreading of texts when needed. They are much appreciated. Our administrative assistant, Nancy Levis, and our secretary, Barbara Tierno, helped in numerous ways. As always, Grace Houghton has helped us with the finer points of editing and English grammar.

Last, this work has been the inspiration of Ali A. Mazrui, the Schweitzer Professor for the Humanities and the Director of the Institute of Global Cultural Studies. He has been an example of integrity and intellectual courage for all of us.

Acronyms and Abbreviations

AAPS	African Association of Political Science
ACRI	African Crisis Response Initiative
AD	Alliance for Democracy
AEC	African Economic Community
AFDL	*Alliance des Forces Démocratiques pour la Libération du Congo-Zaire*
AFL	Armed Forces of Liberia
AFRC	Armed Forces Revolutionary Council
AGSIM	American Graduate School of International Management
ALF	African Leadership Forum
AMF	American Mineral Fields
AMODEG	*Associação Moçambicana dos Desmobilizados de Guerra*
APC	All People's Congress
APP	All People's Party
AWEPAA	Association of European Parliamentarians for Southern Africa
BDF	Bong Defense Force
CAR	Central African Republic
CASS	Center for Advanced Social Science
CCAT	Joint Commission for Territorial Administration
CCE	Constitutional Commission of Eritrea
CCF	Cease-Fire Commission
CCFADM	Joint Commission for the Formation of the Armed Forces
CEDEAO	*Communauté économique des états de l'Afrique de l'Ouest*
CEEAC	*Communauté économique des états de l'Afrique centrale*
CD	Campaign for Victory (Nigeria)
CDF	Civil Defense Forces

CIS	*Comité international de suivi* (International Follow-up Committee)
CNS	*Conférence national souveraine*
CODESRIA	Council for the Development of Social and Economic Research in Africa
COMESA	Common Market for Eastern and Southern Africa
COMINFO	Intelligence Commission
COMPOL	Police Commission
COPAX	*Conseil pour la paix et la sécurité*
CNA	National Electoral Commission
CNE	National Electoral Commission
CORE	Commission for the Reintegration of Demobilized Combattants
CSF	Cease-Fire Commission
CSC	Supervision and Monitoring Commission
DCP	Democratic Center Party
DDR	Disarmament, Demobilization, and Reintegration
DOP	Declaration of Principles
DRC	Democratic Republic of the Congo
DTU	Demobilization Technical Units
ECA	Economic Commission for Africa
ECOMOG	Economic Community Monitoring Group (Economic Community of West African States Monitoring Group)
ECOWAS	Economic Community of West African States
ESF	Economic Support Fund
EU	European Union
FAC	*Forces armées congolaises*
FAR	*Forces armées rwandaises*
FADM	*Forças armada de defesa de Moçambique*
FEDECO	Federal Electoral Commission
FIS	Islamic Salvation Front
FLN	National Liberation Front
FNLA	*Frente Nacional de Libertação de Angola*
FRELIMO	Front for the Liberation of Moçambique
GDP	Gross Domestic Product
Gécamines	*Générale des carriéres et des mines*
GPA	General Peace Agreement
ICRC	International Committee of the Red Cross
IGAD	Inter-Governmental Authority for Development
IGNU	Interim Government of National Unity

IGSR	Institute of Government and Social Research
IMF	International Monetary Fund
INEC	Independent National Electoral Commission
ING	Interim National Government
INPFL	Independent National Patriotic Front of Liberia
ISRSG	Interim Special Representative of the UN Secretary General

| JCMC | Joint Cease-fire Monitoring Committee |
| JMC | Joint Military Commission |

LDF	Lofa Defense Force
LNC	Liberian National Conference
LNTG	Liberian National Transitional Government
LPC	Liberia Peace Council

MINURCA	*Mission des Nations Unies en République centraficaine*
MISAB	*Mission interafricaine de surveillance des Accords de Bangui* (Inter-African Mission to Monitor the Bangui Accords)
MLC	*Mouvement de libération congolais* (Congolese Liberation Movement)
MNR	Mozambique National Resistance
MP	Member of Parliament
MPLA	*Movimento Popular de Libertação de Angola*

NCCE	National Commission for Civic Education
NDA	National Democratic Alliance
NDPL	National Democratic Party of Liberia
NGO	Non-Governmental Organization
NIF	National Islamic Front
NPFL	National Patriotic Forces of Liberia
NPRC	National Provisional Ruling Council
NRA	National Resistance Army
NRM/A	National Resistance Movement/Army
NSC	National Security Council (USA)
NUP	National Unity Party

OAU	Organization of African Unity
OECD	Organization for Economic Cooperation and Development
OIC	Organization of the Islamic Conference
ONUC	*Opération des nations unies au Congo* (United Nations Operations in the Congo)
ORH	Operation Restore Hope

PDD	Presidential Decision Directive
PDP	People's Democratic Party
RCD	*Rassemblement congolais pour la démocratie* (Congolese Rally for Democracy)
REC	Regional Economic Communities
RECAMP	*Renforcement des capacités africaines de maintien de la paix*
RENAMO	*Resistencia Nacional Moçambicana* (Mozambique National Resistance)
RPA	Rwandese Patriotic Army
RPF	Rwandese Patriotic Front
RRA	Rahanweyn Resistance Army
RSLMF	Republic of Sierra Leone Military Forces
RSS	Reintegration Support Scheme
RUF	Revolutionary United Front
SADC	Southern African Development Community
SAP	Structural Adjustment Program
SLA	Sierra Leonean Army
SLPP	Sierra Leone Peoples' Party
SNA	Somali National Alliance
SNF	Somali National Front
SNM	Somalia National Movement
SPLA	Sudan People's Liberation Army
SPLM	Sudan People's Liberation Movement
SPM	Somali Patriotic Movement
SRSG	Special Representative of the Secretary General (UN)
SSD	Special Security Division of the Sierra Leonean Police
SSDF	Somalia Salvation Democratic Front
UAD	United Action for Democracy (Nigeria)
UD	Democratic Union
ULIMO	United Liberation Movement of Liberia for Democracy
ULIMO-J	United Liberation Movement of Liberia for Democracy-Johnson
ULIMO-K	United Liberation Movement of Liberia for Democracy-Kromah
UMHK	*Union minière du Haut-Katanga*
UMA	*Union du Maghreb arabe* (Arab Maghreb Union)
UNAMIR	United Nations Assistance Mission for Rwanda
UNAVEM	United Nations Angola Verification Mission
UNHCR	United Nations High Commissioner for Refugees
UNICEF	United Nations Children's Fund
UNDP	United Nations Development Program

UNITA	*União Nacional de Indepêndencia Total de Angola* (National Union for the Total Independence of Angola)
UNITAF	Unified Task Force
UNOHAC	United Nations Office for Humanitarian Assistance Coordination
UNOMIL	United Nations Observer Mission in Liberia
UNOMOZ	United Nations Operation in Mozambique
UNOMSIL	United Nations Observer Mission to Sierra Leone
UNOSOM	United Nations Operation in Somalia
UNPP	United National People's Party
UNPROFOR	United Nations Peacekeeping Operations in the Former Yugoslavia
UNTAC	United Nations Peacekeeping Operations in Cambodia
UPDF	Ugandan People's Defense Forces
USC	United Somali Congress
USIP	United States Institute for Peace
WPF	World Food Program
ZDF	Zimbabwean Defense Force

I

The Causes of War and the
Consequences of Peacekeeping

The Causes of Warfare
and the Implications of Peacekeeping
in Africa

Ricardo René Laremont

The horror of civil war and genocide haunted us at the end of the twentieth century. Whether it was murder in the "killing fields" of Cambodia, "ethnic cleansing" in Bosnia and Kosovo, or the planned, systematic killing of over five hundred thousand persons over a three-month period in Rwanda in 1994, the world stood idly as mass murder was repeatedly committed under our gaze on the Cable News Network.

Organized, systematic murder spared no part of the world. From Phnom Penh to Beirut to Sarajevo to Freetown, mass murderers were permitted to engage in their trade while the world stood by. Often these killers sheltered themselves from international control or criticism, claiming that their activities were part of the resolution of "internal matters" that were beyond the supervision of international legal bodies or review by international humanitarian norms.

Since 1970 Africa has suffered more than thirty wars; most of these have had intrastate origins. A recent study has documented that from 1990 to 1997 sixteen wars took place in Africa. Fourteen were intrastate conflicts (Algeria, Angola, Chad, Ethiopia, Liberia, Mozambique, Rwanda, Sierra Leone, Somalia, South Africa, Sudan, Uganda, Western Sahara, and Zaire); only two were interstate (Chad/Libya and Rwanda/Uganda).[1] These wars have killed millions and created more than eight million refugees and internally displaced persons.[2]

This book is preoccupied with the causes of warfare and the consequences of peacekeeping and other forms of conflict resolution in Africa. For most of the twentieth century until the end of the Cold War, most security analysts focused primarily on conflict *between* states. With the end of the Cold War, the nature of warfare has changed. Most of our concern is now focused on conflict *within* states. These intrastate conflicts and proposed suggestions for their resolution preoccupy us in this volume.

The causes of warfare have shifted emphasis since the end of the Cold War. During the period of superpower Cold War rivalry, many wars and tensions in Africa were often encouraged by the United States and the Soviet Union (as evidenced by the proxy wars in Namibia, Angola, and Mozambique). With the departure of the Soviets from the world scene and from the African continent, the Western powers of the United States, France, and Great Britain have concomitantly retreated from Africa and lowered the importance of Africa's geo-strategic role. Hence, despite the existence of disintegrating societies and failing states in Africa, the West has responded reluctantly. The interest is not there. Despite this lack of interest, the West has felt obligated to respond intermittently to disasters—whether of ecological or man-made origins—in a series of African states. Yet one only needs to recall the West's failure to respond adequately in a variety of states (including Somalia, Rwanda, Burundi, Liberia, Sierra Leone, Zaire) to realize that intervention by the West even for humanitarian purposes is both unreliable and unpredictable.

In this era of ambivalent responses by the West, Africa has still remained the location for devastating warfare. Since the 1970s war has been continuous. It also, more recently, has undertaken much more macabre dimensions. We now observe the routine amputation of limbs in Sierra Leone, the banal explosion of thousands of land mines in Angola and Mozambique, and the bizarre evisceration of putative enemies—including women—in Algeria. This violence has destroyed much of our optimism for peace in the post–Cold War world.

THE CAUSES OF WARFARE

Why does this violence occur? The standard academic response has been that violence and war occur in Africa because of irreconcilable ethnic differences and conflict. In this volume Crawford Young (in an article entitled "Pluralism, Ethnicity, and Militarization") and Francis Deng (in "Sudan: An African Dilemma") analyze how ethnicity and race continue to divide African societies. Crawford Young's article takes a pan-African standard of analysis while Francis Deng's article focuses on the Sudan. In both cases, the authors explain how the putatively artificial distinctions of race and ethnicity become important and relevant to systems of social subordination and the provocation of war. Despite much postmodernist philosophical, anthropological, and sociological critiques of the artificiality of race and ethnicity as ontologically real categories of analysis, on a political level the changing contours of ethnicity and race still remain real factors in the provocation of war.

At the end of the twentieth century it remains clear that "differences" concerning ethnicity, race, nationalism, and religion remain central to the explanation of violence and warfare. To some extent these factors that encourage intrastate warfare have superceded geo-political or geo-economic factors that provoke interstate warfare. (There are some notable exceptions: Pakistan-India, India-China, Iran-Iraq, perhaps North Korea.) In Africa, the reality is that we have diverse ethnic or national communities living in geographical units called states that are in fact multiethnic or multinational in composition. Uniethnic identity and multiethnic or multinational states are the norm in Africa. This contradiction has been exacerbated by the geographical configuration of states that have their genesis in the colonial period.

Nations and states have not cohered in much of Africa. Why is this so? It would seem that much of the explanation for the causes of warfare and violence in Africa lies in the disorderly creation of nations and states that emerged as a result of the colonial period. The nations and states that we have in Africa now are the result of geographical units created by European imperialists who divvied up Africa beginning at the Congress of Berlin in 1885, partitioning Africa into entirely artificial territorial units. Whereas these units served the geo-economic and geo-political interests of imperial Europe, they had the effect within Africa of either arbitrarily dividing already established communities on the one hand or uniting essentially dissonant communities on the other. Hence, in contemporary Africa, we can observe English-speaking Yoruba peoples in Nigeria and French-speaking Yoruba peoples just across the "border" in Benin. These forced divisions are unnatural and artificial. Because of this forced creation of artificial states, the process of state creation and nation building in Africa has been most unnatural, leading to very unstable nation-states. In Europe, by contrast, the absence of imperial intervention in nation formation led to a process of nation and state formation that was more natural and organic.

To worsen matters, in the immediate postcolonial period African leaders themselves made critical decisions that reified those artificial colonial borders and the artificial communities that resided within them. At a critical moment in 1963, the Organization of African Unity (OAU) made a decision to accept the colonially defined borders that African states had inherited from Europe.[3] The leaders within the OAU did so because, in the immediate postcolonial period, African political leaders focused upon the reality that postcolonial states were quite fragile and could be easily destabilized. When the OAU made its decision to accept and honor inherited colonial borders, African governments were more interested in consolidating the state than in examining the social causes of divisions within their own borders. To have examined the social components of nation formation would have led, at least in their initial estimation, to the further disintegration of these newly created states. From the OAU's viewpoint, state creation was needed to assure immediate political survival; nation building would have to be addressed later. This immediate goal of state creation and consolidation was understandable; in the long term, however, it would prove to be destabilizing. Whereas in Europe national identities were developed *before* the creation of the state (to create the *nation-state*), in postcolonial Africa a reverse process was at work. The state—preferably a strong, centrally controlled state—was to be created first. Attention would be given to building the nation afterwards. This reversal of the process—the creation of the state before the nation—lies at the root of many security crises in Africa. In this volume we examine this phenomenon in a variety of cases and elaborate the sources of conflict in a remarkably broad variety of countries.

THE END OF THE COLD WAR AND THE BEGINNING OF THE NEW WORLD DISORDER

Most of the analyses in this book focus on post–Cold War, intrastate causes of warfare in Africa. Two of our analyses, however, (the analyses of Mozambique by João Honwana and Angola by J. Michael Turner), have focused on two conflicts that were firmly rooted in the Cold War and that emerged from rivalries between the United States and the Soviet Union. Warfare in Africa during the Cold War was often exacerbated and made more deadly by superpower intervention. Yet in retrospect we can assess that even during the period of superpower intervention in Africa, Africa was still of peripheral importance to the United States and the Soviet Union. Africa only came into play when used as a playing field for warfare within larger geo-strategic games. Besides Angola and Mozambique, which are examined by Turner and Honwana, superpower rivalry also flared in Ethiopia, Somalia, Egypt, Namibia, and Zaire. When the Cold War ended and superpower rivalry between the United States and the Soviet Union subsided, the superpowers withdrew. Warfare in Africa after the Cold War, however, has increased rather than dissipated. Superpower intervention and rivalries, therefore, cannot continue to be claimed for warfare in Africa. This forces us to shift our analysis from Cold War explanations to the examination of new questions that, we hope, will provide new answers for establishing security frameworks for Africa.

At the eclipse of the Cold War—and, more specifically, just after the formation of the unique multinational, UN-sponsored coalition that defeated Iraq in the 1990–1991 Gulf Conflict—US President George Bush announced what he called a "New World Order." In President Bush's vision of the New World Order, he charted a new world security framework that called for United States leadership in international affairs while imagining an expanded use of the offices of the United Nations to endorse peacekeeping and peacemaking around the world. After the Gulf War, UN peacekeeping initiatives flourished. During the 1990s alone, the UN deployed thirty-two peacekeeping missions. Of those thirty-two missions, thirteen were in Africa. In the early 1990s the UN expanded its role in peacekeeping, believing that it would finally fulfill its hoped-for role as provider of neutral auspices for conflict resolution around the world.

Within this "New World Order," the UN, under US leadership, would play a greater role in the management of international conflict. This era of United States–dominated, aggressive multilateralism in collective security began in the 1990s just after the Gulf War, which for one brief and anomalous moment brought together a unique coalition of former adversaries as diverse as the United States, the Soviet Union, Egypt, and Syria to defeat Iraq, which had transgressed the territorial sovereignty of Kuwait. During this period in the early 1990s, the United States effectively seized control of the Security Council, which gave its imprimatur first to the Gulf War and then to Operation Restore Hope, which was a Pentagon-drafted plan to restore order to Somalia. In light of the apparent military omnipotence of the United States after the spectacularly quick victory in the Gulf War, the Security Council during this period ceded its leadership to resolve international conflict to the United States, even if that required US dominance of the Security Council and its peacekeeping operations. It then quickly gave the US its approval to commence Operation Restore Hope in Somalia as well as a series of other peacekeeping operations. In the immediate post–Gulf War era, the UN entered an aggressive era of multinational peacekeeping, preferring that approach for dealing with conflict and war.

Peacekeeping and peacemaking undertaken by the UN and the Security Council historically, however, has had mixed results. The deployment of UN peacekeeping troops has tended to be both tortuous and highly problematic because decisions to deploy peacekeeping forces cannot be made without the unanimity of the Security Council's five permanent members (the United States, Great Britain, France, Russia, and China). This has made rapid deployment of UN forces very often impossible. This procedural constraint has effectively limited the UN to intervening in traditional peacekeeping scenarios that require it to be "invited" in after the combatants have put down their arms and agreed to a cease-fire.

Enthusiasm for UN-sponsored peacekeeping and peacemaking in Africa lasted through the fall of 1993. Beginning with its peacekeeping mission in Somalia, the United Nations (and, also, the United States) learned how difficult peacemaking and peacekeeping would be. Led by the United States, the United Nations deployed peacemaking and peacekeeping troops in Somalia in December 1992. This operation was called Operation Restore Hope. Barely two seasons later, in October 1993, the United States withdrew its forces after eighteen of its soldiers were killed during military operations there. As a result of this withdrawal, the larger UN operation failed and Somalia remains a nonexistent or failed state. The failure in Somalia would have greater and more devastating effects when genocide occurred in Rwanda in 1994. The reversals of UN efforts in Somalia and also the former Yugoslavia chilled America's and the international community's appetite for internationally sponsored peacekeeping and peacemaking initiatives in Africa and elsewhere.

Somalia was a turning point. After Somalia, paralysis set in concerning international peacekeeping in Africa. Consequently, when the genocide began in Rwanda in 1994, the international community stalled as hundreds of thousands of persons were killed within a very short time period. Many of these deaths could have been prevented if international and regional military forces had intervened in a timely manner. The failure of UN peacekeeping and peacemaking in Somalia directly contributed to the failure of the United States to endorse United Nations intervention to prevent genocide in Rwanda. The reversal in Somalia also led to hesitation in Bosnia, Serbia, and Croatia. Nevertheless, it is still patently clear that Africa needs an effective security regime that can restore and maintain peace—even if that peace is short lived.

The international community's view and approach to peacekeeping was profoundly affected by what transpired in Somalia. Much of the failure to engage seriously the security problems of Africa or to come up with solutions stems from the failure to deal effectively with that crisis. The consequences of the intellectual stasis resultant from the

Somalia intervention became evident when the international community paused and agonized over how to respond to the unfolding tragedy in Rwanda. The failure to respond in Rwanda, as hundreds of thousands of people died, highlighted the crucial need for the creation of rapidly deployable military forces—probably supported by regional groups—that could intervene to prevent genocide and restore peace.

If the United Nations and the United States are increasingly reluctant to intervene in Africa, it is then incumbent upon African leaders to discuss and determine whether regional approaches to peacekeeping and peacemaking are preferable to UN-sponsored, multilateral intervention. In Africa we have seen international efforts at peacemaking and peacekeeping (examples: Mozambique, Angola, and Somalia) and regional approaches (examples: Sierra Leone and Liberia). All are discussed in this volume.

Given the extensive extant warfare within Africa and the effects that war has on polit-ical and economic development, scholars and public policy analysts have asked whether there is now a need for regionally based "crisis intervention" teams of soldiers and diplo-mats positioned in Africa that will deal with emerging crises. Too often, international forces and agencies such as those controlled by the United Nations cannot act quickly enough to deal with war and humanitarian crises as they arise in Africa. By the time wars in Africa come to the attention of a generally inattentive world community, it is often too late. It is, therefore, necessary to ask the question of whether it would be bet-ter to have regional forces in place that could rapidly deploy to deal with genocide, civil wars, and *coups d'état.* Because of the United Nations' incapacity to act quickly, disparate regions of the world have had to consider the creation and deployment of regional peacekeeping forces. Arguably, regional peacekeeping groups may have superior knowl-edge of local conflicts and will have stronger incentives to resolve them than the United Nations.

Because of these problems and time lags involved in responding to crises from New York, Washington, London, or Paris and because Africa is not presently central to the geoeconomic and geopolitical ordering of the world, both France and the United States have more recently come forward with proposals to create regional diplomatic and mil-itary forces that would be charged with policing the peace in their regions of Africa. The French proposal is called RECAMP *(Renforcement des capacités africaines de maintien de la paix)* and the United States calls its proposal ACRI (African Crisis Response Ini-tiative). Both proposals reveal a desire by France and the United States to avoid con-tributing forces directly to peacekeeping in Africa—thereby letting Africans police themselves—while maintaining political influence and military linkages to African states. The proposals are designed to meet two goals: To extricate the French and the Americans from direct involvement in African peacekeeping (which may be politically unpopular at home) while maintaining a certain influence within Africa. These two pro-posals provide lower cost, lower risk solutions to maintaining influence.

If one supports the concept of regional peacekeeping initiatives—and this approach must be considered because it is relatively clear that the United Nations and the larger industrialized states like the United States and France will play a smaller role in African peacekeeping—the next set of thorny questions involves the placement, training, staffing, recruitment, and financial support of these regional peacekeeping forces. Placement of these forces is important because if, for example, South Africa and Nigeria are chosen as the locales for the placement of regional peacekeeping forces in southern Africa and western Africa respectively, does this decision not turn these two states *ipso facto* into regional political and military hegemons? If Uganda or Kenya were chosen to keep the peace in East Africa, would that decision overly empower them in the region? How do we create regional peacekeeping and peacemaking forces and, at the same time, avoid the creation of regional imperialists?

There are powerful reasons for creating regional peacekeeping forces. There are also particular dangers. Regional forces and arrangements have particular biases and motives that they bring when they try to resolve regional disputes. The political interests of militarily powerful states do not disappear when they participate in the creation of regional peacekeeping or peacemaking forces. States may use "peacekeeping" forces to further their more narrow geo-political objectives rather than more broad humanitarian objectives. Despite this concern, the question nevertheless remains: Should regional peacekeeping forces be discouraged because they may be used as a ruse to encourage local military and political hegemons? Or should they be encouraged because they may have the capability and the interest to respond more rapidly to humanitarian crises than the United Nations?

While Somalia may have amounted to a case of peacekeeping failure and Rwanda was an example of a tragic failure to act, it is important to emphasize that not all United Nations peacekeeping ventures in Africa have been failures. The ONUMOZ (United Nations Operation in Mozambique) peacekeeping operation in Mozambique stands, notably, as a lonely success. The United Nations deployed a creditable force there that was adequately supplied and staffed; the force also had the substantial support of the former combatants in Mozambique. Using a combination of military force, diplomatic and political initiatives, and considerable economic aid, the United Nations in Mozambique was able to restore peace and reset Mozambique on a path to constructive development. In this volume, João Honwana explains the reasons for the UN's success in Mozambique. J. Michael Turner and Hussein Adam, on the other hand, explain the deficiencies of UN operations in Angola and Somalia.

Given US and UN hesitation to act in Africa, as evidenced by the failure to intervene to prevent genocide in Rwanda, an enlarged discussion is needed concerning the necessity to create regionally based "African Rapid Deployment Forces" that can deploy rapidly to avert humanitarian crises in Africa. These must be considered as alternatives to UN-sponsored international peacekeeping involvement.

REGIONAL PEACEKEEPING FORCES: AN ALTERNATIVE?

The first real on-ground attempt to test the applicability of regional peacekeeping approaches in Africa occurred with the deployment of ECOMOG (the Economic Community Monitoring Group) in Liberia in 1990.[4] ECOMOG was and is a regional military force created in 1990 by ECOWAS (the Economic Community of West African States) to serve as a regional peacekeeping force in West Africa. The direct deployment of regional forces by ECOMOG in Liberia constituted a fundamental change in how African forces dealt with the question of the suppression of war. Before Liberia, African forces, under the leadership of the OAU, practiced UN-style peacekeeping rather intervention to restore or create peace (known as peacemaking). Under traditional peacekeeping procedures, peacekeeping forces enter combat zones as neutral agents to enforce a cease-fire agreement between combatants that has already been agreed. They do not enter a militarily hostile environment to restore peace. The latter can be characterized as peacemaking. For example, in the first OAU attempt at peacekeeping (in Chad in 1980), peacekeeping forces entered in the fray after being invited by the former combatants (Chad and Libya) to maintain the peace. In Liberia, by contrast, ECOMOG intervened to restore peace rather than to maintain the peace. In the initial ECOMOG operation, Ghana, Guinea, Sierra Leone, and Nigeria contributed troops. Later, Benin, Burkina Faso, Gambia, Ivory Coast, Mali, Niger, and Senegal participated. Throughout the ECOMOG operation, however, Nigeria clearly controlled the command of troops. Nigerian management and dominance raised questions concerning whether Nigeria should emerge as a more powerful actor within ECOMOG and within West Africa more generally. There may be advantages and disadvantages to having Nigeria as a powerful military and political power within West Africa.

Assessing ECOMOG purely as a military and political operation, however, despite inadequate staffing and lack of coordination, ECOMOG still accomplished a modicum of success. It eventually installed Charles Taylor in Liberia as head of a new but unstable government, and violence abated. After the ECOMOG operation in Liberia, ECOMOG was called again to act in Sierra Leone in 1997. ECOMOG deployed there to restore the rule of Sierra Leone's duly elected President Ahmad Tejan Kabbah who had been deposed in a *coup d'état*.

ECOMOG operations provide an example of the problems involved in creating regional security arrangements in Africa. First, these operations were precariously financed and they did not receive the best, most recent, and most effective military equipment. Second, ECOMOG as a military force, because it has been commanded and staffed principally by Nigerians, has occasionally come to express the foreign policy preferences of Nigeria, even while it has been essential in reestablishing the peace in Liberia and Sierra Leone. Despite concern about the regional empowerment of Nigeria, however, support of ECOMOG may be necessary because it has had some success in dealing with and attenuating warfare in West Africa. Nevertheless, the clear danger of empowering and funding ECOMOG lies in the certainty that by doing so Nigeria will be encouraged to be a regional hegemon. Are we, therefore, faced with a Hobson's choice: The empowerment of Nigeria via ECOMOG or failure to respond to emerging humanitarian catastrophes in West Africa? Similar arguments concerning the creation of regional hegemons could also be asked concerning South Africa's role within SADC (Southern African Development Community).

Because the United Nations and the international community have demonstrated that they lack the will and interest to deploy and sustain peacemaking and peacekeeping forces consistently in Africa, questions arise when considering how best to create and support regional peacekeeping forces to do the job while attending to short-term security concerns and long-term concerns of selective empowerment and regional stability. Among the questions to be addressed include the following: Which states will create and participate in those forces? Who will sustain them with personnel and financial support? How and where will they be trained? How will they have access to adequate armaments? Who will command these multinational and perhaps multilingual troops? Where will they be based? Who will have the authority to permit their deployment? Under what circumstances will they be permitted to deploy? Will there be preexisting protocols in place that will provide legal bases for the legitimation of intervention? Thorny though these questions may be, they must be addressed if Africa will create the regionally based peacekeeping and peacemaking forces that it needs. Because of the evident reluctance of the international community to reengage in Africa, analysis of these issues is necessary and desirable.

If regional peacekeeping and peacemaking forces will be a trend in the future of Africa, it seems that one of the primary questions that will have to be addressed will be whether and under what conditions military intervention will be authorized. As W. Ofuatey-Kodjoe argues in this volume, the deployment of regional forces often involves a violation of the territorial integrity and sovereignty of the target state. To intervene without protocols for intervention would be to create a security regime that could turn from intervention for humanitarian purposes to regional imperialism. This would be both unadvisable and unacceptable. If regional intervention forces are created, they cannot be deployed in a willy-nilly, capricious manner; they must be deployed subsequent to regional consensus and pursuant to compliance with either procedural or legal protocols.

Even granting the eventual need for protocols for intervention, can we not in the short term at least advocate that genocide and humanitarian excesses cannot be allowed to reign in Africa? Are there not profound humanitarian reasons justifying at least multilateral if not unilateral intervention? Can we say that humanitarian intervention by regional forces may be permissible where the state has imploded and does not exist? How can we say that state sovereignty has been violated by the intervention of a regional peacekeeping force where no "state" really exists to restore civil order? Perhaps at a minimum we can assert that "humanitarian intervention" by regional forces to avert genocide may be permissible in cases where the state has clearly failed or imploded (e.g. Somalia, Rwanda, Liberia, or Sierra Leone). The ethical question of international responsibility in the face of genocide has been debated and many parties have been called to act, particularly after the lessons of World War II. The question is, Where should that responsibility lie now that Africa is being ravaged by war and genocide? Perhaps in cases of dissolved or imploded states, intervention to reestablish peace and order should be warranted and justifiable. After order has been reestablished and the genocide and mutilations have abated, only then can we claim that a "state" exists that can assert claims of sovereignty that need to be respected. After the reestablishment of the state and order, it can be argued that intervening forces are obligated to depart.

In the conditions of failed states, we should be able to claim that various states within a region can join together to act to end genocide and physical mutilation. Multilateral, regional intervention should be permissible and legitimate under these circumstances. Walter Clarke has argued,

In territories where there is no state, as in Somalia, or where it is disputed, ineffective, or unclear sovereignty, as in Afghanistan, Bosnia, and Liberia, responsible countries of the world must be prepared first to offer their good offices to mediate political solutions and provide resources to facilitate the return to order. If, in time, these peaceful efforts are unavailing and it is perceived that substantial portions of the populations of the afflicted territories are suffering from unacceptable inhumanities, common morality then requires that responsible states, preferably in coalition, mount a coordinated political-military intervention to create the conditions that may lead to the restoration of civil order. Intervening forces must have the mandate to take those measures necessary to promote public safety, including the use of force against recalcitrant members of the society.[5]

Some kind of security regime needs to be devised that will be capable of intervening to prevent genocide, physical mutilation, sanctioned violence *en masse* and the creation of refugees and internally displaced peoples.

THE WILD CARD IN AFRICAN WARFARE: ALTERNATE SOURCES OF FINANCING AND MERCENARIES

What is troubling in post–Cold War Africa has been that new sources of financing have replaced the financial support for war that was previously provided by the United States, the Soviet Union, and other parties. War in Africa quickly becomes complicated when material resources—such as diamonds or petroleum—become available to combatants as alternate sources of financing for their wars. In particular, access to diamonds and revenues generated from their black market sale have enabled warring groups in Angola, Liberia, Sierra Leone, and the Democratic Republic of the Congo to make the arms purchases that have enabled them to continue warfare. After petroleum, diamonds are Africa's second largest export. In this new era of war financing, access to these resources by combatants has created parallel financing opportunities for the purchase of sophisticated weaponry. In these deals involving diamonds, petroleum, precious metals, and other resources, transnational corporations have been willing co-conspirators in war because they have been willing to "do business" with combatants as long as their access to these valuable raw materials is not denied. The implications of this kind of financing are particularly well explained in the essays provided by Georges Nzongola-Ntalaja, Yusuf Bangura, W. Ofuatey-Kodjoe, and J. Michael Turner.

This transnational corporate collaboration with insurgents is crucial for their survival. For example, in the heat of Laurent Kabila's military operations to topple Mobutu

Sese Seko in Zaïre, Jean-Raymond Boulle, Chairman of American Mineral Fields (AMF) flew in his own corporate plane to strike a deal with Kabila, even as Mobutu's government was falling. In Liberia during the civil war, now-President then-insurgent Charles Taylor was able to finance resistance to ECOMOG's efforts at peacemaking and peacekeeping because, allegedly, he had access to $200 million to $250 million dollars a year from the sale of timber, rubber, and other natural resources. In his dealings, Taylor's principal partners were the Firestone Tire and Rubber Company and Sollac (a French mining company).[6] In Angola, Jonas Savimbi has been able to continue to fund his war against the central government in Luanda because he controls the province of Luanda Norte, which is a diamond-rich region. Furthermore, he covets expansion into neighboring Shaba province in the Democratic Republic of the Congo, another diamond-rich region. According to *Diamond International,* UNITA's (National Union for the Total Independence of Angola) diamond income in 1996 alone amounted to $800 million, eighty percent of Angola's diamond output.

In the Congo access to and control of minerals seem to be at the heart of military aspirations. Besides the presence of petroleum and diamonds in the country, strategic minerals are valuable commodities. The Democratic Republic of the Congo controls two-thirds of the world's reserves of cobalt, one-tenth of the world's copper supply, and significant reserves of uranium and manganese. Control of areas where these metals are mined is essential for those who desire economic and political power. During the period of Mobutu's rule, Mobutu himself controlled the exploitation of much of the Congo's riches. His near monopoly of access to these resources made him an extraordinarily wealthy man. In the post-Mobutu era, the underlying economics of political power and warfare in the Democratic Republic of the Congo has not changed. Various forces (from the central government in Kinshasa to Angola, Zimbabwe, Rwanda, and Uganda) all intend to divvy up the Congo because, by partitioning the country, they would have access to these valuable resources.

With the profits from the sale of these resources, combatants finance the purchase of arms or, even, armies. In post–Cold War Africa, companies that provide security or mercenary services like Sandline, Gurkha Security Guards, MPRI, and Executive Outcomes can provide personnel, tactical, and logistic support to either governments or insurgents who are willing to pay the price. Executive Outcomes, a very effective military force operating from South Africa, has provided its services in Angola, Sierra Leone, and other hot spots in Africa. These specialists in warfare emerged from crack, decommissioned battalions in the South African army, including the thirty-two Buffalo Battalion, Koevoet, Recce squadrons, and the Civil Cooperation Bureau. Units from Executive Outcome have played decisive roles in battles, particularly in Angola and Sierra Leone.

CONSEQUENCES: CHILD SOLDIERS, REFUGEES, STUNTED DEVELOPMENT

One of the saddest events of the last ten years of the twentieth century has been the emergence of large armies of children in Africa who have known only war and who have never had an opportunity to obtain an education or enter the nonmilitary sector of the economy. Indeed, war—as an industry and as a means of employment—has in some areas largely replaced many nonmilitary sectors of the economy—like agriculture and light industry—as a means of livelihood for tens of thousands of African children. In Sierra Leone, there were at least six thousand child combatants, and, according to UNICEF, up to five thousand orphaned, lost, or abandoned children on the streets of Freetown, the capital of Sierra Leone. In Uganda, UNICEF estimates that as many as eight thousand children have been abducted by rebels since 1995. At least six thousand of the fighters in Liberia were children under fifteen, and ten thousand were aged fifteen to eighteen. In many cases children have been inducted into war by being kidnapped or removed from their families and, as was prevalent in Sierra Leone, drugged into submission.

Besides these child soldiers, conditions of warfare, genocide, and other forms of humanitarian abuse have created a situation at the beginning of the twenty-first century wherein one-third of the world's refugees—five million people—reside in Africa. Besides these refugees, another sixteen million people are "internally displaced" within their own countries and often have no access to humanitarian assistance. The worsening refugee problem is inextricably linked to warfare and human rights abuses.

The failure to attend to the prevention and the resolution of armed conflict in Africa has had a clear impact on the development of stable economies on the continent. During the 1990s, economic growth for all of Africa varied between 2.5 percent and 3 percent per year and this figure was distorted by revenues generated by petroleum exporting countries like Nigeria, Angola, and Gabon. Removing these countries from the total would reveal that during the 1990s, continental Africa experienced little or zero growth during the decade. During the 1990s, forty per cent of Africa (240 million people) tried to live on less than $1.00 a day. Continental Africa needs to raise its growth rates to averages of eight percent per annum to satisfy the needs of its burgeoning populations.[7] Funds that are being spent on armaments and military personnel are being diverted from investments in physical infrastructure and in education. Significant, large-scale investments in education and physical infrastructure will be needed for Africa to catch up with the economic growth that was experienced by much of the developing world during the 1990s. As long as many areas of Africa are preoccupied by war, this development will be difficult to achieve.

OUTLINE OF THE BOOK

In June 1999 the authors of this present volume gathered at the Rockefeller Foundation's Bellagio Study and Conference Center to discuss the policy options of regional versus UN-sponsored peacekeeping and peacemaking operations in Africa. Numerous case studies were commissioned including Angola, Mozambique, the Democratic Republic of the Congo, Sierra Leone, Liberia, the Sudan, Somalia, and the Eritrean-Ethiopian war, among others. The scholars, military officers, and diplomats involved in the conference endeavored to examine both the successes and failures of UN-sponsored and regionally sponsored peacekeeping and peacemaking ventures as well as the costs and benefits of each. The results of these discussions and research are provided in this volume. The volume is organized in three sections: I. The Causes of War and the Consequences of Peacekeeping, II. Case Studies, III. Political Issues.

After this introduction, Ali A. Mazrui and Robert L. Ostergard, Jr., in their article "From Pax Europa to Pax Africana," argue that the historical role of peacekeeping and peacemaking has been dominated by countries outside Africa. With the collapse of the Cold War, Africans are now being asked to manage their own conflicts. They explain that while there are potential hazards in this policy, the continuing influence of external actors in Africa's conflicts does not bring about needed African solutions and that peace, in the final analysis, must be achieved by Africans on Africa's terms.

Crawford Young then provides an article entitled "Pluralism, Ethnicity, and Militarization." In this article, Young merges an analysis of ethnic politics, the centralization of state power and the militarization of the state, and post–Cold War resistance to the state to provide a nuanced explanation of how these factors contribute to contemporary conditions of conflict in Africa. In his analysis, he explains how colonialism and colonial institutions contributed the seeds of conflict. He then goes on to explain postcolonial factors. His perspective is pan-African and panoramic.

A series of case studies follow, beginning with Francis Deng in "Sudan: An African Dilemma." Deng directly addresses a question that confronts all students of African politics: How can a political and geographical unit known as a state, which was created by European colonialists, be reexamined so that diverse peoples (in this case Arab, African, Afro-Arab, Muslim, Christian, and Animist) can co-exist peacefully? Deng recognizes the existence of separate cultures in the Sudan and he argues that impulses towards self-determination between the geographical North and the geographical South are deeply rooted. He examines whether the partition of the country or autonomy for southern Sudan are needed to obtain peace.

Georges Nzongola-Ntalaja, in "Civil War, Peacekeeping, and the Great Lakes Region," explains why at least seven African countries have involved themselves militarily in the Democratic Republic of the Congo. The economic and political stakes are quite high, given the Congo's mineral riches and geographic centrality. Besides explaining these economic and political concerns, he cogently explains the ethnic factors involved in the genocide in Rwanda, and he analyzes options regarding regional and international peacekeeping in the area.

W. Ofuatey-Kodjoe, in "The Impact of Peacekeeping on Target States: Lessons from the Liberian Experience," assesses the short-term and long-term impact of ECOMOG operations in Liberia. His view of ECOMOG's and ECOWAS' efforts in Liberia is dim; he views both their military and diplomatic efforts as faulty. On the military side, he claims that the ECOMOG force was not sufficiently large to accomplish its objective quickly. In terms of diplomacy, he claims that ECOWAS was unimaginative. Ofuatey-Kodjoe also argues that ECOMOG's and ECOWAS' failures encouraged the spread of the war to Sierra

Leone. He questions the salutary effects of military intervention for allegedly humanitarian purposes; he believes these interventions are probably unjustifiable from the viewpoint of international law and fraught with logistical and tactical problems when they are deployed. He advocates enhanced diplomacy and diminished military operations as a means of resolving conflict in Africa.

In "Strategic Policy Failure and State Fragmentation: Security, Peacekeeping, and Democratization in Sierra Leone," Yusuf Bangura provides a complex analysis of the factors that led to civil war in Sierra Leone. Besides providing background on the causes of the Sierra Leone war, he assesses ECOMOG strategy and operations in Sierra Leone. He strongly endorses the need for a regional peacekeeping force like ECOMOG in West Africa, but he insists that such a force can only be employed as a stop-gap measure to restore peace and order in the short term. He argues that peace in Sierra Leone can only be restored with reform of the electoral system, changes in recruitment of soldiers and officers in the army, the removal of diamonds as a source of financing for warfare, and the provision of a massive social and educational program for Sierra Leone's youth, which has been seriously damaged by the ferocity of the war.

Hussein Adam, in "The International Humanitarian Intervention in Somalia, 1992–1995," explains the origins of conflict and the implosion of the state in Somalia. He claims that the disintegration of Somali society was patently evident and observable over time and that few political actors, either from the region or internationally, intervened early enough, in a diplomatic fashion, to arrest the disintegration. He notes that when UN and US forces did deploy in Somalia, UN Representative Ahmed Sahnoun undertook a creditable diplomatic effort to resolve the conflict but was removed when the US and the UN shifted its emphasis from diplomatic to military initiatives. When United States diplomatic and military officers changed policy and began hunting for the arrest of General Aidid (a local warlord) as a central element of its approach to resolve Somalia's problems, the hunt for Aidid unleashed virulent anti-American sentiments that shifted and escalated the conflict to attacking UN and US peacekeepers and peacemakers. When UN and US forces undertook heavy losses in October 1993, Operation Restore Hope came to an end. Adam argues that peacemaking to restore order should be an option where the state has clearly imploded but he emphasizes that for peacemaking to succeed, diplomacy is as important—if not more important—than military tactical maneuvers.

In "Mozambique: What Nexus among Peacemaking, Peacekeeping, and Development?" João Honwana explains how peace was attained in Mozambique. He explains that much of the eventual success of the peace process had its origins in discussions sponsored by the Sant'Egidio Community (a Roman Catholic lay organization) in Rome, which brought RENAMO (Mozambique National Resistance) and FRELIMO (Front for the Liberation of Mozambique) to a neutral forum where they could discuss their differences. The negotiations in Rome led to a General Peace Accord in 1992 and successful multiparty elections in 1994. The Rome discussions began a process of mutual understanding between the combatants. This development would later prove essential because the implementation of the Peace Accord during the period from 1992 to 1994 encountered difficulties. Without the base of mutual understanding first established in Rome and then encouraged by UN representative Aldo Ajello, it is likely that the peace process in Mozambique would have failed. Honwana emphasizes the role of mediation, diplomacy, and disarmament in the peace process. Unlike many of the cases discussed in this volume, there is less emphasis placed on military intervention and more discussion of the importance of mediation and diplomacy. The lesson in Mozambique seems to be that peace is more easily attainable when the combatants truly want peace and when the United Nations has adequate diplomatic and material resources to support the process. This raises important questions: Must diplomacy always precede military peacekeeping? Is diplomacy the only or best answer? Or, must military intervention never be considered, even in the face of genocide or humanitarian abuses?

In contrast to Mozambique where peace has been attained, J. Michael Turner in "The Perpetual Civil War in Angola: The Failure of Peacekeeping and Democratization" explains why war has been the status quo in Angola since 1961. Ethnic strife, superpower intervention and manipulation, and profound struggles over valuable resources combined in Angola to create a volatile political mix. Turner contrasts peace processes and peacekeeping efforts in Mozambique and Angola. Whereas in Mozambique the combatants agreed to a 1992 General Peace Accord in Rome which adhered, in Angola the 1991 Bicesse Accords and the 1994 Lusaka Protocol were never honored. Whereas in Mozambique the UN committed sufficient resources to implement disarmament and the organization of elections, the UN commitment in Angola was paltry. Turner points out that neither the commitment of the combatants nor the investment of resources by the UN was sufficient in Angola to accomplish the objectives of attaining peace. When one adds the government's considerable access to petroleum revenues to purchase armaments and UNITA's access to diamond revenues to do the same, one understands how sophisticated weaponry continues to flow into Angola. The lack of political will to end the war together with seemingly unlimited resources to purchase armaments have combined to sustain a war that has lasted almost forty years.

Following Turner's article is a last section that deals with political issues and processes that are relevant to securing peace and democracy in Africa. In "Military Disengagement from Politics and Constitutionalism in Africa: Challenges and Opportunities," Julius Ihonvbere laments the militarization of African societies and politics, which he says results from lack of consensus among political elites, the fragmentation and weakness of civil society, the existence of ineffective governmental bureaucracies, and the failure to control the political and pecuniary aspirations of military officers. This arrogation of political power to military officers has led to a culture where constitutional norms and democratic institutions are trivialized. Ihonvbere argues that, in order to rein in the military, it is important to expand civic education from the grass roots up so that civil society can be reconstructed to serve as an effective counterweight to the assertion of power by military elites. He emphasizes the value of a democratic constitution and believes that the masses must be involved in country-wide processes whereby they become active politically and contribute to the creation of a meaningful, living document known as a constitution. He asserts that a constitution that is not created by elites but that emerges from the masses and which is the result of widespread consultations and debates will ultimately be more enduring. Ihonvbere believes this process crucial because it helps create trust in government and contributes directly to the creation of a more vibrant and plural civil society, which is essential for democracy to endure.

Ricardo René Laremont and Habu Galadima, in "Lessons for the Transition to Democracy in Africa: The Experience of the Military in Argentina, Brazil, Chile, Nigeria, and Algeria," engage in a comparative analysis of transitions from military rule in five countries. They describe the roles that military officers can play in the transition to civilian rule and discuss the problems the military encounters during transitions as well as their interaction with democratizing civilian elites and the masses. They emphasize that transitions are variable but, in the final analysis, elite consensus for democracy as a preference is indispensable for the eventual consolidation of democracy. Furthermore, they emphasize that governments have been rendered more stable when the economic management of the state rests in the hands of civilian leaders who can be rejected at the polls rather than military officers who cannot.

NOTES

1. Michael J. Dziedzic, "Policing the New World Disorder: Addressing Gaps in Public Security during Peace Operations," in *Toward Responsibility in the New World Disorder,* ed. Max Manwaring and John T. Fishel (London: Frank Cass, 1998), p. 135.

2. Kofi Annan, "The Causes of Conflict and the Promotion of Durable Peace and Sustainable Development in Africa," pp. 2–3.

3. Charter of the Organization of African Unity, Article 2-1-C and 2-1-F.

4. Prior to the ECOMOG effort in Liberia, the OAU sent peacekeeping forces to Chad in 1980. That intervention will be characterized as a pan-African intervention rather than as a regional peacekeeping intervention.

5. Walter Clarke, "Failed Visions and Uncertain Mandates in Somalia," in *Learning from Somalia: The Lessons of Armed Humanitarian Intervention* (Boulder, Colo.: Westview Press, 1997), pp. 13–14.

6. William Reno, *Warlord Politics and African States* (Boulder, Colo.: Lynne Rienner, 1998), pp. 99–100.

7. The World Bank, *The World Bank Group in Africa* (Washington, DC: World Bank, 1998), p.1.

2

From Pax Europa to Pax Africana

Ali A. Mazrui and Robert L. Ostergard, Jr.

When the colonial order ended in Africa, a myriad of problems confronted the new African nations resulting from centuries of European control. The most prevalent of the problems became horrifyingly apparent. The legacy of the Westphalian system was playing havoc in ways unforeseen by both Europeans and Africans. Shortly after the period of decolonization, political conflict erupted in many of Africa's newly independent states. While the legacy of imposed borders is often pointed to as a significant cause of Africa's conflict, most of Africa's wars, ironically, are not *about* those borders. In fact, those same borders were embraced by African leaders in the wake of colonial rule. Since then, African leaders have defended the question of borders and territorial integrity and discouraged challenges to them. However, the territorial borders themselves are not always or necessarily the issue in Africa's conflicts because most conflicts are within borders rather than across them. Rarely have threats to African states come from other states; rather, conflict has emerged from disputes among groups within those borders. In light of political turmoil and economic crises, the major question that has arisen in the postcolonial period has been who will keep the peace in Africa?

The most obvious answer to the question has been the one least employed—Africans themselves will keep the peace. Those often involved in resolving Africa's conflicts have been the former colonial powers (Britain and France mostly), the United States, and the United Nations. Three questions become important in Africa's legacy of peacekeeping. First, why have outsiders played the dominant role in African peacekeeping? Second, why have Africans been unable to end their own conflicts? And finally, what is the domestic impact of peacekeeping intervention in Africa's conflicts? To answer these questions, it is important to explore the role of outside forces in Africa's conflicts.[1]

THE COLONIAL EXPERIENCE: BRITISH AND FRENCH INTERVENTION

Some interventions can be traced to different types of colonial experiences that African nations underwent. It seems as though postcolonial differences arise depending upon whether Britain or France was the colonizing power. While all European colonial powers shared a moral imperative to spread "superior" Western culture and values, significant differences emerged between colonial powers in the administration of their territory in Africa. The British system of indirect rule was designed to allow indigenous people to govern locally under Britain's administration. The system allowed for the preservation of culture and customs, but as Wallerstein notes, it also was designed to keep distance between the British and their African subjects.[2] The French, on the other hand, were more paternalistic. There was no indirect rule; instead the French encouraged "assimilation" of African subjects into French society. The French aspired to implant France in Africa, culturally, linguistically, economically, and politically.

While volumes have been written about the impact of these two different forms of colonial administration, for our purposes it is important to note how these prevailing systems affected postcolonial relations between Britain and France and their former colonial possessions, particularly with reference to peacekeeping and intervention.

The initial inclination was for Britain to maintain influence in all its former colonial possessions. The British Commonwealth and admission to the Commonwealth was seen as a *rite de passage* for former colonies.[3] However, political reality quickly caught up to Britain's desire for a strong global presence. Once it became apparent that Britain had slid from a global hegemon to a regional power, Britain's interest in maintaining the Commonwealth diminished, and so did its interest in Africa.

Prior to the 1970s, British intervention in African crises was much more pronounced than afterwards. Under the guise of the Commonwealth, Britain was quick to intervene from 1964 onward after a string of East African military mutinies occurred. At the request of the victors in Zanzibar, President Julius Nyrere of Tanganyika sent a police contingent to help restore order there. Tanganyikan troops took advantage of the reduced strength of the police to mutiny, demanding higher wages and the further Africanization of the military officer corps. Troops in Kenya and Uganda followed suit, mutinying against their respective governments. The governments of Tanganyika, Uganda, and Kenya all requested and received British help in putting down these mutinies.[4]

France's relationship with its former colonies took a different path than did Britain's. In part, France's move to solidify its position in sub-Saharan Africa was a reaction to its own disastrous adventure in the Algerian civil war. In trying to maintain its influence in sub-Saharan Africa, the French government concluded a series of military agreements that would assure its presence on the continent. Twelve African states signed military agreements with France between 1960 and 1961, some bilateral, some multilateral.[5] Mali and Upper Volta refused to sign agreements initially, fearing French intervention in their internal affairs. The refusal was more the exception than the rule. Military agreements assured France an exclusive position in Francophone Africa, preserving French military bases in several key countries.

The initial plans to maintain a dominant military presence ultimately became politically unfeasible due to the exorbitant costs. French troop levels were reduced from 58,000 to 21,300 in 1964 and reduced again to 6,400 during the 1965–1970 period.[6]

Despite the troop reductions, France maintained an active presence in Africa through the creation of the *Force intarmies d'intervention,* which was deemed politically more acceptable than having a large military contingency permanently stationed in Africa. France put the force to use on multiple occasions. Direct French intervention occurred when foreign invasions, civil wars, rebellions, and threats to French-supported leaders emerged. Between 1962 and 1995, nineteen interventions occurred: Senegal (1962), Gabon (1964, 1990), Chad (1968–72, 1978, 1983, 1986), Mauritania (1977), Zaire (1978, 1991), Central African Republic (1979), Togo (1986), Comoros (1989, 1995), Rwanda (1990–93, 1994), Djibouti (1991), Benin (1991), and Sierra Leone (1992).[7] These represent an extensive list of French involvement in African domestic conflicts on an overt level. French covert intervention was also prevalent, providing monitoring and penetration of opposition groups to French clients as well.[8]

The most extensive of France's overt interventions came in Chad. French intervention in Chad was first utilized in suppressing Chad's civil war. However, with Libyan support of opposition forces in Chad, French support for Chad's government became more important and extensive. In 1983, direct French intervention was deemed necessary when Libyan troops launched a major offensive in Chad, while placing claims to a large segment of land, the Aouzou Strip.[9] With support, Chadian President Hissein Habre was able to push Libyan troops back, but it was apparent that his success was due to French intervention.

France's postcolonial goals of sustaining a French-African community to preserve its influence in Africa brought French aspirations into conflict with British goals in Nigeria's Biafran War (1967–70). The fear of genocidal reprisal upon Ibo secessionists in the war brought international sympathy that helped prolong the war. France's intervention in the war, however, was stimulated by its desire to obtain exclusive oil rights in secessionist Biafra, while promoting the breakup of Nigeria. Nigeria's breakup would have increased the relative strength of Francophone African states in West Africa.[10] For Britain, by contrast, its interests were served by supporting the Nigerian federal government. By supporting the federal government, Britain hoped to maintain access to Nigerian petroleum.[11] British military aid was sent for this purpose, providing the needed resources to put down the Biafran revolt.

The British and the French record of intervention for peacekeeping has not been altogether successful. While conflict was derailed in some of these instances of intervention, often the solution imposed was a military solution without addressing the underlying issues in Africa's conflicts. In Arab north Africa, the essential elements at the heart of conflict have tended to be religious, while in Black sub-Saharan Africa, the roots of conflict are predominantly ethnic. Ex-colonial intervention has not been successful at addressing these issues. Instead, British and French attempts at ending conflict have generally involved the preservation of self-interest instead of settlements that are in Africa's interests. But even in this regard, differences emerge between British and French intervention in Africa. In part, this is due to the colonial legacy. For Britain, the impact of indirect rule made it easier for the British to disengage from Africa and to place considerable distance between itself and its former colonies. For France, disengagement from Africa's affairs has been difficult because if France were to disengage politically and militarily from Africa, it would begin the disassembly of France's foreign policy of French cultural influence (Francophonie) that it deems so important. If this were to occur, France's cultural and political role in Africa would begin to evaporate.

UNITED NATIONS PEACEKEEPING IN AFRICA

The newest initiatives in Africa by the United Nations have, for the most part, been a post–Cold War phenomenon.[12] During the Cold War, the United Nations played a prominent role in the process of liberating Africa from colonial rule.[13] However, the United Nations' role in peacekeeping during that process was hindered by ideological bipolarity and lingering colonial sentimentalities. The one United Nations peacekeeping operation that did occur during the Cold War, in the Congo (ONUC, 1960–1964), provided an example of the paralyzing effect that Cold-War policies could have on United Nations operations.

Shortly after independence from Belgium, troops in the Congo mutinied against their Belgian officers. With the authority of the Congolese government, Belgium responded by deploying troops in the capital, Leopoldville (Kinshasa). The provincial premier of Katanga (later Shaba) province, Moïse Tshombe, backed by local Belgian administrators, declared the province's independence. The key to Katanga province's secession involved the presence of Belgian troops, who supported Tshombe and who courted mining interests in the province. The attack on Matadi provoked retaliation against whites throughout the country. The retaliations escalated Belgian involvement and a further massive Belgian intervention, unauthorized by the Congolese government of Patrice Lumumba. At the request of the Congolese government, United Nations troops were deployed to the Congo to quell the problem.[14] On the one hand, the ONUC operation was considered successful in the sense that it was able to prevent the breakup of the Congo, and possibly deter other secessionist movements in Africa.[15] On the other hand, the ONUC operation revealed disagreements among the United States, Britain, France, and the Soviet Union over what to do in the Congo.

The United States was in full support, politically and economically, of the peacekeeping operation. Britain and France, however, saw problems. Britain had a vested interest in the Congo, with a financial stake in Belgium's mining operation in Katanga province.[16] Britain's support for the operation was, at best, lukewarm. France opposed the operation by withholding financial support and undertaking obstructionist policies. The French government, sympathetic to Belgium's cause, convinced the governments of central Africa not to grant overflight rights to aircraft transporting troops to the Congo. France also allowed recruitment or mercenaries for the Katanga secessionist movement.[17] The Soviet Union initially supported the deployment of United Nations troops in the Congo as a way of supporting national liberation movements that were dedicated to decolonization. After the assassination of Lumumba, however, the Soviet Union withdrew its support for the operation and refused to contribute financially to it.[18]

The Congo crisis thus presented a case study of how peacekeeping by the United Nations should not be carried out. Durch summarizes the problems aptly: ". . . ONUC's fundamental problem was that . . . there were no disinterested parties. All of the rivalries of the Cold War and all of the tensions of African decolonization . . . tugged at the operation and distorted it. . . . Given all of the international struggles for power, it is perhaps not surprising that at one point or another every Congolese political faction considered ONUC the enemy."[19] The Congo experience exemplified the divergent interests at play in Africa, with little attention paid to what was actually needed to bring peace to the crisis-stricken country. For the remainder of the Cold War, the United Nations participated in humanitarian relief efforts and mostly unsuccessful peacemaking operations. Peacekeeping was not to reappear on the United Nations agenda in Africa until after the Cold War. The table below illustrates this clearly. The earliest United Nations peacekeeping intervention in Africa occurred with the Congo crisis in 1960; however its next opportunity for peacekeeping occurs in 1989, when United Nations troops were deployed to monitor Cuban troop withdrawals from Angola (UNAVEM I).

Table 2.1
United Nations Operations in Africa, 1960–Present

Location	UN Operation	Dates
Angola	UNAVEM I	1989–1991
	UNAVEM II	1991–1995
	UNAVEM III	1995–1997
Central African Republic	MINURCA	1998–2000
Congo	ONUC	1960–1964
	MONUC	1999–Present
Ethiopia/Eritrea	UNMEE	2000–Present
Liberia	UNOMIL	1993–1997
Libya/Chad	UNASOG	1994
Mozambique	ONUMOZ	1992–1994
Namibia	UNTAG	1989–1990
Rwanda	UNAMIR	1993–1996
Sierra Leone	UNOMSIL	1998–1999
	UNAMSIL	2000–Present
Somalia	UNOSOM I	1992–1993
	UNOSOM II	1993–1995
Uganda/Rwanda	UNOMUR	1993–1994
Western Sahara	MINURSO	1991–Present

Source: United Nations Peacekeeping Operations [Web Page]. United Nations Department of Public Information, [cited October 1, 2000]. Available from http://www.un.org/Depts/dpko/dpko/ops.htm.

Since the end of the Cold War, United Nations intervention for peacekeeping in Africa dramatically increased, as the veil of the Cold War that had long suppressed domestic conflict was lifted. The demise of the Cold War in Africa has brought about contradictory issues: the increasing demand by the international community for democratic governance in Africa amidst the decline in interest in Africa within the international community. The result has been the eruption of domestic conflict at a higher rate than any time in Africa's postcolonial history. The danger of conflict in Africa goes beyond civil wars because many of Africa's civil wars have spillover effects on neighboring states.[20]

The United Nations since the end of the Cold War has increased its role in peacekeeping in Africa and on other continents; this has placed tremendous financial and manpower burdens on the organization. Many of these peacekeeping interventions have brought some level of success. Its two worse cases of failure, the prevention of genocide in Rwanda and the Somalia operation led by the United States, helped to bring about a reassessment of United Nations activities in Africa and America's role in peacekeeping operations. For the United Nations, the reassessment involved reexamination of procedures and criteria for entering a peacekeeping mission; for the United States, Somalia was a defining moment in American post–Cold War foreign policy.[21]

AMERICAN INTERVENTION: THE COLD WAR AND BEYOND

The impact of the Cold War had domestic and international ramifications for much of the developing world. Africa was no different in this regard. Decolonization in the shadow of the Cold War brought a new dimension to the question of who would keep the peace in Africa. In the context of the Cold War, a third answer to that question came in the form of American intervention in African conflicts. American intervention in Africa followed a pattern of American self-interest that relegated Africa's needs to America's.

Historically, America's interest in Africa evolved from social and economic considerations. In its early stages, America's relationship with Africa was purely economic, with America being the final destination for many of the slaves in the trans-Atlantic slave trade. With the end of American slavery after the Civil War, policymakers maintained at least a peripheral interest in Africa, mostly for its economic potential. By the 1870s, the United States was preoccupied with Reconstruction, but by 1883 President Chester Allen Arthur was pushing the United States to open significant economic ties in the Congo. With the start of King Leopold's African International Association in 1884, members of the United States Congress were pushing to support Leopold's brutal policies in the Congo. By opening up economic ties and supporting Belgian interests, the hope was that Africa could provide a substantial export market to help lift the suppressed textile industry in the United States south. But other members of Congress had more sinister reasons for supporting a United States Africa policy—namely to export newly emancipated Africans and African Americans back to Africa. Doing so, of course, would have alleviated labor surpluses and unemployment in the southern United States while promoting exports to Africa.[22]

America's economic interests continued in the wake of World War II, though in the context of the emerging Cold War. As a major source for copper, cobalt, gold, diamonds, manganese, and other strategic minerals, the United States saw economic importance and strategic importance in keeping those resources out of Soviet control.[23] With the beginning of the Cold War, American "manifest destiny" took on anticommunist zeal, which took on harsher tones in other regions of the world.[24] Still, this rhetoric played a significant role in shaping America's policies toward Africa. With America preoccupied in Asia and Latin America, the United States was content to leave France as the safe-guard against communist expansion in Africa. However, this did not keep the United States out of Africa's conflicts, and where it seemed that Soviet penetration was poten-tially successful, the United States used a number of resources to assist in curtailing their advances.

The first real test of America's commitment to halting Soviet expansion in Africa occurred in the Belgian Congo. America's reaction to United Nations operations in the Congo (ONUC) was at first supportive. ONUC was designed to maintain the political independence of the Congo, while preventing the occurrence of civil war and securing the removal of all foreign military, paramilitary, and advisory personnel not under the United Nations Command.[25] More than nineteen thousand UN troops were committed to the operation. However, the operation itself was not successful per se and its failure heightened American security concerns in the region. Ultimately, the Congo crisis came to an end with the assassination of Patrice Lumumba, an event in which United States' actual complicity has been difficult to determine.[26] From the United States' perspective, the assassination of Lumumba dealt a blow to Soviet ambitions.[27] For Africans, Lumumba's assassination ushered in one of the most corrupt and brutal dictatorships in modern African history. Subsequently, for more than thirty years, Mobutu Sese Seko enjoyed American and French support because he was one of Africa's staunchest anti-communist leaders. America's intervention in the Congo was one of its strongest efforts to prevent what was perceived to be Moscow's attempt to spread Communism in Africa. However, from the end of the Congo crisis, the United States was content to leave most of Africa in the hands of the French and British. Involvement by the United States in Africa was inconsistent and geographically limited mostly to the Horn of Africa and southern Africa.

In the Horn of Africa, American involvement emerged from Cold War interests and considerations. With the fall of Emperor Haile Selassie in 1974 to a military revolt and the installation of a pro-Marxist government, the United States took the opportunity to supply military aid to Somalia in its ongoing battle with Ethiopia over the Ogaden terri-tory. The United States was particularly interested in striking a deal with the Somalis over the use of Soviet-constructed military installations at Berbera. Support for Soma-lia in trying to settle the dispute between itself and Ethiopia was therefore predicated on two aspects: the Marxist alignment of the Ethiopian government and the securing of American military installations in Somalia, which would allow greater surveillance of the Middle East, North and East Africa, and the Persian Gulf. Hence, the Cold War was the determining factor in support for Somalia and opposition to Ethiopia. Southern Africa would prove to differ little in this regard.

The Reagan doctrine of unwavering support for anticommunist movements in the developing world became the basis of America's interest in southern Africa in the 1980s. However, support for anticommunist movements was not immediately forthcoming in southern Africa. Under Assistant Secretary of State for African Affairs Chester Crocker the administration developed a regional policy of "constructive engagement" in southern Africa. The policy sought to "eliminate sources of instability and conflict among the states of southern Africa . . . in order to create possibilities for peaceful change and development within those states."[28] Constructive engagement was applied to Angola and Mozambique, both of which were embroiled in anticommunist insurgencies. While the policy was in force during the entire length of the Reagan administration, it was constantly under pressure from conservative groups in the United States who demanded a stronger showing of support for anticommunist movements in Angola and Mozambique. In both cases Soviet aid to these governments brought domestic pressure from conservative groups and Congress to apply the Reagan Doctrine.[29] In the case of Angola, the Reagan Doctrine came into full force and provided limited success to ending the violence in Angola. In Mozambique, when it was revealed that RENAMO was engaged in the large scale slaughter of civilians, any attempts to fully apply the Reagan Doctrine to Mozambique ended and another chapter in America's strategic concerns in Africa slowly came to a close. The ideological basis of American foreign policy in Africa would become apparent in the early 1990s in the wake of the Cold War.

The disappearance of the Soviet "threat" in Africa after the Cold War also marked the beginning of the United States' diplomatic departure. Within three years of the fall of the Berlin Wall, the State Department's Bureau of African Affairs lost seventy positions, and consulates in Kenya, Cameroon, and Nigeria were scheduled to be closed. The United States Agency for International Development's Africa desk lost between thirty and forty officers out of a total of a normal staff size of 130.[30] The end of the global ideological tug-of-war between the United States and the former Soviet Union marginalized Africa in United States foreign policy and in the international community. Africa's strategic usefulness had come to an end. However, the ramifications of Africa's marginalization would haunt the United States and the international community, contributing to major policy errors in the post–Cold War period.

American intervention in Africa in the post–Cold War period was defined at first by international and public opinion and later by the legacy of policy failure. The United States' first significant attempt at peacekeeping intervention in the post–Cold War period occurred under United Nations auspices in Somalia (UNOSOM I and UNOSOM II). The objective of the insertion of American military personnel in Somalia was to contain devastating famine and to bring an end to the anarchy in Somalia that was exacerbating that famine. The policy would, in hindsight, mark a significant turn in American policy on intervention. It was the first time that American troops were introduced to a country in order to provide humanitarian relief, a significant departure for the United States from its long-standing anticommunist strategic interest policies in the Horn of Africa.[31] The operation in Somalia, in essence, became the turning point of United States peacekeeping policy in Africa in the post–Cold War period.

With the overthrow of President Siad Barre in 1991, Somalia was plunged into anarchy by warring clans, which contributed to famine conditions within the country. Initial American assistance came in the form of donations through private groups and through United Nations programs. As United Nations peacekeeping troops met opposition in distributing food relief to people in Somalia, the United Nations Security Council passed resolution 794 requesting a United States-led force to enter Somalia. The initial deployment of troops in 1992, however, illustrated the laxity and complacency in which the United States Department of Defense and its commander approached the Somalia operation. Marines landing in Somalia were met by reporters and television crews on the beaches in Somalia, resembling more of a Hollywood production than a military operation. The fanfare of the initial landing quickly dissipated as the reality of the problems in Somalia confronted American troops and their allies.

American troops faced opposition from Somalia's clan leaders and even from the general population itself. Initial hopes of providing relief to the Somali people were shattered as American troops found themselves confronted by strong opposition to their presence.[32] Following prolonged fighting between American forces and Somali clans and the death of several American soldiers, the United States withdrew from Somalia. It became apparent to policymakers that the initial intervention plan underestimated the cost of the intervention in terms of manpower and finances. Significant political and cultural barriers confronted American forces in Somalia that had not been anticipated.

The events in Somalia, however, had a longer impact beyond the immediate failure in Somalia itself. When genocide in Rwanda confronted the United States and the international community, few offered peacekeeping solutions. As one analyst noted, "Rwanda was unfortunate to have erupted when it did—while the tears of Somalia were still fresh on the cheeks of America."[33] With Somalia fresh on their minds, American policymakers and the international community turned a blind eye to events in Rwanda. Secretary of State Madeleine Albright recognized the issue, ". . . we—the international community—should have been more active in the early stages of the atrocities in Rwanda in 1994 and called them what they were: genocide."[34] The secretary's blunt admission was at the forefront of a complete reevaluation of American policy toward Africa. Part of the reevaluation was designed to place responsibility for Africa's political and humanitarian problems in African hands. For Africa, the idea was not new. But past attempts at African peacekeeping solutions by Africans have produced mixed results.

AFRICAN PEACEKEEPING INITIATIVES

The post–Cold War period has placed responsibility for Africa's problems in African's hands, almost by default. Given the lack of interest by the international community in

Africa, the options for maintaining peace have narrowed, perhaps for the better. In one sense, the idea of Africans handling their own crises has tremendous appeal, particularly given that the will of others was the determining factor in settling Africa's crises during the Cold War. In another sense, the increasing involvement of African nations in peacekeeping begs the question: what will be the domestic impact of peacekeeping interventions both on the foreign participants and the host country? The answer to this question lies in what form the peacekeeping takes. Africa's options for dealing with conflict include regional organizations, regional integration, unilateral action (international vigilantism), and rapid reaction forces.

Regional Organizations

The Organization of Africa Unity (OAU) was the first regional organization to attempt peacekeeping in Africa. The irony of OAU peacekeeping initiatives rests in the debate over colonial borders that occurred during the formation of the OAU in 1963. Leading the debate was Ghana's President, Kwame Nkrumah, who said in advocating the abandonment of colonial boundaries, "only African Unity can heal this festering sore of boundary disputes between our various states."[35] Others, such as President Modibo Keita of Mali argued that "We must take Africa as it is, and we must renounce any territorial claims, if we do not wish to introduce what we might call black imperialism in Africa. . . . African unity demands of each one of us complete respect for the legacy that we have received from the colonial system, that is to say: maintenance of the present frontiers of our respective states."[36] The new doctrine accepting the colonial borders was presented in 1964. The question became whether the OAU could help settle disputes over those borders.

The OAU met limited success in its attempts to keep the peace in African disputes. Perhaps no other case illustrates the problems the OAU encountered than the Chad/Libya peacekeeping initiative. Prior to French intervention in Chad, the OAU had attempted to bring peace to the country that had been rocked with factional fighting since its independence from France. By 1978, Chad was on the brink of collapse with more than ten groups fighting for control of its capital, Ndjamena. An attempt by Nigeria to broker a settlement in Chad led to a brief cease-fire that eventually failed, leading to the return to factional fighting. When Libya made its intentions to intervene in Chad known along with its intent at "full unity" with Chad, the OAU took up the matter of Chad and Libya. Many of the leaders at the 1981 Nairobi meeting expressed concern over Libyan intentions and agreed to dispatch a peacekeeping force to Chad.[37]

The introduction of the peacekeeping force in Chad, however, proved to be a disaster for the OAU. Several problems plagued OAU peacekeeping operations in Chad. From a logistical standpoint, the operation suffered from poor planning and coordination. Moreover, countries that had initially committed troops never sent them. As a result, the operation did not have adequate manpower to carry out a successful peacekeeping operation. Militarily, the operation called for the immediate withdrawal of Libyan forces from Chad. This, however, created a power vacuum that was immediately filled by factions led by Hissein Habre, who took control of Chad's government. From a political standpoint, the mandate for the operation was quite ambiguous, leaving much room for interpretation on the part of the peacekeepers, Libya and Chad. But, probably most important, the reasons for the failure of the OAU mission in Chad was that the leaders who committed the troops to Chad did so half-heartedly. They saw the war in Chad as nothing more than a by-product of the Cold War, with significant outside intervention. Libya was pro-Soviet while Chad's government was pro-West, particularly pro-French. Hence, the Chad-Libya conflict was simply another proxy war, not much different from the 1960 war in the Congo and later Angola.

Other attempts at OAU peacekeeping were made after Chad. But the roles played by political actors outside Africa (the United States, France, Britain, and the Soviet Union) limited any significant contribution that the OAU could make to resolving crises or keeping the peace. Outside intervention by the United States, the United Nations, or other powers brought resources to influence outcomes in directions favored by *them* rather than solutions preferred by *Africans*. Similarly, the OAU has limited its capacity to intervene to maintain the peace. Given that most of Africa's wars have been intrastate wars, the OAU has been prohibited by its own charter (Article 3, Clause 2) that expressly forbids the OAU from intervening in internal conflicts. The result has been an artificial distinction between intrastate conflict and interstate conflict, given that intrastate conflicts most often have spillover effects in Africa.[38] The inherent problems that the OAU faces in peacekeeping operations is acknowledged by its support for subregional peace-keeping operations.

Subregional organizations have acted to maintain peace in Africa, most prominently the Economic Community of West African States (ECOWAS) and its monitoring group ECOMOG. ECOMOG intervention in Liberia (and later Sierra Leone) is covered extensively elsewhere in this volume. Suffice to say here that ECOMOG succeeded in stopping the expansion of the fighting in Liberia, but it too confronted organizational, logistic and political problems. Among these was the command structure of the force in Liberia, the dominance of Nigeria within the force, and the superordination of Nigeria's interests over Liberia's.[39] Despite ECOMOG's lack of experience and the disarray in Nigeria, Liberians had their say at the ballot box. While Liberians eventually voted for Charles Taylor—the architect of the civil war—to be their president, at least his election emerged from free democratic choice. Nevertheless, the fumbling but historic role of ECOMOG in Liberia underlies this choice.

Regional Integration

Regional integration involves voluntary agreements among states to limit political, ethnic, and economic conflict. The idea is not new and in fact came into being with the union of revolutionary Zanzibar and Tanganyika in 1964. The benefits of such a union included greater political and economic stability within the resulting Tanzania. In the post–Cold War era, the notion of integration has taken on wider support. One such system would involve having Africans administer an international trusteeship over countries in conflict. A second option would involve the recolonization of weaker African states by stronger ones.[40] Such a union was proposed at the time of the Hutu-Tutsi conflict in Rwanda. The idea was to incorporate Rwanda and Burundi into a federation with Tanzania, which would help to alleviate the ethnic divide between Hutu and Tutsi.[41]

Unilateral Action (International Vigilantism)

International vigilantism occurs when one country occupies another to restore and maintain order. In 1971, Idi Amin Dada overthrew the government of Milton Obote in Uganda. President Nyerere of Tanzania roundly condemned the coup, refusing to have any dealings with Amin. Nyerere, however, was not prepared to use force in order to overturn the coup and put Obote back in power. In 1979, Nyerere was forced to change his mind after Idi Amin's Ugandan forces invaded Tanzania as part of Amin's persistent regional destabilization efforts. Nyerere ordered Tanzania's troops to march to Kampala with the specific goal of ousting Amin from power. Subsequently, he established a Tanzanian protectorate over Uganda before multiparty elections could be held. In doing so, two mistakes became clear. First, the duration of the protectorate was too short, and, second, he pushed Obote back into power. Both decisions had catastrophic effects for Uganda. The protectorate itself was beneficial, though it was not well focused to resolve some of the problems in Uganda. The second Obote administration in Uganda turned out to be a tragedy, only to be ended by Yoweri Museveni's military triumph in 1986.

Rapid-Reaction Forces

The three options covered (regional organizations, regional integration, and international vigilantism) have all had limited success and, in some cases, detrimental affects on the long-term prospects for African peacekeeping. Despite these limitations, it is clear that the international community will be less inclined to intervene in African affairs, given the high costs, limited resources, and lack of strategic interest in Africa. In some regard, even the international community itself, particularly the United States, recognizes this situation. These reasons motivated the United States proposal for the African Crisis Response Initiative (ACRI) in 1996.

The ACRI was first conceived in the aftermath of the Rwandan genocide. On a tour through Africa, then-Secretary of State Warren Christopher proposed the establishment of a ten-thousand-man crisis force that would be sponsored by the West. The response from the United Nations was positive, but the initial reaction of African countries was mixed. Some nations such as Ethiopia, Senegal, and Mali backed the proposal from the start. Others such as Zimbabwe, South Africa, and Tanzania were uncommitted. Tanzania actually rejected monies from the United States earmarked for peacekeeping training as not being in conjunction with its national interests.[42]

African countries have perceived problems with the ACRI. First was the issue of command: who would deploy the force? The issue addressed concerns that African countries had about deploying forces at the request of non-African countries. The deployment of the ACRI force would be at the control of African participant countries at the request of regional and international organizations such as ECOMOG, the OAU, and the United Nations. Perhaps another obstacle to the initiative's implementation involved its source: the West.[43] Some African leaders perceived that the ACRI was conceived by the West so that it would do the West's bidding on the continent. In this sense, the perception was no different from the historical legacy of Western intervention in Africa's conflicts. Instead of direct intervention by the West, African countries would follow policy dictates by the West. The United States moved to allay African fears by emphasizing that the ACRI would not produce a standing army, but would be a crisis team engaged in traditional peacekeeping when called to do so by Africans themselves. This clarification helped to bring Uganda into the plan, which the United States saw as important for the success of the ACRI.

Opposition to the ACRI was not limited to African nations. France has expressed severe concerns about further United States encroachment in its sphere of influence. But as Warren Christopher reminded the French, old spheres of influence have gone by the wayside. Countries cannot consider groups of countries as being their "private domains."[44]

It is true that the ACRI may decrease French influence in Africa, but this may not necessarily be problematic through African eyes. For example, the decrease in French or American external influence may present opportunities for African countries to exert their own regional hegemonic prowess. South Africa has been hesitant to take up such a role in southern Africa. Nevertheless, it has increasingly come under pressure to take more active roles in resolving the conflict in the Democratic Republic of the Congo and Angola. Its reluctance to do so comes at a crucial time in the history South Africa. While South Africa struggles with its domestic problems, the opportunity to exert regional influence within *Pax Africana* may be slipping.

ANALYSIS AND CONCLUSIONS: THE DOMESTIC CONSEQUENCES OF PAX AFRICANA

Of the four sources of peacekeeping in Africa—the former colonial powers, the United Nations, the United States, and Africans themselves—the first three have had a dramatic influence over Africa's international relations. Since decolonization, African foreign relations have been conducted either in the shadow of its former colonizers or in the shadow of the Cold War. Attempts at African peacekeeping can be seen as an attempt to exert an African international relations devoid of external influence, as difficult as it might be. Additionally, the first three options for peacekeeping and intervention in Africa have had a significant impact on domestic politics in Africa. The twists and turns in the course of nations' histories in Africa have been heavily influenced by the interests of the former colonial powers and the ideological battle in the Cold War. With Africa set to take on a more active role in its own peacekeeping, will there be long-term domestic consequences as well? In this sense, we are interested in the impact of peacekeeping and intervention on both the peacekeeper and the host country.

When the former colonial powers left Africa, they made the implicit assumption that liberal democracy and its institutions would control problems encountered by the new African governments. The political legacy of colonialism involved the implementation of the Westminster model of government. It failed. Because of the failure of the of liberal parliamentary governments, any of the governments of Africa succumbed to military coups in the postcolonial period. The politicization of the military came as a result of a crisis of purpose for the military in Africa: Why did the military exist? What was the military's *raison d'être*? Most postcolonial governments did not have external enemies against whom their armies could be deployed. Who was the military "other?" In the absence of an external other, the military created its own purpose, a domestic "other" that took the form of either ethnic, or regional (internal north-south divisions as in Uganda), or sectarian (Muslim, non-Muslim as in Sudan), or all three (regional, ethnic, and sectarian as in Nigeria). The result has been an ongoing wave of instability that has removed democratically elected governments and has threatened Africa's political stability even after the Cold War.

Patriotism among the military in postcolonial Africa has needed a worthier sense of mission than ethnic, regional, and sectarian strife. Does regional involvement give the military its *raison d'être*? Until the military coup in the Ivory Coast in December 1999, ECOMOG as a regional organization seemed to be making progress in delegitimizing military coups in West Africa. The strong response from ECOMOG and Nigeria against the military coup in Sierra Leone seemed to make a strong statement against future coups in West Africa. The neutralization of the Sierra Leone coup, however, was not strong enough to avert the military coup in the Ivory Coast. Yet this may not be the end of the story. The movement towards delegitimizing military coups as a source of political change will take time, but it is an important step toward the consolidation of democratic norms in Africa. In this sense, the military's *raison d'être* is the guardian of the democratic order, and not the guardian of selfish praetorian interests.

Because the peacekeeping countries are the enforcers of the democratic order, the domestic consequences back home could become a double-edged sword. One result could be a more stable political environment, at least in the short term. The military is occupied with a new sense of purpose in this regard, relieving it of its search for the domestic "other." Governments may then have the ability to carry out their duties without fear and threats of political military intervention. With the military's having a direct stake in protecting democratic institutions abroad, reluctance to intervene at home may build. But the possibility still exists for civil-military relations to decline in the wake of extensive peacekeeping operations.

Peacekeeping could also provide the long-term basis of domestic political instability in some African countries. For the peacekeeping country domestically, resentment may build on the part of the military toward civilian rulers for sending them on what would be missions without achievable goals. One consistent problem in maintaining an African peacekeeping force involves the availability of resources for maintaining such a mission. The availability of resources becomes an even greater issue when African governments are confronted with their domestic economic problems. Is it possible for African peacekeepers to be sent on a mission without adequate resources? The possibility certainly exists, with dire consequences for civil-military relations at home and in the host country. In the host country, the potential consequence would be the breakdown of the peacekeeping mission and the return to conflict. The potential backlash may jeopardize civilian control of the military. The reprofessionalization of Africa's military toward civilian control cannot include morale-damaging missions that are inadequately funded and not supported politically.

One positive element of the ACRI is that the West is willing to fund the initiative. This may alleviate the resources issue. But does this mean that the West will want to control the actions of the ACRI? The logical conclusion seems to be in the affirmative, which could add to domestic tensions for those engaged in the peacekeeping process. Moreover, does advanced training of Africa's military forces by the West provide for better peacekeeping forces or better coup-making forces? The skills learned in training and in peacekeeping are also a double-edged sword. As easily as they can be deployed in an external environment, so too can they be deployed domestically.

Despite these hazards, part of the political development process and part of the movement towards Pax Africana must involve having Africans take charge of Africa's affairs. The influence of external actors has proven to be one source that exacerbated problems left by the colonial powers after decolonization. The continuing influence of external actors in Africa's conflicts does not bring about African solutions. While outside assistance may be useful, it must be done on African terms. This means that Africa must not only take responsibility for maintaining the peace on their continent, but also for consolidating democratic governments that have emerged in the post–Cold War period. Democratic trends in Africa are real, but still very fragile. Democratization within individual countries, however, is only part of the process of resuming control over Africa's destiny. Pax Africana is the continental face of this process of self-determination, provided that the goals and means are in tune with Africa's interests, and not the interest of outside powers.

NOTES

1. In this sense, the lines between "peacekeeping" and military "intervention" have become blurred and we recognize this issue as an integral part of this essay.

2. Immanuel Maurice Wallerstein, *Africa, the Politics of Independence: An Interpretation of Modern African History* (New York: Vintage Books, 1961), p. 65; Ali Al Amin Mazrui, *Africa's International Relations: The Diplomacy of Dependency and Change* (London and Boulder, Colo.: Heinemann, Westview Press, 1977), p. 103.

3. Crawford Young, "The Heritage of Colonialism," in *Africa in World Politics: Post–Cold War Challenges,* ed. John W. Harbeson and Donald S. Rothchild (Boulder, Colo.: Westview Press, 1995), p. 29.

4. Jan Jelmert Jørgensen, *Uganda: A Modern History* (New York: St. Martin's Press, 1981), p. 254.

5. John Chipman, *French Power in Africa* (Cambridge, MA: Basil Blackwell, 1989), pp. 116–117.

6. Ibid., p. 121.

7. Ibid., p. 124.; Shaun Gregory, "The French Military in Africa: Past and Present," *African Affairs* 99, no. 396 (2000): 435–448.

8. Crawford Young, "The Heritage of Colonialism," pp. 32–33.

9. For a detailed account of French involvement in Chad, see Keith Somerville, *Foreign Military Intervention in Africa* (London & New York: Pinter Publishers; St. Martin's Press, 1990), and Ali Al Amin Mazrui and Michael Tidy, *Nationalism and New States in Africa from about 1935 to the Present* (Nairobi, Kenya: Heinemann, 1984), p. 207.

10. Mazrui and Tidy, *Nationalism and New States,* p. 206; see also John J. Stremlau, *The International Politics of the Nigerian Civil War, 1967–1970* (Princeton, NJ: Princeton University Press, 1977), specifically pp. 109–142, 224–254.

11. James Mayall, *Africa: the Cold War and After* (London: Elek, 1971), p. 157.

12. We need to distinguish here between peacekeeping (the deployment of personnel/troops either to facilitate negotiations toward conflict settlement or to enforce a negotiated settlement) and peacemaking (the actual negotiation of a settlement to conflict). Other forms of United Nations intervention have included electoral monitoring and humanitarian assistance.

13. Donald F. McHenry, "The United Nations: Its Role in Decolonization," in *African Independence: The First Twenty-five Years,* ed. Gwendolen Margaret Carter and Patrick O'Meara, (Bloomington, Ind.: Indiana University Press, 1985), pp. 31–44; Mazrui, *Africa's International Relations.*

14. Mazrui and Tidy, *Nationalism and New States,* pp. 199–200.

15. McHenry, "The United Nations," p. 43.

16. William J. Durch, "The UN Operation in the Congo," in *The Evolution of UN Peacekeeping: Case Studies and Comparative Analysis,* ed. William J. Durch, (New York: St. Martin's Press, 1993), p. 324.

17. Ibid.

18. McHenry, "The United Nations," p. 43; Durch, "The UN Operation in the Congo," pp. 323–324.

19. Durch, "The UN Operation in the Congo," p. 345

20. 'Funmi Olonisakin, "African 'Homemade' Peacekeeping Initiatives," *Armed Forces and Society* 23, no. 3 (1997): 350.

21. For the most comprehensive dissection of the Somalia operation from start to finish, see John L. Hirsch and Robert B. Oakley, *Somalia and Operation Restore Hope: Reflections on Peacemaking and Peacekeeping* (Washington, DC: United States Institute of Peace Press, 1995).

22. Walter LaFeber, *The Cambridge History of American Foreign Relations, Vol. II: The American Search for Opportunity, 1865–1913,* ed. Warren I. Cohen (New York: Cambridge University Press, 1993), pp. 84–85.

23. Statement of the Assistant Secretary of State for African Affairs, House Foreign Affairs Committee, 20 April 1967 in *Contemporary U.S. Foreign Policy: Documents and Commentary,* ed.

Elmer Plischke (New York: Greenwood Press, 1991), p. 667. See also Richard Nixon, "United States Foreign Policy for the 1970s: Building for Peace," in Plischke, p. 667.

24. Mazrui, *Africa's International Relations*.

25. United Nations Department of Public Information, *Completed Peacekeeping Operations* United Nations, http://www.un.org/Depts/DPKO/Missions/onuc.htm.

26. See Gregory F. Treverton, *Covert Action: The Limits of Intervention in the Postwar World* (New York: Basic Books, 1987).

27. American interpretations of Soviet actions in Africa were inaccurate at best. As Ulam notes, "The Soviet Union's main objective in Africa has not been the establishment of Communist regimes in this or that nation, but a deepening of estrangement of African politicians and intelligentsia from the West and the prevention of an orderly pattern of political development . . ." Adam Bruno Ulam, *Expansion and Coexistence: Soviet Foreign Policy, 1917–73*, 2nd ed. (New York: Praeger, 1974), p. 642.

28. James M. Scott, *Deciding to Intervene: The Reagan Doctrine and American Foreign Policy* (Durham, NC: Duke University Press, 1996), p. 117. See also George Pratt Shultz, *Turmoil and Triumph: My Years as Secretary of State* (New York & Toronto: C. Scribner's Sons, 1993), p. 1112, for a discussion of the formulation and implementation of the "constructive engagement" policy.

29. The Reagan administration's policy in Angola and Mozambique became a quagmire of confusion. While pragmatists such as Crocker and Secretary of State George Shultz advocated constructive engagement, Central Intelligence Agency Director William Casey actively undermined the policy by trying to supply covert aid and assistance to both rebel groups in Angola and Mozambique. The split-track policy caused problems in articulating a clear approach in both cases. For additional details see Scott, *Deciding to Intervene*, chapters 5 and 7, and Shultz, *Turmoil and Triumph*, chapter 50.

30. Marguerite Michaels, "Retreat from Africa," *Foreign Affairs* 72, no. 1 (1992): 96–98.

31. Peter J. Schraeder, "U.S. Intervention in the Horn of Africa amidst the End of the Cold War," *Africa Today* 40, no. 2 (1993): 7–28.

32. For an excellent sociological analysis of the problems faced by soldiers in Somalia, see Laura Miller and Charles Moskos, "Humanitarians or Warriors? Race, Gender and Combat Status in Operation Restore Hope," *Armed Forces and Society* 21, no. 4 (1995): 615–639.

33. Glenn T. Ware, "Just Cause for Intervention," *United States Naval Institute Proceedings* 123, no. 12 December (1997): 53.

34. Norman Kempster, "In Africa, Albright Vows 'New Chapter' in Ties; Diplomacy: It's Time for the U.S. to Work with Budding Democracies to Transform the Continent, Secretary of State Says." *The Los Angeles Times*, 10 December 1997, p. 4.

35. Proceeding of the Summit Conference of Independent African States, Addis Ababa, May 1963, vol. 1, sect. 2, in Saadia Touval, "The Organization of African Unity and African Borders," *International Organization* 21, no. 1 (1967): 104.

36. Ibid.

37. Olonisakin, "African 'Homemade' Peacekeeping Initiatives," pp. 350–351.

38. P. Mweti Munya, "The Organization of African Unity and Its Role in Regional Conflict Resolution and Dispute Settlement: A Critical Evaluation," *Boston College Third World Law Journal* 19 (Spring 1999): 577.

39. Paul Omach, "The African Crisis Response Initiative: Domestic Politics and Convergence of National Interests," *African Affairs* 99, no. 394 (2000): 79–80.

40. One of the original proponents of this system was Ali A. Mazrui. The idea was met with severe criticism. For the exchange between Mazrui and one of his chief critics, Archie Mafeje, see Archie Mafeje, "'Benign' Recolonization and Malignant Minds in the Service of Imperialism," and Ali A. Mazrui, "Self-Colonization and the Search for Pax-Africana: A Rejoinder," in *Codesria Bulletin* 2 (1995); Mafeje, "'Recolonization' or 'Self-Colonization' in Pursuit of 'Pax Africana': Another Response to a Reactionary Thesis," and Mazrui, "Pax Africana: Between the State and Intellectuals" in *Codesria Bulletin* 3 (1995); Said Adejumobi, "Ali Mazrui and His African Dream," and Yusuf Bangura, "The Pitfalls of Recolonization: A Comment on the Mazrui-Mafeje Exchange," *Codesria Bulletin* 4 (1995).

41. Sam Kiley, "African Intellectuals Offer Colonial Cure for Ailing Continent," *The Times* (London), 22 October 1994.

42. Paul Omach, "The African Crisis Response Initiative," p. 87.

43. Ibid., pp. 87–88.

44. Adekeye Abdajo and Michael O'Hanlon, "Africa: Toward a Rapid-Reaction Force," *SAIS Review* 17, no. 2 (1997): 154–155.

3

Pluralism, Ethnicity, and Militarization

Crawford Young

Seeking the intersection and identifying the interaction of three distinct domains of social process is the task of this paper. By pluralism, a term of multiple connotations, I intend to convey the acknowledged and legitimate existence within the polity of diverse currents of ideology, interest, and identity, whose autonomous organizational expression is tolerated, even nurtured. Genuine pluralism implies a liberalized political environment, and is normally paired with democratic governance.

Ethnicity defines the primary terrain of collective identities in contemporary Africa. This subjective domain of social consciousness, defined by a variable array of attributes such as language, culture, shared historical narratives, kin metaphors of belonging, and beliefs, is fluid, interactive, multilayered, contextual, and evolving: at once primordially capable of mobilizing strong passions and deep fears, instrumentally available for political activation, and in continuous instance of social construction. Everyone has ethnicity, indeed likely multiple forms and layers; paraphrasing Ernest Gellner on nationalism, a person must have an ethnicity as "he must have a nose and two ears; a deficiency in any of these particulars is not inconceivable and does from time to time occur, but only as a result of some disaster, and it is itself a disaster of a kind."[1]

Militarization, in the African context, refers to the gradual increase in the role of armed force in the life of the state. At the terminal colonial base line, African constabularies were small and lightly armed. One may suggest that the militarization of social process has evolved in three stages. In a first period, now-independent states, facing a new security logic, and viewing their military as a visible badge of sovereignty, rapidly Africanized the leadership, began to increase the size, and initiated some enhancements in armament and mission. Small navies and air forces were created for the first time. In a second phase, beginning in 1965, a dramatic wave of military power seizures (Ghana, Algeria, Nigeria, Congo-Kinshasa, Central African Republic, Burkina Faso, and Benin within a few months) established security forces as key political players. The coup became the principal instrument, indeed virtually the sole means of incumbent displacement; although this pattern slowed in the late 1980s, by my count eighty-four successful coups have occurred since the Free Officers in Egypt pioneered the tactic for Africa in 1952. In a third stage, beginning simultaneously with the fall of the Berlin Wall and the roll of the Huntingtonian "third wave" of democratization into Africa, two crucial novel dimensions of militarization appeared.[2] Firstly, insurgent forces succeeded in destroying regimes (Somalia, Liberia, Sierra Leone), or actually taking power (Eritrea, Ethiopia, Rwanda, Congo-Kinshasa, Congo-Brazzaville, Chad, Guinea-Bissau). Secondly, an armed seizure of power from the periphery brought the dissolution or disintegration of existing security forces, a process leaving in its wake fragments of militia regrouping under diverse guises, and a large flow of arms into informal markets.

How, then, can one weave together these three strands of macropolitical process, which cumulatively define a large share of the parameters of postcolonial political itineraries of the African state? Each will be examined in turn. In the concluding section, I will endeavor to assemble the parts.

The pact of decolonization, setting aside the small number of liberation war instances, erected pluralism as core principle. The terminal colonial state retreated from its earlier systematic exclusion of the subject and dismantled much of its autocratic superstructure. Political space appeared for the subject to assert citizenship, through an array of organizations articulating diverse interests. Above all, political movements contesting the colonial state itself could emerge. Beginning in the 1940s, electoral competition became a central feature of the terminal colonial arena, both locally and nationally. Although in a number of countries a dominant nationalist party emerged, the rules of the game did not permit forcible elimination of opponents. For the withdrawing colonial power, respectable retreat required replication of the liberal democratic constitutional procedures and structures modeled on the metropole. For the nationalist successor elites, pluralist rules of engagement permitted a rapid mobilization of domestic constituencies drawing upon the accumulated vexations of colonial subordination, and the future expectations of the benefits certain to flow from the dissolution of imperial barriers to African ascension. At the moment of independence, an ephemeral pluralist political order prevailed in much of the continent.[3]

With a tiny handful of exceptions (Botswana, Mauritius, Gambia), this initial pluralist moment in African politics proved short lived. New regimes, often aware of their own fragility, sought a legitimating discourse which justified a consolidation of their power and elimination of challenges to their authority. Two core arguments appeared for the depluralization of the polity.

The combat against the three demons of poverty, ignorance, and disease required the mobilization of all national energies behind the incumbent regime. Any divisive struggle over power itself necessarily subtracted from the social vitalities requisite for the larger battle. The absolute priority accorded to the combat against underdevelopment enjoyed general international acceptance as well. The erection of single-party systems engendered little hostile commentary externally, and indeed was celebrated by a segment of the academic analysis, particularly where it appeared to rest upon effective mass mobilization in anticolonial struggle.[4]

The second master thesis in support of the centralization, unification, and monopolization of power in the hands of state managers was the ethnic question. Open political competition would inevitably mobilize and politicize cultural cleavages in the polity, ran the argument. Such divisions would fatally weaken national resolve in the war against underdevelopment, and open a dangerous rear entry for imperialist influences. Communally defined struggle confounded rather than constructed democracy by transforming elections into mere ethnic censuses, and by construction of political process as a dramaturgy of cultural battle for domination and distribution, rather than a competition of alternative policy visions. The alleged absence of enrooted class divisions in African societies, the legitimate foundation for competing parties, further justified the single-party formula, in the eyes of the independence generation of leaders.[5] Securing the affective attachment of the citizen to the polity through naturalization of a discourse of nationhood came first.

Pluralism was thus banished in favor of state expansion and nation building. Ruling parties insisted that the organizational infrastructure of civil society accept absorption into the dominant political formations as mere ancillary structures. The parties in turn became fused with the state apparatus, extensions of the will of the ruler. Civil society, in the process, returned to the gelatinous condition (to borrow the evocative Gramsci metaphor for Czarist Russia)[6] which characterized it during high colonialism. Although the project of the "integral state" nurtured by a number of rulers in the 1960s and 1970s always fell far short of its hegemonic pretensions,[7] the political marginalization of the subject was comprehensive.

Pluralism reappeared fitfully in the years prior to the African surge of the third wave of democratization in this decade. On occasion, when military regimes were swept away by popular pressures, as in Sudan in 1964 or 1985, a brief democratic interlude appeared. In other cases, military rulers found themselves unable to generate a text of legitimation, and restored liberal constitutional orders of brief duration (Ghana in 1969 and 1979, Nigeria in 1979, Burkina Faso in 1977). A managed pluralism was restored to Senegal by Leopold Senghor in 1976, and Hosni Mubarak in Egypt in the middle 1980s, along with a toleration for public debate and latitude for the media.

The progressive weakening of most African states by the end of the 1970s, as the magnitude of the economic impasse became evident, and the legitimacy of once-seemingly potent regimes frayed, began to open new space for civil society. In South Africa, a profound pluralization of political life occurred in the 1980s through the rapid proliferation of the "civics" as vehicles for oppositional action by the racially excluded.[8] Many states became increasingly unable to deliver basic services, save perhaps on a rental basis. Credibility of the state apparatus corroded as its demoralized and sporadically compensated agents diverted their energies to survival pursuits. Society, abandoned by its would-be hegemon, had to organize itself to assure satisfaction of basic needs.[9] International nongovernmental organizations operating in Africa multiplied rapidly, opening new resource channels for their domestic counterparts. Donor governments, increasingly suspicious of the integrity of state structures, began to funnel assistance through the nongovernmental organization sector. Thus even before the vast contagion of democratization in the early 1990s, precursors of pluralism were appearing.

The extraordinary moment of democratic enthusiasm which swept the continent at the beginning of this decade perhaps began with the October 1988 urban riots which shook Algeria, for long a prototype of the seemingly impregnable single-party under military management. Although the political opening initiated there was aborted in 1992 when Islamist forces appeared poised to win power by electoral process, a legitimated party monopoly was beyond restoration. Even more seminal in opening a new era of pluralism was the veritable seizure of power by civil society in Benin, through the vehicle of a national conference assembling the *forces vives* of the nation, which at once declared itself as repository of sovereignty. Mimesis took hold; a wave of national conferences followed in Francophonic Africa, sweeping perennial incumbents from power in Madagascar, Congo-Brazzaville, and Niger. A third detonator of the previous order was the release of Nelson Mandela and legalization of the African National Congress at the beginning of 1990. For a brief instant of euphoria, a powerful confluence of internal and external forces propelled the surge of democratization. American ambassadors in Cameroon, Central African Republic, Kenya, and Congo-Kinshasa contravened diplomatic usages with trenchant public criticism of incumbents for procrastination in liberalization; French President François Mitterand rattled the 1990 La Baule Francophone summit with a warning that French support would become more tepid for states under its sway who resisted the democratic currents. A triumphalist discourse attended each new multiparty election.

Little by little, the immense hopes invested in the transformative capacity of multiparty democracy subsided. Wily incumbents such as Paul Biya in Cameroon, Omar Bongo in Gabon, and Daniel Arap Moi in Kenya discovered methods for conceding much of the form but less of the substance of political liberalization. Well-lubricated party machines such as the *Parti Socialiste* in Senegal, the *Parti Démocratique de la Côte d'Ivoire* in Ivory Coast, or the *Ralliement Constitutionel Démocratique* in Tunisia proved able to adapt effectively to more open rules of the game. In other instances, such as Togo or Equatorial Guinea, the observation of the ritual of a theoretically competitive election was a shabby charade. The relatively sanguine academic interpretations of the African third wave[10] gave way to more restrained or even downright skeptical readings.[11] Influential writers referred to the patterns of democratic politics emerging in Africa as "illiberal democracy"[12] or "virtual democracy."[13]

Simultaneous with the democratic contagion another and far darker pattern appeared, as unexpected as the wave of liberalization, and at first little noted as a trend: the veritable disintegration of states. State collapse was a product of many of the same forces which yielded political opening: a progressive delegitimation of the patrimonial autocratic state, an accelerating decomposition of the state apparatus resulting from prolonged economic crisis. The small insurgent force led by Charles Taylor entering Liberia at the end of 1989 triggered a rapid disintegration of the enfeebled and widely despised regime of Samuel Doe. The complete disappearance in 1991 of state institutions in Somalia, with no mechanism in view for restoration of a formalized apparatus of rule, made it clear that a new outer stage of state decay was possible. Not long after, Sierra Leone was added to the list. To differing degrees at various points in this decade, the two Congos, Burundi, Rwanda, Central African Republic, Angola, Comores, and Guinea-Bissau could reasonably be expected to appear on a roster of failed or collapsed states.[14]

The incubus of state collapse and limits to democratization notwithstanding, the third wave in Africa—if its initial energy was long spent—left behind substantial elements of pluralization. Claims to state and regime monopolies of power have largely vanished. Significant political space is opened to associational life. Human rights are better respected, and domestic groupings join the international human rights community in a vigilance of monitoring which would have been beyond imagining in the 1960s. Opposition media in most countries coexist with an official press, and private radios make their appearance. Although the international system and the donor community had diminished their pressures for multiparty democracy and gave greater weight to stability in the face of rising levels of civil violence, the global environment exerted pressures for external presentability. A respectable state, at the turn of the century, had to display the formal appearance of a liberal constitutional polity. For the first time in the twentieth century, no credible ideological justification for a state which suppressed pluralism subsisted. Thus, even if an ethos of pluralism did not permeate, a retreat to the hegemonic pretensions of earlier decades was impossible to contemplate. Sheltered by at least a partial pluralism, and in spite of the innumerable terminological disputes about its exact meaning, something reasonably labeled "civil society" was now part of the political landscape.

Ethnicity constitutes the second major strand in this analysis. Here one encounters important alterations both in dominant interpretive understandings of the ethnic phenomenon, and the ways in which it finds recognition and acknowledgement in the political process. African independence happened to coincide with a particular moment in the politics of cultural pluralism. Class politics were fully legitimate and entirely natural; ethnic politics were a debased form, redolent of intrusion of a pathological traditionality into the realm of modernity.

In retrospect, 1960 appears as an apogee of the nation-state as universal normative model for the contemporary country. The coincidence of the launching of the African independent polity, territorially based upon the peculiar logic of the colonial partition, with the overpowering doctrine of nation-building as quintessence of progress, strongly influenced both political practitioners and interpreters: "the curse of the nation-state," as Basil Davidson retrospectively labeled it.[15] Africa, viewing its ethnic divisions, devoutly wished their disappearance. In 1959, Sekou Toure famously observed that "In three or four years, no one will remember the tribal, ethnic or religious rivalries which, in the recent past, caused so much damage to our country and its population."[16] "Tribe" was the normal term employed, a lexical practice which in itself constituted the identity as a backward form; "nationality" or "ethnic group" were labels used for European categories. The tribe was an essentialized category, even if discovered by colonial classificatory systems.[17] A pure tribe was a rural collectivity; migrants to urban domains and thus exposed to the solvents of modernity became "detribalized."[18]

Yet to be discovered was the dialectic between ethnic consciousness and its political uses. The white blanket of racialized colonial domination had concealed such phenomena at submerged fringes of social process. Africanization and pluralization on the eve of independence brought ethnic competition to the surface. Politics, one came to appreciate, in the delectably edible Nigerian metaphor, was about "slicing (or sharing) the national cake." In this imagery, the resources of the state were divisible into visible servings, with ethnic communities watching the cake cutting with a vigilant eye, determined to secure equitable proportionality in the size of the pieces, and to ensure that transparency accompanied the slicing. This master metaphor captures a core dimension of ethnic politics: distribution and domination as the driving forces—the relative size of the servings, and whose hand holds the knife. To an older, mechanically primordial understanding of ethnicity was added a new, instrumental dimension. Ethnicity was activated—and defined—by competitive struggle for utilities within the domain of the state to allocate, or for relative advantage in the social spheres where group interaction occurred—most notably the urban sector.

Another aspect of the ethnic phenomenon gradually acquired recognition, growing out of the instrumentalist dissolution of the primordial hypothesis. The shifting terrain of struggle produced changing definitions of the groups in presence. Moreover, the fluidity of boundaries and instability of the categories raised questions as to the ancestral antecedents of the contemporary identity maps.

During the 1980s, a new interrogation of the ethnic phenomenon emerged, which privileged the continuous role of social process in identity dynamics. Ethnicity was not a timeless essence, but contingent, contextual, and changing. Constructivist modes of interpretation came of age, influenced by diverse currents of postmodernist reflection. Such seminal works as the Benedict Anderson reconceptualization of nationalism as "imagined communities" beckoned a closer inspection of the nature of ethnic consciousness.[19] Various monographs made clear the magnitude of the transformations in ethnic cartography since the precolonial era.[20] Colonial states insisted upon superimposing an ethnic template upon subject societies as the basis for its administrative structure; few precolonial states or societies employed a formalized classificatory system of this nature. Over time, such cultural taxonomies tended to acquire the familiarity of long-standing public usage, and indeed African intermediaries of the colonial state might find their interests tied to the official classifications. Early ethnic monographs prepared by administrators, missionaries, or anthropologists codified the unit and provided a "geobody" by a printed map, often with an imaginatively maximalist representation of its territorial domain.[21] Missionary societies, faced with the strategic necessity of translating the scriptures, had fateful choices to make in evangelical soci-olinguistics.[22] Once equipped with a written form and deployed in schoolroom and chapel, the newly standardized version, following a pathway parallel to the nationaliza-tion of the "King's English" or Parisian French, acquired a status and authority eclipsing the regional dialects thus unified. In turn, the use of the standard version as medium for Bible translation elevated its prestige through association with a sacred text. Thus enhanced, its diffusion through primary schools and catechism reconfigured ethnic consciousness around its contours.

The recognition of ethnicity as socially constructed at times verged into the excess of perceiving contemporary categories as not simply "imagined communities," but entirely invented ones, a mere product of colonial machination; in some of the polemics sur-rounding the Hutu-Tutsi conflagrations in Burundi and Rwanda such arguments are sometimes heard, especially in sources relying upon Tutsi identity narratives. Precolo-nial Africa was not an identity *tabula rasa;* the important point is that, departing from patterns of social consciousness prevalent in the nineteenth century, perhaps grossly distorted or misunderstood by alien systems of classification placed upon them, con-temporary ethnicity has experienced dramatic evolution. With a rapid expansion of urban centers after World War II, important new arenas of social interaction and collec-tive self-definition brought a new dynamic. So also did the emergence of an active urban associational life, and especially competitive political parties. The politization of ethnic consciousness which ensued added a new vector of ferment to the social construction process.

Thus the hermeneutics of cultural pluralism have been radically transformed since the hour of African independence. So also is the global normative environment with respect to cultural diversity. Around the world the homogenizing discourse of "one nation, one people," ascendant in 1960, gives way to competing visions of "multicultur-alism," a term first given official currency in Canada in the early 1970s. An acknowledg-ment of communal diversity as a normal condition of the polity, to merit moral or even constitutional recognition, supplanted an older view holding "national integration" as core state imperative.[23]

Both the changes in dominant modes of interpretation and the international norma-tive order impact ethnicity in Africa. Perhaps more than in any other world region, at the independence baseline, ethnicity, castigated as "tribalism," was declared politically ille-gitimate. Ethnic self-expression was permissible solely in the private sphere. Only the nation, embodied in the ruling single party, was legitimate public collectivity. Ethnic associations, which had flourished in the terminal colonial period, were usually banned. Yet the initial hope, even belief, that the solvent of modernization would progressively relegate ethnic consciousness to the realm of harmless folklore, did not materialize; as Vail puts it, ethnicity "failed to cooperate with its many would-be pallbearers."[24] The pallbearers included many academic analysts as well as African leaders and intellec-tuals.

Although banished from official discourse, ethnicity crept back into the interstices of political life through the innumerable crevices in the seemingly hard outer shell of the state. The progressive embedding of patrimonial practice into the conduct of public affairs honeycombed the political realm with clientelistic networks, within which ethnicity usually supplied the cementing basis of affinity. For the subject, access to the state for a discretionary favor was more readily achieved through the soft entry point provided by a claim to metaphorical kinship. For the ruler, in the sensitive domain of regime security, an "ethnic security map" was widely employed in the top command structures of the armed forces.[25] As state decline become widespread in the 1970s, ethnicity became an important form of social survival capital for the individual.

By the time that repluralization of the polity occurred in the 1980s and 1990s, the intellectual and political mood with respect to ethnicity had changed. The premise that macrohistorical process inexorably diminished the valence of ethnic consciousness vanished. Partly as counterpoint to the discredit brought upon states by the failings of patrimonial autocracy, ethnic consciousness became a domain of civic virtue.[26] Cultural authenticity finds inscription through ethnicity, a heritage to be treasured rather than an indelible stain of primitivity. Far from being a simple artifact of tradition, ethnicity and modernity were twins.

Yet ethnicity mobilized in conflict could harbor the wilder passions; cultural consciousness possessed an ineffable affective dimension. The ethnic self is partly defined in relation to an "other," a potential source of anxiety and fear, and possible target for demonization. The Rwanda and Burundi tragedies served as grim warning as to the possible consequences of ethnicity run amok, severing the bonds of civility through which difference normally found negotiation in African and other societies. Cultural plurality can, but need not, lead to a "war of visions" within the polity, whose sources and dynamic in producing an interminable civil war in Sudan are so painstakingly analyzed by Deng.[27]

Thus ethnicity, though no longer widely stigmatized, is viewed with political ambivalence. In a number of countries, the formation of political movements on an ethnic or religious basis is constitutionally proscribed (for example, among others, Eritrea, Tanzania, Nigeria, Algeria). The new constitutional arrangements which accompanied political liberalization in many countries have experimented with electoral systems designed to foster power sharing and avert zero-sum regional struggles, in many cases including a turn to some dosage of proportional representation.[28] No one has followed the audacious Ethiopian constitutional model of restructuring the administrative subdivisions of the country on an explicitly ethnic principle, and investing the ethnic provinces with an unrestricted right of self-determination, including a right to secession. Thus far, one must hasten to add, the realities of power exercise in post-Mengistu Ethiopia leave no place for exercise of such a right, with residues of the Leninist past still evident. In Nigeria, proposals for a post-transition sovereign national conference constituted on the basis of ethnic representation stirs deep apprehension among many citizens. Unconstrained ethnic confederalization might well trigger a chain reaction of disintegration.

Indeed, here and there one finds continuing traces of an older discourse. If we juxtapose doctrinal pronouncements on the ethnic question by former Ugandan ruler A. Milton Obote (1962–1971, 1980–1984) and Yoweri Museveni (1986–   ), the identity of perspective is striking:

> ...if the pull of the tribal force is allowed to develop, the unity of the country will be endangered. To reduce it to its crudest form, the pull of the tribal force does not accept Uganda as one country, does not accept the people of Uganda as belonging to one country, does not accept the National Assembly as a national institution but as an assembly of peace conference delegates and tribal diplomatic and legislative functionaries, and looks at the Government of Uganda as a body of umpires or referees in some curious game of "Tribal Development Monopoly."
>
> — former President A. Milton Obote[29]

> A leader should show the people that those who emphasize ethnicity are messengers of perpetual backwardness. This process of undermining a sectarian mentality of "my tribe, my religion" is linked with the process of modernization and overcoming underdevelopment. . . . Eventually, the society will be transformed and modernized. The moment that process takes place, one's tribe or religion cease to be of much consequence.
>
> — President Yoweri Museveni[30]

Thus one detects a deep ambivalence with respect to ethnicity in the moral economy of the partially liberalized African state. Bearer of cultural authenticity yet potential catalytic agent of civil conflict; irreducible competitor of the state-as-nation for the supreme affective attachment of the citizen; free-floating social energy refractory to state control: ethnic consciousness is reproduced and evolves by its own logic and rhythms, although influenced by the political context provided by state action. Cultural pluralism can perhaps be managed, but not dissolved.

The third analytical domain to explore is militarization. I return to the three stage process identified in the opening of this paper: expansion, politicization, and escape to the societal periphery. The first two stages merit brief treatment, and the third requires more sustained examination.

Withdrawing colonial powers followed a clear priority in relinquishing authority to their nationalist successors. The political realm was first opened to associations, parties and electoral representation, and eventually ministers. Next, on the eve of independence, came the senior ranks of the bureaucracy. Full control of the security realm was invariably retained until the flags of independence were raised, save in the instance of successful armed liberation struggles, not treated here.

Terminal colonial constabularies were overwhelmingly lightly armed infantry units, intended only for internal security. Further, they were structured on a pan-territorial basis; the *Force Publique* served as security force for all three Belgian-ruled territories, while the "Senegalese" units of the French army were not territorialized. East, West, and Central Africa had British-officered regional forces, though territorial units might exist. The colonial security logic which governed recruitment, and particularly in the British case "martial race" theories imported from India, meant that African colonial army personnel were often drawn from different regional and social milieux than the nationalist leadership.[31] With dazzling opportunities open to the educated elite in the political and public service arenas, army careers before independence held little attraction for young men from areas in which the educational infrastructure was relatively dense. To boot, the constabulary role in disciplining, policing, or repressing nationalist political mobilization carried a repellent stigma.

The security imperative for the newly independent states posed a series of dilemmas. The Weberian definition of a state itself resonated in the minds of new rulers: a compulsory association enjoying a monopoly of the legitimate use of coercion. Emblematic of the nature of the challenge was the moment of intense discomfort experienced by the Burkina Faso (Upper Volta) territorial government in 1959, when warriors of the Mossi paramount ruler, the Moro Naba, assaulted the territorial assembly; the now-autonomous regime had no security force, and escaped unscathed only because the spear-bearing warriors dispersed when a few gendarmes fired into the air.[32] Far more traumatic for Africa as a whole was the 1960 "Congo crisis," when the giant new state found its security capacity paralyzed five days after independence when the entirely Belgian officer corps fled following a troop mutiny. In a different way, the chain reaction mutinies in Tanzania, Kenya, and Uganda in 1964, mastered only by recourse to British intervention, demonstrated the urgency of a reliable security force.

Reliability was critical; so was a projection of sovereignty, through the immediate territorialization of armies. Continued exercise of the top command by European officers could not be long tolerated, though it lasted till 1961 even in Ghana, and 1965 in Nigeria. Security reasons dictated expansion as well, both in force size and into the naval and air force realms previously left in metropolitan hands. To act as independent states in the "anarchical society"[33] of world politics, African nations required at least a few coins of the currency of force. Kwame Nkrumah, recalls the last British commander in Ghana, was determined to have a navy and air force as well as an army second to none in Africa;[34] although his ambitions were exceptional in scale, they were not in kind. In Uganda, at the time of independence the Uganda Army consisted only of a single battalion of seven hundred extricated from the pan-territorial King's African Rifles. A second battalion doubling army size was created in the first year, with expansion then accelerated due to perceived security threats within and without.[35] In Nigeria, which had only 7,600 troops in 1958, the army size had doubled to fifteen thousand by 1966, then swelling to 250,000 during the civil war. Only very slowly did its force level recede to 150,000.[36]

In the first stage, then, the military was nationalized and enlarged, though usually still relatively modest in size. Its Africanization largely shed the colonial stigma. The prospect of rapid promotion within the officer corps for the first time made military careers an attractive option to the educated young. As well, the emergent military could bask in the reflected glory of an academic literature of virtually hagiographic nature, extolling its role in developing nations. Armies, ran the argument, as servants of the nation were uniquely credentialed as bearers of a nation-building vocation. The discipline and hierarchy seemingly characteristic of security forces qualified them for leadership in the political realm as well. A rigidly merit-based promotion system assured that the higher ranks were screened for competence. Their supreme devotion to the interest of the state, and their purportedly apolitical character, endowed the military with special qualifications as technocratic agents of development.[37]

Politization, the second stage, soon followed, with the wave of military power seizures in 1965–66. The initial intervention was often motivated by a political impasse amongst civilian politicians, as in Nigeria, Congo-Kinshasa, or Burkina Faso, or their discredit, as in Central African Republic or Ghana, and justified by the claim that military power exercise was merely temporary. But soon, in a large number of instances, military rulers sought ways to prolong their rule. The justifications supplied for a coup might provide entry legitimacy, but could not serve over time. In a large number of countries, such as Sudan, Togo, both Congos, Mali, Burkina Faso, and Rwanda, military rulers appropriated the form and discourse of the single-party system, dissolving prior structures and imposing their own from the summit. As well, a number stole the ideological clothing of the radical intelligentsia; it is striking that, of the regimes that formally labeled themselves Marxist-Leninist in the 1970s, all but Angola and Mozambique were led by army officers, none of whom had any known knowledge or interest in such doctrines prior to power seizure. Strategic elements from the political class were coopted into the governmental and political apparatus. But the security forces remained the ultimate guarantors of the military ruler. And absolute control of the military instrument was the prerequisite for remaining in power.

The coup became the institutionalized means for regime change by the late 1960s. By that time, about forty percent of African states were headed by rulers of military origin, a percentage that remained stable until the liberalization era opened. The impact upon the military was of prime importance. Although most military regimes soon became largely civilian in ministerial and regional administrative posts, nonetheless key political roles were open to core security operatives. Over time, these became avenues for immense wealth: the Mobutu-Abacha syndrome. Career ambitions for younger officers began to incorporate visions of a detour into the political or entrepreneurial realm. Conspiracy and the webs of affinity it spun penetrated the barracks, intruding complex factions into the security forces. As Peters argues for the Nigerian army, the military had taken on the character of a factionalized political party, with ambitious junior officers needing a godfather at the summit to advance.[38]

Whether or not a head of state was of military antecedents, security forces enjoyed at this stage important leverage for satisfaction of its material aspirations in equipment and facilities. During the 1970s, before structural adjustment pressures began to bite, military expenditures in Africa rose faster than in any other world region, admittedly from a relatively low base.[39] The military instrument was firmly entrenched at the core of the state, and in the center of the political arena.

Along with the expansion in its scale and political role came a deflation in its public standing. Nothing in the actual performance of soldiers as rulers in Africa validated the worshipful treatment by academic analysts in the early 1960s. As African publics, by the 1980s, came in many lands to perceive states as simple predators, their soldier-presidents shared the opprobrium with their civilian counterparts. Deepening economic difficulties began to result in arrearages in military pay, particularly for garrisons distant from the capital. In turn, as army units began to live off the land, extortionate behavior towards civil populations bred animosity and contempt. The representation of the military in the monograph radically altered, shredding the earlier image.[40] No less a specialist in security studies than the late Congo-Kinshasa President Mobutu Sese Seko had, in a celebrated 1974 speech, castigated his own army, "costly and unproductive," as the seventh of ten scourges which were ravaging Congolese society.[41]

The third and present stage of militarization opens in the 1980s, when slowly spreading theaters of endemic civil conflict appeared. Some of these now extend back decades: southern Sudan, Western Sahara, Angola. They were understood as particular zones of unrest, with specific histories and protaganists. However, as the 1990s wore on, the conflict locations have tended to enlarge, flow together and interpenetrate, and to attract a larger number of participants. Entrenched armed formations at the periphery of existing states acquired the capacity to reproduce themselves over time, and to effectively resist the efforts of the internationally recognized state actors to eliminate them. In a vast arc stretching from the Horn to the South Atlantic, ten states now belong to a single theater of armed strife: Somalia, Ethiopia, Eritrea, Sudan, Uganda, Rwanda, Burundi, both Congos, and Angola. Djibouti, Central African Republic, and Chad perch precariously on the sides of this cauldron. A second, smaller zone in West Africa embraces four states in a similarly interpenetrated conflict theater: Liberia, Sierra Leone, Guinea-Bissau, and Senegal. Thus about a third of African states are embroiled in these conflict patterns, whose common thread is the loss of the monopoly of military means by the state.

A closely related phenomenon is the development of a new pattern of armed power seizure: by an insurgent group from the periphery, rather than by military coup at the center. The latter practice, although still occurring (Gambia 1994, Niger 1996 and 1999, Nigeria 1993, Comores 1999, Burundi 1993), is much less frequent than in previous decades. In its place comes the triumphant march into the capital from the countryside. The pattern setter was the National Resistance Army of Yoweri Museveni in Uganda in 1986; following in this mold were Idriss Deby in Chad in 1990, Isaias Afeworki in Eritrea in 1991, Meles Zenawi in Ethiopia in 1991, Fred Kagame in Rwanda in 1994, Laurent Kabila in Congo-Kinshasa in 1997, Denis Sassou-Nguessou in Congo-Brazzaville in 1997. In addition, armed strikes from the periphery destroyed regimes in Somalia, Liberia, Sierra Leone, and Guinea-Bissau.

Although coups and insurgent takeovers are both armed displacement of incumbents, there are profound differences in impact. The military instrument normally remains intact with a coup, even if the leader is not the commander. An insurgent military victory results in the dissolution of the existing army. Army fragments dissolve into the periphery, often taking their weapons with them. As well, the armament stock of government forces can disappear into informal markets. Particularly dramatic in this respect was the simultaneous collapse of the two large Horn armies of Somalia and Ethiopia in 1991, whose Cold-War patrons had made them a pair of the most lavishly equipped security forces on the continent.

Supplying the context for this new pattern of regime displacement is the broader phenomenon of state weakening, widespread if differentially experienced. In the most grotesquely deteriorated polities, such as Congo-Kinshasa, two decades of unremitting decline had ravaged the public infrastructure of the country. The state had long since ceased providing any significant services to its hinterland. Hyperinflation destroyed the currency; two dollars, worth one zaire in 1974, could purchase 42 billion zaires by 1996. What resources the state could still collect from diamonds and what remained of its mineral production largely went to sustain the shrinking security and patrimonial apparatus of personal Mobutu rule.[42] To a less extreme degree, a number of states exhibited aspects of this syndrome of decay. Battered by economic crisis, beset by a disengagement of civil society in the face of a delegitimized public authority deemed predatory, they had a sharply diminished capacity to confront armed challengers.

One product of this situation is a vast increase in weaponry of the sort employable with lethal effect in insurgent warfare: automatic guns, rocket-launchers, land mines. Weapons flow comes not only from dissolved armies, but from continued acquisition by dissident militia, either by purchase on the basis of valuable resources they control (diamonds, gold, coffee, timber), or by supply by neighboring states, and by governments seeking to combat them. One source reports that in the last couple of years the Burundi government and Hutu rebel formations have signed forty-seven contracts for arms supply or training with a large number of countries.[43] In Uganda, the government estimates thirty-five thousand AK-47s are in the hands of Karamojong; as a preemptive move, a number of these young men are retained for $10-monthly payments as auxiliaries.[44] In many African capitals, AK-47s are available on the black market for $50 or less. A number of governments today face a populace which is well armed, a radical contrast with the 1960 situation; the colonial state had effectively disarmed the subject.

The warlord appears in Africa as a distinctive category of political actor, whose nineteenth-century precursors were the merchant-warriors such as Msiri, Tippo Tip, or Rabah who erected mercantile states based on slave and ivory traffic. But in modern times, until the 1990s, the warlord term was rarely heard. William Reno traces a convincing portrait of this type of political figure, of whom Charles Taylor of Liberia is a prototype.[45] A number have developed impressive mercantile skills over the years, and frequently benefit from permeability of borders and collusion if not support from neighboring states. Their autonomy is assured by well-armed militia, and effective control of a high-value resource base.

The diffusion of sophisticated military knowledge is another important factor. In contrast to the rudimentary skills of the 1964 Congo rebels, the 1996–97 astonishing sweep of the Kabila forces, with critical Rwandan encadrement, was a military masterpiece. The key command structure of such forces often include elements who have received advanced military training and experience. The top leaders of the Rwandan Patriotic Front (RPF) had learned their tactics in the Museveni NRA. The core of the Taylor movement in Liberia was trained in Libya, as were a number of the Sierra Leone rebels led by Fodoy Sankoh. The 1998 Congo rebels had both Rwandan and Ugandan military advisors (and soldiers), and former officers of the Mobutu army. A recent research paper by a Malian officer notes that the Tuareg revolt in the 1990s was impossible to defeat militarily, in contrast to a similar uprising in 1962–64, successfully repressed at the price of considerable brutality. A key difference was leadership of the insurgents by "Afghans," or Tuareg veterans of the anti-Soviet combat in Afghanistan.[46] The hydra-headed *Groupes Islamiques Armés* in Algeria contain similar elements.

An important new factor is the demonstrated capacity of such militia to sustain their action over extended periods without discernable support, or even in the face of animosity from the local populace. Such is clearly the case for the Lord's Resistance Army and Alliance of Democratic Forces in Uganda, as well as the sundry militia operating in Liberia and Sierra Leone during this decade, and probably for the GIA fractions in Algeria, the Cobras, Zulus, and Ninjas in Congo-Brazzaville, and the *Rassemblement Congolais pour la Démocratie* insurgents in Congo-Kinshasa. Aversion toward insurgents does not mean support for the central government, however, as repressive military action conducted by state forces imposes high costs on local populations (the Ugandan efforts at forced regroupment in Acholi, for example).

A chilling new tactic which now finds systematic and deliberate employment is the use of the child soldier. Recruitment through abduction of young adolescents first came to notice in the guerrilla strategy of the *Resistência Nacional Moçambicana* (RENAMO) during the 1980s.[47] Adolescent children, often abducted by force, when isolated from their kin and communities, subjected to terror, and forced to commit violent acts, can become fierce foot soldiers. The weapons in use are not heavy, and the successfully "turned" child soldier may be less inhibited by fear than their adult counterparts. Drugs and supernatural immunization are also efficacious instruments of control and manipulation. So also is their knowledge that their home communities may not welcome them back; the boys may be feared as uncontrollable sociopaths, and the girls damaged beyond repair by sexual abuse and exposure to AIDS.[48]

Beyond abducted children, the militarily experienced core of such militia can readily find a pool of impoverished, disaffected, unemployed youths with poor prospects in the urban slums and refugee camps. The lethal ethnoregional militia recruited in Congo-Brazzaville by former President Pascal Lissouba (Zulus, later Cocoyes), Brazzaville potentate Bernard Kolelas (Ninjas), and present ruler Denis Sassou-Nguesso (Cobras) first terrorized Brazzaville in 1993, then unleashed a new round of neighborhood cleansing and looting in 1997, are a depressing example. Once constituted, such bands easily escape the control of their patrons. Their street combat in Brazzaville in the latter half of 1997 resulted in 10,000 to 15,000 officially admitted deaths, and vast material destruction. They were generally recruited in the secondary provincial towns, and afforded some military training and sporadic payment. Roadblocks were erected to verify ethnic or regional identities, relying on name, language, accent or other perceived markers, and to extract payments. Exemplary punishment might be visited upon those failing to pass the identity test, or, particularly for the Cobras, belonged to the despised class of politician-profiteers. The atmosphere of arbitrary violence is captured in the following testimonial:

At a check point, the Cobras who were searching [a young soldier in civilian clothes, well known in the neighborhood] found a revolver on him. He argued that the militiamen knew who he was and should be able to understand that, as a soldier, he needed a gun for his personal security. He was taken to a piece of wasteground. A few moments later, the Cobra who had executed him returned brandishing the jeans which his victim had been wearing as proof that he had accomplished his mission, shouting out "I've sent him on his way."[49]

The widespread looting, in the eyes of its youthful practitioners, found justification in the sins of the political leadership and indeed in the older generation which had visited misfortune upon them. The violence and banditry of the militia form part of a larger social pathology, which will not be easily erased. Here the conclusions of Bazenguissa-Ganga merit reflection:

The process of democratic transition in Congo in the early 1990s had a marked effect in disseminating the use of political violence throughout a large section of society.... Hence an analysis of the violence of the period, considered in terms other than as a dysfunctioning of the democratic process, can reveal much about the way in which political practice in Congo has been transformed. This amounts to a redefinition of common social experience and popular conceptions of social status, the true subject of the various conflicts which have been so tragically militarized.[50]

When civil strife continues over time, it tends to generate a multiplication of militarized fragments. Governments seek to combat insurgencies by arming local militia (the Kamajors in Sierra Leone, various factional armed groups in southern Sudan, diverse "Mai-Mai" and Hutu refugee groups in Congo-Kinshasa, village paramilitary forces in Algeria). This in turn produces a pattern of wars within wars, which become the more refractory to peace-making efforts.

Yet another novel set of actors are the ubiquitous private security forces available for rent on the international market. The commercial success and often military effectiveness of Executive Outcomes is only the most conspicuous example. Mercenaries made

their appearance in Africa in the 1960s, but the higher order of professional and commercial sophistication of current international private security forces make them
another potent new factor.[51]

Lastly, the transborder nature of many such conflicts deeply implicate neighboring
states, and create interpenetrating security logics. Rwandan and Ugandan backing for
first the *Alliance des Forces Démocratiques pour la Libération du Congo-Zaire* (AFDL),
then the RCD, is driven by their frustration at the use of Congo sanctuary and bases by
the Interahamwe and former Rwandan army elements, and the ADF. In turn, Congo
arms Interahamwe as auxiliaries, making the Hutu insurgents a more deeply feared
threat to Tutsi survival. Similar interpenetration of conflict is found in Guinea-Bissau-
Senegal, Angola, and both Congos, Uganda-Sudan, Eritrea-Sudan, Eritrea-Ethiopia, and
Ethiopia-Sudan.

How, then, do pluralism, ethnicity, and militarization tie together in the search for an
African future which does not simply reproduce the past? These analytical trails con-
verge upon the issue of the state.[52] The quest for an efficacious state, capable of assur-
ing political order, providing basic services to civil society, and administering a liberalized polity and society is far more arduous than imagined in 1960, or at the outset of the
democratizing impulse in 1990.

In the moment of enthusiasm which accompanied political opening, doubtless the
degree to which the relatively strong state structures of the terminal colonial era had
weakened was underestimated. Perhaps more than the relatively low per capita income
levels of most African states, the huge challenge of transition finds definition here.
Democratization per se, Adam Przeworski and Fernando Limongi argue, is not contingent in some deterministic sense on the level of economic development.[53] But sustainability is affected by level of development and the capacity of the state to bring improvement. Nothing in the evidence supplied by three decades of overwhelmingly autocratic
modalities of rule validates the argument that a return to the authoritarian past is
appropriate therapy. Indeed, there is food for reflection in the fact that the sole African
polities to enjoy high levels of sustained growth approximating that of the now-tar-
nished Asian model are Botswana and Mauritius, both of whom had held out against the
authoritarian tide. But pluralization of the polity, however indispensable, needs to proceed in tandem with a restoration of state capacity.

An important array of political lessons with respect to ethnicity have been learned,
which suggest ways and means of accommodation of diversity.[54] In a more pluralist
polity, ethnicity cannot easily be confined to a purely private realm. Yet through design
of electoral systems, various formulas for regional distribution of power or decentralization, cultural sensitivity in educational and language policies, and a rule-of-law state
respectful of group as well as individual human dignity, the pluralist multicultural
polity is possible. The overwhelming majority of countries in the world are culturally
plural, and the majority today are at least partially democratic; in most cases, communal violence does not arise.

Neither does affording political space to ethnic expression give an inexorable stimulus to separatist sentiments. Although secessionism finds a number of African examples, closely inspected the degree to which separatist claims have been publicly grounded in territorial rather than ethnic claims is striking. Eritrea and, de facto, Somaliland are the only instances of effective separation, both involving the restoration of colonial territorial units. Katanga, Biafra, and southern Sudan, whatever the degree of ethnic definition of the social energies propelling separation claims, rooted their demands in the territorial frame of an existing administrative subdivision.[55] In the Casamance case, widely believed to be an expression of Diola ethnic unrest, the claim for separation on close examination draws, as in the Katanga case, on arguments of the regional administrative specificity of the zone, ironically originally advanced by French settlers.[56] On the other side of the coin, one can only be struck by the refusal of collapsed states to utterly disintegrate. The ease with which Kabila marched across the Congo in 1996–97 demonstrates how little there was to stop a determined bid at separation, whether ethnic or regional. Even though, in 1999, the country was splintered into multiple zones of relative military influence, and its civil violence drew into the vortex seven foreign armies, no demand for separation was heard. To a surprising degree, the territorial frame of the colonial partition has been naturalized in the social imaginary.

On the militarization front, a scrutiny of the theaters of civil strife reveals a striking paradox. Ethnic consciousness certainly figures in the dynamics of conflict, influencing patterns of participation and responses to violence. But, with the important exceptions of Rwanda and Burundi, ethnicity per se does not drive the conflicts nor define their origins. Warlords may manipulate and use ethnicity, but they are not ethnic entrepreneurs. The Lord's Resistance Army in Uganda and its precursor, the Alice Lakwena Holy Spirit Movement, originate in particular circumstances facing the Acholi community arising from the heavy involvement of soldiers from this region in the massive violence of the Obote Luwero Triangle military repression campaigns in 1982–1984, and their perceived vulnerability in the new order imposed by Museveni. But the eclectic and often bizarre discourse of Holy Spirit and LRA was never formulated as an ethnic agenda.[57] In recent years, the great majority of LRA participants and their victims are both Acholi.

The new patterns of militarization of society and the periphery pose a large threat to the African future. Weakened states lack the capacity to bring most of the present conflicts to an end by military means, nor can any states now rely upon extra-African force to subdue their tormenters. In these circumstances, only some kind of negotiated settlement can bring the violence to an end. Such accords will require some form of legitimation through invocation of a formally democratic process. They will also necessitate security guarantees to any ethnic community which may believe itself at risk. The most striking success of such a formula is Mozambique, with a degree of power-sharing and political incorporation of the former insurgents. In this instance, peace has been accompanied by significant economic recovery, at least as measured by macro-economic indicators, a large degree of demilitarization of society, and a restoration of the state writ throughout the territory. Democracy, however virtual or illiberal, becomes the only available antidote to institutionalized disorder. The harmonious accommodation of ethnicity and a gradual retreat from militarization can only take place within a pluralist order.

NOTES

1. Ernest Gellner, *Nations and Nationalism* (Ithaca: Cornell University Press, 1983), p. 6.

2. Samuel P. Huntington, *The Third Wave: Democratization in the Late Twentieth Century* (Norman: University of Oklahoma Press, 1991).

3. For elaboration of these arguments, see Crawford Young, *The African Colonial State in Comparative Perspective* (New Haven: Yale University Press, 1994).

4. One may recollect such influential works as Thomas Hodgkin, *African Political Parties: An Introductory Guide* (Harmondsworth: Penguin, 1961); Immanuel Wallerstein, *Africa: The Politics of Independence: An Interpretation of Modern African History* (New York: Vintage, 1961), and Ruth Schachter Morganthau, *Political Parties in French-Speaking West Africa* (Oxford: Clarendon Press, 1964).

5. Most eloquently argued by Julius Nyerere, *Ujamaa: Essays on Socialism* (London: Oxford University Press, 1968).

6. Antonio Gramsci, *Selections from Prison Notebooks* (New York: International Publishers, 1971).

7. On the integral state notion, see Crawford Young, "Zaire: the Shattered Illusion of the Integral State," *Journal of Modern African Studies* 32, no. 2 (1994): 247–64.

8. Stephen Zunes, "The Role of Non-violent Action in the Downfall of Apartheid," *Journal of Modern African Studies* 37, no. 1 (1999): 137–69.

9. See, for example, the masterful study of this dynamic by Aili Mari Tripp, *Changing the Rules: The Politics of Liberalization and the Urban Informal Economy in Tanzania* (Berkeley: University of California Press, 1997).

10. For an example, see my 1994 contribution, "Democratization in Africa: The Contradictions of a Political Imperative," in *Economic Change and Political Liberalization in Sub-Saharan Africa*, ed. Jennifer A. Widner (Baltimore: Johns Hopkins University Press, 1994), pp. 230–50.

11. Larry Diamond, "Is the Third Wave Over?" *Journal of Democracy* 7, no. 3 (1996): 20–37; Richard Joseph, ed., *State, Conflict and Democracy in Africa* (Boulder, Colo.: Lynne Rienner Publishers, 1999); Michael Bratton and Nicolas van de Walle, *Democratic Experiments in Africa: Regime Transitions in Comparative Perspective* (Cambridge: Cambridge University Press, 1997).

12. Fareed Zakaria, "The Rise of Illiberal Democracy," *Foreign Affairs* 76, no. 6 (1997): 22–43.

13. Joseph, "The Reconfiguration of Power in Late Twentieth Century Africa," pp. 57–80.

14. For analysis of this new phenomenon, see I. William Zartman, ed., *Collapsed States: The Disintegration and Restoration of Legitimate Authority* (Boulder, Colo.: Lynne Rienner Publishers, 1995); Jennifer A. Widner, "States and Statelessness in Late Twentieth Century Africa," *Daedalus* 124, no. 3 (1995): 129–54.

15. Basil Davidson, *The Black Man's Burden* (New York: Times Books, 1992).

16. Sekou Toure, *Toward Full Reafricanisation* (Paris: Présence Africaine, 1959)p. 28.

17. James C. Scott, *Seeing Like a State: How Certain Schemes to Improve the Human Condition*

Have Failed (New Haven: Yale University Press, 1998).

18. For an overview of the literature on ethnicity in Africa, see Crawford Young, "Nationalism, Ethnicity, and Class in Africa: A Retrospective," *Cahiers d'Études Africaines* 26, no. 3 (1986): 421–95.

19. Benedict Anderson, *Imagined Communities: Reflections on the Origins and Spread of Nationalism* (London: Verso, 1983).

20. Particularly influential, for Africa, were a pair of edited volumes providing numerous compelling cases of identity changes over time; Jean-Loup Amselle and Elikia M'bokolo, ed., *Au coeur de l'ethnie: Ethnie, tribalisme et état en Afrique* (Paris: Editions de la Découverte, 1985), and Leroy Vail, ed., *The Creation of Tribalism in Southern Africa* (Berkeley: University of California Press, 1989).

21. On the potent effects of mapping the social imaginary, see Thongchai Winichakul, *Siam Mapped: A History of the Geo-body of a Nation* (Honolulu: University of Hawaii Press, 1994).

22. For an engaging example of sociolinguistic mission politics, see Dmitri van den Bersselaar, "The Making of 'Union Ibo,'" *Africa* 67, no. 2 (1997): 273–95.

23. Especially striking is the incorporation of multiculturalism into concepts of nationhood in Latin America, long a stronghold of melting-pot ideologies presuming the eventual dissolution of indigenous identities. See, for example, Donna Lee Van Cott, *Indigenous Peoples and Democracy in Latin America* (New York: St. Martin's Press, 1994).

24. Vail, "Introduction: Ethnicity in Southern African History," p. 2.

25. The "ethnic security map" notion derives from Cynthia Enloe, *Ethnic Soldiers: State Security in Divided Societies* (Athens: University of Georgia Press, 1980).

26. This argument builds upon the classic Peter Ekeh article, "Colonialism and the Two Publics in Africa: A Theoretical Interpretation," *Comparative Studies in Society and History* 17, no. 2 (1975): 91–112.

27. Francis M. Deng, *War of Visions: Conflict of Identities in the Sudan* (Washington: Brookings Institution, 1995).

28. See the masterful survey of electoral systems and their impact on cultural pluralism by Ben Reilly and Andrew Reynolds, *Electoral Systems and Conflict in Divided Societies* (Washington: National Academy Press, 1999).

29. Cited in Nelson Kasfir, *The Shrinking Political Arena: Participation and Ethnicity in African Politics, with a Case Study of Uganda* (Berkeley: University of California Press, 1976), p. 209.

30. Yoweri Kaguta Museveni, *Sowing the Mustard Seed: The Struggle for Freedom and Democracy in Uganda* (London: Macmillan, 1997).

31. Ali A. Mazrui, *Soldiers and Kinsmen in Uganda: The Making of a Military Ethnocracy* (Beverly Hills: Sage Publications, 1975).

32. Pierre Englebert, *La révolution burkinabe* (Paris: Karthala, 1986).

33. To recall the evocative characterization by Hedley Bull, *The Anarchical Society* (New york: Columbia University Press, 1977).

34. H. T. Alexander, *African Tightrope* (London: Pall Mall Press, 1965), pp. 11–16. The cautious Alexander formula was a battalion a year.

35. Amii Omara-Otunu, *Politics and the Military in Uganda 1890–1985* (New York: St. Martin's, 1987), p. 51.

36. Jimi Peters, *The Nigerian Military and the State* (London: Tauris Academic Studies, 1997), p. 77.

37. Illustrative of this perspective were John J. Johnson, ed., *The Role of the Military in Undeveloped Countries* (Princeton: Princeton University Press, 1962), and Morris Janowitz, *The Military in the Political Development of New Nations* (Chicago: University of Chicago Press, 1964).

38. Peters, *The Nigerian Military*, p. 224. For other examples, see Omaru-Otunnu, *Politics and the Military*, pp. 78–137; Crawford Young and Thomas Turner, *The Rise and Decline of the Zairian State* (Madison: University of Wisconsin Press, 1985), pp. 248–75.

39. According to defense expenditure data collected by Robert West.

40. Representative of this literature was Samuel Decalo, *Coups and Army Rule in Africa: Studies in Military Style* (New Haven: Yale University Press, 1976).

41. Young and Turner, *The Rise and Decline of the Zairian State*, p. 248.

42. Colette Braekman, *Le dinosaure: le Zaire de Mobutu* (Paris: Fayard, 1992); Jean-Claude Willame, *L'autumne d'un despotisme: Pouvoir, argent et obéissance dans le Zaire des années quatre-vingt* (Paris: Karthala, 1992); Crawford Young, "Zaire: The Anatomy of a Failed State," in *History of Central Africa: The Contemporary Years since 1960*, ed. David Birmingham and Phyllis M. Martin (London: Longman, 1998), pp. 91–130.

43. Al Venter, "Arms Pour into Africa," *New African* 370 (January 1999): 11.

44. I am indebted to Mustafa Mirzeler, who conducted field research amongst the Jie 1995–1997, for this information.

45. William Reno, *Warlord Politics and African States* (Boulder: Lynne Rienner Publishers, 1998.

46. Lt. Col. Kalifa Keita, "Conflict and Conflict Resolution in the Sahel: The Tuareg Insurgency in Mali," Strategic Studies Institute, U.S. Army War College, May 1998.

47. Margaret Hall and Tom Young, *Confronting Leviathan: Mozambique since Independence* (Athens: Ohio University Press, 1997), pp. 165–70.

48. See the moving testimonials by former Sierra Leone child soldiers in Krijn Peters and Paul Richards, "Youths in Sierra Leone: 'Why We Fight,'" *Africa* 68, no. 2 (1998): 183–210. See also Ruddy Doom and Koen Vlassenroot, "Kony's Message: A New Koine? The Lord's Resistance Army in Northern Uganda," *African Affairs* 98 (1999): 5–36, and Robert Gersony, *The Agony of Northern Uganda: Results of a Field-Based Assessment of the Civil Conflicts in Northern Uganda* (Kampala: USAID, 1997).

49. Jacques Mbanza, "La guerre comme un jeu d'enfants," *Rupture* 10, no. 2 (1997): 12, cited in Remy Bazenguissa-Ganga, "The Spread of Political Violence in Congo-Brazzaville," *African Affairs* 98 (1999): 46. This article provides an incisive if chilling analysis of the militarization of politics in that land.

50. Bazenguissa-Ganga, "The Spread of Political Violence," p. 54.

51. Reno, *Warlord Politics*.

52. Such was a major conclusion of a conference convened by Richard Joseph in 1997, bringing together a number of scholars who in one way or another had past associations with the Africa Demos project at the Carter Center, led by Joseph, to take stock of democratization. Joseph, ed., *State, Conflict and Democracy in Africa*, reproduces most of the papers.

53. Adam Przeworski and Fernando Limongi, "Modernization: Theories and Facts," *World Politics* 49, no. 2 (January 1997): 155–83.

54. See various of the essays in Crawford Young, ed., *Ethnic Diversity and Public Policy: A Comparative Inquiry* (London: Macmillan, 1998).

55. Crawford Young, *The Politics of Cultural Pluralism* (Madison: University of Wisconsin

Press, 1976), pp. 450–504.

56. See the revealing evidence supplied by Michael Lambert, "Casamance: Ethnicity or Nationalism?" *Africa* 68, no. 4 (1998): 585–602.

57. For colorful details, see Heike Behrend, "Is Alice Lakwena a Witch? The Holy Spirit Movement and Its Fight against Evil in the North," in *Uganda Now: Between Development and Decay,* ed. Holger Bernt Hansen and Michael Twaddle (London: James Currey, 1988), pp. 162–77.

II

Case Studies

4

Sudan

An African Dilemma

Francis M. Deng

The crisis of nationhood currently afflicting the Sudan represents two aspects of the dilemmas that confront African countries as they strive to build nations on the foundations emerging from the colonial state. One is the lack of cultural roots to the modern African state which was fashioned on the European model in virtual disregard for indigenous values and institutions. Although Africans have adopted and assimilated this model, it remains a poor copy of its European original. The other aspect of the African dilemma is that colonialism separated ethnic groups and brought others together in the process of state formation, creating diversities that were eventually rendered conflictual by gross inequities in the sharing of power, national resources, and development opportunities. The founding fathers of African independent states tried to contain the threat of disunity and fragmentation by re-affirming the colonial borders and often by opting for one-party political systems. While they largely succeeded in preserving unity, diversities and disparities have remained sources of tension and conflict within state borders.

The ensuing contest over state power, resources, and institutions often created conflict among identity groups, each of which sought to capture the state, break away, or pursue its own autonomous development. The state, therefore, ceased to be the embodiment of the collective national will. This created a crisis of national identity that can result in vacuums of responsibility for the security and general welfare of the citizens who fall outside the dominant identity framework of the state. With violent conflicts often resulting in humanitarian tragedies, the victims of these tragedies, especially if not members of the dominant groups, become dispossessed by their own governments, unprotected, unassisted, even persecuted. In their desperation, they can only turn outside the state framework to seek and receive humanitarian assistance and sometimes human rights protection from the more compassionate international community. But even here, the outside world and the needy victim community are often confronted by a negative assertion of state sovereignty as a barricade against foreign scrutiny and intervention.

However, in reapportioning responsibility in the post–Cold War era, national sovereignty is acquiring a new meaning. Instead of being perceived as a means of insulating the state against external scrutiny or involvement, it is becoming increasingly postulated as a concept of responsibility. This requires a system of governance that is based on democratic popular citizen participation, constructive management of diversities, respect for fundamental rights, and equitable distribution of national wealth and opportunities for development. For a government or a state to claim sovereignty, it must establish legitimacy by meeting minimal standards of good governance or responsibility for the security and general welfare of its citizens and all those under its jurisdiction. Otherwise, it can expect scrutiny and, in extreme cases, humanitarian intervention.

This paper places these African dilemmas in the context of the civil war that has raged intermittently in the Sudan since independence, the acute crisis of national identity that has impeded progress in the peace process, the critical choices the parties must make in light of the identity crisis, what must be done by the international community to help move the peace process forward, and the extent to which the Sudanese situation lends itself to a peacekeeping operation by the international community.

OVERVIEW OF THE CONFLICT

The civil war in the Sudan is essentially a conflict of identities between the Northern and Southern parts of the country. The North, roughly two-thirds of the country's territory and population, is Arabized and Islamic. The South, the remaining third, is more indigenously African in race, culture, and religion. However, Christianity, initially introduced by Western missionaries, has become widely accepted as one of the central features of Southern identity, and the modern counterpart to Islam in the North. Despite the complexities of the country's racial and cultural configuration, this North-South dualism offers a useful guide to the national identity crisis behind Sudan's "war of visions." As the war has intensified and polarized the country, religion has emerged as the pivotal factor in the conflict.

The revivalist ideology of the ruling National Islamic Front, NIF, that seized power on 30 June 1989 through a military coup, is the culmination of a long-standing aspiration of the dominant political forces in the North toward the creation of an Arab-Islamic state. It should be noted that in the Sudan Islam is closely associated with Arabism as a racial and cultural concept. The Southern-based Sudan People's Liberation Movement with its military wing, the Sudan People's Liberation Army, SPLM/SPLA, represents the latest in a long chain of armed struggle by the indigenous African peoples in the Southern part of the country, whose modern leadership is overwhelmingly Christian. Since independence, the South has resisted Northern domination and its twin ideologies of Arabization and Islamization. The irony is that the stated goal of the SPLM/SPLA, unlike that of its predecessors, is not the secession of the South, but the creation of a new, secular, pluralistic Sudan, free of discrimination on the grounds of race, ethnicity, culture, or gender. This goal has been interpreted as a euphemism for the de-Arabization and de-Islamization of the country, or, to put it in other words, the Africanization of the

Sudan. The radicalism of the NIF regime and the extreme version of the Islamic state it has been pursuing can be explained as a reaction to the threat posed by the Southerners and their secularist allies in the North. To the NIF, dominant traditional parties in the North have been too weak or too compromising in their efforts to create an Arab-Islamic state in the Sudan. The crisis has now gone beyond the North-South divide as the military dictatorship of the NIF has brought together opposition parties from both the North and the South in a collective struggle for democracy under the umbrella of the National Democratic Alliance. Nevertheless, the North-South conflict remains the most important challenge to the nation.

It can be argued that both sides of the North-South ideological divide have a just cause. The North seeks cultural and religious legitimacy to its concepts of nationhood, while the South resists the domination and assimilation which is inherent in the Northern vision of an Arab-Islamic state. Behind the Northern Arab-Islamic fervor and the Southern Africanist identity of resistance is a historical baggage in the evolution of these conflicting identities. The essence of the country's unique complexity and anomalous identity can be summed up in what Ali Mazrui has described as "the multiple marginality of the Sudan" between Africa and the Arab-Muslim world.[1] This crisis now threatens the viability of the Sudan as a united country.

Although national unity is desirable for a variety of reasons, it should not be viewed as an end in itself. Rather, unity should be seen as the means to achieving the ends of equitable social and economic development, political participation, and protection of rights of citizenship. This should preclude discrimination on grounds of ethnic, religious, linguistic, or other form of exclusive identity. When a system is so oppressive to a people's sense of identity and cultural integrity, and when their rights to political participation, economic development, access to essential services, and so forth are being denied, the reconciliation of competing claims within the unity framework may not be possible. Secession, therefore, becomes a right that ought to be permissible: "The moral justification and the political force of the principle of self-determination are linked to the notion that government should be based on the consent of the governed: that people have a right to associate freely into an entity organized to govern itself, thereby giving expression to the consent of the governed."[2]

The question of whether or not the principle of self-determination applies to the Sudanese context raises questions about the respective "peoples" involved and whether the right of self-determination is exercisable within the framework of national unity or through secession. The case of the South can be argued on two grounds. One is the extent to which Southern Sudanese represent a "people" with distinct racial or cultural characteristics that constitute a sense of nationhood. The second is whether the grievances of the South could be adequately addressed within the framework of unity or whether, conversely, secession is justifiable.

It is often argued that thinking of the Sudan in terms of North and South is an oversimplification that obscures the complexities of the country's commonalities and cross-cutting diversities. According to this line of argument, there has been so much racial and cultural mixing across the North-South divide that the results defy any exclusive racial, ethnic, or cultural classifications. Equally, although there are more Muslims in the North than in the South, religion is also not a reliable indicator of the differences. As for economic and social indicators, it is argued that while the North, taken as a whole, is more advanced than the South, it has pockets of underdevelopment that may be worse off than parts of the South. And yet, it is widely recognized that the South is more indigenously African in racial, cultural, and religious terms than the North, and that it has generally lagged far behind the North in political and economic development. Indeed, while genuine anomalies do exist, attempts to minimize the differences between the two parts of the country have been viewed with suspicion as politically motivated Northern machinations.

The issue of whether the problems between the North and the South can be solved within the framework of unity or whether they require partitioning the country has also been controversial. There are those who argue that the differences do not justify such a radical solution as partition. Others believe that all attempts to find solutions within the framework of unity have failed and that only partitioning the country stands a chance of providing a durable solution to the chronic civil war that has devastated the country since independence.

The historical process that has separated the Arab Muslim North and the African South and the anomalies between the two has its roots in the Arabization and Islamization of the North and Southern resistance to Arab-Islamic domination and assimilation.

ARAB-ISLAMIC ASSIMILATION IN THE NORTH

Sudanese contact and interaction with the Middle East via Egypt date back thousands of years before Christ, taking the form of trade in ivory, gold, and other commodities. Arab traders settled among the indigenous population and integrated themselves with the advantages of wealth, which promoted pro-Arab association to the extent that eventually the Sudanese identified with the Arabs, both genetically and culturally. The process intensified after the advent of Islam in the seventh century, when the Arab Muslim empire invaded Sudan and, without victor or vanquished, concluded peace accords with the northern peoples of Nubia and Beja.[3] These accords established remote Arab controls over the country, opened the channels of communication with the Arab world, guaranteed freedom of movement for the Arabs, protected Arab trade, and safeguarded Arab settlement, but otherwise left the Sudanese in relative peace and independence.

Although the Arab settlers were traders and not rulers, their privileged position, their more cosmopolitan and universalizing religious culture, and their superior material wealth combined with the liberal assimilationist Arab Islamic tradition, opened gates to universal Islamic "brotherhood," and made them an appealing class for intermarriage with the leading Sudanese families. As Arabs did not come with their wives, and as Islam did not permit the marriage of Muslim women to non-Muslims, intermarriage was a one-way street. It is generally accepted that the descendants of the Arabs succeeded to the leadership positions of their maternal families through the system of matrilineal succession then prevalent in the North. The patriarchal system then took over and perpetuated the Arab-Muslim male line. The children identified with the paternal line, and, in the course of time, the Arab element predominated. The pre-Islamic system was not so much overthrown as "turned inside out."[4]

Sufi orders are widely acknowledged as having played a pivotal role in blending Islam with indigenous traditions to produce an eclectic approach to religion.[5] These religious orders known as *tariqahs,* which spread through wandering teachers, were decentralized in organization, reflecting the lack of centralized structures in Sudanese Islamic communities. They also provided an alternative basis of support for the local holy men and holy families, thereby adding a dimension of religious diversity to the community. Islamic orders with more centralized organizational approaches began to come to the Sudan by the beginning of the nineteenth century. The Turko-Egyptian administration of the Ottoman Empire, which ruled the country from 1821 to 1885, introduced Islamic orthodoxy, but Sufi orders flourished nonetheless. In 1885, Mohamed Ahmed, the Mahdi, overthrew the Turko-Egyptian administration and tried to suppress the Sufi orders in favor of orthodox Islam. Although the Mahdi died shortly after his miraculous victory, he established the Mahdist state that lasted until the Anglo-Egyptian reconquest of 1898. While the Mahdi was initially hostile to the Sufi orders and tried to eliminate them, his efforts proved unsuccessful. Indeed, the school of thought which he founded, the Ansar, eventually turned into a sect and his descendants emerged as the principal religious and political rivals of the previously dominant Khatmiyyah order, led by the Mirghani family. Contrary to orthodox Islam, their descendants inherited the spiritual leadership which in due course became transformed into a theocratic political dynasty. With a superstitious zeal that is also un-Islamic by orthodox standards, the unsophisticated followers of these spiritual leaders see them as divine, with supernatural powers to bless, curse, and destroy in a worldly context. Sufist Islam is thus as worldly in its orientation as traditional African religious beliefs and practices. Also like African indigenous religions, it is more tolerant of diversity in religious expression than the centralized orthodox Islam of the modern state.

The main following of the two families in their traditional strongholds divided the country into the western regions for the Mahdi and the north and east for Mirghani, with the central regions split between them. Popular support for these families grew rapidly along these lines. During the Anglo-Egyptian rule (1898–1956), colonial exploitation of these religious leaders was countered by an ambivalent reaction toward them from the educated class. This reaction gave rise to radical movements representing both secularism and Islam which, though antagonistic, had antisectarianism as a common objective.[6] These were the Communist Party and the two Brotherhoods, the Muslim Brothers and the Republican Brothers, the last two differing in their interpretation of the Islamic doctrine, one orthodox and the other liberal to the point of being secular.

The Muslim Brothers embraced the traditional Shari'a with a political ideological twist. Their radicalism was conceived from within a revivalist vision into tradition that provided the rationale for the forward postulation of a modern Islamic state. The Republican Brothers, on the other hand, reinterpreted Shari'a in the context of historical criticism. Their ideological argument was that principles that were appropriate for seventh century Arabia could not be equally suited to twentieth-century conditions. They did not consider it the divine purpose to follow literally a bygone code whose moral imperatives could be construed as less than that demanded from the contemporary generation, including human rights, social justice, and international peace.[7]

The irony is that while holding views which diverged radically from traditional Islam, the Republican Brothers remained devoted to Islam, its ideals, and practices from a spiritual and moral point of view. The Muslim Brothers on the other hand politicized Islam and equipped themselves with the tools of modernity to pursue power and state control in a pragmatic, Machiavellian fashion that became virtually divorced from the spirituality of religion, except as an instrument of power and control.[8]

The difference between the Republican Brothers and the Muslim Brothers may well be in the degree to which Islamic ideals are an end or the religion is a means to other objectives. The first represents the Republicans, the second the Muslim Brothers, or at least its dominant faction. The differences, indeed the conflicts, between the two wings of the Islamic path increased with time and with a helping hand from the 1983 "September Laws" of the military ruler, Jaafar Nimeiri, enacted in alliance with the Muslim Brothers and which eventually resulted in the public hanging of the pious, elderly leader of the Republican Brothers, Mahmoud Mohamed Taha on 18 January 1985, condemned of the Islamic crime of apostasy.[9]

From the foregoing, it is obvious that despite ethnic or tribal diversity, the North has consolidated an identity based on Arabism and Islam. Indeed, the Islamic platform of the Muslim Brothers, now the National Islamic Front, has been shared by virtually all political forces in the North, the main difference being the contest over power and the degree of commitment to the religious agenda, with NIF being the most radical and uncompromising proponent of the agenda. Although Arab identity has always been acknowledged, this nationalist Arab-Islamic agenda is an elite concept that first emerged with the movement for independence from European domination.

The psychological roots of exaggerated attachment to Arabism indeed go deep into the history of the threatening and even humiliating relations with the Christian West. Edward Atiyah, a Syrian who first taught at the Gordon Memorial College in the 1920s and then made a career in government service, vividly described the attitude of his contemporaries among the newly educated class of northern Sudanese. He arrived in 1926 to find students displaying mixed emotions—excitement about the outside world with its superior knowledge, power, and wealth, and a sense of self-pity for being backward, poor, and ignorant, all of which evoked "a collective feeling of smallness and inferiority" and provoked in many cases both a "strongly assertive individual attitude and an inordinate self-conceit."[10] According to Atiyah, identification with the Arab East was as much a reaction against Western domination as it was an escape from the inferiority of the African background. Sudanese emphasized their Arab descent, excluding from their consciousness any association with Africa and the negroid elements, and they found great consolation in the renaissance of the Arab East. But as that renaissance had not much to offer in tangible terms, they sought comfort and encouragement in the past glory of the warlike Arabs who, inspired by their religion and the spirit of the Prophet, had swept victoriously through Christendom. "Had not the Arabs been the masters and teachers of the world when the now mighty Europeans were steeped in medieval night? Had they not translated Aristotle into Arabic and transmitted to the European barbarians the first gleams of the light of Greece? But the greatest consolation of all, the one beyond doubt and dispute, the safe and sure anchorage of their being was the knowledge that in their Book and Prophet they possessed the Ultimate Truth. In this serene knowledge they felt superior to all outsiders.... Truly that knowledge was a rock of comfort."[11]

Muddathir Abd al-Rahim, a leading Islamist and northern expert on the South, confirms Atiyah's observation by explaining that a dominant theme in the writings and verbal utterances of the literate northern Sudanese at that time was the need for unity and solidarity based on the principles of Islam and Arabism rather than on Sudanese nationalism. Having been defeated and humiliated by the Anglo-Egyptian forces, the Sudanese, he explains, needed psychological reassurance, which they could not find in their past or in contemporary African identity. Instead of helping them to regain their lost self-confidence, Africa threatened to accentuate their feeling of inferiority in comparison with both the British and the Egyptians. "Almost involuntarily, therefore, the Sudanese ... turned their backs on Africa and became passionately attached to the glorious past of Islam, which, together with the richness of classical Arabic culture and thought, provided the necessary psychological prod."[12]

Abd al-Rahim probed the psychological denial of the African dimension of Sudanese identity, which the politically conscious Northern Arab Muslim did not regard as a source of glorification or self-gratification. Their African present and past was to them a part of the so-called *Jahiliyya*, the Age of Ignorance or Darkness, with which they could therefore not identify themselves. Islam as a total system, "a religion, a civilization, a way of life, and a polity, was the central fact in life and the main object of loyalty. It was through its association with Islam that Arabism also had become a subject of pride, not only among the Arabs but throughout the Muslim world ... where ... people ... proudly explain their Arab connections and ancestry (true or imagined) as well as their Islamic identity."[13] Another northern Sudanese scholar observed that, "It was the citadel of Islamic culture that stood as a guarantee against the submersion of The Sudan in the jungles of the heathen Africa, the source of magazines and books that were the intelligentsia's link with the world beyond, the cradle of the nationalist movement and its heroes."[14]

The foremost northern specialist on the South, Muhammad Omar Bashir, observed that "Northern Sudanese generally identified themselves with the Arab world through ... Egypt ... the window through which they viewed the outside world." He then went on to explain that it was natural for them to do so, since "they were undoubtedly more Arab than African in their culture.... Besides, the Africans in the Southern Sudan, who were among the most backward peoples on the continent, could hardly inspire their Arab compatriots with any desire to identify with Africa."[15]

Sudan's foreign policy after independence was dominated by two main ideological themes: identification with the Arab world and the ambivalences of East-West relations. The latter in part reflected the domestic rivalry between the dominant religious elements and the radical left, the religious factor combining with continuing ties with Great Britain and the West, yet countered by the pull of the left toward the Eastern bloc. The connection with Africa trailed behind these factors, and it was based more on geography rather than on genuine racial, ethnic, or cultural affinity.

Muhammad Ahmed Mahjoub became foreign minister of the newly independent Sudan in a coalition government in 1956, and he held the position until the military coup of 1958. He became prime minister when parliamentary democracy returned in 1965, lost the premiership briefly in June 1966, and resumed it in May 1967, remaining in power until another coup overthrew his government in 1969. Known for his tough line against the southern rebel movement, Mahjoub "was noted during his periods of power for his antipathy to the South."[16]

The irony of his position toward the South, expressed in some of the most repressive and atrocious policies of the history of the conflict, is that he was highly admired in the North as a man who stood for the ideals of democracy and respect for human rights, which was supposedly the essence of the title of his memoirs, *Democracy on Trial.* Mansour Khalid, who observed him at close range, has written that "Mahjoub was a democrat, in temperament, style of government, as well as in his private life."[17] The context for which Mahjoub advocated democracy was of course the North, and his plans nearly always excluded the South. Although Mansour Khalid "quoted and requoted" his memoirs on democracy, Mahjoub's own "narrative ... tells a different story about this great democrat; the way he acted and behaved in the South, a world that lies beyond what the ruling elite consider to be the Sudan."[18]

The intention here is not to rehash the destructive and divisive role this otherwise democratic leader for the North played as a colonial ruler in the South; rather it is to show how his Arab-Islamic orientation, which was dividing his own country internally, motivated and shaped his policies and actions externally, especially among the Arabs. Muhammad Ahmed Mahjoub was undoubtedly most prominent in Arab circles: physically towering, a brilliant lawyer, exceptionally articulate in both English and Arabic, and a distinguished poet in Arabic, a language he loved exceedingly. Mahjoub even sought to champion the cause of Arabism better than the Egyptians did, by questioning the extent of Egypt's commitment to the cause of Arab nationalism: he argued that Egypt had by far the richest Arab heritage and the largest Arab population. Arabs had therefore looked to Cairo as the citadel of pan-Arabism. However, Cairo has not always fulfilled this role. As political leaders, Mohammed Abdu, Saad Zaghloul, Mustafa Kamil were *Egyptian,* not *Arab,* nationalists. "As political thinkers and writers, Lutfi El Sayid, Taha Hussein and Al-Aggad were Egyptian, but not Arab, nationalists.... When the revolution of 23 July 1952, brought Gamal Abdul Nasser and his colleagues to power, they were not much better than the thinkers, writers and politicians in their outlook towards pan-Arabism."[19]

Mahjoub's pride in Arabism, apparent in his portrayal of the Arab past glory and yearning for its revival, recalls the picture painted by Edward Atiyah about the manner in which his students at the Gordon Memorial College, where Mahjoub studied, identified themselves with the historical glory of Arabism and Islam, denying their African reality to combat the sense of inferiority inflicted on them by Western conquest. Mahjoub first acknowledged "the glorious past of Islam," which unified the Arabian peninsula, and moved the mainly Arab armies to the conquest of the Persian and Byzantine empires, beginning from the seventh century and contining until the thirteenth. With patriotic pride in this "glorious epoch," Mahjoub exalted the "wisdom and brilliance" of some of the Caliphs under the Unmayad and Abbasid caliphates who made numerous achievements in different fields.[20] Then he lamented the decline of the Arabs as a forceful element: "The power of the Abbasids was eventually extinguished by the Mongolian hordes of Genghis Khan and his successors.... The real power moved into the hands of non-Arab Muslims...."[21]

To Mahjoub, then, Arabism was more than the Arabic language and culture and the Islamic religion. Being Arab was something in the blood—genealogy, ethnicity, or race—real or assumed, but sustained by historical association and a rising sense of embracing nationalism. Mahjoub did not stop at merely reflecting the past and contemporary realities of the Arab identity and its politics; he postulated pan-Arabism as an objective to be pursued with vigor. And indeed, much of his illustrious diplomatic career was devoted to the promotion of Arab nationalism. Acting as a spokesman for the Arab delegations in introducing a draft resolution on the situation in the Middle East in 1958 in the wake of the Iraqi revolution, which triggered American and British intervention in Lebanon and Jordan, Mahjoub made the blood component of the Arab identity explicit: "I am not speaking this time in the name of the delegation of the Sudan," he said. "It is my honour and privilege to speak in the name of all ... the ten Arab States which are related not only by a common language or a common heritage of history and culture, but also by blood."[22] Mahjoub stressed that the resolution was cosponsored by all the Arab states as a result of frank deliberations among themselves over what they regarded as a dispute between family members. "We have had strong ties in the past; we have strong ties at present, and we all aspire to a glorious future for Arab nations in order to contribute once again to the human heritage in the fields of knowledge and human welfare."[23] His aspiration for the Arabs was euphoric:

For us, Arabs, this will be the beginning of a glorious future. It will be the beginning of strengthening our ties, co-operating among ourselves, and being tolerant with each other. We shall, no doubt, do all that is possible to realize our hopes and aspirations, and co-operate among ourselves wholeheartedly. We hope that we will be able to contribute to the well-being of our Arab nation, whether that nation remains distributed among different independent states, in a regional organization, or under any form of government to which the peoples of the Arab lands will agree, or become one state.... Once more, the light will come from ... [the East]. "Our ... mission henceforth will be the pursuit of human perfection, peace and security and not destruction and annihilation of the human race.[24]

Ismail al-Azhari, one of the legendary figures of the nationalist struggle, who was to become the first prime minister and later president, expressed Northern Sudanese identification with Islam and Arabism in unequivocal terms in an address to the Round Table Conference on the problem of the South in 1965:

I feel at this juncture obliged to declare that we are proud of our Arab origin, of our Arabism and of being Moslems. The Arabs came to this continent, as pioneers, to disseminate a genuine culture, and promote sound principles which have shed enlightenment and civilization throughout Africa at a time when Europe was plunged into the abyss of darkness, ignorance and doctrinal and scholarly backwardness. It is our ancestors who held the torch high and led the caravan of liberation and advancement; and it is they who provided a superior melting-pot for Greek, Persian and Indian culture, giving them the chance to react with all that was noble in Arab culture, and handing them back to the rest of the world as a guide to those who wished to extend the frontiers of learning.[25]

Most Northern Sudanese deny any ideological identification with the revivalist policies of the NIF, which they view as a minority elite party, whose extremist version of Islam is not in the least representative of the country. To a large extent, they are right. What they underestimate, however, is the extent to which the NIF has manipulated the broader identification with Islam and Arabism to promote their own interpretation that leaders of the other dominant political parties, which are also religiously based, find difficult to challenge effectively. In a way, the NIF has pulled the religious rug from under the sectarian religious leaders and has blackmailed them into an ineffective opposition based not so much on challenging the Arab-Islamic foundation of the NIF ideology, but rather on the extent to which the regime has violated fundamental principles of democracy and international human rights.

The renowned historian Robert O. Collins, whose scholarly career has been devoted to the study of the Sudan, gave a penetrating analysis of the NIF regime in a paper presented at the Fourth Triennial Meeting of the International Sudanese Studies Association held at the American University in Cairo on 12–14 June, 1997. In that paper, he noted that the officers who seized control of the Sudan government on 30 June 1989, were committed to build a *New Sudan* from the debris of a lost generation of Sudanese in search of an identity. The *New Sudanese* would be defined by Islam and the Qur'an to be interpreted and enforced by the doctrines of the National Islamic Front (NIF) and to be promulgated in Arabic, the language of the Qur'an. To be Sudanese required conformity to this rigid ideology. Those who could not conform to its creed would be excluded. Collins notes that the Sudanese have been searching since independence for an identity that has often made the seekers ever more desperate for a definition of their nationality. The Sudanese have learned by their terrifying sacrifices of two million people during this past half century that the best definition of "Sudanese" is perhaps no definition at all: "The search for the Sudanese has absorbed journalists, scholars, wise men and fools. It has revived ethnic historicism and relieved religious rivalries. It has stimulated dreams of a beneficent future made possible by an open not a closed society in which there is a free and unrestricted exchange of ideas that are a fundamental part of Sudanese society in recognition of worth defined not by creed but by humanity."

In the face of NIF's ideological dictate, "the dilemma of the Southern Sudanese is no different from their Northern Sudanese brothers, only more acute, more complete. In order to prosper or even survive, the choice presented to them by the Government of National Salvation is not choice at all ... The message of the NIF may appeal to the subterranean streak of religious xenophobia that lingers in the Sudanese soul on the frontiers of Islam." In the end, Collins sees two paths: "One branches east to the fundamental security of a long and established Muslim society. The other forks to the west and its secular administrative and scientific traditions. Many Sudanese have fled from the Islamists into exile. Some have attempted to cross from one culture and religion to another in order to escape from the labyrinth of the Islamists in the Sudan, but they are no near the end of their journey than at the beginning. Beguiled by rhetoric and cash some have returned to the Southern Sudan as mercenaries for the Islamists to prosper in the din and thunder of Sudanic war." But for most Southerners, the Islamists have only sharpened the line of confrontation. "Determined to impose their vision of a *New Sudan*, the Islamists seek to resolve by the Book or the Sword the conflict with those Africans equally determined to defend the integrity of their own culture history."[26]

But for Hassan al-Turabi, since the Islamists represent a superior culture and religion, with God on their side, they are sure to prevail. An account by William Finnegan in *The New Yorker* of 25 January 1999 provides a remarkable insight into the frame of mind of this political and religious thinker and spokesman of the Islamic revolution:

At one point, he was trying to convince me not just that his poor, hungry, war-torn backwater "is becoming a very important country" but that his terrifying police state "is a free country," and added, "Monopoly is only for God." He mixes economic libertarianism with high-flown disquisitions on art, science, and religion. ("An artist is submitting to God. A scientist is doing the same.") ... I asked Turabi about the war. He said that John Garang was jealous of the former rebels who had joined the government, which struck me as unlikely. To explain the situation in the South to me, Turabi thought to use an American analogy—the Civil War. "The Confederacy no longer exists," he said. "Most of the niggers of yesteryear, they are in Chicago now. It is just the same here, with millions of southerners having come to the North. With better roads, which we plan to build, virtually all of them will come to the North. They are becoming conscious of the fact that there is such a thing as a job, et cetera. They will no longer want to sit under a tree just waiting for the fruit to fall."

Finnegan reflected on Turabi's comments: "The idea that the people of Sudan's South—herders and farmers with the most physically demanding lives imaginable, people as deeply wedded to their lands as any set of tribes on earth—are lazy and are looking forward to moving north en masse to work for the hated Djellabah [Arabs] struck me as so deeply foolish that it was almost funny. Nobody laughed, though. And Turabi nattered on."[27]

Ironically, Northern fervent identification with the Arab identity not only overlooks the fact that even those who qualify as Arabs are in fact an Afro-Arab hybrid, but also misrepresents the North as monolithically Arabized. It must be emphasized that despite the dominance of the Arab-Islamic elements, there are non-Arab communities in the North, which, though large in numbers proportional to the Arabized tribes, have been paradoxically marginalized and partially assimilated by their conversion to Islam and adoption of Arabic as the language of communication. These groups are particularly noticeable in the West, where the Fur have retained their indigenous characteristics, in the East where the Beja tribes have resisted total assimilation, and certainly along the borders with the South, where the Nuba and the Ingassana are becoming recognized as having a lot in common with the South. Even the Nubians who border Egypt in the North and who have had more intense interaction with the Middle East through the Egyptian connection, have resisted total assimilation by retaining their indigenous languages and other cultural characteristics.

While these racial and cultural anomalies challenge the stereotype of the Arab North and the African South, the North-South cleavage remains the most formidable barrier to a sense of shared national identity. Unlike the process of Arabization and Islamization in the North, which occurred through persuasion rather than coercion, North-South relations have been for the most part adversarial. Indeed, southern identity can best be understood as one of resistance to the North.

SOUTHERN IDENTITY OF RESISTANCE

What is particularly significant about the southern confrontation with the North, whether prior or subsequent to the advent of Islam, is that while the Arabs persistently invaded the South for slaves, they never penetrated sufficiently, far less attempted to settle. Swamps, flies, tropical humidity and the fierce resistance of the tribes kept the contact marginal, even as it was devastatingly violent. Furthermore, since the Arab Muslim was interested in the actual or potential value of the Negro as a slave, he did not desire to interact and integrate with him in the manner experienced by the North. To convert the Negroes of the South to Islam would have meant that they could not be justifiably raided for slaves.

Although the Turko-Egyptians and the Mahdists invaded the South to extend their control, and might therefore be distinguished from the ordinary commercial slave-traders, their raids also involved slavery and were in fact indistinguishable from those of ordinary slave-hunters. For that reason, local memory conceptually fuses them and associates them with the total destruction of the South. Indeed, it was not until the Turko-Egyptian government opened the Bahr el-Ghazal and Equatoria provinces and established more security from outside invaders that the slave trade became well established and assumed large proportions.[28]

The Anglo-Egyptian condominium rule, while objectionable in principle, gave the South the only period of peace, tranquility, and relative independence in the form of "tribal" autonomy that they had experienced for centuries. However, the British did not develop the South, but kept it isolated from the North as "Closed Districts" to evolve along indigenous lines with the Christian missionaries playing a modest "civilizing" role. The separation of the administrative set up and of the educational system, which envisaged the South more in the context of East Africa than in the national framework of the Sudan, meant that graduates from the southern intermediate schools went to Makerere College in Uganda for higher education, and the future of the South was contemplated in the context of East Africa rather than the Middle East.

With the rise of political consciousness in the North, the independence movement, spearheaded by northern elites collaborating with Egypt, began to manifest aspirations for the integration of the South into the national political process. The first step was taken by the Graduates Congress in 1942 that demanded from the government, among other things, the abolition of restrictions placed on trade and intra-Sudanese travel, and the unification of the educational system of the country. By 1944, an Advisory Council was formed in the North, which, though it did not legislate, wielded much influence. The South did not participate in the Council. Indeed, the possibility of its being separated from the Sudan and annexed to one of its neighbors to the South or left completely independent was still in mind. A Report of the Fabian Colonial Bureau in 1945, while stating the political and economic interests of the North in the South, concluded: "On all other grounds the South ought not to be united to the Arab North. In human terms it belongs to the Africa south of it."[29] The same year the Fabian report was published, the policy of the government was still to act upon the fact "that the people of the Southern Sudan are distinctly African and Negroid, and that our obvious duty to them is therefore to push ahead as far as we can with their economic and educational development on African and Negroid lines, and not upon the Middle Eastern Arab lines of progress which are suitable for the Northern Sudan."[30]

In 1946, the Governor-General set up an Administration Conference to help determine steps to be taken toward the devolution of power to the Sudanese. Again, the South did not participate in that conference. When northern members demanded the unification of the South and the North, participants were flown to the South for an impressionistic enquiry into the conditions there. They returned to recommend the unity of the South with the North, to begin with the participation of the South in a Legislative Assembly which was to be formed. That year, under pressure from Egypt and the northern Sudan, James Robertson, the Civil Secretary, decided to reverse the separatist southern Policy in favor of ultimate unity of the Sudan.[31] The new policy stipulated that while the peoples of the Southern Sudan were distinctly African and negroid, "geography and economics combine (so far as can be seen at the present time) to render them inextricably bound for the future development to the Middle Eastern and Arabicized Northern

Sudan."[32] On the assumption that the outcome of the negotiations between Britain and Egypt on the future of the country would be a united independent Sudan, the Civil Secretary argued that "it is the Sudanese, Northern and Southern, who will live their lives and direct their affairs in future generations in this country."[33]

Even then, the ultimate unity of the country was not seen as a foregone conclusion, as the British still seemed to hope that the North might change its mind and reject the South as a financial burden: "It may be that the feeling which now exists among a few of the wisest Northern Sudanese, that they should not, when self-governing, be asked to shoulder the financial and communal burden which they believe the South will always prove to be, may become an important political policy among them. But we should now work on the assumption that the Sudan, as at present constituted, with possibly minor boundary adjustments, will remain one."[34]

The British administrators in the South protested against the new policy on the ground that it was one-sided, and suggested that a southern Administrative Conference be held in the South. The Civil Secretary agreed and the Juba Conference was held on 12 June 1947 to seek Southern views on the issue of whether and how the South should be represented in the proposed assembly.[35] To the argument often made that the South opted for unity at the Juba Conference, Sir James Robertson explained in his memoirs that "No decision could be made by the conference, since members had not received a mandate from their people. The only decision resulting from the conference was taken by myself. I decided that I would, after what I had seen about the Southerners who attended, endorse the recommendation of the administrative conference and ask the Governor-General in council to accept the proposal that the new Legislative Assembly would be representative of the whole Sudan."[36]

Things developed much faster than had been predicted, even by the British administration. In 1953, northern parties agreed with Egypt and Britain on a transitional period of self-government that would lead to self-determination in three years. The South was not represented in those negotiations. As the southern statesman and jurist, Abel Alier, has observed, during the accelerated march to independence, "The British Civil Secretary [James Robertson] was preoccupied with how to win the Northern Sudanese intelligentsia away from the Egyptian government in the contest between the two Condominium powers. . . . Robertson believed that safeguards for the South were bound to drive Northern Sudanese political leaders over to Egypt which was craftily championing the Northern Sudanese case for unconditional unity of the two regions of the Sudan."[37] As Tim Niblock observed,

Although the South could not now be deprived of that distinct cultural identity which had been safeguarded and fostered by earlier policies, the emphasis was placed on conditioning southerners to increased contacts with northerners, drawing the South into national political institutions, and making southern education compatible with the educational systems established in the North. With less than seven years before southerners had to cope with the politics of national self-determination, however, it was too late.[38]

With the signing of the Anglo-Egyptian Agreement in 1953, a southern nationalist movement began to take organized form. The gist of this movement was that the South had not been accorded its due share in the decision processes leading to self-determination; that the constitutional set-up envisaged for the independent Sudan did not give due recognition to the southern identity; that under the unitary system, the South would be politically subordinated to, and dominated by, the North; and that unity with the North was only possible under a federal system of government.

But things had gone well beyond the control of the South. What remained was the formal implementation of the steps outlined in the 1953 agreement between Britain and Egypt. Northern participation was to guide the country through self-rule to independence. The Parliament that was elected in 1953 to determine the country's future decided on August 16 by a unanimous vote to carry out the requisite steps toward exercising the right of self-determination. On August 29 a resolution was passed for the holding of a nationwide plebiscite to ascertain the wishes of the Sudanese people. This decision was quickly reversed. "The political parties realized that the organization of a plebiscite in a country as vast and diversified as the Sudan with its largely illiterate population, in the south especially, would create many problems and solve none. Moreover, it would be virtually impossible to conduct a plebiscite in the south since the [1955] mutiny had caused a collapse in the security and administrative system."[39]

When the critical moment of agreeing on the declaration of independence came, in the words of Mohamed Ahmed Mahjoub, one of its principal authors, the leaders of the nationalist movement "worked feverishly" over "the next few days," to persuade the South to accede. "We encountered some difficulty in convincing the Southerners so we inserted a special resolution to please them, pledging that the Constituent Assembly would give full consideration to the claims of Southern Sudanese Members of Parliament for a federal government for the three Southern Provinces."[40] On 19 December 1955, the Sudanese Parliament adopted a unanimous resolution in favor of the declaration of independence, which became effective January 1, 1956. Whether Northern members intended to take this pledge seriously or not can only be judged from the cursory reference to it and the subsequent dismissal of the southern claim without anything near a "full consideration."[41]

The crisis of legitimacy, however, went beyond the southern Sudan and affected other marginalized parts of the country. As Tim Niblock observed: "To much of the population in the less developed fringe of Sudan, then, the Sudanese state as it emerged at independence seemed a distant and alien entity, just as it did in the colonial era. The peoples of southern Sudan, and most of those in western and eastern Sudan, had little access to the benefits which the state bestowed (education, health services, remunerative government jobs, etc.). The state personnel who faced them . . . appeared to share little of their cultural or ethnic background."[42]

Rather than endeavor to win the South, northern perspectives since independence have focused on blaming the separatist policies of the British for their encouragement of a southern identity based on traditional systems with the influence of Christianity and Western culture. Consequently, their remedy has persistently been aimed at undoing this history through Arabization and Islamization, to remove the Christian Western influence and to integrate the country along the lines of the northern model.[43] The exception to this pattern was the 1972 Addis Ababa agreement during Nimeiri's rule which granted the South regional autonomy and thereby ensured peace and national unity until its unilateral abrogation by the government in 1983, when the war was resumed.

The Addis Ababa Agreement, however, appears to have also had the effect of arousing the fears of the extremists on both sides. It was particularly perceived by the right wing factions of Arabism and Islam as a victory for their adversaries—southern Christians and secularists—not to mention military dictatorship. And of course, there were southerners who saw the agreement as a virtual surrender. As one Northern observer noted: "Despite important concessions from the Northern parties, there was still little common ground. The Northerners, while offering some regional devolution of power, stopped short of federation; the Southerners, while accepting a unified Sudan, wanted the loosest of confederation."[44] Another Northerner wrote: "The Addis Ababa agreement . . . brought peace and the establishment of the Southern Region, and cast the May regime . . . in a more favourable light in the West, especially after its violent break with the communists the previous year. The southerners now actively supported Nimeiri, and in fact were the main prop of the regime. . . . The Islamists and their allies were very suspicious about the Addis Ababa agreement, and were certain that it had secret clauses of an anti-Islamic character."[45]

According to the Islamic scholar Abdelwahab El-Affendi, a serious debate ensued among the Islamists about allowing the South to secede if that was necessary for the establishment of an Islamic state in Sudan. In fact the call for a united Muslim front that would include the major political parties—Umma Party, Democratic Unionist Party, and their own Islamic Charter Front, was justified by the Brothers on the grounds of the need to meet "the new challenge of the South which demanded from the North unity in defence of its interests and its cultural identity against the [Christian] missionary, imperialist, racist monster."[46] It was clear to the Muslim Brothers that "any association based on Islam automatically excludes non-Muslim citizens."[47]

Nimeiri was faced with a dilemma. On the one hand, he needed the South which was proving to be his main source of security. On the other hand, he continued to be threatened by the rightist, mostly Islamic opposition groups. He chose the latter and embraced the Islamic agenda. Although he himself was overthrown by a popular uprising in 1985, his policies eventually led to the rise of the Islamists to the summit of power. It is now widely accepted that their seizure of power on 30 June 1989 was prompted by the prospects of an imminent agreement between the government and the SPLM/SPLA that would have compromised the Islamic agenda.

For the North, the appeal of the South lay in its weakness and underdevelopment, which made it a raw material to be molded, ideally into the Arab-Islamic pattern of the nation rather than the Christian-Western patterns of the colonialists. As a northerner has stated, "The paradoxical result is that the stronger the South grows, the more the Muslim Northerners feel challenged, and the stronger becomes their attachment to their religious identity."[48]

As the South improves itself with education and develops a modern identity reinforced by Christianity, Western culture, and military strength, the emerging parity between the competing models makes the South too strong to disregard or to manipulate. But the more seriously grievances of the South are considered, the clearer it becomes that they cannot be redressed within the Arab-Islamic status quo. As a result, the South begins to pose a real threat to the system: either the national framework is fundamentally restructured, the South decisively defeated and dominated, or the country risks disintegration. Sudan remains poised between these difficult choices. And with the realization that the needed compromises are difficult to make, the regime in Khartoum becomes even more inclined toward adopting a hard line, hoping to break the back of the SPLM/SPLA and make those groups more amenable to accepting far less than they are currently demanding.

But even with the national situation working in favor of the Arab-Islamic model, the government cannot stabilize the nation without the cooperation of the SPLM/SPLA, and this movement cannot be expected to endorse the northern vision for the nation. The prospects that such polarized positions will be bridged may well depend on the development of a third centrist force. Such a force seems to be in the making in the current cooperation of the SPLM-SPLA with northern opposition groups. While much of this cooperation may be purely tactical, it could conceivably prove to be midwife for other alternative arrangements, since the identity picture of Sudan is a murky one. By virtue of its ambiguities, it offers potential in varied directions. Which way the future will go remains the challenging question for building or dismantling the emerging nation.

THE DILEMMAS OF DIVIDED NATIONALISM

The foregoing historical overview indicates that the North and the South constitute relatively distinct "peoples," that the North was involved in the process that led to self-determination and independence, while the South was excluded, and that the people of the South are now entitled to exercise that right. The entitlement of the people of the South to that right is no longer in question. Indeed, it constitutes the core of the peace initiative undertaken by the neighboring countries of the Inter-Governmental Authority for Development (IGAD) in 1993. The initiative brought promising signs and gained considerable international support, especially from the Friends of IGAD, a group of Western donors concerned with the cause of peace, stability, and development in the Sudan. This group recently reconceptualized their role as that of IGAD Partners, with a greater level of involvement and support for the IGAD process.[49]

When IGAD neighbors of the Sudan first became involved in the search for peace in the country, they brought into the equation several advantages. Some of them had been supported by the Sudan Government in their war against the Mengistu regime in

Ethiopia and were therefore "friends" who could count on the cooperation of the regime in Khartoum. The new leaders in Ethiopia and Eritrea had lived in the Sudan and were well informed on the sources of the conflict. They realized that the problems of the region were interconnected and that the peace, security, and stability of the neighboring countries were indivisible and should be approached regionally. They also realized that for any peace arrangement to succeed and endure, it had to address the deep-rooted causes of the conflict. They saw the justified grievances of the people of the South as the underlying cause of the conflict that had to be addressed. They sought to achieve this goal through the Declaration of Principles (DOP) which upheld the right of self-determination for the South, but postulated national unity as an objective that should be given a chance. This required creating appropriate conditions for mutually agreeable unity, including separation of religion and state, regional decentralization, (perhaps entailing a large measure of autonomy through federal or confederal arrangements) pluralistic democracy, and respect for fundamental rights and civil liberties. When the mediators realized that the Government of the Sudan was reluctant to create those conditions, and seemed to rely on a military solution, they relaxed their diplomatic efforts and sought to influence the balance of power in the field with the view to persuading the parties that the war was not winnable and that they should therefore embrace a negotiated settlement in earnest. It was believed that the collective will of the regional powers would eventually bring pressure to bear on the parties and ensure a just and lasting peace.

Optimism about the IGAD process is now fading. In spite of some important achievements, such as securing agreement on self-determination for the South, the mediators have not been able to follow through with new initiatives or consolidate the gains made. In view of the glaring inadequacy of the current process, the worsening of the humanitarian situation, and the escalating cost of the war in terms of civilian suffering, the international community is no longer justified in leaving the challenge of peace solely to IGAD. No progress now seems possible without a rigorous and sustained involvement from the international community.

The basis for such involvement must, however, remain anchored on the IGAD Declaration of Principles which recognized the right of self-determination for the South, although it recommended that unity be given a chance, and suggested arrangements that could facilitate unity. These principles were endorsed by the 1995 Asmara Declaration of the National Democratic Alliance (NDA) in which all the opposition groups from the North and the South are members. The internal settlement of April 1997 between the government and factions of the SPLM/SPLA that had defected from the movement also concedes the right of self-determination to the South. And in the Nairobi talks of April 1998, the government also accepted self-determination for the first time in direct negotiations with the mainstream SPLM/SPLA.

Nevertheless, the positions of the parties remain ambiguous on the issue of self-determination due to a combination of factors, some of them internal, and others external to the country. A common element in these factors is the general assumption that self-determination is synonymous with secession. There is a generally shared fear in the North, in Africa generally, and indeed in the international community, that self-determination might lead to the fragmentation and disintegration of the country. This danger is compounded by the immense diversities that characterize both the North and the South. It has been argued that without the South there would be no North.[50] This is probably even more true of the South where the confrontation with the North has been the uniting factor. It is feared that once the North-South confrontation is removed, divisions within the North and the South would proliferate and aggravate internal conflicts. There is also the argument that neither the South nor the North is economically viable alone. During the colonial period, it was the South which was regarded as dependent on the North and non-viable as an independent entity. But more recently, with the discovery in the South of oil reserves in commercial quantities, the mammoth Jonglei project aimed at retrieving the vast waters of the Southern Sudd region for irrigation in the North and Egypt, and the vast arable land with adequate rainwater, not to mention the yet-unexplored mineral resources believed to exist in abundance, the South has emerged as a potential source of national wealth. The concern for nonviability has therefore shifted to the North. Beyond the national interests of the Sudanese themselves, there is also a general concern that partitioning the Sudan would not only break a vitally important Afro-Arab strategic bridge, but also open a Pandora's box that would encourage a separatist wave across the continent. But voices are increasingly being heard in Africa and internationally arguing that the Sudanese, particularly in the South, have suffered too much for far too long in the name of a national unity that has proved to be ill-founded, that unity is not an end in itself, and that it is time to give the people of the South the right of self-determination, which all would agree they have never freely and genuinely exercised. Besides, most observers would agree that Africa has consolidated the principle of preserving colonial borders so that justified exceptions can no longer endanger the legitimacy of those borders generally.

It is becoming increasingly evident that the North-South division makes national unity an elusive goal. As a Northern Sudanese Islamist scholar has noted, "What we are witnessing is the clash of two antagonistic cultural outlooks, both of which are experiencing a revival."[51] Addressing the progress of Islam and Arabism among the Northerners in the face of the increasingly self-assertive Africanism among the Southerners, he argued that "The close association between Islam and Northern Sudanese nationalism would certainly rob Islam of an advantage [in the South as] it remains beset by problems similar to those that limited the appeal of the SPLA's Africanism [in the North]."[52] In his view, "Northern Sudanese, who strongly identify with their Arab heritage, are in no danger of being seduced by Africanism. But, equally, Islamic ideology is by definition, unacceptable to non-Muslims. Its association with Arab Northern self-assertion makes it even more unpalatable to Southerners."[53] Even before the National Islamic Front (NIF) seized power to establish an Islamic state, Crawford Young made this assessment:

The integral Islamic state desired by some in the north is beyond reach. Whatever its ethical virtues, such a political formula can never be imposed on the south, either by military force or by a now-shattered state apparatus. The alternative to splitting the Sudanese state is a political settlement acceptable to the south. The SPLA leadership's commitment to unity is not shared by many of its cadres and the rank and file. It cannot persist indefinitely if the dominant Islamic-oriented forces in the northern political equation continue to insist on that which they lack the means to enforce and can never achieve by persuasion.[54]

This assessment, carried to its logical conclusion, makes the quest for a uniting national identity sound increasingly utopian and unrealistic. This is indeed the conclusion which some scholars and politicians from the North have reached. One scholar observed that "it is virtually impossible for a viable system of government and administration to be created, let alone survive, in a deeply divided and heterogeneous nation in which political parties are primarily organized on sectarian, ethnic, and religious lines."[55] According to another, "It is thus unlikely in the given circumstances, that the conflicting demands of the two major camps could eventually be satisfied within one state. . . . A multi-state solution may be the only way to preserve what is left of that once much loved oasis, and could be the only substitute to an illusory 'united country.'"[56] In a book published before the NIF seized power, Abel Alier, the highly respected senior statesman who, apart from President Nimeiri himself, made the 1972 Addis Ababa Agreement possible, argued prophetically that "a violent and reactionary revolution in the northern Sudan determined to adopt a theocratic system of government and an all-out Arab nationalism making no provision for African nationality . . . could well spell the end of a Sudanese nation-state."[57]

These dilemmas have had considerable impact on the perspectives of the parties, the mediators, and other interested actors in the peace process. Rather than confront the issues and available options realistically, the peace process has become a game of wits, semantics, and tactical moves. The SPLM/SPLA is aware that the overwhelming majority of the South, given a genuine choice, would opt for secession, but realizes that for precisely that reason, the North will never sincerely grant the South the right of self-determination, unless it is absolutely compelled to do so. Otherwise, the North will give only lip-service recognition of self-determination and hope to manipulate the process to predetermine the outcome. Meanwhile, to win allies in the North against the government in Khartoum, the SPLM/SPLA emphasizes unity as a goal, while advocating the right of the South to self-determination as a residual, fall-back option. The message that comes across is inherently and perhaps intentionally ambiguous. The undeclared strategy or the hidden agenda seems to be that the South could only exercise the right of self-determination meaningfully, that is to have the choice of secession open to it, if and when it has liberated itself militarily, and that to achieve that end, it will continue to need its allies from the North, especially among the Nuba and the Ingassana.

There are, however, Southerners, admittedly a small minority, who believe that Sudan is African, that they have a sizable population of assimilated "Southerners" among the so-called Arabs of the North who should not be abandoned, and that in the long run there is more to be gained from unity than from secession. By the same token, this unionist sentiment from the South, especially when espoused by the leadership of the SPLM/SPLA and backed by credible military force, threatens the Arab-Islamic establishment in the North and radicalizes even more the Islamists who are set on creating an Arab-Islamic state in the Sudan. Ironically, this radicalization also tends to divide the North profoundly.

Northern opposition parties in the National Democratic Alliance (NDA) confront a similar dilemma and adopt comparable tactics. On the one hand, partly as partners with Southerners in the opposition and partly out of conviction about the legitimacy of the Southern cause, they have come to accept the right of self-determination as a matter of principle. But they remain committed to the unity of the country, not only as an objective, but also as a self-fulfilling prediction in the exercise of self-determination. Since most Southerners are known to prefer secession, this confidence in the predictability of unity either betrays the lack of sincere intention to let the South exercise that right or a blind faith in the declared position of the SPLM/SPLA and the belief that the leadership of the movement will somehow deliver the South.

The government, seeing self-determination for the South endorsed by all the major political forces in the country and by the international community, decided to join the game. First, it offered an alternative process which ostensibly recognizes the Southern right to self-determination through an agreement with defectors from the SPLM/SPLA, who had paradoxically endorsed the government agenda for the country. These splinter groups, while demanding independence for the South, agreed on a referendum to be exercised at an appropriate time, after the country had achieved a satisfactory degree of stability and reconstruction. In the meantime, they would join forces with the government to preserve the unity of the country against enemies inside and abroad, a euphemism for the SPLM/SPLA and its allies. When that process was exposed and discredited as flawed and disingenuous, the government decided to accept self-determination through the IGAD process. Even then, it is still widely believed by the SPLM/SPLA and its NDA allies that this acceptance of self-determination is merely a tactic to buy time for military advantage.

Viewed from the perspective of the government, none of the options placed before it can provide a comfortable basis for a negotiated settlement to the conflict. Clearly, the government would not want to accept responsibility for a process that might lead to partitioning the country, even if they saw that as the ultimate way out of the national predicament and may indeed be their secret preference. At the same time, it is difficult to see how the NIF regime, whose *raison d'être* is the creation of an Islamic state, can compromise enough to win the South within the framework of unity without losing its power base; nor can the South be expected to endorse the Arab-Islamic agenda of the regime as a basis for unity. Furthermore, any settlement between the government and the SPLM/SPLA that maintains the unity of the country, but excludes Northern opposition parties from sharing power, is certain to be opposed by them. Only a settlement that enjoys a national consensus would be sustainable as a basis for a durable peace and unity in the country. On the other hand, how practical is such a national consensus? Certainly not on the basis of the declared positions of the parties.

To complicate the picture even more, regional actors are not necessarily in accord with a concept of self-determination that might lead to partitioning the country. Egypt, operating individually and through the Arab League, has campaigned vigorously against self-determination, fearing that it would lead to the secession of the South and the creation of a non-Arab state in the upper Nile region, where it has strategic water interests. This is in addition to its interest in protecting the Arab-Islamic identity of the Sudan, its historic claims over the Sudan, and its geopolitical interests in the country and in the larger region. As for the IGAD neighbors, their principled support for the Southern right to self-determination also runs against their national interest in curtailing the regional threats of Islamic fundamentalism in the Sudan, which is better attained by removing the NIF regime and replacing it with a more ideologically amicable alternative. Ironically, self-determination that might lead to the secession of the South risks strengthening the regime to continue its Islamic agenda at both the regional and international levels. Since the government has been accused of involvement in international terrorism, this regional concern is shared by significant elements in the international community, foremost among them the United States and the West in general.

If unity is to be desirable enough to win voluntary support from the South, rather than to be imposed by the North, self-determination should motivate the North to strive harder to offer conditions for unity more desirable to the South than they have so far done. This is possible only if the threat of secession is real. To rule out secession as a matter of principle is to remove pressure on the government and endorse the status quo against the south. The only other alternative would be to bring about a radical change of government that might create a new political climate more favorable to unity. But this cannot, of course, be an object of negotiations or third-party mediation.

Given the combination of the North-South dichotomy with the cross-cutting racial and cultural linkages across the dividing line, several alternative arguments recommend themselves for the campaign associated with self-determination. One argument assumes the overriding goal of national unity and builds on those elements most likely to achieve it. A major factor in this argument is that the racial and ethnic composition of the country does not support any claims to Arab purity, since there is a significant African element in the North that still links the population to the non-Arab groups within the North and the South. If Arabism as a racial and a cultural concept is not representative of the North, it certainly is not representative of the country as a whole. The message of this argument essentially means telling the North that it has been laboring under a notion of Arab identity that is fictitious, not sufficiently supported by genetics or history, but that has divided the nation in a way that can no longer be sustained. If Northerners value the unity of their country above their self-perception that they are Arabs, then they must courageously scrutinize their self-identification, explore the bonds of common ancestry with their non-Arab compatriots, and endeavor to help build a nation that is grounded on the uniting factors and enriched by its diversities. A similar message would also be targeted to southerners to make them realize that what divides them from the North is not as profound as has always been assumed, that a significant part of the northern population comprises the progeny of their African ancestors and ancestresses who were captured and taken away from the South as slaves, and that the challenge of building a united and strong nation now makes it incumbent upon them to close ranks and explore their common origins.

A second line of argument recognizes that the identities of North and South have evolved into sharply contrasting racial, cultural, and religious self-perceptions. These divisions are further characterized by different standards of living and varying levels of economic, social, and cultural development. In the North the sense of pride and dignity the Sudanese Arabs gain from their self-perceived heritage would prevent them from shedding their Arab skin to resume their long-discarded African identity, at least not in the sense advocated by the non-Arab Sudanese. The southern Sudanese, too, are proud of their tribally rooted ethnic and cultural identity—which has survived recurrent Arab invasions for slaves—and contemptuous of a race they consider bent on subjugating and humiliating the black race. They would rather take the northern Sudanese for what they claim to be—Arabs. The fact that these Arabs deny their visible black African genetic origins is all the more reason to condemn them as renegades. The only unity that can be sustained on the basis of this duality is one founded on a diversified confederal coexistence.

An extension of the second alternative would lead to a third choice of policy. If indeed the differences between the North and the South are so wide and deep, there is every reason to believe that problems based on race, ethnicity, religion, culture, and language, crowned with regionalism, will remain and undermine any form of unity. However broad or limited the scope of a unified national framework, the same principles of identity that impede full unity and integration would operate to divide the country. The inevitable conclusion is that even a loose framework of unity may not be mutually accommodating enough to be sustainable. In that case, the only remaining option is to partition the country. Partition may indeed allow each side to consolidate its internal front on the bases of shared values and institutionalized practices. With the realization that friendly and cooperative relations are essential to regional security, economic growth, and prosperity, the two nations may eventually begin to build new bridges and come back together on the basis of genuine need for cooperation and regional integration without the domination of one by the other.

Given the history of broken promises and agreements between the North and the South, any peace accord in the future should be backed by international guarantees. This raises the question of whether such guarantees should be through peacekeeping operations and whether such operations should be undertaken by the subregional organization, IGAD, the OAU, or the United Nations. Whichever of these is involved, the complexity and volatility of the Sudanese situation and the martial culture of its people with a history of violent resistance to foreign intervention suggest that considerable force would be needed for peace enforcement or peacekeeping. Such a force is unlikely to be authorized by any of the organizations mentioned above and would in any case not be advisable. What would be more practical and appropriate would be a modest mission of observers or monitors whose task would be to oversee the implementation of the peace accord and report to the pertinent authorities.

The issue of whether such a force should be from the neighboring IGAD member countries, from other OAU members, or from the United Nations can be debated on several grounds. Having observers or monitors from the neighboring countries could soften the element of foreign intervention. But those neighbors nearly all have their own interests in the Sudanese conflict, which would raise questions about their neutrality. And yet, durable peace in the Sudan would enhance regional security and stability, while a return to hostilities would pose a threat to the region. Sudan's neighbors should therefore have an interest in ensuring the success of the peace agreement.

Forces from other OAU countries or from the United Nations would be more removed and therefore more neutral, but by the same token would have less incentive to ensure the success of the peace agreement. In comparative terms, troops from African countries, whether under the OAU or the UN, would probably be less objectionable than troops from non-African countries, even though the latter would be more neutral on the issues. Considering the risk factor and the costs involved, the deployment of African troops is likely to be more practical than the deployment of non-African UN forces.

In any case, it would be important to prepare the troops adequately for service in the Sudan. The complexities and sensitivities of the racial, ethnic, cultural, and religious factors involved in the conflict are likely to elude a casual observer. Minor acts that reflect insensitivity to these factors could provoke a violent reaction that could be counter-productive, as the experience of the UN in Somalia demonstrated. A brief but intensive training should sensitize the troops to the social and cultural context, the challenges of the situation, and the ways in which the troops should conduct themselves under the circumstances.

These scenarios do not, of course, address the problem of internal divisions in both the North and the South and the danger they pose for the further disintegration of these entities. The danger for the South is admittedly greater than for the North where Islam, the Arabic language, and a broad cultural assimilation may serve as unifying factors. But the case of the South has to be seen in the context of divisive maneuvers by the North. If an agreement were reached on a mutually acceptable arrangement, this complicating factor would be significantly reduced, if not removed. Both the North and the South would then deal with their internal diversities in much the same way other African and Arab countries manage their internal ethnic or tribal differences.

MOVING THE PEACE PROCESS FORWARD

It is now widely accepted that the war in the Sudan has gone on for far too long, has cost far too much, and must therefore be stopped. The most practical way to stop it is to build on self-determination for the South, which all parties in the peace process have agreed upon. The practical steps forward must be based on the following principles:

First, self-determination for the South must be stipulated as a genuine goal to which all the parties must sincerely and transparently commit themselves. In particular, since there is credible evidence that the stated goal of the SPLM/SPLA leadership for the creation of a new united Sudan emanates from lack of confidence in the commitment of the government to the right of self-determination for the South and since this stated position does not represent the aspirations of the overwhelming majority of the people of the South, both the government and the SPLM/SPLA must reaffirm their unequivocal and credible commitment to self-determination for the South.

Second, self-determination should not be viewed as synonymous with secession, but instead should be seen as offering a genuine choice between unity and secession. This should motivate those desirous of national unity to strive harder to create conditions favorable to the option of unity in the referendum on self-determination. But negotiating the unity package should not become an obstacle to peace. The Government should be asked to table the best package it is prepared to concede and have that as the alternative to secession in the referendum.

Third, the NDA needs to be involved in the negotiations along with the SPLM/SPLA and the negotiations must address the issues of governance, pluralistic democracy, and respect for human rights, which are of grave and urgent concern to the North.

Fourth, despite official reservations from the Government, both parties want the United States to be more actively involved in the search for peace. Accordingly, the United States, in collaboration with IGAD and its partners, should organize a peace conference in which top leaders must take part, to commit themselves to these principles and their urgent implementation and with the OAU and the UN as essential observers. International assistance, particularly from the United States, needs to be offered to the IGAD negotiating team to make that a credible and effective mechanism to advance the peace process.

Fifth, for self-determination to be credible, international mechanisms for observing and monitoring its structures and procedures of implementation to ensure that it is free and fair, must be agreed upon and put in place in collaboration with the OAU and the United Nations. The required steps should include international guarantees for a sustainable cease-fire, negotiating an interim administration and security arrangements in the South, and initiating the process for an internationally supervised referendum in which the choice will be between secession and the best unity package the Government is prepared to offer without protracted negotiations.

In conclusion, it should be reiterated that the parties now know all the dimensions of the conflict and what is required to bring an honorable peace that all can accept without undue loss of face. Only a credible and sustained involvement of third parties, representing the international community, can ensure achievement of peace with justice. It is also important to underscore that self-determination for the South has become recognized as a right that cannot be denied, wherever it leads. Undoubtedly, unity is a laudable goal, but the best guarantee for unity is for the leadership, especially at the national level, to rise above factionalism and to offer the entire nation a vision, both in words and deeds, that would inspire a cross-sectional majority of the Sudanese people, irrespective of race, ethnicity, region, or religion, to identify with the nation and to stand together in collective pursuit of their common destiny. Only through mutual recognition, respect, and harmonious interaction among African and Arab populations throughout the country does the cause of unity stand the chance of winning the test of self-determination. Only under those conditions does the Sudan stand a chance of achieving and ensuring a just and lasting peace. And only then can the Sudan live up to its postulated role as a true microcosm of Africa and a dynamic link between the continent and the Middle East.

NOTES

1. Ali Mazrui, "The Multiple Marginality of the Sudan," in *Sudan in Africa*, ed. Yusuf Fadl Hasan (Khartoum: Khartoum University Press, 1971), p. 240.

2. Abdullahi A. An-Na'im, "The National Question of Constitutionalism: Secession and Constitutionalism" in *Constitutionalism and Democracy: Transitions in the Contemporary World*, ed. Douglas Greenberg et al. (Oxford: Oxford University Press, 1993), p. 108.

3. For the texts of the agreements, see Abd el-Fatah el-Sayed Baddour, *Sudanese Egyptian Relations* (The Hague, M. Nisheff, 1960), pp. 17–20, and Yusuf Fadl Hasan, *The Arabs and the Sudan* (Edinburgh University Press, 1967), pp. 22–24.

4. Yusuf Fadl Hasan, *The Arabs and the Sudan*, p. 90. The current tendency, however, is to dispute the matrilineal theory and to see the process more in terms of the dominance of the Arabs in the power process with a degree of magnanimity and a relatively harmonious interaction that favored the Arab-Islamic identity as a symbol of upward mobility. See, for instance, Lloyd Binagi, *The Genesis of the Modern Sudan: An Interpretative Study of the Rise of Afro-Arab Hegemony in the Nile Valley A.D. 1260–1826* (Temple University, Ph.D. Dissertation, 1981). Abdullahi A. Ibrahim addresses this very point: "Scholars adhering to the model have not taken into account the parameters of power attending the Arab/African encounter in the Sudan." Abdullahi A. Ibrahim, *The Northern Sudanese: An Anthropology of Hybridity*, unpublished proposal, December 1991, p. 3.

5. For Sufi orders in the Sudan, see Tom Niblock, *Power and Class in the Sudan: The Dynamics of Sudanese Politics 1898–1985* (Albany: State University of New York, 1987). See also K. D. D. Henderson, *Sudan Republic* (London, Ernest Benn Ltd., 1965), p. 23.

6. For studies of these two movements, see Mohamed Nuri El-Amin, *The Emergence and Development of the Leftist Movement in the Sudan During the 1930s and 1940s* (Khartoum: Khartoum University Press, 1984); and Hassan Mekki Mohamed Ahmed, *Harakat El Ikhwan El Muslimeen Fil-Sudan 1944–1969* (Khartoum, Khartoum University Press, 1987).

7. For the philosophy of their founding leader, Mahmoud Mohamed Taha, see Abdullahi An-Na'im, *The Second Message* (Syracuse, NY: Syracuse University Press, 1987).

8. An insider and admirer, Abdel Wahab El-Affendi, described the pragmatic approach of the leader of the Islamic movement, Hassan al-Turabi, as approximating cynicism. "There is in Turabi's discourse an objectivity that an outsider might be excused to deem as cynicism. Turabi's

explanations for his actions and those of his movement sometimes look more like the theses of a social scientist than of a movement's ideology." Abdel Wahab El-Affendi, *Turabi's Revolution: Islam and Power in the Sudan* (London: Grey Seal, 1991), p. 179.

9. On Mahmoud Mohamed Taha's trial and execution, see Abdullahi Ahmed An-Na'im, "The Islamic Law of Apostasy and its Modern Application: A Case from the Sudan," *Religion* 16 (1986): 197. Sadiq al-Mahdi also opposed September Laws. See his views in his *Islam and the Problem of the South*, published by the author (Khartoum, 1984).

10. Edward Atiyah, *An Arab Tells His Story: A Study in Loyalties* (London: John Murray, 1946), pp. 141–42.

11. Ibid., p. 142.

12. Muddathir Abd al-Rahim, "Arabism, Africanism and Self-Identification in the Sudan" in *The Southern Sudan: The Problem of National Integration*, ed. Dunstan M. Wai (London: Frank Cass, 1973), p. 38.

13. Ibid., p. 39.

14. Mohamed Omer Beshir, *The Southern Sudan: From Conflict to Peace* (London: C. Hurst and Co., 1975), p. 134.

15. Ibid.

16. Cecil Eprile, *War and Peace in the Sudan 1955–1972* (London: David and Charles, World Realities, 1974), p.162.

17. Mansour Khalid, *The Government They Deserve: The Role of the Elite in Sudan's Political Evolution* (London and New York: Kegan Paul, 1990), p. 280.

18. Ibid., pp. 280–81.

19. Muhammad Ahmad Mahjoub (Mahjub), *Democracy on Trial: Reflections on Arab and African Politics* (London: Deutsch, 1974), p. 63.

20. Ibid., p. 74.

21. Ibid., p. 74.

22. Ibid., p. 97.

23. Ibid., p. 98.

24. Ibid., pp. 98-99.

25. Quoted in Deng, *Dynamics of Identification: A Basis for National Integration in the Sudan* (Khartoum: Khartoum University Press, 1973), p. 74. Sadiq al-Mahdi, in a discussion with the author about how polarized the country had become along racial and religious lines, said, "I have no problem whatsoever with my own identity. I know I am an Arab and a Muslim. But I also know that there are others in this country who are not and whom we must accommodate. The other Northern parties would want to impose their Arab and Islamic identity on the whole country. Which of us offers a better alternative for the country?" Sadiq did not at all present himself as also an African. The issue for him was which of the varying degrees of Northern commitment to Arabism and Islam was more accommodating and therefore acceptable to the South.

26. Robert O. Collins, "Africans, Arabs, and Islamists: From the Conference Tables to the Battlefields in the Sudan," unpublished revision of a paper presented at the Fourth Triennial Meeting of the International Sudanese Studies Association at the American University in Cairo, Egypt, 12–14 June, 1997, pp. 2–8.

27. William Finnegan, "The Invisible War," *The New Yorker*, 25 January 1999, p. 72.

28. Generally speaking, northern Sudanese are extremely sensitive to any mention of slavery and will argue that the Arabs were not the only ones who engaged in the slave trade. But as Gabriel Warburg has argued, "While historically Sudanese Muslims neither invented slave raids

nor were the first to introduce them into the Sudan, the fact remains that European or Egyptian ivory and slave traders, both of whom preceded the Sudanese, left this region once it ceased to be profitable. The Northern Sudanese, on the other hand, sought to establish themselves in the South on a permanent basis, and hence their legacy as one-time slavers has made it difficult for them to convince their Southern brethren of their benevolent intentions." Gabriel R. Warburg, "National Identity in the Sudan: Fact, Fiction and Prejudice," in *Asian and African Studies* 24 (1990): 151–202; 153.

29. Fabian Society, *The Sudan: The Road Ahead* (London: Gollanz, 1945), p. 25.

30. Secret Dispatch No. 89 of 4 August 1945.

31. See Memorandum on Revision of Southern Policy CS/SCR/1.C.1, 16 December 1946; Appendix VIII of Muddathir Abd Al-Rahim, *Imperialism and Nationalism.*

32. Ibid., p. 255.

33. Ibid., p. 255.

34. Ibid., p. 255.

35. This conference is often cited by northerners as the occasion when the southerners decided for a fully united Sudan, but this is a disputed view. For the southern viewpoint see the Government of Sudan, Report of the Commission Enquiry, *Southern Sudan Disturbances, August, 1955* (Sudan: McCorquedale, 1956), pp. 18–19. The speech of the representative of the Southern Front at the Round Table Conference on the Southern Problem, Deng and Oduho, *The Problem of the Southern Sudan;* Oliver Albino, *The Sudan, A Southern Viewpoint* (London, Oxford University Press, 1970), pp. 25–28. See also Bona Malwal, *People and Power in the Sudan* (London, Ithaca Press, 1981), pp. 24–30; Dunstan Wai, *The African Arab Conflict in the Sudan* (New York: African Pub. Co., 1981), pp. 42–44; and Abel Alier, *Southern Sudan: Too Many Agreements Dishonoured* (Exeter: Ithaca Press, 1990), pp. 20–21.

36. James W. Robertson, *Transition in Africa: From Direct Rule to Independence* (London: Hurst, 1974), pp. 108–9.

37. Abel Alier, *The Southern Sudan*, pp. 21–22.

38. Niblock, *Power and Class in the Sudan,* p. 156.

39 Mohamed Omer Beshir, *Revolution and Nationalism in the Sudan,* (London: Rex Collins, 1974), p. 182.

40. Mahjoub, *Democracy on Trial*, p. 57.

41. Khalid, *The Government They Deserve*, p. 231. And as Tim Niblock noted, "Southerners remained peripheral to the debate over independence arrangements during 1955, except when their votes were needed in Parliament. Such attention as northern political parties did give to southern Sudan, moreover, was motivated by short-term political interest and often had destruc- tive consequences. Promises were made by northern politicians in the course of the 1953 elec- tions which bore little relation to what these politicians intended, or were able, to do." *Power and Class*, p. 215. After reviewing the constitutional and political developments leading to the decla- ration of independence, Bona Malwal concluded: "We have gone into these lengths in quoting from the pre-independence documents in order to prove that the sovereign state called Sudan is at best an illegitimate child and at worst non-existent. Geographical Sudan does exist—as a piece of real estate—But the nation called Sudan does not.""Address to the Sudan Studies Association," p. 15. Commenting on this event, a northern scholar has observed that "Sudan's declaration of independence, in the words of one of its authors, was thus a take-in: a fraudulent document obtained through false pretenses and subterfuge; that does no honour to the northern political

establishment." Khalid, *The Government They Deserve*, p. 231.

42. Niblock, *Power and Class*, p. 146.

43. As an Islamist scholar has observed, "For Ikhwan [Muslim Brotherhood], the South was perceived as a distant, vaguely symbolic place. Like the rest of the educated [Northerners], Ikhwan only saw in the South the alienated, lost brother, who had to be retrieved through the spread of Islam, the Arabic language and better communications." Abdel Wahab El-Affendi, *Turabi's Revolution*, p. 148.

44. Mohamed Beshir Hamid, "Confrontation and Reconciliation Within an African Context: The Case of Sudan," *Third World Quarterly* 5, no. 2 (April, 1983): 322. Peter Woodward viewed the Addis Ababa Agreement as "dependent regionalism" which was "designed to give sufficient regional powers to appease the South, while creating enough ties to band the region into the Sudan as a whole." Under the system the North provided patronage to the South to support national unity. The South was thus attached to rather than incorporated into the national political system. *The Unstable State*, pp. 142–46.

45. Abdel Wahab El-Affendi, "Discovering the South: Sudanese Dilemmas for Islam in Africa," *African Affairs* 89, no. 358 (July 1990): 378.

46. El-Affendi, "Discovering the South," p. 378.

47. El-Affendi, "Discovering the South," p. 378.

48. El-Affendi, *Turabi's Revolution*, pp. 44–45.

49. John Obert Voll, "Northern Muslim Perspective," in *Conflict and Peacemaking in Multiethnic Societies*, ed. John V. Montville (Lexington, MA/Toronto: Lexington Books, 1990), p. 389.

50. El-Affendi, "Discovering the South," p. 371.

51. El-Affendi, "Discovering the South," pp. 371, 387–88.

52. El-Affendi, "Discovering the South," pp. 371, 387–88.

53. El-Affendi, "Discovering the South," pp. 371, 387–88.

54. Crawford Young, "Self-determination and the African State System," in *Conflict Resolution in Africa*, ed. Deng and Zartman (Brookings, 1991), p. 345.

55. Kamal Osman Salih, "The Sudan, 1985–1989: The Fading Democracy," *The Journal of Modern African Studies* 28, no. 2 (1990): 199–224.

56. El-Affendi, "Discovering the South," pp. 388–89.

57. Abel Alier, *The Southern Sudan*, p. 277.

5

Civil War, Peacekeeping, and the Great Lakes Region

Georges Nzongola-Ntalaja

Since 1990, the Great Lakes Region has been a theater of civil war in one or all of the four core countries of this geographical area: Burundi, Congo-Kinshasa, Rwanda, and Uganda. Although civil war is not a new phenomenon in all of these countries, the level of violence and the destruction of the productive infrastructure of development have increased significantly. The mobilization of so many young people, including boys, for military service in rebel armies and numerous militias has led to a strong militarization of the region. Major consequences include the evolution of warlordism, the transformation of state armies into informal economic networks of looters and smugglers, and the generalized insecurity for millions of men, women, and children.

Efforts at regional and international peacekeeping have failed largely because the political and economic preconditions of a durable peace have not been met. These include political settlements that take into account the diverse interests of groups whose objectives are often difficult to discern, the consistent application of severe sanctions against those parties violating signed agreements, and the creation of economic and social opportunities likely to constitute a viable alternative to militarism for young people. Overall, the persistence or recurrence of armed conflict, despite regional and international conflict resolution efforts, is often due to the fact that these efforts deal more with the symptoms, or surface manifestations of conflicts, rather than with their underlying causes.

This study examines the civil war situations in the Great Lakes Region with a view to understanding their causes, substance, and consequences for peace and security in Central Africa. The focus of analysis is the current situation in the Congo, which serves as a revealing moment for all the social cleavages and the conflicts they generate in the region as a whole. After analyzing the war that began in August 1998 in its historical and geopolitical contexts, I shall attempt to assess the prospects for peacekeeping, demilitarization, and development in the Great Lakes Region.

THE HISTORICAL CONTEXT OF THE GREAT CONGO WAR OF 1998–1999

The war began on 2 August 1998, simultaneously as an invasion of the country by Rwanda and Uganda and a rebellion against President Laurent-Désiré Kabila by Rwandan-backed units of the Congolese Armed Forces (*Forces armées congolaises,* FAC). The civilian leadership of the rebellion, which constituted itself a few days later, was made up of a disparate alliance of three groups that had nothing in common, except their opposition to the Kabila regime.[1] The first group comprised virtually all of Kabila's former Tutsi associates in the Alliance of Democratic Forces for the Liberation of the Congo (*Alliance des forces démocratiques pour la libération du Congo,* AFDL). This was an umbrella organization of the groups that Rwanda and Uganda assisted in overthrowing President Mobutu Sese Seko. Former Mobutu allies seeking to regain state power made up the second group. The third and last group consisted of non-Tutsi intellectuals and former AFDL officials who saw the Kabila regime as a form of Mobutuism without Mobutu.

Faced with foreign aggression, a rebellion supported by two of his erstwhile allies, and intermittent raids from Burundi, Kabila sought and obtained military intervention from Zimbabwe, Angola, Namibia, and Chad. This widening of the war to armies from at least eight African countries and many armed rebel groups, including Hutu extremists from Rwanda and Burundi, has engendered deep antagonisms and rifts in the Great Lakes Region and across Central and Southern Africa. In an environment already marked by poverty and deep-rooted conflict,[2] the physical and moral devastation that war has brought will have serious long-term consequences for peace, security, and sustainable human development in the region.

For a better understanding of the war and its implications for peace and development in the region, it is necessary to replace it in its proper historical context. This analysis involves an understanding of the major sociopolitical disruptions that culminated in the fall of the Mobutu regime and Kabila's rise to power, on the one hand, and on the other, the regional context of deep-rooted conflict in Rwanda, which made this transition possible.

The Disintegration of the Mobutu Regime

In the Congo, the democracy movement, which arose in 1956 with the struggle for independence, persisted in various forms and at different levels of intensity as a fight against the neocolonial state and Mobutu's dictatorship and reign of terror throughout the 1960s, 1970s, and 1980s.[3] In the 1990s, this prodemocracy struggle became an integral part of the continent-wide democratization process that sought to transform the postcolonial state from a patrimonial and clientelist system, in which the bulk of public resources constitute the private domain of an autocrat and his entourage, to the rule of law under state institutions that function in an impartial manner in the interest of the community as a whole. This implied ending the one-party system of government and replacing it with a pluralistic system of multiparty democracy, which is seen as more favorable to economic and social development.

The end of external protection for dictators in the post–Cold War era, the political conditionalities imposed by Western and international donors, and above all the internal pressures by the democracy movement combined to weaken the Mobutu regime and lead to its rapid disintegration. For President Mobutu, the series of events that gave a signal of his eventual demise included 1) the May 1990 massacre of students at the University of Lubumbashi, which brought about the suspension of the external assistance that helped to sustain his repressive apparatus; 2) the looting incidents of 1991 and 1993 by the military, which resulted in the quasi-total destruction of the modern commercial sector, the loss of thousands of jobs, and the growing informalization of the whole economy; and 3) the Sovereign National Conference (*Conférence nationale souveraine*, CNS), the culminating point of the process of undermining his authority by the democracy movement.

Held in Kinshasa between 7 August 1991 and 6 December 1992, the CNS was a national forum designed to establish the truth about the past, to promote national reconciliation, and to adopt a legal and institutional framework for the transition to multiparty democracy. Its 2,842 delegates represented all strata of the Congolese population. Its comprehensive examination of what had gone wrong with the country and its attempt to chart a new and better course for the future have left an important legacy of freedom and popular empowerment in the Congo. Unfortunately, because of errors by the opposition and skillful manipulation by Mobutu, the CNS failed to accomplish one of its primary objectives: the establishment of an orderly and nonviolent transition to democracy.

The Genocide in Rwanda

This failure coincided with a generalized situation of crisis in Central Africa, whose defining moment was the 1994 genocide in Rwanda. The roots of this genocide lie in the history of ethnic identity construction and mobilization under colonial rule. Originally, the categories "Hutu" and "Tutsi" were not ethnic. They referred to social ranks associated with occupation, cattle ownership, and proximity to the royal court. The colonial policy of divide and rule transformed these social status differences into more rigid lines of ethnic cleavage, while giving preference to the Tutsi in education and civil service positions until the mid-1950s. Since the Tutsi elite were heavily involved in the struggle for independence, the Belgian colonialists opted for the promotion of a Hutu counter-elite as a counterweight to the Tutsi. The Hutu took advantage of the new recognition and social status to end Tutsi dominance in Rwanda in 1959, three years before independence.

The 1994 genocide was a logical outcome of an ideology and a politics of exclusion that had generated earlier episodes of large-scale massacres of Tutsi beginning in 1959.[4]

The events of 1959 resulted in the flight into exile of thousands of Tutsi and the establishment of a Hutu republic in Rwanda. Democracy and majority rule came to be defined in exclusively ethnic terms as "Hutu Power."[5] The Tutsi who did not leave the country after the 1959 pogrom and subsequent massacres became an oppressed minority inside Rwanda, as they were denied equal opportunities in education, employment, and other entitlements through a rigid quota system. Those who settled as refugees in neighboring countries and abroad were denied their right to return home by the Hutu governments of Grégoire Kayibanda (1962–73) and General Juvénal Habyarimana (1973–94). In 1988, representatives of the worldwide Tutsi diaspora met in Washington, DC, and decided to use all means necessary to exercise their right of return.

This goal appeared reachable once Yoweri Museveni took over state power in Uganda in 1986. The Tutsi diaspora in Uganda, the most politically organized of all Tutsi communities in exile, had helped him wage a successful armed struggle. Rwandan Tutsi comprised approximately forty percent of Museveni's army, with Tutsi officers serving in key positions of chief of staff and chief of military intelligence. Fred Rwigyema, who also served as Uganda's Minister of Defense between 1986 and 1989, held the position of chief of staff of the National Resistance Army (NRA), while Paul Kagame, the current Rwandan strongman, directed intelligence operations.[6] With Museveni's assistance, the Rwandese Patriotic Front (RPF), the political organization of Rwandan refugees in Uganda, launched military operations against the Habyarimana regime in October 1990.[7]

The RPF offensive did not succeed in overthrowing Habyarimana. France, Belgium, and Mobutu's Zaire came to the dictator's rescue and prevented an RPF victory. General Rwigyema, the RPF leader, was killed in battle. He was replaced by Paul Kagame, who had to interrupt his military training in the United States to assume the leadership of the Rwandese Patriotic Army (RPA) and the war effort. Under the auspices of the Organization of African Unity (OAU) and neighboring states, negotiations were held between Habyarimana's government and the RPF to resolve the conflict peacefully. In 1993, these negotiations resulted in the signing of the Arusha accords, which contained a cease-fire agreement and protocols on wide ranging subjects including the rule of law, power sharing, integration of the two armed forces into a single army, repatriation of refugees, and resettlement of internally displaced persons.

The genocide that took place a year later was planned and executed by hardliners in President Habyarimana's entourage as part of their violent backlash against the democratization process in Rwanda. Members of the *akazu*,[8] who included the First Lady and her brothers, the hardliners did their best to undermine the Arusha peace agreement. Accordingly, they unleashed their genocidal machine against the Tutsi and moderate Hutu leaders on April 6, 1994, in the wake of the assassination of Habyarimana as his plane was about to land at Kigali Airport. The Rwandan head of state was returning from a one-day conference in Dar es Salaam, Tanzania, on the implementation of the Arusha Accords. In the absence of conclusive evidence or a thorough international investigation in Habyarimana's death, a strong hypothesis remains that the plane was shot down by the "Hutu Power" extremists in the President's own entourage. This speculation exists because they were the ones who stood to lose the most from a process of national reconciliation involving the return of Tutsi exiles and power sharing between Habyarimana, the RPF, and Hutu moderates. A different hypothesis attributes the assassination to the RPF, as a calculated move on their part to create a war situation likely to help them take over state power.

In three months, between eight hundred thousand and one million people were killed in a genocide spearheaded by elements of the Rwandan Armed Forces (*Forces armées rwandaises*, FAR) and the extremist Hutu militia known as *interahamwe*, or "those who work together." The act of killing was so generalized that even priests and nuns are said to have taken part in it. As Gourevitch points out, killing "was not regarded as a crime in Rwanda; it was effectively the law of the land, and every citizen was responsible for its administration."[9] Obviously, the definition of who a citizen was in "Hutu Power" ideology did not include the Tutsi, as the latter could not be expected to carry out the civic duty of killing against themselves. Since they did not belong to the "Hutu nation," they were defined as outsiders to be ethnically cleansed from Rwanda. Consistent with the demonization peculiar to final solution scenarios of ethnic cleansing and genocide, Tutsi were depicted as being less than human. There were "cockroaches," or troublesome insects to be crushed without mercy.[10] With the international community looking on, the genocide ended only with the victory of the RPA over the FAR and the *interahamwe*.

The defeated forces fled together with nearly two million people across the border into the Congo. Protected by the French, who had intervened in June in a supposedly humanitarian mission (the *Opération Turquoise*), the *génocidaires* were able to relocate their regime on Congolese soil, with the entire Rwandan state treasury and nearly all the equipment of the FAR. The failure to deal forcefully with the Hutu extremists, who used the UN refugee camps as staging points for raids into Rwanda, is one of the major factors of the present crisis in the Great Lakes Region. In October 1996, the RPF regime took the initiative to destroy the UNHCR refugee camps in Kivu and, consequently, the bases of the FAR and *interahamwe* in the Congo. It was this drive against those responsible for the genocide that served as the engine of the seven-month war, which eventually ended with Mobutu's overthrow and Kabila's rise to power in Kinshasa on 17 May, 1997.

Kabila's Rise to Power

The Rwandans had already recruited and trained Congolese Tutsi from both South Kivu (the Banyamulenge) and North Kivu who would compose their Trojan horse in the fight against Hutu extremists and their Congolese backers. To legitimize the move by a coalition of African states including Angola, Eritrea, Rwanda, Tanzania, Uganda, and Zimbabwe to get rid of Mobutu,[11] Museveni and Kagame proposed the idea of using Kabila, a former guerrilla chief turned ivory and gold trader, as the leader of an instant Congolese liberation struggle.

It is evident that after creating the AFDL on 18 October 1996, nearly two months after the beginning of the offensive from Rwanda,[12] Kabila and his new Congolese associates did not have the kind of military organization capable of defeating the otherwise weak and demoralized army of Field Marshall Mobutu. The *kadogo* or child-soldiers whom they recruited during the long march from Goma to Kinshasa were valuable only for purposes of intimidation against civilians. The one solid Congolese faction in the seven-month war was made up of the *Tigres* or mostly Katangan auxiliaries of the Angolan army who were brought back home for the good cause. They engaged in serious combat against Mobutu's white mercenaries, his praetorian guard, and Jonas Savimbi's men at Kisangani, Lubumbashi, and Kenge, respectively.

All other military operations were the work of Rwandan soldiers and units of Congolese Tutsi trained in Uganda and Rwanda. General Kagame himself has boasted about the crucial role Rwanda played in the 1996–97 war.[13] That role, which included acts of genocide against Hutu refugees in the Congo, has yet to be investigated thoroughly for crimes against humanity and gross violations of international humanitarian law by Rwandan military officers and their field commander, James Kabarebe.[14] Like most of the Rwandan authorities today, Kabarebe is a product of the Tutsi diaspora in Uganda. Until 13 July 1998, he served as chief of staff of the FAC, the new Congolese national army, and many of his trusted unit commanders were equally officers of the RPA.

The Rwandan military tutelage in the Congo became more and more cumbersome as President Kabila sought to assert himself as the supreme leader of a sovereign state. His 27 July 1998 decision to send Commander James and his Rwandan comrades-in-arms back home, apparently to preempt a coup d'état, was the immediate cause of the rebellions that shook Goma and Kinshasa six days later. Although the leaders of the Goma rebellion turned out to be Congolese, Commanders Jean-Pierre Ondekane and Sylvain Buki were trusted lieutenants of Commander James, who had placed them in charge of this strategic military location.

Circumstantial evidence for anti-Kabila activities by the Rwandans and their Congolese allies before July 27 includes the fact that nearly all Congolese Tutsi in high government positions left the country by the end of July. The best explanation for this move is undoubtedly their own involvement in the plotting against Kabila. As a group, Congolese Tutsi were no longer threatened with expulsion from the Congo, the very issue that had sparked off the Banyamulenge rebellion of 1996. What is evident is that Kigali and Congolese Tutsi close to the RPF have taken it upon themselves to speak in the name of the entire Tutsi community in the Congo by assimilating its interests with those of the RPF regime in Rwanda. This is a danger for Congolese Tutsi, who became victims of officially inspired hatred and violence after 2 August 1998.[15] They have become the biggest losers in the present conflict.[16] The authentic leaders of the Banyamulenge understood this from the very beginning of the second Congo war, and this is the reason why they refused to join it.[17]

THE GEOPOLITICAL CONTEXT AND IMPLICATIONS OF THE CONGO WAR

The existence of groups that straddle national boundaries like the Banyarwanda, both Hutu and Tutsi, creates the possibility that identity-based conflicts originating in one country may easily be exported to another country. The two Congo wars since 1996 are in many ways the continuation of the civil war in Rwanda, with the same belligerents fighting each other in a different land. However, as Emmanuel Lubala has pointed out, there is more than a simple "geographical transfer of the Rwandan conflict."[18] The Rwandans have succeeded in introducing into the Congo, the Kivu region in particular, a culture of deep-seated enmity and violence that was hitherto unknown. Just as the Congo can be affected by conflicts originating or taking place in neighboring countries, its own conflicts may have severe repercussions in the other countries of Central, Eastern, and Southern Africa. This is due in large part to the country's enormous size, geographical location and bountiful resource endowment.

The Congo's Geography and Resource Endowment

The Congo occupies an area of 905,568 square miles (2,345,409 sq. km) in the heart of Africa, and is connected to the Atlantic Ocean by a coastline of 25 miles (40 km) containing the mouth and lower reaches of the Congo River. It is the third-largest country in Africa after Sudan and Algeria, and it shares borders with nine other countries in Central, East, and Southern Africa. It is centrally located in a vast area of linguistically and culturally related peoples, the overwhelming majority of whom speak Bantu languages. The country's ties to its immediate neighbors are reinforced by the fact that many of its ethnic groups straddle national boundaries. Examples include the Kongo, who are also found in Angola and Congo-Brazzaville; the Ngbandi, in the Central African Republic; the Azande, in Sudan; the Alur, in Sudan and Uganda; the Hutu, Tutsi and Twa, in Rwanda and Burundi; the Bemba, in Zambia; and the Lunda, in Zambia and Angola. With Lake Tanganyika, the second-largest lake in Africa and fifth-largest in the world separating them, Tanzania does not share a land border with the Congo. However, it played a major role in Congolese history before colonialism as the origin of the Nyamwezi/Teke state of Katanga and of the Arab-Swahili slave traders from Zanzibar, who brought Islam and Kiswahili to the Congo.

Economically, the Congo has enormous wealth in natural resources. Known primarily as a minerals-producing country, it has such an ecological diversity that it is also rich in nonmineral goods, including forest and water resources. Approximately seventy-seven percent of the total land area of 885,781 square miles (2,267,600 sq. km) is made up of forests and woodlands, including the tropical rain forest in the equatorial zone; the Mayombe Forest near the west coast, another important source of marketable timber; and the productive woodlands and grasslands of the savanna zones north and south of the equator. The natural vegetation comprises many valuable tropical trees such as ebony and mahogany, which are indigenous, as are wild rubber trees, palm trees, raisin-yielding trees, plantains, and bananas. Coffee, tea, and cotton plants are also major agricultural products.

The animal life of the Congo is as profuse as its vegetation. Large and small mammals, birds, and reptiles are found all over the country, while rivers and lakes are stocked with many kinds of fish. There are seven great lakes in the country, four of which are located along the eastern border in the Great Lakes Region, and hundreds of rivers and smaller lakes. The whole country is drained by the Congo River and its many tributaries. The second-longest river in Africa and fifth-longest in the world, the Congo River is probably first in the world with respect to hydroelectric potential. Part of this potential has already been harnessed through the Inga Dam to provide electricity to the Congo and some other countries, including Zambia and Zimbabwe.

The Congo has a wide array of minerals, including copper, cobalt, tin, zinc, gold, diamonds, iron ore, silver, and cadmium. Minerals not yet exploited in large quantities include rare metals needed for space aeronautics in the twenty-first century such as europium, niobium (or columbite), tantalum, and thorium. According to the Marek Enterprise, Africa contains fifteen percent of the world's niobium reserves and eighty percent of its tantalum deposits. Of these African reserves, the Congo alone has sixty percent of the niobium and eighty percent of the tantalum.[19] These metals, together with other highly valued resources like methane gas from Lake Kivu, are found in the northeastern region of the country, which was quickly occupied by Rwanda and Uganda during the early phases of the second Congo war. Although it is not a major oil producer, the Congo exploits some crude oil offshore, in its territorial waters along the twenty-five-mile strip of the Atlantic Ocean.

Until the collapse of the formal economy in 1991, copper and cobalt from the Katanga Province were the mainstay of the national economy. The state mining company, the *Générale des carrières et des mines* (Gécamines) also produced zinc, coal, and other minerals. Its colonial predecessor, the *Union minière du Haut-Katanga* (UMHK) produced the uranium that Americans used to make the first atomic weapons, the bombs they dropped at Hiroshima and Nagasaki. A major consequence of this development was that the United States found for itself a vital national interest in the Belgian Congo, and this was extended in the postcolonial period to imply a Western stake in preventing the Soviet Union and its allies from gaining influence in Central Africa.

Since 1991 and the end of the Cold War, external interests in Congo's minerals and other resources have come from three sources: the major powers, transnational corporations, and a number of African countries. Each of these three constituencies has played a role in the evolution of the political situation in the Great Lakes Region in general, and in the Congo in particular.

The Major Powers

The two major powers that have shown interest in the region are the United States and France. Since both of them have a strategic interest in rare metals, they would like to see their transnational corporations have access to these resources. For this reason, and for fear that such resources might fall in wrong hands, they cannot remain indifferent as to who holds state power in the various countries of the Great Lakes Region. More importantly, the global interests of the US as a superpower and France's neocolonial alliances and stakes in Central Africa require that they remain engaged in this region.

The United States sees its major interest in Africa as fighting against transnational threats including Islamic fundamentalism, terrorism, narcotrafficking, and humanitarian disasters. A close ally of Eritrea, Ethiopia, Uganda, and Rwanda as guardians on the frontline vis-à-vis the Islamist threat from Sudan, Washington supported their sponsorship of Kabila to remove former ally Mobutu from power. Kabila's incompetence, erratic behavior, and friendship with states to which the US is hostile like Cuba, Libya, and Sudan have not endeared him to American policymakers. Until July 1998, US military personnel were training Rwandan troops in counterinsurgency, and a US military and diplomatic team was sighted at the Rwanda-Congo border when the war broke out on 2 August 1998. Officially, the team was there "to assess the Rwandese government's ability to prevent another genocide."[20] There could be no better expression of support for Rwanda's aggression in the Congo, which Kigali justified in terms of preventing another genocide. Thus, despite official statements that Rwanda and Uganda had to withdraw their troops from the Congo, both countries continued to receive assistance from the United States and the World Bank.

As the number one power in Central Africa, France has had a major stake in the region's political dynamics. Paris supported the Habyarimana regime against the RPF, and intervened in Rwanda to rescue his followers in June 1994. There is no doubt that France intervened to stabilize the Mobutu regime and to help rehabilitate the discredited dictator internationally. The rehabilitation had in fact begun in October 1993 at the Francophone countries summit in Port Louis, Mauritius. It continued with efforts by the Western Troika (US, France, and Belgium) to withdraw support for Etienne Tshisekedi, the prime minister elected by the CNS, in favor of Léon Kengo wa Dondo, a Mobutu protégé who had strong support from the Bretton Woods institutions as a supposedly competent technocrat. The fact that Kengo presided over the greatest pillage of the country's wealth during his previous two terms as prime minister (1982–86 and 1988–90) escaped the attention of institutions and people who were mostly interested in debt recovery. During his third term (1994–97), he and his Interior Minister Gérard Kamanda wa Kamanda did their best to help Mobutu block the transition to democracy.

The Western hostility to the democracy movement in the Congo, the astonishing longevity of the Mobutu regime, and the country's economic and social collapse are interrelated. They are part of a strategic calculation basically favorable to French interests in Central Africa. In an article published in 1979, Jean-Pierre Alaux argued persuasively that, according to this strategy, "the ruin of Zaire is better for Western interests than a strong and independent state likely to support the struggle against white Southern Africa."[21] Now that Southern Africa has been politically liberated and the Cold War over, a strong and independent Congo would still be a threat to French hegemony in Central Africa, by becoming a rival to France for influence in its *chasse gardée*, the resource-rich countries of Cameroon, Central African Republic, Congo-Brazzaville, and Gabon. This is the meaning of Jacques Foccart's cryptic remark about France's "evident interest" in the Congo's potential as a regional power.[22]

Transnational Mining Corporations

The second source of interest comes from transnational mining companies. Mining transnationals from all over the world have joined their South African counterparts in a new scramble for mining concessions and exploration rights all over Africa. All of them are hopeful of cashing in on the new opportunities of the post–Cold War era, including the push toward privatization and the fact that Africa does possess a large supply of resources, which by and large have been depleted in the developed countries.[23]

One of the main reasons for their attraction to the Congo—in spite of the economic ruin of the country and its political turmoil—is the relatively high mineral contents of Congolese copper, cobalt, and gold ores, which are among the highest in the world.[24] Thus, although their long-term interests require political stability, investors seeking mining contracts do not seem to shy away from war-ravaged countries with a fabulous resource endowment, like the Congo. Likewise, they have no respect for diplomatic formulae like national sovereignty and territorial integrity that may stand in the way of short-term profitability. They make deals with whomever controls a mineral-rich territory, including warlords and invaders, as they have done in northeastern Congo with the AFDL, Rwanda, the Ugandan warlord Brigadier James Kazini, and the rebels of both the Congolese Rally for Democracy (*Rassemblement congolais pour la démocratie*, RCD) and the Congolese Liberation Movement (*Mouvement de libération congolais*, MLC).[25]

The abundance and diversity of Congo's minerals had given the country its colonial-era distinction as a "geological scandal." In the wake of the real life scandals of the wild rubber atrocities of King Leopold's Congo Free State,[26] colonialism established a system of mineral exploitation that consisted of extracting raw materials for exports, with little or no productive investments in the country from which they were extracted, and little or no effort to protect the environment. In the Congo since independence, this system has remained intact as a national curse, in that its enormous wealth attracts so many outsiders who eventually find local collaborators to help them loot the country's natural resources. As in Leopold's days, the national wealth is monopolized by the country's rulers and their foreign business partners to the detriment of the mass of the people, who remain among the poorest of the poor in the world today. This is the real scandal of the Congo.

For the Mobutu regime, as for his successors, all that did matter, and seems to matter today, is the amount of money foreign businesses are prepared to pay up front to win lucrative contracts, and the percentage of earnings that will later go back to political authorities or warlords. Rebel groups, beginning with Kabila's AFDL, have discovered that making deals in this manner is a good way of raising money for warfare. In one transaction in May 1997, the AFDL received an initial payment of $50 million from Consolidated Eurocan Ventures of the Lundin Group of Vancouver, Canada, for a copper and cobalt investment deal worth $1.5 billion, with the remainder $200 million to be paid over four years.[27] Jean-Raymond Boule, the principal owner of American Mineral Fields, a company registered in Canada but operating from the State of Arkansas in the US, even loaned his executive jet to then-rebel-leader Kabila for his visits to liberated cities in the Congo and diplomatic missions in Africa.

African Interests 1: Uganda, Rwanda, and Burundi

Mining transnationals are not the only external forces likely to fish in troubled waters. Some African leaders, like President Museveni of Uganda, have tried their best to divide up the Congo among rival warlords for purposes of maintaining political influence in the country and access to its vast resources. Kampala's support for Jean-Pierre Bemba's MLC, which was created by Uganda as a response to the lack of popular support for the RCD in the Congo, and its strong backing for the faction of the RCD led by Ernest Wamba dia Wamba are indicative of a strategy aimed at the Somalization of the Congo.

Museveni's generals and other military commanders have been more successful in making business deals than in waging war in the Congo. Thus, beginning with his half brother, General Salim Saleh, and the Army Chief of Staff, Brigadier Kazini, the major activity of the Ugandan Peoples Defense Forces (UPDF) in northeastern Congo has been the systematic looting of natural resources and consumer durables. A regime of pillage reminiscent of the Leopoldian regime has been established, with Ugandans and Rwandans dividing up among themselves the gold, diamonds, timber, coffee, and tea of the northeast. Whereas senior officers have engaged in high-value pillaging, including the award of mining concessions to private operators, junior officers, and the noncommissioned ranks have found their loot in vehicles, refrigerators, stoves, and all kinds of electronic goods, which they seize from Congolese citizens at gunpoint. Excluding the Rwandan desire to get rid of the Wamba faction of the RCD, the military clashes of August 1999 between Rwandan and Ugandan troops in Kisangani were basically a case of fighting over turf and resources.[28]

It follows, then, that the need to end rebel incursions from the Congo that Uganda and Rwanda use as a justification for their aggression is a pretext for hiding their expansionist aims in northeast Congo. As pointed out above, RPA officer Kabarebe was the chief of staff of the FAC. With respect to Uganda, President Kabila had authorized the stationing of a UPDF battalion on Congolese soil to police the Congo-Uganda border. How, then, can Kampala and Kigali accuse Kabila for having failed to put an end to rebel incursions when they were directly involved in the management and activities of Congolese security forces until July 1998? Rwandan leaders, President Pasteur Bizimungu in particular, have on several occasions spoken about the need to redraw colonially inherited boundaries. Thus, the security imperative has to be understood in a broader sense as comprising the need for a buffer zone of economic and military security for these impoverished lands, one of which (Rwanda) is overpopulated.

There is no doubt that a major concern of the RPF regime in Kigali is the threat posed by the *génocidaires* in the ranks of the *interahamwe* and the former FAR, who are still committed to finishing off the deadly task they had set for themselves in 1994. But if the RPA could not contain rebel incursions along the 136-mile (217 km) border between Rwanda and the Congo, what makes Kagame and his military strategists think that they can wipe out the threat by unleashing their troops all over the vast Congo? In their arrogant belief that they can hunt down and kill the last Hutu extremist, the Rwandan militarists are determined to take advantage of the collapse of the Congolese state and army to set up at the most a puppet regime in Kinshasa, or at the very least a buffer zone of security, including Tutsi settlement and economic exploitation, in eastern Congo. They have already shown their true intentions by giving mining concessions for the exploitation of rare metals in the occupied territory to foreign firms,[29] and by making sure that Rwanda, and not Uganda, takes the lion's share of Congo's resources. As the Ugandan daily *The Monitor* has commented with respect to the bloody row between the UPDF and the RPA in Kisangani, "though the Ugandans made money, they got crumbs as Rwanda took the lucrative deals."[30]

Burundi, the third partner in the anti-Kabila coalition in the region, has also sought to justify its limited military involvement as arising out of the need to stop incursions of Hutu extremists based in the Congo. Until the imposition of economic sanctions in the wake of the coup d'état of July 1996 by Major Paul Buyoya, the Bujumbura Free Trade Zone was the major market for gold smuggled from the Congo.[31] With Kampala and Kigali deeply involved in the gold trade, Bujumbura could not afford to be left out of the scramble for Congo's riches.

African Interests 2: Angola, Zimbabwe, Namibia, and Chad

Of the four countries that came to Kabila's rescue, three are members of the Southern African Development Community (SADC): Angola, Namibia, and Zimbabwe. They justify their intervention in the Congo war as support for a fellow SADC member facing external aggression, in accordance with international law and the UN and OAU charters. While this is true, there is no doubt that the personal motivations of the leaders involved as well as the economic and geopolitical interests of their countries did influence the decision to intervene.

For Angola, these interests were basically twofold. First, Angola needed to protect its petroleum and diamond exploitation zones, particularly the oil-rich area from the northwest to Cabinda, which is partitioned by a slice of Congolese territory. The occupation of the Atlantic region of the Congo by the anti-Kabila alliance in August 1998 was a clear and present danger for Luanda, not only for its potentially negative impact on industry and commerce, but also in view of the alleged collaboration between the alliance and Savimbi's UNITA. Second, the Luanda government feared that Savimbi would once again use the Congo as a rear base for his rebellion, as he did during the Mobutu regime. More than the other two countries, Angola has an evident interest in the stability of the Congo, a country with which it shares a long land border of 1569 miles (2511 km). Having already intervened in the Congo through the Katanga gendarmes in 1977 and 1978, and more decisively in 1997 in both Congos by helping to put Kabila in power in Kinshasa and restoring the *ancien régime* of Denis Sassou-Nguesso in Brazzaville, the Angolan government was eager to establish its credentials as a regional power in Central Africa.

Both Angola and Namibia followed Zimbabwe in advocating a military role for SADC in the Congo. Zimbabwe took the initiative in making their intervention a collective defense action against an external threat through the SADC Organ for Politics, Defense, and Security, chaired by President Robert Mugabe.[32] Its military involvement has been the heaviest of all of Kabila's allies, with as many as ten thousand troops. While a lot of attention has been given to a leadership rivalry between Zimbabwe and South Africa, perhaps more important in the decision to intervene were the economic interests of the country and its governing elite.

It is widely reported that the Kabila government owes millions of dollars to Zimbabwe for military equipment and supplies obtained during the seven-month war of 1996–97. After the regime change in Kinshasa, a number of Zimbabwean businesses and state enterprises extended credit to the Congo for the purchase of goods in various sectors, but have not received payments from the Congolese as expected. With its population of approximately 49 million people, the Congo represents an attractive market for Zimbabwean goods and services, inasmuch as Zimbabwean textile, agro-industrial, and other enterprises are losing ground, even at home, to competition from South Africa and suffering from the detrimental effects of globalization. In the area of clothing, for example, the textile factories of Bulawayo are having a hard time competing with better quality imports.

The Zimbabwean governing elite are determined to make good on their investment in the Congo. During the civil war in Mozambique, Zimbabwe sent thousands of troops to help the FRELIMO government fight the RENAMO rebels. After the civil war, there were no dividends for the sacrifices made, as South Africa, the very country that had armed RENAMO and tried to destroy Mozambican society and economy, reaped the lion's share of the benefits of peace. Zimbabweans are determined not to be short-changed this time around. They hope to reap some concrete benefits from their military intervention in the Congo.

Already, Billy Rautenbach, a Zimbabwean businessman with interests in transportation and automobile assembly, has been appointed the managing director of Gécamines, the Lubumbashi-based state mining company specializing in copper and cobalt.[33] With a strong military presence in Mbuji-Mayi, Zimbabweans are said to be shipping diamonds home on a regular basis, by air.[34] If this is true, then Zimbabwe, like Rwanda and Uganda, is financing its war effort with the Congo's resources. In addition to Rautenback and Leo Mugabe, the Zimbabwean president's nephew, General Vitalis Zvinavashe, Commander of the Zimbabwean Defense Force (ZDF), is among a select group of individuals who have personally benefited from the war. His trucking company was used to carry supplies for Zimbabwean troops in the Congo from Harare to Lubumbashi.[35]

The economic and geopolitical interests of Namibia and Chad in the Congo are not as easy to determine. If Namibia followed Zimbabwe rather than South Africa in adopting a hawkish position, it could very well be out of a desire to register its freedom to differ with its powerful neighbor on important issues, or to reaffirm its commitment to territorial integrity and the inviolability of colonially inherited boundaries in view of the secessionist threat in the Caprivi Strip. On the personal level, Presidents Sam Nujoma and Kabila seem to get along so well that Namibia was the first foreign country to name a street in Kabila's honor in the capital city of Windhoek. What Namibians need the most from the Congo is water. An agreement has been reached between the DRC and Namibia on collecting the waters of the Congo River before they flow into the Atlantic Ocean and transporting them by pipeline to Namibia. The problem now is finding the financing for this ambitious project.

Chad withdrew its troops from the Congo following the April 1999 Sirte (Libya) cease-fire agreement between Kinshasa and Kampala. The lack of reliable information on its intervention has resulted in unconfirmed accounts that make the country a proxy for France, Libya, or both. A possible explanation of its involvement is that given its rich experience with civil wars, Chad intervened as a result of pressures from the Francophone states of Central Africa under the leadership of President Omar Bongo of Gabon. These countries would like to see the Congo remain engaged with other countries of Central Africa, rather than turn eastward and southward to English-speaking countries. Although it has joined the SADC and the Common Market for Eastern and Southern Africa (COMESA), the Congo remains a member of the Economic Community of Central African States and its security organs, the United Nations Standing Advisory Committee for Security Questions in Central Africa, and its Peace and Security Council (*Conseil pour la paix et la sécurité*, COPAX).

PEACEKEEPING AND POSTCONFLICT DEVELOPMENT IN THE REGION

What are the prospects for peacekeeping, demilitarization, and development in the Great Lakes Region? With so many actors involved and fundamental interests at stake, conflict resolution has proven extremely difficult. Moreover, a lasting peace cannot materialize unless there is a satisfactory resolution of the insurgencies in Uganda and, above all, the Hutu-Tutsi conflict in Rwanda and Burundi. Peace building must therefore be seen as a long-term process whose essential prerequisites are peacekeeping and post-conflict development in the Congo, the one country that has the potential to play a stabilizing role in the region. In other words, the long-term stability of the Great Lakes Region cannot be sustained without an effective government, a well-trained national army, and a healthy economy in the Congo.

Achieving this triple objective will require the active involvement in the peace process by all relevant subregional, regional, and international actors such as SADC, the OAU, and the UN. The remainder of this study consists of an examination of the options for peacekeeping and peacemaking under the auspices of these organizations. More specifically, the peace agenda will be examined with respect to the comparative advantages or disadvantages of regional versus international peacekeeping, and the conditions for a lasting peace, in the Great Lakes Region.

Regional and International Peacekeeping in the Great Lakes Region

The Central African region, and the Congo in particular, has had a long experience with both regional and international military intervention for peacekeeping and peace enforcement. The UN mission in the Congo (*Opération des Nations Unies au Congo*, ONUC), from 1960 to 1964, was then the largest and most ambitious operation ever undertaken by the United Nations, with nearly twenty thousand troops at its peak strength plus a large contingent of civilian personnel for nation-building tasks.[36] External interventions to help the central government deal with insurgencies have also taken place in 1964, 1977, 1978, and 1991. Moreover, the Congo itself has intervened in peace enforcement bilaterally in Burundi (in 1972), and in peacekeeping under the auspices of the OAU in Chad (in 1982).[37] OAU observer missions have been deployed to both Rwanda and Burundi, and a UN peacekeeping mission was actually present in Rwanda during the genocide of 1994. The lessons learned from these and other experiences in Central Africa for peacekeeping and peacemaking should prove useful for designing an appropriate agenda for peace in the Great Lakes Region.

The first and most important lesson is that the comparative advantages and disadvantages of regional versus international peacekeeping cannot be established in a priori fashion. What appears to be a comparative advantage for regional actors, for instance, their greater knowledge of the political situation in the country at war, may be counterbalanced by their partiality with respect to the warring parties. However, given the lack of interest in Africa within the international community today, subregional and regional actors might constitute the only line of defense between order and chaos. The role that Nigeria has played in Liberia and Sierra Leone is very instructive in this regard.

Consistent with the idea of seeking African solutions to African problems, political authorities in Africa are willing to take the lead in dealing with security issues subregionally and regionally. They do insist, however, that the international community must be implicated in the peace process. This position goes beyond mere preoccupation with the problem of financial resources and logistics. It also has to do with the principle that the United Nations must retain primary responsibility for the maintenance of international peace and security in accordance with chapters VI, VII, and VIII of the UN Charter. In 1998, for example, there was African resistance to the idea of deploying a UN peacekeeping force with exclusively African contingents in the Central African Republic, for fear that this might call into question the international character of the operation as well as the responsibility that the world community as a whole should assume for its success. The inclusion of a token presence of Canadian and French troops in the United Nations Mission in the Central African Republic (*Mission des Nations Unies en République Centrafricaine*, MINURCA) seemed to allay African fears in this regard.[38]

There is growing consensus in Africa that peacekeeping and peacemaking should be a joint undertaking by intergovernmental organizations at the subregional, regional and international levels. Since the establishment in 1993 of its Mechanism for Conflict Prevention, Management, and Resolution, the OAU is expected to play a major role in coordinating peace efforts with both the United Nations and the major subregional groupings, which are component parts of the OAU/AEC system.[39] A model for such tripartite cooperation is provided by the regional and international peacekeeping efforts in the CAR since the national reconciliation pact of 25 January 1997 known as the Bangui Accords. These were negotiated between January 11 and 18 under the auspices of an International Mediation Committee appointed at the December 1996 France-Africa Summit at Ouagadougou and consisting of Burkina Faso, Chad, Gabon, and Mali.

Both the UN and the OAU gave financial support toward the work of the International Follow-up Committee (*Comité international de suivi*, CIS), headed by the former Malian President, General Amadou Toumani Touré, and the Inter-African Mission to Monitor the Bangui Accords (*Mission interafricaine de surveillance des Accords de Bangui*, MISAB), a peacekeeping force of eight hundred troops from Burkina Faso, Chad, Gabon, Mali, Senegal, and Togo, which relied on logistical support from the French troops stationed in the CAR. Like the ECOMOG in Liberia and Sierra Leone, the CIS and MISAB were a basically successful experiment in African solutions to African problems, with minimum but indispensable external support. On April 15 and 16, 1998, the CIS, after having stabilized the situation in the CAR, formally turned over its authority and peacekeeping duties to the United Nations, with the MISAB being replaced by MINURCA.

Lessons from the CIS experience in the CAR might prove useful for collaboration between the UN, the OAU and the SADC as active partners in conflict resolution and peace building in the Congo. The Lusaka Agreement of July 10, 1999 on the DRC recognizes the limits of international peacekeeping intervention by providing that the belligerents themselves be transformed into peacekeepers until the deployment of a UN peacekeeping force authorized by the Security Council under Chapter VII of the UN Charter. These temporary peacekeeping operations are to be carried out under the dual supervision of a Joint Military Commission (JMC) constituted by the parties and a UN/OAU observer group. If successful, such collaboration between former belligerents involving the disengagement of forces, the disarmament and encampment of armed and criminal groups, and the withdrawal of foreign forces, can lay the groundwork for a lasting peace in the Great Lakes Region.

More reassuring for the long-term consolidation of peace is the expected deployment of a UN force with peacekeeping and peace enforcement powers. Such a force, in current UN parlance, is of necessity "multidisciplinary," in the sense that it must comprise a wide range of activities that are crucial for the peace agenda:

These include the supervision of cease-fire agreements; regrouping and demobilization of armed forces; destruction of weapons surrendered in disarmament exercises; reintegration of former combatants into civilian life; designing and implementation of demining programmes; facilitating the return of refugees and displaced persons; provision of humanitarian assistance; training of new police forces; monitoring respect for human rights; support for implementation of constitutional, judicial and electoral reforms; and support for economic rehabilitation and reconstruction.[40]

Should such a force materialize as stipulated in the Lusaka Agreement, it must be built upon lessons learned from two memorable UN operations in the area, ONUC, from July 1960 to June 1964; and the United Nations Assistance Mission for Rwanda (UNAMIR), from October 1993 to April 1996. Of the two operations, it was UNAMIR that exemplified UN failure not only in preventing genocide, but also in providing assistance for postconflict peace building and national reconciliation. Major General Roméo Dallaire, the Canadian who served as Force Commander in an UN peacekeeping operation designed to oversee the 1993 peace agreement between the government and the RPF, warned his superiors in New York in January 1994 about arms caches by Hutu extremists, and informed them of his intention to destroy them. He was told not to do such a thing, as this was not part of his mandate.[41] As the genocide began in April, the UN Force was considerably reduced in numbers instead of being reinforced. Because of the Somali syndrome, the US government blocked every proposal for an active UN role in stopping the genocide. For the United States, saving money was more important than saving lives.

Having failed to stop the genocide, the UN was equally unhelpful with respect to postconflict development in Rwanda. For over two years, UN agencies and the international community as a whole spent approximately $1 million a day to care for Rwandan refugees in the Congo, many of whom were killers, while ignoring the surviving genocide victims inside Rwanda and doing very little to assist the RPF government in coping with the multiple tasks of economic reconstruction and national reconciliation. The Lessons Learned Unit of the UN Department of Peacekeeping Operations explains the situation as follows:

While UNAMIR did bring with it a fleet of white vehicles and an array of equipment, these were to sustain the Mission . . . and not to help rebuild the country. This display of apparent wealth in the face of a population traumatized by genocide and civil war made the Government feel that UNAMIR was not responsive to its needs. . . . The expanded UNAMIR, once fully deployed, had the technical capability, in its doctors, engineers, telecommunications technicians and logistics (light and heavy vehicles, cement mixers, helicopters, generators) to perform peace-building tasks. The inhibition lay in the mandate, as senior officials were constantly reminded that the military technicians and their equipment were financed by assessed contributions to support UNAMIR and not the Government and people of Rwanda. That task was development oriented, they were told, and the responsibility of that lay with the specialized agencies, which operate on the basis of voluntary contributions.[42]

So what was the "expanded UNAMIR" actually doing in postgenocide Rwanda that required so many technical people and so much equipment? Over thirty years earlier, ONUC had engaged in peace-building activities, with a clear mandate from the Security Council. Long before the second United Nations Operation in Somalia (UNOSOM II), the Congo mission had broken new grounds in the evolution of UN peacekeeping with respect to preventive diplomacy, peace enforcement, and the leading role of the Secretary General in shaping the mandate of peacekeeping missions.[43] Before that, UN peacekeeping operations involved mostly the monitoring of cease-fires and keeping two well-defined belligerents apart, as they dealt with conflicts between states rather than civil wars.

The Congo crisis of 1960 erupted in early July, less than one week after independence, following the mutiny of Congolese troops. The flight of European civil servants and the breakdown of law and order were followed by a unilateral intervention of Belgian troops on July 10 and the secession of the mineral-rich Katanga Province on July 11. In an international context dominated by decolonization and the Cold War, this created a tense situation. It was so tense that UN Secretary General Dag Hammarskjöld took the rare step of formally notifying the Security Council under Article 99 of the UN Charter concerning a potential threat to international peace and security.[44] After ONUC was established, Hammarskjöld departed from previous practice, by which the Council itself kept direct control over peacekeeping operations, in naming a Special Representative of the Secretary General (SRSG) as the overall manager of the UN operation, and the person to whom the Force Commander must report.[45] In addition to the SRSG, a position of chief of civilian operations was also created in ONUC.

A major problem with the UN operation in the Congo, and one that was partly responsible for the death of both Hammarskjöld and Prime Minister Patrice Lumumba, was their diametrically opposed interpretations of the mandate.[46] The text of the mandate is quite clear. The Security Council directed the Secretary General to provide military assistance to the Congolese government to ensure the withdrawal of Belgian troops, to end the Katanga secession, and to restore law and order throughout the country. It also directed the Secretariat to provide technical assistance to the government for ensuring the smooth running of essential services.[47] For Lumumba, what ONUC was supposed to do was crystal clear: help his government send the Belgian troops home; end the Katanga secession, which was made possible by Belgian support; restore law and order; and train Congolese civil servants in running essential services. Hammarskjöld, on the other hand, saw matters differently. Following the conventional logic of peacekeeping, he convinced himself that the Belgians would leave without confrontation once UN troops had restored law and order and brought the situation under control.

While this turned out to be true in the rest of the country, it did not apply to Katanga, whose secession was actively backed by Belgium and the white settlers of Southern Africa. Hammarskjöld was unwilling to use force to expel Belgian military advisers and white mercenaries from Katanga, even after the Security Council implicitly authorized such action on 21 February 1961, in the wake of Lumumba's assassination.[48] Fearful of antagonizing the Western powers with a more forceful stand against Tshombe and the secession, he was mainly interested in using the UN for maintaining law and order and running essential services outside Katanga, as an experiment for his grandiose scheme of world government. For Congolese patriots and many observers around the world, Hammarskjöld was, wittingly or unwittingly, advancing Western interests in the Congo.

U Thant, his successor, ended up doing exactly what Lumumba had insisted upon, namely, using force to end the Katanga secession. But this became possible only after President John F. Kennedy had given the UN a green light to do so in December 1962. By then, maintaining the unity of the Congo was deemed more important to Western interests than the instability that the secession would perpetuate. Moreover, the Belgians and other Europeans who had feared a Congo under progressive nationalists like Lumumba and his followers were relieved that the country was now securely in the hands of pro-Western moderates led by General Mobutu. For the UN managers in the Congo, force could be used because the Katanga problem was now seen "as per se part of an external intervention by Belgians, so that the UN could take measures against the Katangese as needed to end the intervention without choosing sides in an internal conflict."[49] If such a rationalization was needed for UN bureaucrats, the Belgians saw no problem in having Tshombe, their protégé, take a much needed vacation in Spain before returning home "by the big door" seventeen months later to assume the post of Congo's prime minister. Tshombe's triumphant return coincided with the end of the UN mandate in the Congo.[50]

The main lesson from the previous UN operations in the region is that UNAMIR-type missions should be avoided at all costs, while any peacekeeping operation worth the name must encompass the peace enforcement and peace-building features of ONUC. Peace enforcement is needed today to deal with any groups that might refuse to lay down arms or to abide by the agreements they sign. Postconflict development, on the other hand, requires a durable peace so that people can work in security and without fear of being victimized by armed gangs or landmines. The Lusaka Agreement provides a good starting point for the peace process by taking these concerns into account and by establishing a collaborative framework for regional and international involvement in peacekeeping, peace enforcement, and peace building.

Conditions for a Lasting Peace in the Great Lakes Region

The establishment of a lasting peace in the Great Lakes Region is a long process. It involves the demobilization and disarmament of thousands of combatants, including boys, and their reconversion to civilian life; the rehabilitation of millions of people whose lives have been disrupted as a result of the war and its devastation; and the reconstruction of the physical and social infrastructure of production needed to improve their lives. Although a cease-fire agreement and the cessation of hostilities are essential to any peace process, only a comprehensive political settlement can address the root causes of the war and propose the solution likely to prevent the recurrence of violent conflict in the future. The Lusaka Agreement contains all the elements that Congolese civil society organizations have determined as essential to national reconciliation and peace building, namely, a national political dialogue on the transition to democracy; the formation of a broad-based government of national unity for the transition; the adoption of a new constitution; the establishment of a professional and well-trained national army; and the holding of free and fair elections. The challenge for Congolese political leaders, Africa, and the international community is how to translate these fine intentions into concrete realities.

In the political domain, the main strategy for the United Nations, the OAU, and other mediators is to help restart the democratization process that began in 1990 but that has been interrupted by Kabila's rise to power. If Rwanda and Uganda, together with Burundi and Angola, have legitimate security interests along the borders they share with the Congo, these concerns are best addressed by an independent and responsible government, one in which the people have confidence, and which has under its authority a veritable national army. Such a government cannot be imposed from the outside, nor can it be created out of the blue by presidential decree. It can only emerge as an integral part of a democratization process consistent with the legitimate interests and aspirations of the Congolese people.

The most appropriate forum for putting this process back on track is the proposed national debate. Under the Lusaka Agreement, the OAU has been empowered to designate a neutral mediator for this roundtable conference. In many Congolese political and civil society circles, the Italian Catholic group Sant'Egidio has already won support for this role, mainly because of the crucial part it played in the resolution of the civil war in Mozambique. As a roundtable of representatives of all relevant Congolese political and social forces, the national debate is designed to examine the causes of the present crisis and to seek the ways and means of resolving it. The expected outcome is a consensual legal and institutional framework for the transition to democracy, one that includes the provisional institutions of the transition, a minimum government program of action for the transitional period, and a broad-based government of national unity to implement the program. Two specialized institutions are needed for the management of key transitional issues: a constitutional commission to draft a new and permanent constitution for the country, and an independent electoral commission.

For the electoral process itself to be credible, the political preconditions laid down in 1992 by the CNS must be satisfied. These include 1) the commitment to the renunciation of violence and the use of the ballot box as the only legitimate means for acquiring political power; 2) the political neutrality of the security forces and the territorial administration; 3) access by all major political actors to the state-owned media to disseminate their respective political messages; 4) freedom of movement and of expression for all political candidates; and 5) the independence of the electoral commission and of the courts of law, which are responsible for resolving electoral disputes.

In the security domain, four interventions are needed from bilateral and international partners to help ensure a lasting peace in the Congo. The first is the deployment of a peacekeeping force, as already indicated above. The second intervention, and a major task for the peacekeeping force, is to help the Congolese government collect the arms of war that have been disseminated all over the country, including small arms and antipersonnel landmines. The disarmament mission is directly tied to the third intervention, which consists of restructuring the different combatant forces to create a single national and professional army, one that can serve not only to strengthen national unity and the security of the country's borders, but also to guarantee the legitimate security interests of its neighbors. Finally, there is need for a program of demobilization of all fighters who are not retained for the army, the gendarmerie, and the police, and for their reconversion to civilian life. Particular attention should be given to the needs of the *kadogo*, most of whom should be sent to reform schools.

SUMMARY AND CONCLUSION

The deep-seated causes of the Congo war of 1998–99 include the blockage of the democratization process internally and the general crisis of legitimacy of state power in all the countries of the Great Lakes Region. To this must be added the diverse motivations of the political regimes of the countries involved as well as their economic and geopolitical interests. Under these circumstances, the establishment of a lasting peace in the Congo as a condition for peace and stability in the region requires the end of hostilities, the withdrawal of all foreign troops, and a comprehensive political settlement of the problem of democratic transition in the Democratic Republic of the Congo (DRC). For the region as a whole, a lasting peace is impossible without a satisfactory resolution of identity-based conflicts, particularly the Hutu-Tutsi conflict in Rwanda and Burundi. Both the United Nations and the OAU have an important role to play in this process through their peacekeeping and peacemaking mechanisms. Now that the Lusaka Agreement has given them the authority to coordinate the peace process, every effort should be made to enlist the support of the international community to help restore peace and stability to the Great Lakes Region of Africa.

NOTES

1. See "Une alliance hétéroclite sans dynamique intérieure," my interview with *Jeune Afrique Economie* (Paris) 27 (31 August–13 September 1998): 102–3.

2. On the concept of deep-rooted conflict, see *Democracy and Deep-Rooted Conflict: Options for Negotiators, International Institute for Democracy and Electoral Assistance Handbook Series,* ed. Peter Harris and Ben Reilly (Stockholm: International IDEA, 1998), chapters 1 and 2.

3. I have written extensively on this theme during the last thirty years. See, in particular, "Confrontation in Congo-Kinshasa," *Mawazo* 2, no. 2 (December 1969): 19–4; "The Continuing Struggle for National Liberation in Zaire," *Journal of Modern African Studies* 17, no. 4 (December 1979): 595–614; "The Second Independence Movement in Congo-Kinshasa," in *Popular Struggles for Democracy in Africa,* ed. Peter Anyang' Nyong'o (London: United Nations University and Zed Books, 1987), 113–41; and *Le mouvement démocratique au Zaïre, 1956–1996,* Contemporary World Monographs, Center for Interdisciplinary Research in Sciences and Humanities (Mexico

City: National Autonomous University of Mexico, 1997).

4. References for the historical background to the genocide include André Guichaoua, ed., *Les crises politiques au Burundi et au Rwanda, 1993–1994* (Lille: University of Lille I, 1995); René Lemarchand, *Rwanda and Burundi* (New York: Praeger, 1970); Catherine Newbury, *The Cohesion of Oppression: Clientship and Ethnicity in Rwanda, 1860–1960* (New York: Columbia University Press, 1988); and Gérard Prunier, *The Rwanda Crisis: History of a Genocide* (London: Hurst & Co., 1995), French trans., *Rwanda 1959–1996: Histoire d'un génocide* (Paris: Dagorno, 1997).

5. On "Hutu Power" as an ideology of genocide, see Philip Gourevitch, *We wish to inform you that tomorrow we will be killed with our families: Stories from Rwanda* (New York: Farrar, Strauss and Giroux, 1998).

6. For a brief but informative analysis of the Rwandan diaspora in Uganda, see Prunier, *Rwanda*, pp. 87–96.

7. What became the RPF in 1987 was originally established in 1979 as the Rwandese Refugee Welfare Foundation (RRWF). The growing political militancy in the group resulted in its name changing in 1980 to the Rwandese Alliance for National Unity (RANU), and later on to the RPF. For details, see Prunier, *Rwanda*, pp. 87–96.

8. *Akazu,* or "little house" in Kinyarwanda, refers to a clique of insiders who call the shots at the royal or presidential court.

9. Gourevitch, *We wish to inform you,* p. 123.

10. According to Prunier, *Rwanda,* p. 482, *inyenzi,* or "cockroaches" in Kinyarwanda, was the word used to designate Tutsi rebels in 1960–63, "in part by contempt and in part because they moved mostly at night." In the demonization logic of "Hutu Power" ideology, the label was extended to all Tutsi, and not simply the RPA fighters.

11. On the regional role in the fall of Mobutu, see Charles Onyango-Obbo, "So Who Really Did Overthrow Mobutu?" *The East African* (July 1997); and Gérard Prunier, "Forces et faiblesses du modèle ougandais," *Le Monde diplomatique* (February 1998).

12. According to Erik Kennes, "La guerre au Congo," in *L'Afrique des grands lacs: Annuaire 1997–1998,* ed. Filip Reyntjens and Stefan Marysse (Paris: L'Harmattan, 1998), p. 238, low intensity skirmishes "to test the resistance capacity of Zairian troops" began in early August 1996, while the first major attack with heavy artillery from Rwandan territory took place in September.

13. See articles based on Kagame's interviews with John Pomfret in *The Washington Post,* 9 July 1997, and with Mahmood Mamdani in *The Mail & Guardian,* 8 August 1997.

14. Although "Commander James," as he is better known, was usually referred to as "Kabare" in the Congo, it appears that the true spelling of his surname is "Kabarebe." See, for example, Amnesty International, *Democratic Republic of the Congo: A Long-Standing Crisis Spinning Out of Control,* AFR62/033/1998, p. 6.

15. President Kabila and some of his aides launched a hate campaign against the Tutsi in August 1998, resulting in indiscriminate violence by security forces and ordinary citizens against anyone thought to be a Tutsi and the detention of hundreds of Tutsi, allegedly "for their own safety."

16. Colette Braeckman, "Les Tutsis congolais ont déjà perdu la guerre," *Le Soir,* 24 August 1998.

17. Personal Communication from Joseph Mutambo and Müller Ruhambika.

18. Emmanuel Lubala Mugisho, "La situation politique au Kivu: Vers une dualisation de la société," in *L'Afrique des grands lacs,* ed. Filip Reyntjens and Stephan Marysse (Paris: L'Harmattan, 1998), pp. 305–333.

19. See NCN Special Report, "An interim report on the case of moving tantalum and niobium minerals from Congo to Rwanda," http://www.marekinc.com/NCNSpecialTantalum3.html (9 July 1999)

20. Amnesty International, *Democratic Republic of the Congo*, p. 10.

21. Jean-Pierre Alaux, "L'étonnante longevité du régime Amin Dada," *Le Monde diplomatique* (April 1979).

22. The Gaullist *éminence grise* of the Africa policy bureau at the Elysée Palace under Charles de Gaulle and Georges Pompidou and Africa adviser to Jacques Chirac has this to say about the Congo in his memoirs, *Foccart parle: Entretiens avec Philippe Gaillard,* vol. 1 (Paris: Fayard and Jeune Afrique, 1995), p. 310: "You asked me what was France's interest. On this matter there is no ambiguity. Congo-Léopoldville, Zaire today, is the largest country in Francophone Africa. It has considerable natural resources. It has the means of being a regional power. The long-term interest of France and its African allies is evident." (My own translation.)

23. Denis Tougas, "Les transnationales minières à l'assaut du Zaïre comme du Congo," *Info-Zaïre* 127 (23 May 1997).

24. Ibid., p. 3. At Tenke-Fungurume, the mineral content for copper is 4.42%, while the one for cobalt is 0.33%.

25. See, in addition to the Marek report on niobium and tantalum cited above, "The rise of a new colonial power: Uganda's Brigadier Kazini sets up a system of governance for Ituri and Haute-Uele districts in the Congo," http://www.marekinc.com/NCNNewso81902.html (10 August 1999); *The Monitor* (Kampala), 11 August and 14 August 1999; *New Vision* (Kampala), 16 August 1999; and *The New York Times,* 16 August 1999.

26. The most recent book on the Congo holocaust is by Adam Hochschild, *King Leopold's Ghost: A Story of Greed, Terror, and Heroism in Colonial Africa* (Boston: Houghton, Mifflin Co., 1998).

27. Tougas, "Les transnationales minières," pp. 3–4.

28. See particularly *The Monitor* of 11 August 1999. *New Vision* of 16 August 1999 quotes spokespersons for both governments stating that they have no intention of fighting each other and attributing the clashes to "the confusion in Kisangani."

29. See http://www.marekinc.com/NCNSpecialTantalum3.html, op. cit.

30. "What're Uganda, Rwanda beefing over in DRC?," *The Monitor* (Kampala), 11 August 1999.

31. Tougas, "Les transnationales minières," p. 6.

32. For Zimbabwe's role in the SADC peacekeeping strategy, see Michael Nyambuya, "Zimbabwe's Role as Lead Nation for Peacekeeping Training in the SADC Region," in *Resolute Partners: Building Peacekeeping Capacity in Southern Africa,* ed. Mark Malan, ISS Monograph Series, no. 21 (Halfway House, South Africa: Institute for Strategic Studies, 1998), pp. 90–96. General Nyambuya later served as the first field commander of Zimbabwean troops in the Congo.

33. Although Rautenback is reported to be close to Mugabe's entourage, a senior Zimbabwean cabinet minister told me on 11 August 1999 in Harare that he did not understand why President Kabila would appoint such a rogue entrepreneur to head the Congo's number-one parastatal.

34. Personal communication from Mbuji-Mayi.

35. Robert Block, "Zimbabwe's Elite Turn Strife in Nearby Congo Into a Quest for Riches," *The Wall Street Journal,* 9 October 1998.

36. William J. Durch, "The UN Operation in the Congo," in *The Evolution of Peacekeeping: Case Studies and Comparative Analysis,* ed. William J. Durch (New York: St. Martin's Press, 1993), pp.

315–332. According to Durch, "ONUC reached its peak strength in July 1961, with 19,825 troops" (p. 336).

37. The 1974–75 aggression against Angola, in alliance with the United States and apartheid South Africa, falls into a totally different category.

38. Field research notes from the author's study mission for the UNDP on the contribution of the United Nations system to the peace process in the CAR, 1 April–8 May 1998.

39. The five subregional groupings, also known as regional economic communities (RECs) and building blocks for the African Economic Community (AEC), are the Arab Maghreb Union (*Union du Maghreb arabe,* UMA), the Economic Community of Central African States (*Communauté économique des États de l'Afrique centrale,* CEEAC), the Economic Community of West African States/*Communauté économique des États de l'Afrique de l'Ouest* (ECOWAS/CEDEAO), the Intergovernmental Authority for Development (IGAD) and the Southern African Development Community (SADC). In 1998, the OAU launched a major initiative on strengthening cooperation between itself and subregional mechanisms of conflict prevention, management, and resolution.

40. UN Department of Peacekeeping Operations, Lessons Learned Unit, *Multidisciplinary Peacekeeping: Lessons from Recent Experience* (New York: United Nations, 1996), p. 1. Multidisciplinary peacekeeping is part of an overall conflict prevention, management, and resolution strategy whose basic outline is defined in Boutros Boutros-Ghali, *An Agenda for Peace* (New York: United Nations, 1992).

41. Philip Gourevitch, "The Genocide Fax," *The New Yorker,* 11 May 1998, pp. 42–46. Dallaire, on the other hand, "considered such action to be entirely consistent with his rules of engagement" (p. 46).

42. UN Department of Peacekeeping Operations, Lessons Learned Unit, *Comprehensive Report on Lessons Learned from United Nations Assistance Mission for Rwanda (UNAMIR), October 1993–April 1996* (New York: United Nations, 1996), pp. 17–18.

43. In an otherwise good book on UN peacekeeping, Michael Wesley is wrong in claiming that UNOSOM II was the first UN attempt at peace enforcement. See his *Casualties of the New World Order: The Causes of Failure of UN Missions to Civil Wars* (New York: St. Martin's Press, 1997), p. 78.

44. Durch, *The Evolution of Peacekeeping,* p. 319.

45. Before a Force Commander had arrived on the scene, Ralph Bunche acted as both UN Special Representative and Force Commander. See Stephen M. Hill and Shahin P. Malik, *Peacekeeping and the United Nations* (Aldershot: Dartmouth, 1996), p. 38; and Durch, The *Evolution of Peacekeeping,* p. 337.

46. Lumumba was assassinated on January 17, 1961 in Lubumbashi, capital of the Katanga Province, as part of a vast conspiracy involving US President Dwight D. Eisenhower, the Central Intelligence Agency, and his Congolese political enemies, including President Joseph Kasa-Vubu, Army Chief Joseph-Désiré (later Sese Seko) Mobutu, and secessionist leaders Moïse Tshombe of Katanga and Albert Kalonji of South Kasai. Hammarskjöld died in a plane crash on September 18, 1961 near Ndola, Zambia, on his way to negotiate with Tshombe.

47. See Stephen R. Ratner, *The New UN Peacekeeping: Building Peace in Lands of Conflict After the Cold War* (New York: Council on Foreign Relations, 1995; St. Martin's Press paperback edition, 1996), Table 1.1, p. 11.

48. The February 21, 1961 resolution is actually the legal basis that Hammarskjöld's envoys in

the Congo, Deputy Special Representative Mahmoud Khiary and the Representative in Katanga Conor Cruise O'Brien, used for O'Brien's bold attempts to end the secession by force, Operation Rumpunch (August 28, 1961) and Operation Morthor (September 13, 1961). See Conor Cruise O'Brien, *To Katanga and Back: A UN Case History* (New York: Grosset and Dunlap, 1966), for his own account of these events; and Madeleine G. Kalb, *The Congo Cables: The Cold War in Africa From Eisenhower to Kennedy* (New York: Macmillan, 1982), pp. 287–299.

49. Ratner, *The New UN Peacekeeping*, p. 105.

50. Tshombe's government lasted fifteen months only, as he was dismissed by President Kasa-Vubu in October 1965. A month later, Mobutu staged his second and decisive *coup d'état* and went on to rule the country until his demise in 1997.

6

The Impact of Peacekeeping on Target States

Lessons from the Liberian Experience

W. Ofuatey-Kodjoe

One of the unfortunate realities of contemporary Africa is the increasing frequency of intrastate conflict on the continent. Not surprisingly, these conflicts have attracted a number of peace operations. However, unlike traditional peacekeeping which involved the interposition of lightly armed forces on the border between states, in many of these intrastate conflicts it became immediately clear that mass, armed intervention was required to restore peace. Thus many writers have advocated "humanitarian" intervention by international organizations to resolve these conflicts. This so-called "new interventionism" has raised a number of questions, including the legality, ethics, organization, and conduct of such operations.[1] In these discussions, one of the most debated issues has involved the role of regional organizations in the resolution of these internal conflicts. Due to the apparent unwillingness and/or incapacity of the United Nations to take on all these African conflicts, some writers have suggested that African regional and subregional organizations like the OAU (Organization of African Unity), ECOWAS (Economic Community of West African States), or SADC (Southern African Development Community) should take more responsibility for the management and resolution of these regional conflicts.[2]

Initially, there was a great deal of optimism about the effectiveness of these interventions. However, in the wake of the debacles of interventions around the world, new questions have emerged regarding the capacity of such organizations to bring such operations to peaceful resolutions and in ways that would increase the sustainability of democracy, political stability, and development in target countries. In this chapter, I will analyze the short term and long term impact of the ECOWAS intervention in Liberia. The analysis of the short-term effects of ECOMOG (Economic Community Monitoring Group) operations in Liberia will be based on the usual criteria of the objectives of peace operations, that is, its record in bringing the conflict to a quick end through peacemaking, peacekeeping, or peace enforcement. The evaluation of the long-term impact of the operation will be based on its long-range effects on Liberia's potential for political and economic development.

THE ECOWAS INTERVENTION

On 25 August 1990, the Economic Community of West African States (ECOWAS) dispatched a three thousand-man Military Observer Group (ECOMOG) to Liberia to help resolve an armed internal conflict which had broken out in the previous year. On Christmas Eve of that year, a band of Liberians under the leadership of Charles Taylor and Prince Johnson crossed over from the Ivory Coast at Dadane into Nimba County in Liberia with the declared objective of overthrowing the government of President Samuel Doe, and establishing a democratic government. Doe responded by sending two battalions of the Armed Forces of Liberia (AFL) to crush the rebellion. The AFL launched a campaign of terror against the Gio and Mano peoples of Nimba County, plunging the country into a civil war, characterized by the brutal massacre of innocent citizens, causing over ten thousand fatalities, six hundred thousand refugees and 1.5 million (over half the population) displaced persons before the end of that year. On 7 May 1990, after taking several losses, Doe made an appeal to Nigeria and Togo for help, which led to the intervention by ECOWAS.

THE ROOTS OF THE CONFLICT

The Liberian civil war was triggered by the Doe regime's failure to survive a crisis of legitimacy caused by its inability to transform itself successfully from a military dictatorship into an "elected" dictatorship. In this sense, the Taylor insurrection was just one manifestation of deep disaffection with the Doe regime emanating from a wide assortment of groups: students, churches, organized labor, and some army elements. This disaffection had deep roots within sharp contradictions in Liberian society, which produced a variety of economic, social, cultural, and political grievances. However, for many people, these grievances eventually seemed to reduce themselves to ethnic animosities. Thus, ethnicity emerged as a major factor in the Liberian conflict. The depth of this ethnic animosity is evident in the unusual brutality of the civil war in which "all combatants engaged in indiscriminate killing, abuse of civilians and ethnically based executions."[3] Although the sources of the Liberian civil war are to be found in the contradictions within Liberian society, the war itself cannot be fully explained without taking external factors into consideration. These external factors involved the interests of major powers, especially the United States and France, and some major multinational corporations.[4]

ECOWAS AND ECOMOG OPERATIONS

The first action that ECOWAS took with regard to the Liberian crisis was the creation of a Standing Mediation Committee on 28 May 1990, with a mandate to mediate the conflict. On 6 July 1990, the Committee produced an ECOWAS Peace Plan that provided for an immediate cease-fire, establishment of a peacekeeping force, creation of an interim government for Liberia, and the holding of free and fair elections within twelve months, under international supervision. On 20 July Taylor rejected this plan. He then proceeded to capture about 95% of the territory, and on 27 July 1990, he declared himself President of the country. In spite of this development, the ECOWAS Summit decided to implement the peace plan. After re-issuing a call for a cease-fire, ECOWAS created the Economic Community for West African States Cease-fire Monitoring Group (ECOMOG), to be made up of military units from the members of the SMC (Standing Mediation Committee), with additional units from Sierra Leone and Guinea.

ECOWAS established an interim government, not to include the heads of the warring factions, that would govern Liberia, pending free and fair elections to be held within one year. The reaction of Taylor was immediate and extremely hostile. He announced that Nigeria engineered the ECOMOG operation to shore up the Doe regime, and that he would fight "the invaders." In spite of Taylor's opposition, the ECOMOG troops landed in Monrovia on 25 August 1990. Meanwhile, ECOWAS created the Interim Government of National Unity (IGNU) for Liberia, with Dr. Amos Sawyer serving as Interim President, and ECOMOG assuming responsibility for its security. ECOMOG established a twenty-kilometer "security perimeter" around Monrovia and its environs. This was followed by a cease-fire agreement between ECOMOG and NPFL (National Patriotic Forces of Liberia) forces. This stalemate held until 15 October 1992. Any attempts by ECOMOG to break out of this zone were unsuccessful and Taylor seemed unwilling or unable to capture Monrovia.

During the military stalemate, ECOWAS embarked on a number of mediation efforts. Between November 1990 and March 1991, there were three conferences at Bamako (27 November 1990), Lomé (12 February 1991), and Monrovia (15 March 1991). All these attempts failed due to the inability of the NPFL and the IGNU to agree on the main issues of cease-fire, encampment, disarmament, and the creation of an interim government. For the rest of 1991, ECOWAS intensified its diplomatic efforts. At three of four meetings hosted by President Houphouët-Boigny at his country retreat in Yamoussoukro, no agreement was reached. At a fourth meeting, held on 30 October 1991, some compromises were made. However, the agreement quickly fell apart and a subsequent meeting at President Houphouët-Boigny's winter palace in Geneva failed to save it.[5] Meanwhile, the situation on the military front was deteriorating. ECOMOG's attempt to establish buffer zones and blockades bogged down due to continued hostilities between ULIMO (United Liberation Movement of Liberia for Democracy) and the NPFL, and between ULIMO and ECOMOG. Finally on 15 October 1992, while fighting ULIMO elements, NPFL forces attacked ECOMOG forces thus precipitating a collapse of the cease-fire and initiating a two-month siege of Monrovia.

Meanwhile, ECOWAS continued its diplomatic offensive against NPFL. At a 7 November 1994 meeting at Abuja, the ECOWAS Joint Committee called for sanctions against the NPFL, and solicited the cooperation of the United Nations representative for Liberia to implement the ECOWAS peace plan. As a result, the Security Council unanimously adopted Resolution 788, by which it affirmed its confidence in the Yamoussoukro-IV agreements, while condemning the NPFL attacks on ECOMOG forces, imposing an arms embargo on Liberia, and instructing the Secretary General to send a special representative to Liberia to evaluate the situation and make recommendations to the Council.[6] In spite of indications by NPFL that it would comply, ECOWAS in cooperation with ULIMO and AFL forces, launched a full-scale attack on NPFL on 3 January 1993. After some initial successes, ECOMOG was unable to sustain this offensive, and by May the NPFL seemed to have regrouped.[7]

The ensuing stalemate resulted in joint UN/OAU/ECOWAS diplomatic efforts that led to an agreement between IGNU, ULIMO and NPFL in Geneva on 17 July 1993. That agreement was eventually ratified at Cotonou on 25 July 1993. The Cotonou Agreement had both a military and a political component, which formed the basis of subsequent arrangements for the ending of the civil war. The military part of the agreement called for an immediate cease-fire, to be followed by the disarmament, encampment, and demobilization of the warring factions, to be monitored by a Joint Cease-fire Monitoring Committee (JCMC), composed of representatives of the warring factions, ECOMOG, and the UN. The political aspect of the Cotonou Agreement called for the formation of a transitional government to run the country for six months, to be followed by free and fair elections. The United Nations followed the breakthrough with the establishment of a UN Observer Mission in Liberia (UNOMIL) to work with the OAU and ECOWAS in assisting the implementation of the peace agreement. According to Security Council resolution 866 (1993) of 22 September 1993, the UNOMIL would monitor compliance with the terms of the agreement, assist in the administration of the elections, and assist in the provision of humanitarian assistance.

The implementation of the Cotonou Accords ran into some problems. By September 1993, the three factions had nominated their representatives to the various committees of the Liberian National Transitional Government (LNTG). However, by mid-1994, the encampment and disarmament exercises had come to a complete halt.[8] In the meantime, there were violations of the cease-fire on all sides. President Rawlings, the new ECOWAS chairman, attempted to broker a new agreement between the main factions at Akosombo. The Akosombo Agreement of September 1994 called for the usual immediate cease-fire, encampment, and disarmament followed by elections on 15 October 1995. Like the other agreements, this pact also fell apart due to continued fighting over eighty percent of the country. In his report to the Security Council, the Secretary-General remarked that "the political, military and humanitarian developments of the past month have left Liberia in a desperate state."[9]

On 16 August 1995, President Sani Abacha of Nigeria made another attempt to mediate the conflict. He got the factions to agree to set up a new-six man Council of State to head up LNTG-II, chaired by Wilton Sankawulo, with Taylor (NPFL), Kromah (ULIMO-K) and Boley (Liberia Peace Council/LPC) as co-chairs, with Oscar Quiah (Liberian National Conference/LNC) and Chief Tamba Taylor as councilors. The agreement called for elections to be held on 20 August 1996, for which Council members would be eligible. However, the Abuja Accords did not fare better than the others. The new Council was sworn in on 1 September 1995, with great fanfare.[10] However, on December 31 of that year, fighting broke out again between ULIMO-J fighters and ECOMOG soldiers in the Bomi and Lofa diamond-rich areas. The result was the Tubmansburg Massacre, in which some fifteen hundred people were killed.[11] Finally, in the early part of 1996, serious tensions arose between the factions, leading to the worse violence in Monrovia since 1992.[12]

When Abacha became chairman of ECOWAS in August 1996, he summoned all the factions to Abuja, where they signed the Abuja-II Accord on 17 August 1996. This agreement called for a cease-fire by August 20, and elections on 30 May 1997. There was to be disarmament of all six factions, and a new Council, headed by Ruth Perry, was to work with UNOMIL and ECOWAS to prepare for elections. However, with the problems between Johnson and the other councilors, the attempted assassination of Taylor, and fighting among all the factions, the Council members were so deeply divided and mistrustful of each other that the possibility of their effective collaboration seemed out of reach. However, by the end of October, most of the faction leaders had indicated that they would participate in the disarmament and demobilization exercises, which had been scheduled for 22 November 1996.[13] On October 27, Alhaji Kromah and Roosevelt Johnson signed an agreement to cease hostilities in the west and to create a buffer zone between their troops. It was widely believed that the NPFL and LPC were contemplating a similar agreement. This made it possible for a beefed-up ECOMOG (eighteen thousand soldiers) to embark on a ten-week demobilization exercise, which officially ended on 9 February 1997.[14] As of 13 June 1997, an estimated 13,786 weapons and more than 1.24 million pieces of ammunition had been recovered.[15] As a result of this disarmament effort, the country became sufficiently peaceful that UNOMIL and ECOWAS concluded that the country was secure enough for the holding of free and fair elections.

Meanwhile, the Council of State began developing plans for the elections to be held on 30 May 1997, and preparation began in earnest. The elections were held on 19 July 1997. Charles Taylor won the presidential elections, and his National Patriotic Party won twenty-one out of the twenty-six seats with 75.3 per cent of the total vote. On 2 August 1997, Charles Taylor was sworn in as President of Liberia.

EVALUATION OF THE ECOWAS INTERVENTION

As an instrument of conflict management and resolution, ECOWAS used the whole range of techniques that are usually associated with international peace operations. These included peacemaking, peacekeeping, and peace enforcement Thus, the ECOWAS intervention in Liberia was a hybrid operation. Sometimes, ECOWAS used these methods of peace operations sequentially. More often it used them simultaneously. The methods failed to produce the desired outcomes. These failures were due to the fact that the organization was unaware of the challenges and pitfalls encountered in these operations, especially regarding internal wars.[16]

Peacemaking

ECOWAS was involved in fourteen mediation attempts. Twelve of these efforts were mostly dead on arrival. The only two that seemed to have a chance were the Cotonou and Abuja-II Accords. However, these two also presented serious implementation problems, which doomed them to failure. It is true that the violence stopped at the same time as the signing of the Abuja Accords. However, the cessation of the violence was not caused by the Accords itself, but by the war weariness of the factions themselves, and their calculation that the probability that they would be able to achieve their objectives through violence was rapidly evaporating. By the time of the Abuja Accords, the warlords had independently arrived at the conclusion that some kind of power sharing would be much better for them than continuation of the fighting.[17]

In the Liberian situation, the necessary conditions for successful mediation were absent. First, disputes over power and resources are usually the most difficult to resolve. Second, the parties to the conflict had a long history of mutual animosity. Third, and most important, the requirements of the role of mediator were beyond the capabilities and strategies of ECOWAS. To be successful at mediation, a mediator must be able to do at least two things: he must be able to make proposals which have a reasonable chance of being acceptable to the disputants, and he must be able to convince them to accept the proposed compromises.[18] In order to perform these functions, the mediator has to have the trust and confidence of the parties to the dispute. ECOWAS was never able to get and maintain the trust of the factions. At the outset, it was common knowledge that ECOMOG was really a Nigerian attempt to come to the assistance of General Doe, and was bent on destroying Taylor.[19] Under the circumstances, Taylor's refusal to disarm his troops under the supervision of ECOMOG was entirely understandable. The lesson of the murder of Doe after he had allowed his men to be disarmed by ECOMOG troops was not lost on him. As time went on, other parties to the conflict also came to the conclusion that ECOMOG was not to be trusted. For many of the warlords, ECOMOG was just another one of the factions contesting for power while looting the resources of Liberia.

Second, ECOWAS did not present any proposals to help resolve the conflict. In most of the negotiations, ECOWAS simply repeated the demands for a cease-fire, encampment, disarmament, demobilization, and elections. However, since ECOMOG's real objective was to get rid of Taylor, its proposals for elections usually included a clause prohibiting the warlords from participating in the elections. This prohibition clearly revealed ECOWAS's misunderstanding of the stakes involved for the faction leaders and proved to be manifestly unacceptable to them. It was not until ECOWAS dropped the requirement that the faction leaders would not be eligible to participate in the election as candidates that they took serious interest in the negotiations at Abuja in 1996. In addition, ECOWAS was very rigid in rejecting other proposals. For instance in 1992, Taylor offered to have his commanders disarm his men and secure the weapons, pending agreement by ULIMO and other factions to disarm. He also offered to disarm and encamp his men under the auspices of the United Nations. Both of these offers were rejected by ECOWAS out of hand. The unwillingness of the ECOWAS to consider these offers seriously undermined its capacity to mediate. Not only did it deprive the parties of the opportunity to consider other proposals, but it confirmed to Taylor that the real objective of ECOWAS was to eliminate him.

Third, ECOWAS failed to perform the third function of a mediator successfully. The third function of the mediator involves the selling of solutions to the disputing parties. Successful mediation requires a ripeness of the conflict. This ripening occurs when the parties realize that they cannot impose a unilateral solution on the dispute, and that any attempt to do so will result in either an interminable debilitating "plateau" or stalemate, or a catastrophic "precipice" leading to an abrupt decline in their fortunes.[20] In the absence of such a realization, it is the responsibility of the mediator to "encourage" them to reach this conclusion, through actions designed to block unilateral solutions. Due to the partisan actions of ECOMOG, ECOWAS was never able to fulfill this role.

In the beginning, Taylor was in a strong position. He controlled over 95 percent of the country and almost all the wealth of the country. Consequently, Taylor did not see any reason for him to make any concessions. He was determined not to lose at the conference table what he had won on the battlefield. On the other hand, IGNU controlled only the area around Monrovia, with ECOMOG as its security guarantor. Therefore, ECOWAS encouraged IGNU to believe that it was the legitimate government of Liberia, and therefore it did not have to make any concessions to the NPFL. This gave the IGNU a sense of security which encouraged it to be equally uncompromising. Thus by its own actions, ECOMOG was not able to get the warring parties to recognize the "plateau" or the "precipice" which they would have had to endure if they persisted in their attempts to impose a unilateral solution.[21] Thus, in the Liberian case, the objective probability that ECOWAS would succeed in mediating this conflict was extremely low.

Peacekeeping

Until the very end of the ECOMOG presence in Liberia, the peacekeeping activities of ECOWAS were not any more successful than the mediation efforts. The initial mission in the Liberian crisis was to help negotiate a cease-fire, separate the warring factions, and maintain the peace. As Alan James has pointed out, one of the most important conditions for successful peacekeeping involves trust and cooperation among the warring parties. Specifically, they should demonstrate a willingness to stop fighting, establish a cease-fire, and welcome the peacekeeping force.[22] Since Taylor had already declared his determination to fight ECOMOG, the conditions for successful peacekeeping in the traditional sense did not exist, and the peacekeeping function of ECOMOG was dead on arrival. Thus ECOMOG was not only transformed into peace-enforcement operation, but it also became one of the leading contestants for power in Liberia. Viewed in terms of its original mandate, the initial cease-fire that was established between November

1990 and October 1992 should be viewed as a positive accomplishment. However, this cease-fire was due more to a stalemate between ECOMOG and the NPFL rather than any active accomplishment on the part of ECOMOG in keeping the warring parties apart. After this particular episode, ECOMOG was basically unsuccessful in its role of monitoring cease-fires. The cease-fires that were negotiated never held.

In any case, the purpose of the cease-fire was not only to freeze the situation, but also to reduce the capacity of the factions to resume hostilities at the same or higher levels. Thus peacekeeping involves not only cease-fire monitoring, but also the encampment and disarmament of the troops, and the containment of the conflict. The ECOMOG force was never able to reduce the level of military hostilities because it became a partisan rather than an impartial peacekeeping force, and thus provided opportunities for the factions to use the cease-fires for regrouping. Under these circumstances, the factions typically attempted to use the peacekeeping force to improve and consolidate their positions while waiting for the next opportune time to re-initiate hostilities. Thus, ECOMOG increased the scope, the intensity, and the duration of the armed conflict.

Disarmament

The issue of disarmament was particularly sensitive, since the factions knew that giving up their arms would surely mean their demise. The warring factions had very little incentive to surrender their arms because they had no confidence in the impartiality of ECOMOG. At the end, when the factions decided to disarm, they did so because of war weariness among themselves. Their eventual disarmament agreements were made outside the formal accords. To the credit of ECOMOG, it moved with some determination to supervise the disarmament when given the opportunity by the warlords. Even so, many of these warlords, including members of the government, are believed to have private arms caches, and they still have access to arms from their external allies and connections.[23]

Containment

ECOMOG efforts to contain the Liberian civil war also met with little success. Until January 1993, ECOWAS was unable to isolate Charles Taylor diplomatically, or stop him from acquiring weapons for maintaining his insurrection. At the beginning Taylor had the support of Houphouët-Boigny of Côte d'Ivoire, Compaoré of Bourkina Faso, and Qadafi of Libya. In addition, he was able to obtain the cooperation of some overseas business interests—particularly in France and the United States—who helped to finance his war machine.[24] For instance, video-taped evidence left by NPFL elements after they evacuated Harbel, show that the US Charge d'Affaires and President Carter secured assurances from Taylor to safeguard the evacuation of rubber through the port of Buchanan.[25] In addition, ECOWAS was unable to seal the Liberian borders and quarantine the war. Due to the open borders, Taylor was able to export minerals and timber, and receive armed shipments through Côte d'Ivoire.[26]

In March 1991 the civil war spilled over into Sierra Leone, when NPFL sympathizers organized as the Revolutionary United Front (RUF) started an insurrection in Sierra Leone. The Revolutionary United Front (RUF), which was led by Foday Sankoh who was supposed to have trained with NPFL fighters in Libya in the mid-1980s, was generally recognized as an arm of the NPFL. In a few months, the NPFL elements had captured about twenty-five percent of Sierra Leonean territory, prompting Nigeria and Guinea to send troops to repel them. On May 29 of the same year, ULIMO was formed in the Guinea capital of Conakry, and quickly became one of the main factions in the Liberian civil war, although operating out of Sierra Leone and Guinea.[27]

After ECOWAS imposed economic sanctions on NPFL-held territory on 7 November 1992, and after the UN Security Council imposed an arms embargo, ECOMOG appears to have been able to isolate Taylor both diplomatically and territorially. In the second half of 1992, Houphouët-Boigny began limiting arms shipments from Ivorian territory to the NPFL. As a result, ECOMOG became more successful at monitoring the embargo. Starting in February 1993, a beefed-up air and naval component of ECOMOG was able to patrol both Liberian land borders and ports. As a consequence, ECOMOG was finally able to do serious damage to Taylor's war-making capability, leading to an improvement in his willingness to negotiate. However, ECOWAS was not able to sustain the effort, and fighting broke out all over the country in 1994. From mid-1994 until the truce between the factions in 1995, some of the most savage fighting occurred in Liberia, leading to widespread civilian deaths and hundreds of refugees. Throughout this period, ECOMOG officials had to admit that they had neither the troops nor the equipment to control the situation.

Enforcement

With the role of peacekeeper unavailable to ECOMOG, it slid increasingly into the peace-enforcement role. But even in this role, ECOMOG was also unsuccessful. After the 1990 stalemate, ECOMOG made several unsuccessful attempts to disarm the NPFL forces. These attempts failed. On the other hand it was unwilling to disarm the ULIMO forces, since it was fighting side by side with them against the NPFL. Also, it was unable to establish and enforce the buffer zone between ULIMO and NPFL forces as outlined in the Yamousoukro-IV agreement. After the siege of Monrovia in 1992, ECOMOG forces were engaged in many encounters with NPFL combatants, as well as ULIMO and AFL forces. However, it was never truly able to enforce a settlement on the partisans. As the massacres at Harbel, Sinje, Tubmansburg and others show, every effort made by ECO-MOG to enforce the peace ended in episodes of retaliation by the factions.[28]

The conditions that are associated with success in enforcement action usually are 1) a quick identification of the target of the enforcement action, 2) the ability of the group to attack the target with a force superior to that of the target and its allies, and 3) the emergence of a leader willing and able to take responsibility for directing the enforcement action.[29] ECOMOG was never able to fulfill the role of effective enforcement machinery due to its inability to achieve a consensus among its members on these criteria: the target of enforcement, the need to apply massive force, and the leadership of Nigeria.

Identification of the Target

One of the most glaring problems with the ECOMOG intervention was the inability of ECOWAS to develop a consensus as to the target of the enforcement action. While Nigeria had targeted Taylor as the offender, both Compaoré and Houphouët-Boigny were supporting Taylor throughout the war.[30] Thus, as the situation unfolded, and some of the internal actors were eliminated or changed their alliances, it became difficult to make adjustments regarding the objectives of ECOMOG, its character, and its relationship with the factions. Because of these shifting conditions and alliances, ECOMOG often found itself in awkward positions, sometimes fighting alongside ULIMO and the LPC.

Application of Force

ECOMOG's second problem involved the application of superior force to the target. The strategic uncertainties in the development of consensus regarding the objectives of the intervention affected decisions regarding the force levels that were necessary for the ECOMOG operation. At the outset, the ECOMOG was only a three thousand-man force. The size of the force turned out to be grossly inadequate. Whatever limited success ECOMOG had in the field came at times when the force was enhanced with land, sea, and air forces. Part of the problem with the determination of force levels was due to the limited resources of the ECOWAS members, in both men and money.[31] However, another reason for their difficulties was the refusal of Côte d'Ivoire and other countries to participate in the operation.

Leadership

In a formal sense, ECOWAS did not have a leadership problem. Nigeria was certainly the leader of the operation. However, the leadership of Nigeria turned out to be one of the problems of the ECOWAS operation. The heavy-handed way in which Nigeria tried to "lead" the coalition was a source of serious annoyance for many ECOWAS members. More importantly, it was a source of the inability of the coalition to develop serious consensus on the objectives and strategies of the operation. As President Soglo of Benin is supposed to have exclaimed ". . . Nigeria has taken over ECOMOG, and ECOWAS is too divided to have a common policy for a peaceful resolution of the problem."[32] These political problems of ECOWAS seriously affected the effectiveness of field operations. With the confusing command and control situation, the field commanders did not know whose orders to obey. Consequently, they often had to react to the changing conditions in the field on an ad hoc basis, while trying not to fall afoul of the political leadership.

SPECIAL PROBLEMS OF INTERNAL CONFLICTS

As a hybrid peace operation, ECOWAS/ECOMOG was engaged in peacemaking, peacekeeping, and peace enforcement. As we have shown above, peacekeeping is essentially a temporary conflict management strategy that is intended to reduce the level of violence, limit the scope of the violence, and provide opportunities for mediation, conciliation, and humanitarian assistance. The expectation is that peacemaking through mediation would provide a more lasting solution to the conflict, and that through peace-enforcement, recalcitrant partisans would be forced to accept the peace that has been imposed on them. In attempting to achieve these outcomes, many of the failures of ECOWAS were due to the fact that it met with many of the classic problems of peace operations which it could not surmount. However, ECOWAS's problems were compounded by the fact that this operation was an intervention in an internal conflict. These conflicts usually have a zero-sum character about them, with extremely high passions, fueled by primordial animosities and hatreds, and complicated by ethnic patterns of deprivation.[33] In such situations, warring groups usually see themselves as being involved in a long, protracted struggle, the point of which is to seize the governmental apparatus for the benefit of their ethnic affinees, at the expense of other ethnic groups. Under these circumstances, the effectiveness of the techniques of mediation, peace-keeping, and enforcement are severely compromised.

PROBLEMS OF INTERNAL PEACEMAKING (MEDIATION)

Internal conflicts are the most difficult to mediate.[34] As I have discussed earlier, successful mediation is contingent on four factors: 1) the issue(s) of contention in the conflict, 2) the identity of the parties, 3) the status, resources, and skills of the mediator, and 4) the actual strategies used by the mediator in the conflict resolution process. This is because these factors present additional difficulties in internal conflicts. The issues involved in internal conflicts are usually more difficult, there is more likely to be a history of animosity between the parties, and the mediators are more likely to have difficulty developing appropriate strategies for resolving these conflicts.

Issues

Some conflicts are more difficult to resolve than others. For instance conflicts over borders may be easier to resolve that conflicts over scarce water resources. Therefore the inherent manageability or intractability of a conflict will have an effect on how successful mediation of it might be. Ethnic conflicts are regarded as some of the most intractable and enduring and the most difficult to manage and resolve.[35] Such conflicts are even more difficult to resolve when significant natural resources are located in regions inhabited by aggrieved ethnic groups. In Liberia the conflict revolved around issues of ethnicity and resources. Soon after the war broke out Taylor realized that con-

trol over areas rich with timber, rubber, diamonds and other resources was more important than the immediate capture of Monrovia. Thus the Liberian civil war quickly
became a resource war, and most of the fighting involved efforts to control resource-rich
territory.

Parties

The difficulty in resolving a conflict may also depend on the parties involved and
their perceptions of their relations with the other parties to the conflict. For instance,
even conflict over very scarce resources which are usually very difficult may be
amenable to solution if the parties see each other as friendly, with shared common
interests, and with whom they have a history of cooperation.[36] In situations of internal
conflict, there is likely to be a great deal of animosity between ethnic groups. Due to the
prevalence of ethnic patterns of deprivation, many political demands and protest have
been framed in ethnic terms. In some cases such demands are considered to be nego-
tiable demands in normal political life. By the time armed conflict has emerged, however, these political demands become non-negotiable. These non-negotiable demands
in turn encourage an extreme commitment to ethnic identities and a determination to
fight on behalf of their ethnic "group."[37] Under these circumstances, negotiations and
mediation become even more difficult for a number of reasons: there is no room for
compromise, there are no trade-offs, and the factions come to believe that stalemates
are better than losing.[38] Thus under the conditions of internal multiethnicity and hostility among these groups, extreme commitment to ethnic identity is encouraged by
armed conflict, which in turn becomes the *raison d'être* of the partisans, thus making
mediation more difficult.

Mediators

A third factor that affects the outcomes of mediation efforts involves the mediator. As
I have shown earlier, mediators perform three essential roles. They must keep communication between the conflicting parties, they must be able to formulate appropriate
solutions to the conflict, and they must be able to manipulate the parties into accepting
the proposals. Thus it very much matters who the mediators are, how they are viewed by
the partisans, and what skills they bring to the negotiations. Some attributes that a
mediator should have in order to improve his/her chances of success are 1) knowledge
of conflict, 2) the skills of communication, negotiation, and crisis management, and 3)
valued relationships that would make it possible for him/her to make side payments,
and effective threats and sanctions.[39] Most important, the mediator should have the
trust of the partisans.[40] Internal conflicts present special difficulties with regard to the
ability of mediators to perform the functions of communication, formulation of solutions, and manipulation of partisans. Communication involves acting as a channel of
communication between the factions in the conflict. It may be accomplished through

direct face-to-face communication or shuttle diplomacy. In internal conflict there are difficulties involving access to the strategies and demands of the various parties due to the lack of trust. The probability of effective communication with the partisans can be compromised by the partiality of the mediator. In Liberia, the fact that ECOMOG was observed fighting with different factions at different times promoted extreme distrust on the part of the factions, thus inhibiting the ability of ECOWAS to communicate effectively with them.

Formulation of Solutions

In many international conflicts, the contentions usually involve interstate disputes such as border disputes. Therefore the solutions suggested by mediators are usually limited to such external topics as border demarcations. In internal conflict, the issues are usually embedded deep in the fabric of the society. Therefore, the solutions to such problems are related to issues involving the restructuring of society, the creation of a new political system, and the establishment of a new viable government. This situation adversely affects the ability of mediators in formulating solutions to the conflict, since it requires mediators to have a deep understanding of the internal political economy and culture of the target state. Peacemakers seldom have the necessary knowledge of the history and culture of the society to make profound contributions to sustainable solutions to internal conflicts.[41]

Influencing the Factions

The internal nature of a conflict presents the most difficulty for mediators because it involves the manipulation of various parties into accepting the idea of ending the conflict by compromise. As indicated earlier, the chances of successful mediation are based on the perception of the warring factions that if the conflict continues, there will be a mutually damaging stalemate or a catastrophic decline in their fortunes. They, therefore, do not have a chance for imposing their own unilateral solution on the conflict. In internal conflicts it is extremely difficult for the parties to arrive at this conclusion by themselves. Internal conflicts have dynamic cycles involving articulation, mobilization, and insurgency.[42] These cycles have different effects on the factions in terms of their perception of their chances of victory. As a result, at any one time some factions would be very enthusiastic about negotiations while others, believing that their chances of victory were good, would not be ready to negotiate. Therefore, if one group is in a negotiation-friendly stage, and another group is in a negotiation-hostile phase, the probability of mediation success would be significantly reduced. Furthermore, these groups attempt to co-opt peacekeeping forces to their cause, and these forces are almost compelled by the fluidity of the situation to take, and be seen as taking sides, thus compromising their role as mediators. Once that happens, the ability of the mediator to get the partisans to accept compromise solutions is severely eroded.

These dynamic cycles have two additional negative effects. One effect is that there is likely to be a proliferation of groups with no clear objectives other than acquiring enough power to be considered as a having a credible interest on prospective negotiations. Another effect is the tendency of groups to splinter off, especially toward the end of the conflict, in the hope of getting a better deal than their previous group in anticipated negotiations. Under these circumstances, the preparedness of the groups for negotiations is totally confused, and it becomes extremely difficult for mediators to judge the precise moment at which the conflict will be "ripe for resolution."

The difficulties encountered by ECOWAS in its efforts to mediate the Liberian conflict can be attributed to the coming together of these negative factors. Among these convergent factors were conflicts over access to remunerative natural resources, adherence by factions to strong ethnic identities and a strong sense of ethnic grievance, power asymmetry among the major groupings, and the fact that ECOWAS clearly did not have the necessary qualities for successful mediation. Under such circumstances, it was difficult to get the various factions to agree to cease-fires and negotiate. They viewed the negotiations as temporary respites in the war, which they could use to regroup, replenish their armies, and reestablish their contacts with outside weapons suppliers, in what they perceived to be a protracted conflict. Sometimes the factions participated in negotiations under pressure. In these cases, however, negotiated promises were fragile, and the tendency for them to renege on their commitments were predictably high. The splintering of ULIMO, and the defection of various individuals from one faction to another, provide evidence of the shifting groupings which ECOWAS had to face in its effort at peacemaking. Thus the failure of ECOWAS in mediating the Liberian conflict can be explained, at least in part, in terms of the dynamics of internal conflicts. In spite of these natural problems of internal conflicts, some of the blame for the diplomatic impasse should go to ECOWAS. First, ECOWAS was ignorant of the sociocultural factors that led up to the armed conflict. Therefore, it did not have the ability to propose solutions that had some relevance to the conflict. Secondly, it did not have the resources to be able to make the side bets, or provide the rewards and sanctions needed to provide incentives for the parties to bring the issue to a successful conclusion.[43]

In 1990 there were four power contenders in Liberia: the NPFL, the INPFL (Independent National Patriotic Front of Liberia), the AFL, and ECOMOG/IGNU. In 1991 ULIMO joined this group. By 1995 several other factions had emerged. Among these were the Armed Forces of Liberia (AFL), the Lofa Defense Force (LDF), the Bong Defense Force (BDF), and the Liberia Peace Council (LPC). By the end of the conflict there were more than ten factions. All these groups had a sense of ethnic identity and ethnic grievance. Throughout this period the different factions were at different stages of development, and therefore they had different perceptions of their fortunes, and different dispositions towards negotiations. As a result, at any one time some factions were very unenthusiastic about negotiations while other factions were not.

At the end, the Abuja Accords was primarily an agreement between ECOWAS and Charles Taylor, the main protagonists in the war. This agreement confirmed the idea that a negotiated settlement would be most likely when the parties recognized the need to compromise in order to avoid a precipitous drop in their circumstance or an interminable and catastrophic stalemate. The Nigerian leadership and ECOWAS knew that they could not defeat Taylor militarily. For ECOWAS the alternative was a situation in which there would be an interminable commitment to staying in Liberia. Nigeria and ECOWAS wanted to withdraw for reasons including the sheer cost of the operation, in both funds and casualties. However, unilateral withdrawal would have been difficult because ECOWAS would not have been able to claim that it had achieved its purpose of restoring peace and democracy to Liberia. ECOWAS finally recognized that without Taylor such an outcome would be impossible. Therefore, by not dealing with Taylor, ECOWAS was looking at a long period of stalemate. On the other hand, Taylor also knew that he could not take Monrovia by force. The only way he could win would be through elections, and ECOWAS was the only party that could produce the election, which he was fairly confident of wining. For both ECOWAS and Taylor, the idea that there would be elections in which the warlords could be candidates was the perfect compromise. It was a win/win situation for both ECOWAS and Taylor. The deal was probably struck at a meeting between Taylor and Abacha in the summer of 1996. The Abuja Accords was just the device used to ratify the decision. Once the decision was made, all the other factions had to fall in line.

PROBLEMS OF INTERNAL PEACEKEEPING

Peacekeeping under conditions of internal warfare presents special problems. In traditional or border peacekeeping, the practice has been the interposition of a light force between the warring countries, or in a buffer zone between the armies, usually at national borders. Internal peacekeeping activity is more intrusive, and usually involves the policing of cease-fires, and the encampment, disarmament, and demobilization of troops. In some cases, there are added responsibilities such as conducting elections, and the reestablishment of public order. The ability of peacekeeping forces to accomplish these functions depends on a number of factors. First, peace needs to have been established. Insofar as mediation efforts have not yielded a cease fire, it is likely that peacekeeping forces would be under attack from one or another faction within the territory. This condition makes the implementation of peacekeeping unstable and precarious, so that the intervening peacekeeping force will easily slide into a posture of peace enforcement, or become one of the parties to the conflict. As a consequence, the force could lose one of its positive attributes which is to be neutral by intention, composition, and behavior.[44]

Second, in internal peacekeeping the intervening forces do not deploy along a border. Instead, they are deployed throughout the country, as a reaction to the movements of the partisans. This problem may be compounded by such factors as the topography, vegetation, population density, and climatic conditions of the country.[45] Depending on the size of the area to be patrolled, this task can be enormous. Also, there is the problem of the identification and separation of combatants.[46] One consequence of this predicament is the problem of the determination of the force levels necessary for these operations, including the issues of communication, command and control that it poses. The ability of peacekeeping force commanders to project the force levels needed to perform their functions is severely complicated by their access to intelligence regarding the movements of warring parties.

In the Liberian situation, the initial commitment of 3000 troops to ECOMOG was obviously made without consideration of these issues. The result is that ECOMOG was severely handicapped in terms of its ability to be deployed. Not only were the forces seriously inadequate, but intelligence regarding the movements of the factions and assessment of logistical needs was severely compromised, turning the command and control of ECOMOG forces into a huge problem.[47] Under such circumstances, ECOMOG could not function as a peacekeeping force. As reported by the UN Secretary-General, ECOMOG troops had to be withdrawn many times because they were menaced by numerically superior rebel troops. Indeed, during most of its presence in Liberia, only about sixteen percent of ECOMOG troops were fully deployed. It was not until 1996, when the parties themselves committed themselves to peace and the ECOMOG forces were appropriately built up, that ECOMOG could finally play a legitimate role of deploying its forces in enough parts of the country to carry out its functions of encampment and disarmament with some modicum of success.

PROBLEMS OF INTERNAL PEACE ENFORCEMENT

There are also problems associated with peace enforcement in the context of internal conflicts, which are likely to sabotage the entire effort. The first of these problems has to do with the difficulty in identifying the target of the enforcement. This is always a political decision, which has to be negotiated within the high political decision-making command of the organization engaged in the intervention. Nevertheless, in international relations, once the decision has been made it is unlikely to change. However, in internal wars, this is not at all certain. It is more likely that the target will change. One reason for these changes involves political considerations among the members of the group involved in the intervention. The more difficult situation arises when the political decision makers or the field commanders decide that there are other targets that ought to be stopped. Under such circumstances, it is possible for the enforcement force to find itself fighting alongside forces which it had previously decided were the targets of the peace enforcement. Another reason for such changes is the tendency of the factions to try to use the enforcement mechanism to further their own objectives, and to collaborate at times with the force at the expense of other factions. Thirdly, the enforcement troops themselves may find that fighting alongside local factions could be useful to them in their campaigns due to the familiarity of these groups with the terrain and other local conditions. The result of these considerations could be a situation in which the enforcement force will find itself fighting on opposite sides at different times.

As the experience of Liberia has shown, the targeting of one or another of the warring partners was extremely problematic. At the outset, ECOWAS made the decision that Taylor's NPFL was the clear obstacle to the peace process, and therefore it should be eliminated. The official ECOWAS line settled on this interpretation of the events in Liberia, in spite of the disagreement of Houphouët-Boigny and Blaise Compaoré. The result was not to make the ECOMOG pursuit of Taylor more effective but to encourage the various factions to try to pit members of ECOWAS against each other, and thus cause more confusion in terms of the nature and objectives of the operation. Another consequence of this activity was the destruction of the credibility of ECOWAS, since it became very clear that the criteria that ECOMOG was using to decide which side it would fight on had nothing to do with the original mission of ECOMOG but rather the calculations of ECOMOG commanders as to what would benefit them.

Application of Force

The application of force to a target in the context of internal conflict also presents serious problems. As noted earlier, the fact that the conflict is taking place within a country usually complicates the issues of the determination of necessary force levels, intelligence, command and control of the force, and strategies to be adopted in the conflict. Frequently, decisions are made with regard to force levels which turn out to be inadequate as a result of less-than-adequate knowledge of the extent of the area to be patrolled, the strengths of the fighting forces, and their movements. If the enforcement force has to fight several factions at one time, there are additional problems of the availability of forces and their terms of engagement. For instance, in many internal situations, the peace-operations force may be constantly surprised by movements of some factions. Strategic planning becomes extremely complicated because of the need to react to these movements.

Another problem with internal enforcement involves the difficulties in developing strategies and tactics that will do minimum damage to the target country. Under conditions of international conflict, there is less concern for the devastation of the national territory and its resources until after the war. However, in internal wars, the fighting takes place on the national territory in which all sides would have to live after the conflict. Therefore, whether or not the target of enforcement is the right one, destruction of the national territory will occur. The problem of the devastation of national resources is even more acute when the target of the enforcement action keeps shifting as was the case in Liberia. Additionally, the ways in which force is used in enforcement operations do not seem to be based on any concern for national reconstruction and peace building. Since in internal conflicts targets of enforcement are more likely to change, peace enforcement is carried out in ways which are more likely to produce deep destruction of natural and human resources. In Liberia, care has not been taken to do as little damage as possible. This has caused massive problems for reconstruction.

LONG-TERM IMPACT OF ECOMOG

Many historians have observed that war has a profound impact on the society that engages in it, and that the more extensive the involvement, the greater the strain of war making.[48] The effects of warfare on a country at war with itself, with the fighting on its own territory, has to be even more disastrous. Beyond the failures of the ECOMOG intervention in the areas of peacekeeping, peacemaking, and peace enforcement, the intervention has had an impact on Liberia, which will adversely affect its political, economic, and cultural development for a very long time to come. The most significant consequence of ECOMOG participation in the civil wars has been the prolongation and spreading of the war. By many estimates, without the ECOMOG intervention, the civil war could have ended in 1990.[49] While the original ECOMOG contingents remained in Liberia, they did not actively attempt to prosecute and end the war. The only time they made an effort to take the war to the NPFL was in the spring 1993 military offensive which it failed to follow through, due to the ambiguous mandate of the ECOMOG force.

Part of the extremely deleterious consequences of the intervention emerged from the type of warfare in which ECOWAS participated in Liberia. Like many other civil wars in Africa, the Liberian civil war was caused mainly by state failure and the patron-client relationships that had been built up since independence through state military and civilian bureaucracies. Previously, governments had based their viability on revenues derived from the exploitation of natural (mineral and agricultural) resources, supplemented by foreign aid. As these traditional sources of revenue broke down after the Cold War, these governments began to lose their ability to satisfy their local clients on the one hand, and their international supporters on the other. As these states collapsed, their former domestic clients began to look for sources through which they could maintain themselves in the style to which they had become accustomed. At the same time, their international supporters, both governmental and corporate, also began to seek ways of maintaining their access to resources at the same or better prices and conditions, in case their former clients were overthrown. Thus, the war was essentially about attempts by former government officials (like Johnson, Boley, Kromah etc.) to seize control of lucrative national resources and use them to acquire wealth and power.

The objectives of these former government officials was to transform themselves into warlords, seize territory that was resource rich, and loot and exploit these territories to finance their operations. In this effort, they tried to tap into what they considered to be ready-made constituencies (usually but not exclusively ethnic affinees), and foreign governments or companies who wished to have access to those resources. Meanwhile, after trying a variety of legitimizing strategies involving transitions to democracy, these desperate governments, unable to trust their own militaries or bureaucracies, ended up trusting their fortunes to other foreign governments and corporations, including mercenaries and security companies like Executive Outcomes and Sandline.[50] Thus, these wars are devoid of any ideological commitments or concern for international territorial boundaries. They are simply wars for the control of territory, for the purpose of maintaining or increasing the wealth and power of the warlord.

One way in which the ECOMOG commanders prolonged the war was through the practice of recruiting local groups to do the fighting. As it became clear that the objective of the war was not ideological but economic, many other groups who had any access to weapons and a few soldiers began to form their own factions in order to press their claims to power and wealth. ECOMOG commanders found the development of these new groups to be very useful. First, it made it possible for them to recruit individuals and groups to fight on their side with greater efficiency. The locals knew the terrain much better, and they were much less costly to operate. Second, recruiting them would allow the ECOMOG forces to lessen their own involvement, thereby lessening casualty counts, which could prove to be embarrassing at home.[51] This ECOMOG strategy inevitably prolonged and widened the civil war. First, the effect of this strategy of recruiting local fighters was to create a large number of independent factions, each of them "uncontrollable" because they controlled their own sources of financing their operations through smuggling, looting, and commercial activities.[52] Furthermore, there was a tendency for power in these factions to move away from the top towards the commanders of the smaller units. Soldiers frequently changed sides on the basis of their calculation of profits. Therefore there was a high incentive for commanders to control the forces' troops. This situation tended to prolong the war even further, because local commanders were very likely to scuttle any political settlements that could close down their lucrative economic activities, such as mining or timber exploitation. For instance, the refusal of ULIMO-J to disarm was due to the fact that if they disarmed they would lose control of the Bomi diamond and gold fields to ECOMOG commanders.[53]

The Liberian civil war has had some negative effects in the region. In Nigeria, it cost at least six hundred killed and one billion dollars above normal operating costs, at a time when its own debt stood at $35 billion.[54] It has had terrible consequences in other parts of the region. For instance, it contributed to the coup in the Gambia, which overthrew Sir Dauda Jawara. In Sierra Leone it promoted the formation of ULIMO, which was formed in Freetown in part to neutralize the Revolutionary United Front (RUF) and to keep Charles Taylor away from the sources of diamonds in the west.[55] In addition, the war in Sierra Leone has caused numerous coups and counter coups, killed at least fifteen thousand people, and created 1.5 million refugees, one quarter of the population. The worse effects of the war were undoubtedly in Liberia. Due to the nature of the war and the participation of ECOMOG, the intervention has compounded the usual effects of a war fought on the target state. The effects have been the massive devastation and looting of natural resources; death, displacement, and violation of the human rights of populations; political, economic, social, and cultural dislocation of society; and reduction of opportunities for agricultural and industrial development.

Devastation

The most apparent consequence of the war in Liberia has been the sheer physical devastation of the country. There are of course the usual effects of warfare, including the destruction of roads, bridges, power plants, and also many natural resources such as agricultural land, and industrial plants. However, in this particular instance the destruction has gone far beyond these. It is difficult to lay the entire blame for the destruction of the Liberian territory on ECOMOG. However, it certainly has to share some of the blame. As mentioned earlier, ECOMOG commanders wanted to use local factions to reduce their casualties. On the other hand, because of their command over a number of resources, many of these groups wanted to use ECOMOG for their own purposes. Therefore, a mutually destructive symbiotic relationship developed between ECOMOG and these groups, in which it was difficult to delineate clearly where the operations of ECO-MOG began and where the work of other groups ended. The most important incentive to get these locals to join the war effort was to offer them opportunities for looting, shares in exploitative economic activities, and protection. For instance, ECOMOG provided air transport for ULIMO and fought alongside it during Operation Octopus. Also, ECOMOG provided both ULIMO-K and ULIMO-J and the LPC with arms, ammunition, intelligence, and free passage.[56] Thus, ECOMOG's encouragement of a large number of quasi-independent factions, each financing its operations through the looting of natural resources, led to an even greater devastation of rural Liberia.

In addition, many ECOMOG commanders seem to have gone into business for themselves. For instance, ECOMOG collaborated with Alhaji Kromah in mining operations in the Bomi area, and jointly operated timber projects and rubber plantations with George Boley (LPC) near the Ivorian border, (estimated at about $1.5 million a year). Underpaid and ill-equipped ECOMOG commanders have been getting involved in diamonds and iron products and have even been known to be involved in stripping some of the country's assets—railroad stock, mining equipment, and public utilities—for sale to expatriate companies.[57] In this particularly nasty war, ECOMOG has been using the kind of tactics designed to intimidate civilians and to try to starve out areas suspected of rebel activity. For instance, ECOMOG has been known to bomb humanitarian relief convoys and their border crossings in order to stop them from reaching NPFL areas.[58] Such artillery and aerial bombardments have had a catastrophic effect on these areas. It is reported, for instance, that social services in Grabbing, Buchanan, and Grand Bassa were totally nonexistent because of ECOMOG bombardment.[59]

Human Resources

The other easily observed consequence of the war was the number of people who have lost their lives. According to UN estimates, one hundred fifty thousand people have been killed. It is not clear what the demographic breakdown of casualties was. However, it has been estimated that over fifty percent of the soldiers in this war were younger than fifteen years. Therefore, it is not unreasonable to assume that a very high percentage of those killed or maimed will fall into the 12–30 age group. Since these are most productive years among any population, we have to conclude that this loss of human resources will have a devastating effect on the development potential of Liberia. The destruction of the infrastructure in Liberia, and the destruction of educational, health and water facilities present a very grim picture of the difficulty of integrating these young men into national programs of recovery and reconstruction for some time. The new government is just beginning to restart most of the country's schools that have been closed down during the fighting, and also opening centers for the treatment of the significant number of women and children who have been victims of rape and sexual abuse as a result of the civil war.[60] There is also the large number of refugees and internally displaced persons that this war has created. According to most observers, the war has caused upward of seven hundred thousand refugees and over eight hundred thousand internally displaced people. One of the effects of this situation is the endemic sense of insecurity throughout the country. The United Nations Secretary-General reports that there is an estimated 1.8 million persons, mostly women and children, in serious need of humanitarian assistance.[61]

Economic Impact

The effect of the devastation of natural resources has been the almost total destruction or degradation of the infrastructure.[62] When one considers the loss of population, the general sense of insecurity, and the destruction of the infrastructure, it is not surprising that any meaningful activity in either agriculture or industry has come to a halt. One of the effects of the destruction of the countryside has been the wiping out of indigenous agriculture. Also, the pervasive sense of insecurity has discouraged those Liberians who would like to return home to invest in agriculture. The situation of industry is even more bleak. The destruction of whatever limited industrial plant caused by the fighting and the uncertainties associated with long-term returns on industrial activity will limit investment in that area for some time to come. Furthermore, with the downgrading of the physical infrastructure, the productive sectors of the economy are virtually paralyzed. There does not seem to be the available capital or the inclination to recover it.[63]

Political Impact

The most devastating and long-lasting consequence of the peacekeeping intervention in Liberia are the political effects including the transformation of the area into a "zone of anarchy," the collapse of political order, the breakdown of civil society, and the lack of development of structures and norms that can help establish political order in the near future. Postwar politics in Liberia is very much a zero-sum game. President Taylor controls all access to major economic activity. This pattern of governance reveals that he has to reestablish the patrimonial politics that existed before the civil war. In order to accomplish this, he has moved with vigor to establish and control the new Liberian security services and the AFL.[64] Since 1997, he has consolidated his control over the political system so much as to make it almost absolute.[65] The long-term consequences of the war and ECOMOG's role in it are more ominous. The civil war has created certain political conditions which have placed the return of political order to the region in some jeopardy. One of these conditions is the development of a culture of political violence in the region, which will tend to encourage the proliferation of civil wars. Under pressure from the internal threats to their viability, African states will continue to depend on security contractors. Such a development will be antidemocratic in the real sense of the term. That is to say, it would lead to disempowerment of the people in the region and destroy their ability to find solutions to their political problems.

CONCLUSION

The ECOWAS experience is a rare experiment in the practice of conflict resolution in post–Cold War Africa. As such, it represents an attempt by African states to undertake the management and solution of conflict in the region. The success of such attempts would be an important step toward the achievement and maintenance of regional security and regional autonomy in Africa. Thus it represents an impulse toward self-reliance that will develop African organizations with the political will, the capabilities, and the skills to establish a Pax Africana on the continent. Therefore, this development is very significant for the prospects of the resolution of internal armed conflict in Africa. There is no doubt that there will be other instances of internal conflict in Africa, and African states and international organizations will be faced with the problem of resolving these conflicts. Therefore, an evaluation of the performance of ECOWAS and ECOMOG should help to determine what lessons are to be learned that can shed some light on the possibilities and limitations of regional organizations in the management and resolution of internal conflicts.

The starting point of the thinking on this issue is the general prohibition against intervention in international law. This does not mean, however, that there should be a general aversion to the use of international agencies for the resolution of internal conflict. To say that intervention may lead to unwelcome outcomes is not to say that non-intervention will necessarily lead to salutary outcomes. However, it does mean that any such intervention should be taken extremely seriously, and should be the result of a great deal of circumspection. As we have seen in the case of Liberia, intervention was extremely intrusive. Therefore, peace operations are not only capable of exacerbating internal conflicts, they can also have devastating long-range impacts on the political and economic development of target states. From this point of view, it is recommended that such operations can only be justified as exceptions to the general rule against intervention, and that such justification can only be based on the legitimacy of the operation, the legitimacy of the agent or agents, and the legitimacy of the intervention process itself.

The first lesson that the ECOMOG experience suggests is the need for the operation to be legitimate. In this regard an important issue is the legal basis of the intervention. In the case of ECOMOG, the legal basis is somewhat unclear. The justification of intervention in the internal affairs of states on the basis of humanitarian intervention is not unequivocally established, and the Protocol of the ECOWAS Defense Pact has not clearly removed this doubt.[66] Beyond the legal question, there is also the question of the political legitimacy of the operation, or to be more precise, the legitimacy of the objectives which the operation was attempting to achieve. Clearly, in this case there was a great deal of dissension among the ECOWAS members regarding the legitimacy of the peace operation. Of course, the argument that a group of states led by a military dictatorship have a right to intervene in another state to establish a democratic regime is not credible. This is not a purely formal matter. As I have shown, the chance of the success of the operation depends at least in part on the stature of the intervenors, and the legitimacy of the operation itself. One of the recurrent themes in the intervention was the fact that the warring factions in Liberia had no confidence in ECOWAS, and they came to believe that ECOMOG was and behaved like just one of the warring factions. It was in this regard that ECOMOG was most compromised.

In fact, the Nigerian leadership recognized this issue, and that is why they decided to undertake this operation as ECOWAS rather than as Nigeria. By doing so, they were trying to accentuate the legitimacy of the agent and thereby minimize the possible illegitimacy of the objectives of the operation. Clearly, intervention by a regional organization, even taking into consideration all the problems of collective decision making, is much more defensible and preferable than unilateral intervention by Nigeria would have been. Nevertheless, the transformation was not complete, and throughout the ECOMOG presence in Liberia it was clear to all that it was primarily a Nigerian operation, and that the objectives were Nigerian.

Another consideration of the ECOMOG has to do with its prudence. In this regard, the decision to intervene should be based on an accurate assessment of the motivations and capacities of the groups involved in the conflict, and the issues about which they are fighting. On this basis the organization would be able to make a judgement about the negotiability and likely duration of the conflict. Also, it is important to undertake a sober assessment of the resources and capabilities and skills available to the organization, and the strategies that the organization can use to achieve a quick and successful resolution of the conflict. In this regard, African regional organizations should limit their operations to the less ambitious types of operations such as peace observation and fact finding. Mediation should be based on prior assessment of the "negotiability" of the conflict after consideration of the partisans and the issues, and every effort must be made to mediate the conflict by showing the partisans the catastrophic consequences of attempting to impose unilateral solutions. It is particularly important for the organization to be modest in attempting to impose solutions on the basis of its own normative preferences without a sophisticated understanding of the political culture of the target state. As we have seen, the civil war points to the fact that there are serious fissures in Liberia. The course that it has taken points to the fact that an important aspect of these fissures has to do with the ethnic animosities that continue to plague Liberian society. Thus a question that arises is whether it is possible to accomplish satisfactorily the settlement of internal disputes of this nature without taking into consideration the peculiar historical and cultural aspects of such societies.

Finally, it is extremely important that the organization avoid any attempt at enforcement action. As the Liberian situation has shown, the internal situation is so fluid that any attempt at enforcement will enmesh the force in a maze of conflicting alliances with internal groups that will raise doubts about the legitimacy of the force as well as the ability of the force to successfully carry out its mission. Furthermore, and most important, there is a serious probability that the activities of the peace-enforcement troops will have a catastrophic effect on the target state in terms of the destruction of the natural resources and infrastructure, the curtailment of indigenous agriculture, the termination of industrial activity, the creation of refugees and displaced persons, and above all, the dissipation of human resources. There is serious doubt that anything that such forces can do will be enough to compensate for such devastation. Whatever enforcement action is carried out, it must be done in support of mediation, and carried out with clearly established limited objectives, based on envisaged outcomes that are clearly recognizable. The most important consideration should be the impact of these operations not only on the immediate prospects of resolving the conflict, but also on the more long-range consequences of the operation on the target country. When African governments engage in these types of operations, which they undoubtedly should and will, these considerations should make their efforts more consistent with African security and African aspirations for sustainable political, economic, and cultural development.

NOTES

1. For some perspective on humanitarian intervention see Fernando R. Teson, *Humanitarian Intervention: An Inquiry into Law and Morality,* 2nd ed. (Hudson, N.Y.: Transnational Publishers, 1997); Sean D. Murphy, *Humanitarian Intervention: the United Nations in an Evolving World Order* (Philadelphia: University of Pennsylvania Press, 1996); Stanley Hoffman, *The Ethics and Politics of Humanitarian Intervention* (Notre Dame: University of Notre Dame Press, 1996); Gene M. Lyons and Michael Mastanduno, eds., *Beyond Westphalia?: State Sovereignty and International Intervention* (Baltimore: Johns Hopkins University Press, 1995); John Harris, ed., *The Politics of Humanitarian Intervention* (New York: Pinter, 1995); Lori Fisler Damrosch, ed., *Enforcing Restraint: Collective Intervention in Internal Conflicts* (New York: Council on Foreign Relations, 1993).

2. Benjamin Rivlin, "Prospects for a Division of Labor Between the UN and Regional Bodies in Peacekeeping: a Long Term Challenge," in *Agenda for Change,* ed. Klaus Hufner (Oplander: Lesko and Budrich, 1995), p. 147.

3. US Department of State, *Country Reports and Human Rights Practices: 1990,* February 1991, p. 192.

4. For a detailed account of the roots of the conflict see, W. Ofuatey-Kodjoe, "Regional Organization and the Resolution of Internal Conflict: The ECOWAS Intervention in Liberia," *International Peacekeeping* 1, no. 3 (Autumn 1993): 267–271.

5. *West Africa,* 4–10 May 1991, p. 768.

6. *West Africa,* 30 November–6 December 1992, p. 2052.

7. *West Africa,* December 7–13, 1992, p. 2112.

8. *West Africa,* 20–26 September 1993, p. 1171.

9. The United Nations and the Situation in Liberia (DPI April, 1995), p. 13.

10. *Facts on File,* 30 May 1996, p. 387.

11. 19th Progress Report of the UN Secretary General on UNOMIL, 6/26/99, p. 4.

12. 23rd Report of the UN Secretary-General on UNOMIL, p. 24.

13. Ibid., p. 4.

14. Ibid., p. 24.

15. Ibid., p. 4.

16. Dayle E. Spencer and William J. Spencer, "Third Party Mediation and Conflict Transformation: Experiences of Ethiopia, Sudan and Liberia," In *Conflict Transformation,* ed. Kumar Rupesinghe (New York: St. Martin's Press, 1988), p. 194.

17. Ahmadu Sesay, Introduction, *The Future of Regionalism in Africa,* ed. Ralph I. Onwuka and Ahmadu Sesay (New York: St. Martin's Press, 1985). p.13.

18. Ibid., p. 8.

19. *West Africa,* 21–27 September 1992, p. 1607.

20. See I. W. Zartman, *Ripe for Resolution: Conflict and Intervention in Africa* (New York, Oxford University Press, 1989), pp. 255–88.

21. Ibid., p. 268.

22. Alan James, *Peacekeeping in International Politics* (New York: St. Martin's Press, 1990), p. 23. See also Paul Diehl, "The Conditions of Success in Peacekeeping Operations," *The Politics of International Organizations: Patterns and Insights* (Chicago: Dorsey Press, 1989), pp. 173–88.

23. Ahmadu Sesay, Introduction, *The Future of Regionalism in Africa,* p. 15.

24. *West Africa,* 25–31 January 1993, p. 104.

25. *West Africa,* 5–11 April 1993, p. 550.

26. *West Africa,* 8–14 March 1993, p. 366; *West Africa,* 21–27 September 1993, p. 1624.

27. *West Africa,* 7–13 September 1992, p. 1519.

28. Ninth Progress Report of the UN Secretary General on the UNOMIL, UN Doc. S/19945/158, February 1995, paragraph 36.

29. Inis Claude, *Swords into Plowshares* (New York: Random House, 1984), p. 252.

30. Femi Omowunmi, "Liberia: The Lybian, Ivorien and Burkinabe Connection," *The Guardian* (Lagos) 7, no. 4878, (3 November 1990): 1–2.

31. *Africa Research Bulletin* 27, no. 9 (15 September 1990): 9801.

32. *West Africa,* 16–22 November 1992.

33. David Carment, "The International Dimension of Ethnic Conflict: Concepts, Indicators and Theory," *Journal of Peace Research* 30, no. 2 (1993): 138. See also Donald Horowitz, *Ethnic Groups in Conflict* (Berkeley: University of California Press, 1985); Donald Horowitz, "Ethnic Conflict Management for Policymakers," in *Conflict and Peacemaking in Multiethnic Societies,* ed. Joseph Montville (Lexington, Mass.: DC Heath and Co., 1990), pp. 115–133.

34. I. W. Zartman, "Dynamics and Constraints in Negotiations in Internal Conflicts," in *Elusive Peace: Negotiating an End to Civil War* (Washington, DC: Brookings Institution, 1995), p. 4. See also Dayle E. Spencer and William J. Spencer, "Third Party Mediation and Conflict Transformation: Experiences in Ethiopia, Sudan and Liberia," in *Conflict Transformation,* ed. Kumar Rupesinghe (New York: St. Martin's Press, 1988).

35. Kumar Rupesinghe, "Conflict Transformation," in *Conflict Transformation,* p. 71–72; Francis Deng, "The Identity Factor in the Sudanese Conflict," in *Conflict and Peacemaking in Multiethnic Societies;* H. Assess, *Mediation in Civil Wars: Approaches and Strategies—The Sudan Conflict* (Boulder, Colo.: Westview Press, 1987); Anne-Marie Smith, *Advances in Understanding International Peacemaking* (Washington, DC: United States Institute for Peace), n. d.

36. Jacob Bercovitch and Allison Houston, "The Study of International Mediation: Theoretical Issues and Empirical Evidence," in *Resolving International Conflicts: The Theory and Practice of Mediation,* ed. Jacob Bercovitch (Boulder, Colo.: Lynne Rienner Publishers, 1995), p. 22.

37. Zartman, *Elusive Peace*, p. 9.

38. Ibid., p. 10.

39. J. Z. Rubin, "Experimental Research on Third Party Intervention in Conflict," *Psychological Bulletin* 87: 379–91; See also Bercovitch and Houston, *The Study of International Mediation*, pp. 26–27; Louis Kriesberg, "Varieties of Mediating Activities and Mediators in International Relations," in *Resolving International Conflicts*, ed. Jacob Bercovitch (Boulder, Colo.: Lynne Rienner, 1995), p. 231; Timothy D. Sisk, *Power Sharing and International Mediation in Ethnic Conflicts* (Washington, DC: United States Institute of Peace, 1996), p. 101.

40. Jackson, *Meeting of Minds* (New York: McGraw-Hill, 1952), p. 129.

41. Rupesinghe, *Conflict Transformation*, p. 84

42. Zartman, *Elusive Peace*, p. 13.

43. Sisk, *Power Sharing and International Mediation*, p. 101.

44. Diehl, "The Conditions of Success in Peacekeeping Operations," p. 5.

45. Ramesh Chandra Thakur and Carlyle Thayer, eds., *A Crisis of Expectations: UN Peacekeeping in the 1990*. (Boulder, Colo.: Westview Press, 1995), p. 227.

46. Ibid., p. 228.

47. For instance General Dogonyaro reports that after the initial encounter with the NPFL, he was under contradictory orders from the Nigerian High Command and President Amos Sawyer of the IGNU. See *West Africa*, 13–20 October 1990, p. 2650.

48. George J. Andreopoulos and Harold E. Selesky, eds., *The Aftermath of Defeat: Societies, Armed Forces, and the Challenge of Recovery* (New Haven: Yale University Press, 1994), p. 1.

49. Ademola Adeleke, "The Politics and Diplomacy of Peacekeeping in West Africa: The Ecowas Operations in Liberia," *Journal of Modern African Studies* 33, no. 4 (1995): 590.

50. William Reno, "African Weak States and Commercial Alliances," *African Affairs* 96, no. 383 (April 1997): 180–185.

51. Reno, ibid., p. 182.

52. Herbert Howe, "Lessons of Liberia: ECOMOG and Regional Peacekeeping," *International Security* 21, no. 3 (Winter 1996–97): 172.

53. Reno, "The Business of War in Liberia," p. 215

54. Howe, "Lessons of Liberia," p.165.

55. Reno, "The Business of War in Liberia," p. 213.

56. Howe, "Lessons of Liberia," p. 157.

57. Reno, "The Business of War in Liberia," p. 214.

58. *Médecin sans Frontière*, Brussels, 4 March 1993.

59. UN doc. A/50/522, 9 October 1995, p. 9.

60. Ibid., p. 7.

61. Ibid., p. 7.

62. *The Europa World Yearbook*, vol. 2 (London: Europa Publications Ltd., 1998), p. 2106.

63. UN doc. 5/1996/232, 1 April 1996.

64. EIU, *Country Reports*, 19 October 1998.

65. The PRS Group, *International Country Risk Guide*, March 1998.

66. Tom Imobighe, "ECOWAS Defense Pact and Regionalism in Africa," in *The Future of Regionalism in Africa*, ed. Ralph I. Onwuka and Ahmadu Sesay (New York: St. Martin's Press, 1985).

7

Strategic Policy Failure
and State Fragmentation

Security, Peacekeeping, and Democratization in Sierra Leone

Yusuf Bangura

On 6 January 1999, rebels of the Revolutionary United Front (RUF) and soldiers of the former Republic of Sierra Leone Military Forces (RSLMF) invaded the city of Freetown and overthrew the elected government for a second time in less than two years. The invasion resulted in the deaths of more than six thousand civilians in the capital, the abduction of thousands of young men and women by the rebels, the maiming and physical abuse of hundreds of citizens, and the burning of a large number of houses and government buildings. After the government's restoration to power by ECO-MOG[1] in March 1998 the populace was assured that even if the rebellion proved difficult to suppress, it would no longer threaten the integrity of the state or endanger the security of most citizens. The invasion destroyed the government's defense policy and undermined the political order on which the policy itself was based. The Armed Forces Revolutionary Council/Revolutionary United Front (AFRC/RUF) was transformed from an illegitimate organization to one that the government and the international community were willing to do business with despite the former's well-known record of barbarism.

How can this dramatic turn of events be explained? What accounts for the extraordinary failure of the government's strategic policy? What are the implications of the policy failure for the territorial integrity of the state, social integration, and democracy? And what prospects exist for a resolution of the conflict? The reasons for the policy failure are complex, but three are significant. Firstly, the country's governance institutions seem unsuitable for mobilizing the population against the rebellion. Once the AFRC formed an alliance with the RUF, and some important elites from the North and Western Area decided to support or work with the AFRC regime, the geoethnic divisions became magnified. Sierra Leone has a *multi-ethnic bipolar* polity: the dominance of two roughly equal ethnic groups in a multi-ethnic setting. Elite politicization of ethnicity in this type of polity often leads to smaller groups coalescing with either of the larger ones in the competition for power.

The two historic elections of 1967 and 1996 in which power shifted from one political sector to another brought out in bold relief the ethnic bipolarity of Sierra Leone's politics. In bipolar settings with governance institutions that are majoritarian,[2] "in" groups seek to maximize their grip on power whereas the "out" groups scheme to overturn it. Even though the RUF rebellion is not ethnic and the RUF (more Eastern and Southern in composition) and AFRC (more Northern and Western Area) formed an alliance in pursuing a common goal, the conflict has had strong ethnic overtones among the key civil political elites.

The second problem is the failure of the government to develop a coherent and effective security policy. The government's security policy has focused on the training of a professional army, including re-engagement of former RSLMF soldiers. As a result, there has been a serious problem in the recruitment and preparation of citizens for the war; the authorities emphasize professional training methods, conventional skills formation, and military hierarchy. The rebels on the other hand seem to have few problems in replenishing and expanding their military stock by abducting young men in the territories they overrun. It's a classic case of elitism being unable to confront popular,[3] albeit brutal, methods of warfare. Indeed, the failure of the government to make national defense a civic duty renders it dependent on external military forces.

The third problem relates to the failure to address the country's huge youth crisis. Even after two violent interruptions on the life of the government, there has been no systematic, comprehensive and well-funded plan to address the youth crisis in the country. The RUF rebellion is a product of a phenomenal youth crisis that dates back to the long period of misrule of the All People's Congress. The youth crisis is linked to the collapse of the national economy, employment opportunities, and access to education. The demobilization program has been insufficient to lure youths away from the RUF and the AFRC who now control the key mining areas of the country.

The paper is divided into six parts. The next section provides a background to the conflict; section three discusses an outline of the government's strategic policy; section four examines the failure of the strategy; and section five the new twin-track policy. Section six concludes the study by examining the pitfalls of the country's majoritarian presidential democracy as well as the need for democratizing access to military security, redefining ECOMOG's peacekeeping role, and youth rehabilitation.

BACKGROUND TO THE CONFLICT

The Sierra Leone war started when a small group of RUF rebels invaded the country from Liberia on 23 March 1991 and occupied the Eastern border village of Bomaru. The invasion was seen then as Charles Taylor's revenge against the decision of the All People's Congress (APC) government's decision to support ECOMOG's operation in Liberia. However, current research suggests that the invasion could have happened even if Sierra Leone had not participated in the Liberian conflict.[4] Foday Sankoh's RUF and Taylor's National Patriotic Front of Liberia (NPFL) had resolved to assist each other in their plans to overthrow their respective governments. Members of both movements had met in military training camps in Benghazi, Libya, and received the support of Muamar Qaddafi, who was looking for allies to overcome the West's containment of his regime.

The RUF is a product of the recurring conflicts between the explicitly violent government of the APC and increasingly radicalized students in the 1970s and 1980s.[5] A large number of students and three faculty members were expelled in 1985 following violent student demonstrations. Some of the students continued their studies at the University of Ghana, Legon. Growing links with Libyan intelligence officials in the region ultimately led some of the students to undertake military training in Benghazi for a planned "revolution" against a corrupt and dictatorial regime in Sierra Leone. Foday Sankoh, who had been retired as a corporal from the RSLMF in the 1970s on an alleged coup plot, later linked up with the leadership of the Ghana group that was organizing the Benghazi trips.

From Abdullah's account, most of those who trained in Benghazi had a troubled educational and social background, and were heavily involved in drugs. Their life styles have been described as *lumpen,* or in local parlance *raray man.* The student organizations later broke with the movement even before Sankoh launched the invasion in 1991. The movement recruited marginal youths engaged in artisanal mining *(san san boys)* and alienated rural youth who were contemptuous of traditional authority;[6] it also abducted and drugged children to produce vicious behavior. But the fuzzy pan-African radicalism of the student movement left its mark: it continued to espouse issues of equality, liberation, and anti-corruption even when its barbaric war practices vastly contradicted its rhetoric.[7]

In April 1992, after twenty-four years in office, young soldiers who were active in the war front against the RUF overthrew the APC government. They proceeded to form the National Provisional Ruling Council under the leadership of Captain Valentine Strasser. Rashid has analyzed the common urban youth values that connect the RUF and the soldiers in the NPRC.[8] With the state's inability to contain the rebellion, civilians in the East and South organized a people's militia to supplement the efforts of the army. Relations between the army and the *kamajoi* militia were acrimonious but manageable. Pressures for democratic rule intensified in 1995 as citizens came to associate the problems of the war with the army itself. Strasser's deputy, Brigadier Maada Bio, who opened negotiations with the RUF and held elections in February, 1996, which Tejan Kabbah won, overthrew Strasser in January 1996. The transfer of power to Kabbah required the retirement of the top cadres of the NPRC from the army. Their exit returned the balance of power in the military to what it was under the APC. Soldiers with Northern ethnic links regained strength: this intensified the tensions between the army and the *kamajoi* as both sides accused each other either of sabotage or excessive favors from the government.

Kabbah signed a peace agreement with the RUF in Abidjan in November 1996, but Sankoh later reneged on it.[9] The army overthrew the Kabbah government on 25 May 1997, and a major, Johnny Paul Koroma, who was awaiting trial on an attempted coup, was asked to head the regime.[10] The new Armed Forces Revolutionary Council invited the RUF to join their regime; Sankoh was made Deputy President and several RUF members were given posts. Politicians, civil servants, lawyers, businesspersons and other members of the elite who felt alienated from the new Sierra Leone People's Party (SLPP)-led Kabbah government joined or supported the AFRC. A larger proportion of these individuals were of Northern and Western Area origin. ECOMOG later got rid of the violent and predatory AFRC/RUF regime after six days of battle in Freetown on 12 February 1998 and Kabbah was returned to power on March 10.

OUTLINE OF THE GOVERNMENT'S STRATEGIC POLICY

The restored government's strategic policy had three core elements: dependence on ECOMOG; efforts to create a new national army that included "trusted" soldiers of the disbanded RSLMF; and support for local Civil Defense Forces (the CDF). The policy aimed to achieve four basic objectives: to delegitimize the RUF and AFRC; to uphold the rule of law and constitutionality; to defend the government's electoral mandate; and to defeat the rebellion.

Dependence on ECOMOG

Before the military overthrew the elected government on 25 May 1997, ECOMOG was not engaged in the Sierra Leone conflict. ECOWAS (Economic Community of West African States) established ECOMOG as a military observer group in Liberia in August 1990 when that country's war reached a stalemate and widespread atrocities against the civilian population became routine. During the time of the coup, the only foreign soldiers in Sierra Leone were a small contingent of Nigerian troops stationed at the presidential lodge. These soldiers had been posted to Sierra Leone under a bilateral agreement between the two governments (the Status of Forces Agreement). Nigerian troops were transported from Liberia to protect its endangered soldiers in Freetown and at the same time attempt to overturn the coup.

A meeting in Conakry of ECOWAS's Foreign Ministers on 27 June 1997 supported a three-pronged strategy to overturn the coup,[11] and at the ECOWAS Summit Meeting at Abuja on 28 and 29 August, a decision was taken to extend ECOMOG's action in Sierra Leone. The Security Council later endorsed ECOMOG's policies on the comprehensive embargo against the AFRC/RUF in its Resolution 1132 (1997). The main troop contributors to the ECOMOG force were Nigeria and Guinea. Many Francophone countries and Ghana were critical of the military operation but supported the embargo.

In policing the embargo, ECOMOG also tried to broker a peace settlement in Conakry in October 1997. The failure of the regime to honor the Conakry commitments forced ECOMOG to eject it from power in February, 1998. Nigerian military power was to constitute the centerpiece of the government's strategic policy. The hero of the ECOMOG operation, Max Khobe, was given the post of Chief of Defense Staff, since the army of the restored government had defected to the rebels. The down side of Khobe's appointment was that it placed Nigerian military officials in the driving seat of strategic policymaking. Khobe's relations with the Deputy Defense Minister, Hinga Norman, were not always cordial. The success of the ECOMOG component of the government's policy depended on continued Nigerian support, ECOMOG's ability to recapture and defend all major towns and villages, as well as forcing a quick surrender of the remaining AFRC/RUF rebels. It also depended on the willingness of Nigerian policymakers and soldiers to absorb high human and financial costs if the war dragged on.

Creation of a New Army

It took six months after its restoration to power for the government to unveil the other components of its defense policy. The Sierra Leone army had expanded from about three thousand before the war to more than fourteen thousand in 1996. Most of the new recruits had troubled social backgrounds.[12] Low pay and poor provisioning encouraged the bulk of the lower ranks to terrorize and appropriate the personal assets of local people. Senior ranks were also guilty of disloyalty and diamond resource extraction at the war front.[13]

The government held consultations with the public and parliament to popularize its new defense policy. Its proposed new army was to constitute a force of five thousand,[14] with twenty percent drawn from the ex-RSLMF. The policy was based on the belief that a new army that was properly screened and trained to respect the ethics of soldiery and civil authority was unlikely to destabilize the country. Recruitment was to be based on "strict requirements" and "favorable character reference" from notable traditional authorities. Military service was no longer to be a permanent vocation, but would be based on fixed-term contracts renewable every six years.

The president defended the policy of re-engaging 1,000 ex-RSLMF soldiers on the basis of costs. In the words of Kabbah, "it takes eight to nine years for a cadet to become a captain"; "you can therefore imagine the length of time it takes to train a Brigadier." Given the small number of soldiers that would constitute the new elite army, the success of the policy depended on an expanded ECOMOG force, or on the ability of ECOMOG to end the war relatively quickly so that the new army could operate as a postconflict defense force. A force of 5,000 would not have been able to check a rebel group that now included most of the soldiers of the ex-military and the RUF. The "new army" policy also depended on whether the re-engaged ex-RSLMF soldiers would remain loyal to the government and ECOMOG.

Formalization of the Civil Defense Force

The civil defense force first emerged as the *kamajoi* movement in the South and East of the country. The *kamajoi* militia was formed as a rural-based people's militia movement to compensate for failed state policies in providing security in areas that had been devastated by war. In 1996, just before the Abidjan peace accord was signed, the *kama-joi* militia had the RUF on the run, and many believed it was their success that forced the RUF to sign the Abidjan accord. During much of the first year of the elected government's tenure in office, there were a number of military encounters between the *kamajoisia* and the military, forcing the government to set up a commission of enquiry on the issue.[15]

The *kamajoi* movement itself was predated by the *tamaboro* of northeast Sierra Leone, who were recruited to help defend villages in the East. As the war spread to other parts of the country other local defense forces were also formed — such as the *donso* of Kono and the *kapra* in the North. But the *kamajoisia* remained the largest and best organized. When the AFRC and RUF seized power in May 1997, efforts were made by the ousted government to transform these disparate forces into a single civil defense force under the supervision of the deputy defense minister, Hinga Norman. Norman had played a central role in the evolution of the *kamajoi* movement itself. Indeed, the *kamajoi* is believed to owe total loyalty to him.[16] It has been repeatedly suggested that one of the reasons why the civil defense force does not feature prominently in the overall strategy of the government is because of the lack of control of the president over this force. Strengthening this force was seen as undermining the president's grip on power and consolidating that of his deputy defense minister.

In the document that announced the new security policy, the president acknowledged the positive role of the CDF and called for its formalization as a subsidiary force to the new army. Every district was to have a civil defense force which would "report directly to their paramount chiefs." There would also be in each district a CDF Administrator who would work with the military on matters such as training and logistics for CDF participation in national crises. The CDF was conceived as a network of auxiliary local forces, each of which should only be mobilized when a district or chiefdom was attacked. It should "supplement the efforts of the Army and the local police in the defense of their chiefdoms."

Although effort was made to create civil defense forces in various parts of the country, the concept failed to gain much ground in much of the country. No such force was established in the capital. In the North and large parts of the East, effective local defense forces were restricted to only a few towns: for instance, Masingbi in the North and Kenema town in the East. The only areas where the civil defense forces were entrenched were the four districts in the South: Bo, Pujehun, Bonthe, and Moyamba. Besides, the civil defense forces continued to use regional or ethnic labels: *kapra* in the North, *donso* in Kono and *kamajoi* in the South and East. Even when a new force was created in the North to complement the work of the *kapra,* it was given an ethnic label: *gbenthis.*[17] Part of the ethnicization of the civil defense force could be attributed to the strategic policy itself, which perceived civil defense as a fragmented and localized issue. In the government's conception of security the only *national* defense force would be the new army. Presidential power and prestige would be based on the elite army—not on a mass-based CDF.

Delegitimation of the AFRC/RUF

A primary goal of the strategic policy outlined above was the delegitimation of the AFRC/RUF. It is important to put this issue of delegitimation in perspective. For much of the period of the war the RUF was seen by all geoethnic sections of society as illegitimate, barbaric and destructive. One strand of the discourse that helped to stiffen local resistance in the South and East was an elite-driven view that the RUF was an "APC/Northern" device to exterminate the peoples of the South and East, or more specifically the Mende. The fact that the RUF was headed by a Northerner, Foday Sankoh, helped to reinforce this view in the minds of those who believed it even though the vast majority of the RUF fighters came from those two regions. Residents in the North and Western Area on the other hand saw the RUF as a "Mende movement" formed to wrest power from the APC and subsequently Strasser's NPRC military regime; it didn't matter in the perception of individuals who held these views that Strasser's government had a very large number of Mendes and that the war continued even when a Mende (Brigadier Julius Maada Bio) took power from Strasser (a Krio).

Under the Abidjan peace accord of November 1996, the RUF gained legitimacy for the first time. It was absolved of all crimes it had committed in war; it was given an opportunity to convert itself into a political party which donors would help fund; its fighters were given the option to join a restructured army or be resettled in productive civilian life; and it was allowed to send representatives to such institutions as the electoral commission and the peace commission. The RUF was delegitimized again after the overthrow of the elected government and the participation of the RUF in the AFRC regime. The high point of the delegitimation was the travel embargo imposed on key members of both groups by the United Nations Security Council and ECOWAS. Delegitimation slammed the door on dialogue; former soldiers and RUF fighters would only be given favorable treatment if they surrendered.

Upholding the Rule of Law and Constitutionality

Closely related to the goal of delegitimizing the RUF and AFRC was the uncompromising stand taken by the government to uphold the law and defend the constitutional order and its mandate. A large number of elites had been apprehended after the ECO-MOG expulsion of the AFRC from Freetown. These included lawyers, civil servants, academics, journalists, senior army officers, businesspersons, community leaders, and politicians. Some had occupied strategic posts in the AFRC/RUF regime in defiance of the society's rejection of the regime, and others had collaborated with the regime in various not-so-strategic ways. Upholding the law meant subjecting these people to public trials. There were two types of trials: military court martial, which did not have a right of appeal; and treason trials in civil courts.

Four problems emerged as the legal process unfolded. First, there was a loud outcry from family members and sections of the public that many of those arrested played no roles in the coup—that issues relating to competition for jobs and local disputes might have influenced arrest patterns. Second, there were not enough judges to provide speedy trials. This meant individuals, including apparently innocent ones, were held in prison for long periods while awaiting reviews of their cases. Third, whilst most of the guilty civilians were perceived to have committed crimes against the country, many argued they should not have been charged with treason. Critics stated that civilians did not actually participate in the coup, that they only served the regime, and that it was not uncommon for civilians to serve military regimes.[18] Fourth, there was a general perception that the "prison list" of about 3,000, as well as the lists of those brought to trial (120), and those executed (24), were heavily skewed against elites from the North and Western Area. It was reckoned that more than sixty percent of elites who were tried were of Northern and Western Area origin. The trials widened the ethnopolitical divide and undermined efforts to create a united front against the rebels.

THE FAILURE OF THE STRATEGIC POLICY

The success or failure of public policies is not always easy to determine. In many cases objectives may not be rigorously defined or outcomes easily quantifiable. There is also a time dimension in the evaluation of policies. The most astonishing thing about the Sierra Leone war was the rapid collapse of the government's strategic policy less than ten months after its restoration to power. The new security plan was unveiled with much confidence in September, 1998. On 23 November of the same year, the president told the BBC that the war would end "way before the end of the year." By 6 January 1999 the government had lost Freetown to the rebels for a second time, and virtually the entire Northern region, Kono, Kailahun, and most of Kenema district. It is important to capture in some detail the full import of this failure and the tragedy which it portended.

Loss of Mineral Resource Base and Territories

Kono and the Tongo area in Kenema district constitute the centerpiece of diamond production in the country. During the 1960s and 1970s, diamonds accounted for about sixty-one percent of the country's foreign exchange. Today, production is virtually dominated by small- and medium-sized groups, many operating informally.[19] Official diamond exports declined from 2 million carats in 1970 to 132,000 carats in 1989.[20] It is believed that the value of Sierra Leone's diamonds that are traded in diamond markets is worth between US $200 million and US $600 million a year. One source reports that even though Liberia can only produce sixty thousand carats of diamonds a year, it exported 8.3 million carats (about US $601 million) to Belgium between 1997 and 1998.[21] The loss of Koidu in the third week of December meant the rebels could recruit more local miners or young unemployed men to join its rebellion in exchange for armed protection. It facilitated greater Liberian involvement in the war. More than sixty thousand Liberian youths carried the guns of various factions during that country's eight years of civil war. The capture of Kono by the RUF and AFRC was a huge opportunity for these ex-rebels to be exported to Sierra Leone.[22]

The control of Kono and Tongo meant the rebels could tap into international criminal or underground networks that make money out of the misfortunes of countries in conflict. The diamonds of Kono and Tongo could be exchanged for guns, drugs, and mercenaries. There were persistent reports from the local and international press of captured or dead mercenaries after the 6 January invasion. For instance, a lieutenant colonel in the Israeli reserve army, Ya'ir Klein, was among the foreign mercenaries arrested after the invasion. He was indicted by the Colombian government in 1989 on charges of providing arms and military training to one of Colombia's main drug cartels, the Medellin. *The Times* of London of February 11 reported that the rebels recruited "300 Ukrainian mercenaries and hundreds of soldiers from Burkina Faso." A criminal syndicate involving Neo-Nazis from South Africa was also implicated.

Considerable pressure has also been put on the government for lucrative mining concessions or favors: the Sandline affair which involved mining concessions to a British mercenary outfit, Sandline International, and a Thai financier (wanted on alleged criminal charges in Canada) for provision of arms to the civil defense force;[23] pressures by Executive Outcomes for contracts to defend mining sectors;[24] and recent government concessions to Branch Energy to carry out mining operations in areas that are still under rebel control. There is strong competition among mercenaries and dubious companies for Sierra Leone's resources: one section supports the rebels and another the government.[25]

When the strategic policy statement was announced in September 1998, the government was in control of all major towns and, by a rough estimate, more than eighty percent of the country. By 6 January 1999 when the rebels attacked Freetown, most of the North was either under their control or effectively outside of government hands. The same was true of Kono, Kailahun, and much of Kenema. Before the signing of the ceasefire agreement in May, travel to and from the capital was by helicopter. The loss of these territories to the rebels resulted in the fragmentation of the state, with serious consequences for political stability, food security, national integration, and the prosecution of the war itself. Most of the North as well as Kono, Kailahun, and parts of Kenema districts have become no-go areas with widespread rebel atrocities against civilians being reported routinely.

State or territorial fragmentation could further degenerate into social and political fragmentation. Influential Northern politicians located outside the country, who were accused of collaborating with the rebels, had problems reconnecting with the political process at home. Their main objective was to fight their way back into the political process. The territorial gains of the rebels offered an opportunity. Their pronouncements on the war and the atrocities of the AFRC/RUF have been ambiguous. They have been totally opposed to the civil defense force (which they see as an ethnic army intended to defend the ruling party's grip on power) and ECOMOG's military activities. They have instead called for a cease-fire, dialogue, a transitional government, and a national conference to settle the dispute.

Disloyal Soldiers and Nigeria's Faltering Resolve

One of the remarkable features of this war was the government's commitment to the rehabilitation of an army that consistently has proven to be disloyal even under the rule of the NPRC. Many—though not all—of the rehabilitated soldiers proved disloyal in the battles for key Northern towns in December 1998 and Freetown in January 1999. Makeni was lost partly because retrained soldiers turned their guns on Nigerian troops. It is believed that an entire battalion of Nigerian troops may have perished because of this treachery. After the fall of Makeni in late December, the resolve or morale of the Nigerian troops collapsed. More than twelve hundred Nigerian soldiers were believed to have been killed between late December 1998 and January 1999. When the rebels attacked Freetown on 6 January, there were no Nigerian or ECOMOG troops in Freetown proper. They had retreated to the barracks at Wilberforce, Juba, Murray Town, Lungi, and the military headquarters at Cockeril.[26]

The political situation in Nigeria was also undergoing dramatic changes. Even though Nigeria had always taken a strong interest in subregional and continental affairs, ECOMOG occupied a special position in Sani Abacha's political strategy. Despised at home and ostracized internationally, he needed a success story to soften criticism of his regime. His dramatic death in June 1998 changed the situation. The new leader, Abdulsalam Abubakar, seemed less enthusiastic about the operation. Even when the eastern suburbs of Freetown were still under rebel control, Abubakar announced that his goal was to have all Nigerian troops withdrawn from Sierra Leone before his tenure expired on 29 May 1999. During the presidential elections in March all the candidates of the three main parties severely criticized Nigeria's involvement in the Sierra Leone war. Olusegun Obasanjo stated in an interview on 21 February 1999 that he "wondered what (Nigerians) are doing in Sierra Leone and Liberia when Nigeria is peaceful and after all, the nation's wealth is being wasted." The joint All Peoples Party/Alliance for Democracy presidential candidate, Olu Falae, also stated he would withdraw Nigerian troops within a year of assuming power. Influential foreign leaders had to exert pressure on Obasanjo and Abubakar to provide assurances that Nigerian withdrawal from Sierra Leone would not be premature.

Opposition to ECOMOG runs deep in Nigeria. Vocal groups, especially those in the Southwest, who were viscerally opposed to Abacha, questioned the failure to provide information about the financial and human costs of the operation. There was also strong opposition to a policy that was draining the Nigerian budget of about one million dollars a day when the country's basic infrastructure and social services were in ruins. The collapse of oil prices by forty percent in late 1998 and early 1999 also contributed to the weakening of the Nigerian military establishment's commitment to the Sierra Leone operation.

Collapse of the Legal Order

The 6 January invasion led to the release of hundreds of political and other prisoners from the central prisons. Those released included prominent figures who served under, or advised, the AFRC regime and were awaiting the outcomes of appeals on their death sentences. A large number of surrendered soldiers were also released. Many willingly handed themselves back to ECOMOG, but a substantial number fled with the rebels, including former president, Joseph Momoh. The legal order that underpinned the government's strategic policy was shattered. The Central Investigations Department, where records on the trials were believed to have been kept, was razed to the ground. About two hundred fifty policemen and one prominent lawyer were killed; and eighty percent of all police offices were destroyed. Rebels searched desperately for magistrates, judges and lawyers of the government's prosecution team. Most fled or went underground, including the Chief Justice, Desmond Luke, whose house was burnt down. The Chief Justice only returned to the country in April 1999; and the magistrate courts started operating on 12 April 1999 only when the government accepted the demands of judges and magistrates for ECOMOG soldiers to guard their homes and offices.

THE NEW TWIN-TRACK STRATEGIC POLICY INITIATIVE

With the collapse of the legal and security order, the government announced a new two-track policy initiative in January 1999: the vigorous pursuit of dialogue with the AFRC/RUF and intensification of the military offensive. At the core of the new initiative was the gradual relegitimization of the RUF. Foday Sankoh would be released to consult with his commanders in Lomé and offered prospects of eventual pardon on his death sentence if he and his movement could reciprocate and embrace peace. There are problems with the policy itself.

Dialogue

As the twin-track policy unfolded it became clear that dialogue was reluctantly accepted, not willingly embraced. Many government spokespersons, including the finance, information, justice, and deputy defense ministers, as well as the president, initially called for tough action against the states that were believed to support the RUF: Liberia, Burkina Faso, Libya, and Ukraine. The dialogue policy was ultimately imposed on the government by Nigeria, Britain, the US, and key officials within the United Nations. Nigerian official pronouncements during much of January, February, and March emphasized dialogue as the principal way of ending the conflict. Britain announced it would tie its £10 million aid program to progress in the pursuit of dialogue. The United Nations representative in Sierra Leone, Francis Okello, was emphatic about the need for dialogue to restore the authority of the government and end the war. In short, after 6 January, the balance of international opinion shifted in favor of dialogue and relegitimization of the RUF/AFRC.

Once the government finally became convinced of dialogue, it worked hard to make it comprehensive. Foday Sankoh would be allowed to use government facilities to talk to his fighters in the bush; he would also be given conditional release to discuss with his commanders in Lomé and hammer out a policy position that would lead to negotiations with the government; the government would try to mend relations with Liberia by exchanging ambassadors and encouraging civic groups in both countries to visit each other's capital and hold meetings with important leaders; plans to have Liberia and Burkina Faso condemned at the United Nations were dropped; the government established diplomatic relations with, and bought two helicopter gunships from, Ukraine; and it was decided not to oppose Togo's policy of involving Libya, the original training ground of the RUF, in the proposed Lomé talks. The government also mobilized civil society groups in Freetown to support the new dialogue policy.[27]

However, the dialogue policy was pursued from a position of weakness. About seventy percent of the country, including the key mining areas, was outside of government control when Sankoh met his RUF/AFRC comrades in Lomé in 18 April 1999, and the strategic highway that links the capital to the rest of the country was in rebel hands. Pressures from the UN, the UK, and the US led to a cease-fire agreement on 18 May, which took effect on 24 May 1999. The agreement effectively transformed the AFRC/RUF into *de jure* legitimate players in the conflict and implicitly conferred on them the right to hold on to territories under their control until a peaceful settlement was reached or the talks broke down.

Territory, Resources, and Civilization

The key issue in the dialogue policy was whether the AFRC/RUF would heed the strong calls for lasting peace. The AFRC/RUF's policy document demands a four-year transitional government that will include the AFRC/RUF; amnesty for all AFRC/RUF fighters and political prisoners, including those awaiting appeals on their death sentences; withdrawal of all foreign troops; and organization of elections in four years. Firstly, the RUF has always failed to honor commitments made in peace accords. The Abidjan accord stalled when Sankoh refused to send representatives to the key disarmament committee that would have helped UN officials disarm RUF fighters. This was despite the fact that four of his representatives were already working with the government in another important committee—the peace commission.[28] Similarly, even though the AFRC/RUF signed the Conakry accord in October 1997, the regime refused to allow ECOMOG to disarm the ex-RSLMF soldiers and RUF rebels.

Secondly, and ominously, events in Africa and elsewhere suggest that dialogue has only produced the intended results when rebels have used territory as a mechanism to cleanse their record of atrocities and provide a backup for deals that emerge from negotiated settlements. Contemporary rebels, who deliberately use terror as an instrument of war, are aware that their atrocities have alienated them from society. The examples of Mozambique, Liberia, and Angola suggest that effective territorial control and access to resources can encourage rebel groups to return to some form of civility and test their public support in elections. Control of territory over long periods may compel rebels to find ways other than brute force to administer the areas under their control. The scale of violence is likely to decline the longer rebels remain in charge of territories. Decline in violence is not the same as absence of arbitrariness and occasional lawlessness.

Control over territory is, however, not enough to instill civility in rebels who are accustomed to terror and predation. An additional factor is needed: resources or finance. Rebel wars have their own economic dynamic; rebels have to survive to fight wars. They can both extract the resources of the land and exchange the proceeds for food or they can prey directly on the food produced by the local population. If rebels have alternative sources of income to pay for their food they are less likely to terrorize peasants or rural populations. They would seek instead to use their acquired resources to build up patronage networks among their subject population for ultimate political support and power.

The NPFL controlled most of the Liberian countryside as well as the diamonds and key timber and rubber plantations. These resources were valued at well over US$300m a year between 1990 and 1994.[29] With such money, Taylor's NPFL did not need to disturb the peasants very much. The violence of the NPFL in the areas it controlled dropped substantially as the rebel leaders focused on building their resource base and political support among the subject population. The money received from these resources was used to set up a patronage system, which, when combined with threats of a resumption of war, paid off in the elections, in which the NPFL received a stunning seventy-five percent of the votes.

A similar situation occurred in Mozambique. In this case, however, Dlakhama's REN-AMO (Mozambique National Resistance) was dependent on South Africa to finance its brutal war. After it had secured much territory in the northern and central parts of the country, it was able to scale down its atrocities and exploit the country's South-North divisions to win support among the people in the northern and central provinces. The rebels later replaced South African money with donor peace-building funds, which helped them to consolidate their hold on the central and northern provinces. They eventually won 44.8 percent of the parliamentary seats and a majority of the provinces despite their early history of atrocities.

Savimbi's UNITA (National Union for the Total Independence of Angola) in Angola also relied more on the proceeds from diamonds than extraction of resources from peasant communities to conduct its war. This helped his movement to win the confidence of the local population, including a large number of professionals. The movement scored about thirty-four percent of the votes in the elections of 1991, with most of these votes gained in the areas under its rule. However, Savimbi reneged on the peace agreement, refused to surrender the territories under his control, and went back to war. A lesson here is that rebel control of resources may encourage its political representatives to opt for an win-all strategy or resistance to power sharing arrangements that denies them access to their acquired resource base.

The AFRC/RUF are unlikely to honor or fully comply with a power-sharing agreement without territorial and resource support. Territory helps to restore civility and offers power to defend gains in a power-sharing agreement; and resources may facilitate a scaling down of terror and prospects of winning the people's confidence. Complete disarmament, the goal of the Lomé appeasement, seems a forlorn hope.

War and Security

Before the Lomé agreement was signed, the other half of the new strategic policy initiative involved the intensification of the military offensive. This strategy had several important elements: financial, technical, and logistical support from foreign sources; reorganization of ECOMOG; training of a new army; increased support for the civil defense forces; and selective use of mercenaries. The external dimension of the strategy included the government's efforts to increase the number of countries with troop contributions to ECOMOG. Ghana and Mali were prevailed upon to join Nigeria and Guinea in ECOMOG. Western countries agreed to finance the participation of Mali and Ghana in ECOMOG. There was a scaling up of the UK government's support to the Sierra Leone government and ECOMOG by sharing intelligence and providing logistics and training, including increased financial support for ECOMOG by the US and Canada.

Given the uncertainties that now surrounded Nigerian participation in the conflict, a decision was taken to train a new army rapidly. The government reverted to its failed security policy of 2 September 1998: only five thousand soldiers would be trained for the new army, and about two hundred surrendered soldiers who were believed to be loyal would be recruited into the force. Five hundred out of the five thousand soldiers would be trained as cadets in Nigeria and the rest by Britain and Nigeria in Sierra Leone. There are conceptual and practical reasons why a professional army is unsuited for the Sierra Leonean and other African conflicts. National security is everywhere a public good—once it has been provided no section of society can be deprived of its benefits; it is also a monopoly good that is not easily exposed to contestable or market pressures. The monopoly status of security provision gives real powers to those who are put in charge—they are the only legitimate group to carry weapons in defense of the nation or community. New institutional analysis teaches that there are principal-agent problems in all collective actions or public goods provisioning. Agents may behave opportunistically or principals may free ride. With regards to a country's army, the principals are the government and the public, whereas the agent is the army.

Three problems are likely to emerge in military-government-civil relations. First, an army may appropriate rent—higher-than-normal salaries, better perks, etc. Second, it may take over the property of the state and become both the agent and the principal. Third, it may be used by one of the principals—government—to terrorize the other principal, the public. These three developments have informed much of Africa's independence history: soldiers have enjoyed a higher standard of provisioning than average citizens; they have staged more than seventy-five coups since 1960; 42.5 percent of current African leaders first came to power by military means; and governments have repeatedly used armies to quell demonstrations by the public or harass critics.

An additional problem relates to the methods which African governments have employed to solve the principal-agent problem: skewing recruitment in the army in favor of groups that are perceived as loyal, and placing relations or individuals with shared ethnicity in strategic posts. We call this the *personal trust solution,* to be distinguished from professionalization. Given the fear of state take-over by soldiers, governments are unlikely to pursue a policy of ethnic balance in the army, however much they pay lip service to the idea. They are likely to be distrustful of soldiers who have a different ethnicity from the president's or that of his core support base. In the case of Sierra Leone, it is instructive that the Chief of Defense Staff, Max Khobe, has complained that politicians and elites are trying to use ethnicity to sponsor candidates to the new army.[30]

An alternative solution to the principal-agent problem, prevalent in advanced democracies, is professionalization. Professionalization aims to get soldiers to respect civic authority and the democratic system. Professionalization requires resources, incentives, and civic readiness to defend the democratic order. Many of these requirements are in short supply in most African countries with poor economies and weak institutions. Setting up professional armies under conditions of widespread poverty and undeveloped civic institutions is likely to further enhance the power of the professional armies to disregard the mission and interests of the principals and carry out coups. Nigeria is a perfect example of a country where professionalization has improved the skills and capacity of the military to overthrow governments.

Finally, most contemporary wars in Africa deliberately target civilians. These wars are often determined by numbers and simple techniques of self-defense or aggression rather than by superior skills, high-tech, or enhanced training. Superior skills and experience may tilt the balance in a nonconventional war only when the people are fully mobilized to defend themselves and their neighborhoods.

CONCLUSION AND ALTERNATIVES

This paper has highlighted the complex issues which led to the failure of the government's strategic policy on 6 January 1999 and the problems that are likely to affect the current twin-track policy. A salient feature of the policy failure is the fragmentation of the state and its potential to degenerate into social and political disintegration. How can instability, fragmentation and disintegration be overcome? We conclude the paper with a discussion of these issues.

The Pitfalls of Majoritarian and Presidential Democracy

A central issue that has undermined efforts to overcome the rebellion relates to the country's majoritarian presidential system of government. Majoritarian presidential rule has several problems: a dual mandate (executive versus legislature), which can produce a political gridlock;[31] rigidities in removing leaders who have failed to perform in moments of great crisis; extremely limited choice of alternatives (only one: the vice president) if a leader steps down or is removed; and the obvious lack of incentives for plural governance. Evidence from political science suggests that parliamentary forms of democracy have a higher survival rate than presidential ones. Among OECD (Organization for Economic Cooperation and Development) countries, only one country has a presidential system, two have mixed systems and two have semi-presidential arrangements, the rest are parliamentary democracies. A study by Stepan and Skatch, which examined 53 developing countries that tried democratic forms of rule between 1973 and 1989, found that more presidential (forty percent) than parliamentary (eighteen percent) systems experienced a military coup.[32] The survival rate of parliamentary systems was sixty-one percent whereas that for presidential systems was twenty percent.

In Sierra Leone's democratic elections of 1996,[33] the only major institutional change was the electoral rule on proportional representation, and the decision to bar parliamentarians from crossing over to other parties that did not sponsor them in the elections. The acceptance of proportional representation had more to do with the impossibility of conducting constituency-based elections under conditions of war than in a genuine desire to promote proportionality. Parties were each required to submit ranked lists of 60 members for parliamentary elections. Although the electoral rules called for geographical representation in party membership and regionally mixed candidates on party slates for presidential elections, the question of how party lists were to be ranked for parliamentary elections was left entirely to the discretion of registered parties.[34]

In the parliamentary elections, no single party had an absolute majority of the votes, even though the Sierra Leone People's Party (SLPP) won the highest number of seats in the six-party parliament. Also, in the first round of the presidential elections, there was no candidate with a plurality of the votes. However, a second round of voting that required only a contest between the top two candidates produced a winner with about sixty percent of the votes.[35] Thus the elections produced a very plural parliament and a formally monolithic presidency. The two largest parties, the SLPP and the United National People's Party (UNPP), were unable to capture all the votes in their core support areas. Indeed, the other eleven parties accounted for 42.2 percent of the votes, but the voting patterns per province reflected the country's ethnopolitical divide: the SLPP and the smaller National Unity Party (NUP), both of which were seen as Southern and Eastern parties, got the bulk of their votes in the South and East; the Democratic Centre Party (DCP), which had its base in the eastern mining district of Kono, scored predominantly in that district; and the UNPP, People's Democratic Party (PDP), and APC, which were regarded as Northern parties, won most of their votes in the North. In Freetown, the contest was a three-way race between the SLPP, the UNPP, and the PDP. Even in the second round of voting, although Tejan Kabbah of the SLPP scored a higher number of the overall votes, he did not win a majority in any district in the North. Karefa-Smart of the UNPP also performed dismally in the South and East.

It is instructive to note that the results of the 1967 elections were very similar to those of 1996. Although the All Peoples Congress won the largest number of seats (32), this was only marginally better than the SLPP's tally of 28 seats; six seats were won by independents. Again, the APC won all seats in the North as well as the capital, and most of the seats in Kono; the SLPP won most of the seats in the South and two districts in the East. Four of the independents were defectors from the SLPP in the South and East. This bipolarity may be functionally related to the ethnic structure of the country. The two largest ethnic groups, the Mende and Temne, are roughly equal in size and account for slightly over 60 percent of the population. The two groups are also geographically separated, with the Mende located in the South and East and the Temne in the North. All the non-Mende groups in the South and East are each less than five percent of the population. In the North, the Limba account for about 8.4 percent of the national population whereas other groups are less than four percent each. This pattern of ethnic distribution in which the two largest groups vastly outnumber other groups in their respective regions may explain why most groups in the South coalesce around the Mende; whereas those in the North revolve around the Temne, although the Limba, especially under Momoh's presidency (a Limba), have made efforts to change this dynamic.[36]

Table 7.1
Distribution of Seats in the Elections of 1967

SLPP	28
APC	32
Independents	6

Table 7.2
Distribution of Votes among Main Parties, Parliamentary Elections of 1996

Party	Northern Province	Southern Province	Eastern Province	Western Area	Total	%
SLPP	10,331	119,518	84,712	55,327	269,888	36.1
NUP	3,989	3,292	17,450	14,554	39,285	5.3
DCP	2,231	504	30,426	2,465	35,632	4.8
UNPP	98,054	3,426	15,137	47,516	165,219	21.6
PDP	48,697	7,081	2,996	48,076	114,429	15.3
APC	18,438	1,761	2,996	19,272	42,467	5.7

Note: Total votes cast were 750,888. Seven other parties, which failed to gain the required five percent of the national votes, are unrepresented in parliament. These parties accounted for 83,938 votes or about 11.2% of the votes cast. Three of these parties, which account for more than seventy percent of the these votes, drew their support from the North and Western Area; two others received votes largely from the Western Area; and the remaining two from the South/East and Western Area.

Politics is likely to be bifurcated if two relatively equal and politicized ethnic groups constitute more than half of the population. The most extreme examples of bifurcation are Rwanda and Burundi.[37] We refer to this type of bipolarity as a *two-ethnic bipolarity*. Sierra Leone presents a different type of bifurcation, which may be called a *multi-ethnic bipolarity*. In Rwanda and Burundi, the two groups are greatly unequal in size (85 percent:15 percent), are not geographically separated, and are hierarchically structured to breed a discourse of superiority and inferiority. Given the overwhelming numerical dominance of one group, bipolarity would have been avoided in Burundi and Rwanda if other smaller groups had existed in addition to the two groups. Botswana, Lesotho, Swaziland, Madagascar, Equatorial Guinea, and a number of countries in Asia, such as Mongolia, Brunei, Bangladesh, and China, have ethnic social structures where one group accounts for more than seventy percent of the population; but politics in these countries has not taken bipolar ethnic dimensions. Instead, intraethnic political divisions or competition have informed their politics, especially in countries that have been democratizing. We refer to this type of ethnic structure as *unipolar.*

When countries in which three large groups that are roughly equal in size and constitute more than half of the population are examined, a pattern of *tripolar* politics emerges. The clearest example is Nigeria. Malawi is another example of tripolarity, although in this case it tends to have a much stronger regional accent. On the other hand, cases in which most ethnic groups are relatively equal in size or in which no single group is large enough to dominate electoral politics, *multipolarity*, produce a different dynamic: politics may still be influenced by ethnic considerations but the rigid bipolarity or tripolarity that one sees in the other two cases may disappear or be greatly reduced. In the dispersed multipolar set, ethnic politics is likely to be localized.

The more dispersed the ethnic structure, the more ethnic politics at the national level may resemble politics in unipolar settings. Intraethnic politics may be a strong current, and parties may have to appeal to a large cross section of ethnic groups to be electorally viable. Indeed, it has been possible in this set of countries for a single party, which effectively is an ethnic coalition party, to appeal across ethnic divides and win a majority of the votes—Tanzania, Zambia, and Liberia, for instance. Charles Taylor's stunning victory at the polls in Liberia would have been impossible under bipolar or tripolar conditions. From this perspective, Sankoh's RUF/AFRC will find it extremely difficult to repeat Taylor's feat in Sierra Leone short of taking over the government by force. Table 7.3 provides examples of countries in the five cases.

If politics takes a bipolar or tripolar dimension it requires great creativity and effort to construct political institutions that will reflect this diversity and rigidity. Under the constitution, the Sierra Leone president is under no obligation to appoint members of opposition groups in his or her cabinet. The office holder can govern in majoritarian ways even if he or she fails to win the mandate of the electorate as a candidate of first choice. Furthermore, even if the office holder seeks to appoint opposition members in the cabinet, he or she will be under great pressure from his/her party either to restrict appointments to party members or to tilt the appointments decisively in the party's favor. Party members behave this way because of the rules of the game: majoritarianism is an either/or contest. The rules do not encourage political actors to set limits on their demands: "it's our turn to rule; others should wait for their turn when they win elections." Alternatively, those who find themselves outside of power when they believe only a small margin of votes divides them from the winners are unlikely to play by the rules consistently; they will exploit opportunities to organize fresh polls or simply create or support instability.

Table 7.3

A Typology of Ethnic Structures in Africa with Illustrative Examples

Type	Number of ethnic groups	Share of pop. by largest group	Share of pop. by two largest groups	Share of pop. by three largest groups
Two-ethnic bipolarity				
Rwanda	2	90	99	100
Burundi	2	85	99	100
Multi-ethnic bipolarity				
Sierra Leone	20	30.9	60.7	69.1
Multi-ethnic tripolarity				
Nigeria	470	19	38	54
Malawi	15	32	47	58
Multi-ethnic unipolarity				
Botswana	30	70	80	82
Equatorial Guinea	12	75	77	79
Mauritania	8	77	83	84
Multipolarity				
Cameroon	279	5	9	11
Namibia	27	7	13	17
Central Afri. Rep.	68	10	17	23
Mozambique	33	14	23	31
Tanzania	131	15	30	34
Liberia	34	16	28	34

Note: I would like to thank Toshihiro Nakamura, Research Assistant at United Nations Research Institute for Social Development, for compiling the data. The raw data is compiled from the Ethnology Website at http://www.sil.org/ethnologue/

Sierra Leone's two great elections (1967 and 1996) have produced opportunistic behavior by losers on both sides of the geoethnic divide. In 1967 leaders of the SLPP conspired with the army, which was headed by David Lansana (an Easterner), to obstruct the mandate of the APC. The results were delayed and false figures were announced by the electoral office to give the impression of a tie, even though it was obvious that the APC had won, albeit by a slim majority.[38] Lansana instructed the current Deputy Defense Minister, Hinga Norman, who was the aide-de-camp to the Governor General, to detain the winners—Siaka Stevens and some members of his party—at State House when they were about to be sworn in as the new government.[39] Norman carried out the orders and Lansana took over the reins of power for a day before he was overthrown by other army officers. In 1996, when the SLPP won the elections, all six parties agreed to honor the results and took their seats in parliament, but the overthrow of the government in little over a year by the AFRC exposed serious opportunism on the part of leaders of the APC and UNPP. Many of the leaders and elite supporters of these parties failed to defend the democratic order and either joined the AFRC or offered advice to it. This split in the ranks of the national political elite has become endemic and threatens to undermine whatever efforts are taken to end the war.

Political Science has produced a formidable body of thought on institutions that can resolve problems associated with rigid bipolar or tripolar ethnopolitical structures.[40] Two institutional arrangements stand out as particularly important: *federalism* and *consociation,* or what is popularly known as *power sharing,* and electoral designs *for majoritarian outcomes.* Horowitz places more emphasis on electoral reforms, rather than on consociational and federalist arrangements, to create majoritarian but cross-ethnic governments. Creative electoral reforms, such as the alternative vote, the single transferable vote system, and rules on geographical distribution of votes which may encourage vote pulling across geopolitical divides, are useful. However, they may have very limited effects on rigidly bipolar political systems.

Our focus is mainly on the consociational aspects of institutional design. As Lijphart has pointed out, the principles of federalism are embedded in the theory of consociationalism.[41] Consociation has four key elements: a government of national unity, proportionality in the key public institutions, territorial autonomy, and minority veto. The first refers to a "grand coalition" of all the key political parties or elites that have gained seats in elections; the second is about balance in political representation and recruitment of individuals in the civil service and military; the third concerns decentralization or federalism; and the fourth is about the power of minority parties or elites to veto basic constitutional changes that are likely to affect their interests. The fourth element may be superfluous if the other three hold.[42]

The government of Tejan Kabbah started off as a coalition government even though he was under no constitutional obligation to form one. His party entered into an alliance with the PDP for the second round of elections and resulted in the award of five ministerial positions, ambassadorial posts, and parastatal board memberships to the latter. Tejan Kabbah also appointed the leaders of the NUP (John Karimu) and the DCP (Aiah Koroma) into the cabinet, and some members of the UNPP (Jim Funnah, for instance) served as advisers. He has tried to make his government reflect the national character of the country. In August 1998 he even wrote a letter to his party members reminding them that he was elected to serve Sierra Leone and not a section of the country.

The main problem, however, has been the lack of institutionalization of the efforts to create a balanced team in the governance of the country. The coalition with the PDP later degenerated into an informal alliance between Tejan Kabbah and the PDP leader, Thaimu Bangura.[43] Before Bangura's death in March 1999, he and Afsatu Kabbah were the only remaining members of the PDP in the government. Others had lost their posts during reshuffles. There were plans to remove Bangura from the leadership of the party because of the perceived loss of party influence in the government. The coalition was seen as serving only Bangura's interests—not that of the party as a whole.

There were also criticisms by Northern political elites that key politicians from the North, who happened to belong to other parties, were not represented in the cabinet. The split in the UNPP in 1996 is indeed related to the question of post sharing in the government which the leader, Karefa-Smart, had rejected since he wanted the presidency itself, but which his parliamentarians supported. Karefa-Smart later dismissed more than eighty percent of his MPs from the party. Under the new rules on parliamentary membership, this action would have led to their removal from parliament. The latter contested what was obviously a high-handed and self-serving move on the part of their leader. They collaborated with the SLPP and other party parliamentarians to suspend Karefa-Smart from parliament. This was a very unwise and dangerous move, as it alienated from the parliamentary process a political leader with forty-one percent of the popular mandate. When the AFRC struck in 1997 Karefa-Smart and members of his party wing flirted with the regime, opposed the ECOMOG intervention, and called for a national conference; his parliamentarians, however, condemned the coup.

Given Sierra Leone's rigidly bipolar politics there would seem to be no alternative to an institutionalized *unity government*. An institutionalized unity government can be a powerful mechanism for managing the marginal vote difference that divides potential winners from losers in a rigidly bipolar polity. Such a government should be based on the relative strengths of the parties that have accepted the democratic route and are represented in parliament: SLPP, UNPP, PDP, APC, NUP, and DCP. A unity government that is grounded in the principles of democracy does not mean the absence of opposition, as examples of countries that have embraced power-sharing systems have shown.

This arrangement disqualifies armed, unrepresentative, and criminal groups like the AFRC and the RUF. Inclusion of the latter in power-sharing arrangements without an electoral mandate as the Lomé agreement has done is likely to lead to the collapse of democracy, which may sow the seeds of long-term instability and disintegration of the country. The record of power sharing with participation of armed groups whose claims to power have not been tested in elections is instructive: in the three known cases, Liberia before the elections, Guinea Bissau, and Ethiopia, these arrangements broke down and rebels either took over power (Guinea Bissau and Liberia—the latter was checked by ECOMOG) or government forces expelled the rebels from the government (Ethiopia).[44] Rewarding banditry and gross human rights abuses with power is not only a terrible injustice to victims and society; it will make it difficult to reclaim such power by democratic means. It is bound to undermine two fundamental principles of democracy: representation and accountability.

The Lomé agreement of 7 July 1999, which grants the RUF/AFRC eight ministerial posts and other high-level benefits in the public sector as well as unconditional and absolute pardon for committing atrocities, makes a mockery of the basic principles of democracy and human rights. It is the first time that the international community has rewarded armed gangs with a well-known record of atrocities with power without the benefit of a democratic mandate. In Cambodia, Mozambique, Liberia, Angola, Bosnia, Northern Ireland and El Salvador power sharing was at least based on the mandate of the people. For all the horrors of Charles Taylor, it was not the Abuja agreement that gave him power but the people of Liberia in elections.

Democratizing Access to Military Security

An all-inclusive democratic political settlement would require a further democratization of the military institution. The one salient lesson of the war is that areas—Bo, Moyamba, Bonthe, and Pujehun—that have well-established civil defense forces have been able to deter or repel rebel attacks effectively. The democratization of defense requires much more than the training of a few civil defense forces. Neighborhoods and individuals ought to be able to defend themselves if they are confronted with another breakdown of security. This will involve a proper program of military and security education, methods of arms use, ways of guarding homes, securing food and medical supplies, and creative methods of self-defense. It may not require all citizens to carry arms at all times, but they should be in a position to do so when an attack occurs.

There are four additional advantages of such an approach to security. First, it is likely to break the rigid bipolarity that has made it difficult to prosecute the war as a united country. The civil defense force is viewed with strong suspicion by a large number of Northern political elites, including those in parliament; they see the civil defense force as an ethnic *kamajoi* army intended to consolidate the hold of the SLPP on power. Furthermore, efforts to create a new army have been resisted because many in this group see the disbanded RSLMF as their army. Democratization of defense is likely to overcome these constraints. Democratization of defense would also allow those members of the AFRC and RUF who would like to surrender to the government to do so with the knowledge that they would not have to confront traditional enemies; rather, they would have to confront the entire population to which they seek to return. Also the potential danger of having two different official armies—the new army and the civil defense force—that precipitated the coup of 25 May 1997 may nip the idea in the bud.

Second, military democratization will resolve the persistent problems that exist between the president and his deputy defense minister. Sierra Leone may be the only war-torn country with a president who does not have an army that he effectively controls, and a defense minister who enjoys unquestioned loyalty from his militia troops but is unable to take the initiative in prosecuting the war nationally. Military democratization will neutralize the power of political elites in military matters. Individuals would not only play central roles in national and personal defense but it would also be difficult for a single politician to dominate such a force. It is instructive to note that one of the most stable multi-ethnic and democratic countries, Switzerland, is governed not only by a power-sharing system but also has a citizen-based army.

Third, the democratization of military life may provide a solid foundation for building the Sierra Leone nation and citizenship. It is bound to enhance national solidarity and make the work of rebuilding the shattered economy and society less difficult. It will help to break the rigidities that are inherent in the bipolar ethnic political structure of the country. Fourth, military democratization will neutralize the pressures on the government to employ the services of mercenaries. The very concept of mercenaries is antithetical to the democratic state. Mercenaries were used in predemocratic Europe when rulers were afraid, or lacked the capacity, to draft their citizens. Mercenaries are a function of supply constraints. Democratization broadened the tax base of governments and made the draft a civic duty. It explains the revulsion that Western governments have for mercenaries in the twentieth century even though their history is filled with mercenary activities.

Redefining ECOMOG's Peacekeeping Role

ECOMOG has played a useful role in Sierra Leone. Without its intervention in the conflict Sierra Leone would either have remained under the violent and predatory rule of the AFRC/RUF or the war would have become irredeemably ethnic. However, events after January 6 have exposed the limitations of ECOMOG as a regional peacekeeping force in situations of protracted armed conflict. Given the unstable nature of Africa's democratization and the time it would take to build inclusive political and mass-based defense institutions, there is need for a regional framework to regulate Africa's conflicts. The only institutionalized form of military intervention in Africa is ECOMOG in West Africa. In other regions, countries have intervened in wars either unilaterally or bi/multilaterally. Even in Southern Africa, the regional institution, Southern African Development Community, was not used by South Africa and Botswana, the intervention powers, to stem the conflict in Lesotho. A multinational intervention force was put together by France to replace its troops in the Central African Republic, but this force remains ad hoc and depends on the policy directives and financial support of France.

The enhancement of ECOMOG's institutional capacity should be linked to a redefinition of its role in peacekeeping operations. The Sierra Leone operation has shown that a regional peacekeeping force cannot fight a protracted war. ECOMOG lost much of its deterrence value after its highly successful ejection of the AFRC from power because it was expected not only to defend all towns and villages but also to fight the rebels in all corners and bushes of the country. Since there were not enough ECOMOG soldiers to carry out this mammoth task, the rebels very quickly realized that ECOMOG soldiers were not invincible. The lesson here is that a regional peacekeeping force should be used strategically. The force should be used essentially as backup to national civil defense initiatives. Without civil defense capacity, regional peacekeeping operations are unlikely to be effective in long drawn-out wars.

Youth Rehabilitation

At the core of the conflict in Sierra Leone is an extraordinary youth crisis. The 15–29 age group constitutes about twenty-five percent of the population, and more than eighty percent of the population is below forty years. The literacy rate of twenty-four percent is among the lowest in the world. The school enrollment ratio for all levels of education is about thirty percent; in addition, a high proportion of youths fail to complete primary or secondary education each year and have to make a living in the overcrowded informal economy. The urban population grew by about fifty-six percent between 1980 and 1995. Only 1.4 percent of GDP was spent on education in the 1990s. The GDP itself contracted by about 25 percent between 1980 and 1995.[45] As a resource-endowed economy, a large number of youths earn a living by participating in illicit or informal mining. In nonmining towns, economic activity is largely dominated by petty trading.

Abdullah has linked changes in the country's mainstream culture to the progressive deterioration of economic opportunities for youths.[46] A growing number of the country's youths are being exposed to a culture of marginality, which is rooted in drugs, loose morality, violence, profanity, and disrespect for institutions. The marginal sector is the core or "natural" constituency of the RUF/AFRC. Unless bold, radical, focused, comprehensive, and well-financed programs are developed that target the youth specifically, the RUF and the AFRC will continue to feed on this fertile reserve of *lumpen* culture, and recruit or abduct youths for its criminal enterprise.

NOTES

1. Economic Community of West African States Monitoring Group.

2. Majoritarianism refers to electoral rules that are likely to produce a single winner. These can be first-past-the-post rules in parliamentary systems or second-round elections in presidential institutions.

3. Popular in this case means "easy to understand" or "plain."

4. I. Abdullah, "Bush Path to Destruction: The Origin and Character of the Revolutionary United Front/Sierra Leone," *Africa Development* 22, nos. 3 and 4 (1997); I. Abdullah and P. K. Muana, "The Revolutionary United Front: A Revolt of the Lumpenproletariat," in *African Guerrillas*, ed. C. Clapham (London: James Currey, 1998).

5. I. Rashid, "Subaltern Reactions: Lumpens, Students and the Left," *Africa Development* 22, nos. 3 and 4 (1997).

6. P. K. Muana, "The Kamajoi Militia: Violence, Internal Displacement and the Politics of Counter-Insurgency," *Africa Development* 22, nos. 3 and 4 (1997).

7. Paul Richards, in *Fighting for the Rain Forest* (London: James Currey, 1996), argued that the RUF movement was led by "quite highly educated excluded intellectuals." Alfred Zack-Williams, "Sierra Leone: The Political Economy of Civil War, 1991–1998," *Third World Quarterly* 20, no. 1 (1999), embraced Richards' arguments and insights. Neither of the two authors produced evidence to support their claims. In a memo to World Bank officials in Freetown (1997), Richards abandoned his thesis on "excluded intellectuals" and appropriated Abdullah's characterization of the RUF as a *lumpen* movement.

8. See also Arthur Abraham, "War and Transition to Peace: A Study of State Conspiracy in Perpetuating Armed Conflict," *Africa Development* 22, nos. 3 and 4 (1997) for a provocative piece on the convergence of interests between the RUF and the RSLMF; and J. Kandeh, "What Does the Militariat Do When It Rules? Military Regimes in The Gambia, Sierra Leone and Liberia," *Review of African Political Economy*, no. 69 (September 1996) for a comparison of subaltern-type mili-

tary regimes in West Africa.

9. Y. Bangura, "Reflections on the Sierra Leone Peace Accord, *African Development* 22, nos. 3 and 4 (1997).

10. See Lansana Gberie, "The May 25 Coup d'État: A Militariat Revolt?" *Africa Development* 22, nos. 3 and 4 (1997), for a detailed account of the May 25 coup.

11. Dialogue, sanctions, and the ultimate use of force.

12. A. K. Koroma, *Sierra Leone: The Agony of a Nation* (London: Andromeda Publications, 1996), and Gberie, "The May 25 Coup d'État."

13. Abraham, "War and Transition to Peace."

14. Ahmed Tejan-Kabbah, Broadcast to the Nation on Peace and Security, 2 September 1998.

15. Muana, "The Kamajoi Militia"; Gberie, "The May 25 Coup d'État."

16. Muana, "The Kamajoi Militia."

17. Literal translation of *kamajoi, kapra, tamaboro* and *donso* from Mende, Temne, Koranko and Kono respectively is hunter. *Gbenthis* is to complete a task in Temne.

18. Tejan-Kabbah's membership of the constitutional review commission established by the military government of the NPRC (National Provisional Ruling Council) was frequently cited.

19. For studies on the political economy of diamonds in Sierra Leone see Alfred B. Zack-Williams, *Tributors, Supporters and Merchant Capital: Mining and Underdevelopment in Sierra Leone* (London: Avebury, 1995), and William Reno, *Corruption and State Politics in Sierra Leone* (Cambridge: Cambridge University Press, 1995).

20. T. J. Makannah, ed., *The Handbook of the Population of Sierra Leone* (Freetown: Toma Enterprises Limited, 1996).

21. J. Rupert, "Diamond Hunters Fuel Africa's Brutal Wars," *Washington Post Foreign Service,* 16 October 1999, p. A1.

22. In his address to the National Consultative Conference on the peace process in Freetown on 10 April 1999, the "pro-tempore president" of the Liberian Senate, Keikura Kpoto, stated: "I do not come here to argue the merits or non-merits of the Liberian involvement. How can anybody say we are not involved, with tens of thousands of professional Liberian fighters the Liberian government cannot provide jobs for."

23. The Sandline Affair caused a political stir in the UK. It was alleged that British Foreign Office officials and the UK ambassador to Sierra Leone, Peter Penfold, knew about the deal. It was claimed that the deal was a violation of the UN embargo on arms to Sierra Leone. The specific UN resolution however empowered ECOMOG, acting in collaboration with the Sierra Leone government in exile, to police the embargo. The resolution could not, therefore, have applied to the government, but to the illegal AFRC regime.

24. Executive Outcomes were employed by the military NPRC government in 1995 when the rebels threatened Freetown in April of that year. It is believed to have links with Branch Energy, a mining company registered in the UK. Executive Outcomes was being paid one and half million dollars a month to defend the mining industry and fight the rebels. Pressures from the IMF forced the government to suspend the contract.

25. United Nations Commission on Human Rights, Fifty-fifth session, 1991, Report on the Question of the Use of Mercenaries as a Means of Violating Human Rights and Impeding the Exercise of the Right of Peoples to Self-determination. Submitted by Enrique Bernales Ballesteros, Special Rapporteur, pursuant to Commission Resolution 1998/6; 13 January.E/CN.4/1999/11.

26. Nigerian military officials have given the following reasons for ECOMOG's failure to pro-

tect Freetown: the rebels used civilians as shields when they entered the town, making it difficult for ECOMOG to open fire on the rebels; a lieutenant colonel, who has been sent to Nigeria to be court martialed, abandoned his duties at the key entry point of Kissy; ECOMOG lacked military equipment like helicopter gunships and M124s.

27. A national consultative conference of civil society groups in Freetown, which came out in support of dialogue, was held on 10 April 1999. The conference opposed a power sharing deal with the rebels.

28. Y. Bangura, "Reflections on the Sierra Leone Peace Accord."

29. Conciliation Resources, "The Liberian Peace Process 1990–1996," *Accord: An International Review of Peace Initiatives,* ed. Jeremy Armon and Andy Carl, Issue 1, 1996.

30. The Chief of Defense Staff, Maxwell Khobe, is reported to have made this complaint on 14 May 1999.

31. J. J. Linz and A. Valenzuela, *The Failure of Presidential Democracy: Comparative Perspectives, Vol. 1* (Baltimore and London: Johns Hopkins University Press, 1994).

32. A. Stepan and C. Skatch, "Residentialism and Parliamentarism in Comparative Perspective," in *Failure of Presidential Democracy.*

33. For a useful background analysis of the elections and the transition, see J. Kandeh, "Transition without Rupture: Sierra Leoni's Transfer Elections of 1996," *African Studies Review* 41, no. 2 (1998); and "The Interrupted Second Republic," mimeographed paper, 1998.

34. It is worth noting, however, that when sections of the army threatened to disrupt the second round of elections, efforts were made to form a national unity government but the deal came unstuck because Karefa-Smart, who was placed second, refused to accept the vice-presidential post. It is quite possible he had calculated that the number of registered voters in his core constituency, the North and Western Area, was higher than the East and South combined.

35. The second round of elections produced some rather bizarre figures: voter turnout in war-torn districts in the South and East, such as Kailahun, Pujehun and Bonthe, was much higher than the registered voters. The loser, Karefa-Smart, complained. The votes of the winner were arbitrarily reduced by the elections office to a figure that corresponded to a 100-percent turnout for the affected districts. Karefa-Smart accepted the results in the interest of peace (United National People's Party, 1996).

36. Mende: 30.9%; Temne: 29.8%; Limba: 8.4%; Kono: 4.8%; Fula: 4%; Koranko: 3.7%; Kissi: 3.5%; Sherbro: 3.4%; Soso: 3.1%; Loko: 3%; Madingo: 2.3%; Krio: 2%; Yalunka: 0.7%; Vai: 0.3%; Gola: 0.2%; Kroo: 0.2%; Bassa: 0.1%. For analysis of Sierra Leone's ethnic politics See J. Kandeh , "Politicsation of Ethnic Identities in Sierra Leone," *African Studies Review* 35(1992); J. Cartwright, *Politics in Sierra Leone, 1947–1967* (Toronto: University of Toronto Press, 1970); and D. Horowitz, *Ethnic Groups in Conflict* (Berkeley: University of California Press, 1985).

37. Others are Guyana, Fiji, Trinidad, and Northern Ireland.

38. C. P. Foray, "The Road to the One-Party State: The Sierra Leone Experience," Africanus Horton Memorial Lecture, delivered at the Centre of African Studies, University of Birmingham, 9 November 1998; A. K. Koroma, "Sierra Leone"; J. Cartwright, *Politics in Sierra Leone, 1947–1967* (Toronto: University of Toronto Press, 1970).

39. Koroma, "Sierra Leone," pp. 1–26.

40. A. Lijphart, *Democracy in Plural Societies* (New Haven: Yale University Press, 1977); A. Lijphart, "Consociation and Federation: Conceptual and Empirical Links," *Canadian Journal of Political Science* 22, no. 3 (September 1979); A. Lijphart, "The Power-Sharing Approach," in *Con-*

flict and Peacemaking in Multi-ethnic Societies, ed. Joseph V. Montville (Lexington, Mass. and Toronto: Lexington Books, 1990); D. Horowitz, *Ethnic Groups in Conflict* (Berkeley: University of California Press, 1985).

41. Lijphart, "Consociation and Federation."

42. Some notable consociations are Switzerland, Austria, Belgium, Netherlands, Luxembourg, Surinam, Netherlands, Antilles, and Malaysia. Failed consociations are Lebanon and Cyprus. Recent consociations are South Africa, Bosnia, and the Good Friday Agreement for North Ireland.

43. Kandeh, "The Interrupted Second Republic"; J. Kandeh, "Transition without Rupture."

44. J. B. Adekanye, "Power-Sharing and Public Sector Reform: New Approaches to the Distribution and Management of Governmental Power," mimeographed paper (Geneva: United Nations Research Institute for Social Development [UNRISD], 1999).

45. World Bank, *World Development Report* (Oxford and New York: Oxford University Press, 1997); UNDP (United Nations Development Program), *Human Development Report* (Oxford and New York: Oxford University Press, 1994).

46. Abdullah, "Bush Path to Destruction"; Abdullah and Muana, "The Revolutionary United Front."

8

The International Humanitarian Intervention in Somalia, 1992–1995

Hussein Adam

The question is whether Americans will learn from Somalia or recoil from the experience and from peace operations generally.

Chester Crocker

A series of civil wars have led to the collapse of the state in Somalia. Like in Chad in 1980–1982, the collapse of the Somali state in 1991–1992 essentially resulted from a factional civil war that caused the demise of all branches of central government. The capital city, Mogadishu, became a divided city of armed barricades, resembling Beirut during the Lebanese civil war. Somali minorities escaped by sea to Kenya and Yemen recalling Vietnam's boat people. Unlike Liberia where most of the capital did not fall into rebel hands, chaos and anarchy engulfed Mogadishu, making it the epicenter of Somalia's problems. The situation in northern Somalia, former British Somaliland, which declared de facto independence under the Somali National Movement (SNM), reflected to some extent the problem of Eritrea with Ethiopia. A deeper tragedy lay in the formerly peaceful Bay region inhabited by the populous yet poorly armed Rahanweyn Somalis. The war came to them simply as a result of their geography. Siyad Barre left Mogadishu but did not leave the country as Mengistu did in Ethiopia. He barricaded himself and his remnant loyalist troops in his home region of Gedo, from where he launched spoiler wars as RENAMO (Mozambique National Resistance) did in Mozambique. What ensued were continuing civil wars between General Aidid's USC-SNA (United Somali Congress-Somali National Alliance) and remnant Siyad forces, fought mostly on Bay (Baidoa) territories. Journalists termed Bay's plight Somalia's Bosnia. These events created a devastating man-made famine that resulted in "The International Humanitarian Intervention in Somalia, 1992–1995."

One could speculate about the possibilities of various external interventions to rescue Somalia from its self-destruction. According to Ali Mazrui's reflections: "Ideally,

Somalia should have been saved by fellow Africans as a kind of Pax Africana, Africans policing themselves or policing each other. It has been attempted in Liberia by a West African force drawn from several nations ... A second preference would have been a rescue of Somalia by members of the Organization of the Islamic Conference (OIC), a kind of Pax Islamica ... A third preference for the Somali rescue would have been under the League of Arab States—a kind of Pax Arabica or Pax Arabiana ... A fourth preference would have been a truly multinational task force to both pacify and feed Somalia, a kind of Pax Humana which would combine troops from carefully and sensitively selected countries."[1] The fact remains that, when foreign intervention to avert the Somali catastrophe came, it was a US initiative under the umbrella of the United Nations. In the post–Cold War era, with economic difficulties facing most states, the prospects of a single power (other than the United States) taking action to save a collapsing state have diminished considerably. Somalia reflects the proposition that the more complete the collapse of a state, the greater will be the role and magnitude of foreign intervention aimed at reconstruction. The OAU (Organization of African Unity) lacked political will and resources; the OIC (Organization of the Islamic Conference) and the Arab League lacked political will.

STATE COLLAPSE

Around January 1991 and during the ensuing months, Somalia experienced a cataclysmic event, virtually unseen since the Second World War. Somalia witnessed complete state collapse: it was not simply a military coup, a revolution, or a new regime emerging from a partisan uprising. Somalia's collapsed state represented the literal implosion of state structures and of residual forms of authority and legitimacy. The visible collapse of the Somali state has lasted for practically a full decade. In some respects, the country seems to have reverted to a nineteenth-century status, a back-to-the-future scenario. Like all collapsed states, the Siyad military state collapsed because it could no longer perform the functions required for it to pass as a state. Siyad's brutal repression and his concentration of power in the hands of his clan elite led to a national uprising.

The opposition groups used their own clans as their organizing base, creating armed clan-based protopolitical organizations such as the Somali National Movement (SNM, for the northern Isaq clan-family), the Somali Salvation Democratic Front (SSDF, for the Majerteen, Darod clan-family), the United Somali Congress (USC, for the Hawiye clan-family), the Somali Patriotic Movement (SPM, for the Ogaden, Darod clan-family), and so forth. At present there are twenty-six such clan-based political factions.

The phenomenon of state collapse represents a major analytical challenge to the social sciences. Siyad's leadership provides an example of the close relationship between state collapse and the role of "rogue" leadership. A major cause in the collapse lay in the mismanagement, pillage of resources, brutal military repressions, and abuses by a dictatorial regime that left the majority of the population without a stake in the existing system. Under Siyad Barre, Somalia became one of the most indebted states in Africa, with a debt service ratio of over 180 percent and a meager revenue base. The clan-based armed oppositions challenged Siyad's military dictatorship at a time when the end of the Cold War reduced the opportunities for extracting adequate military, technical, and financial resources from external sources. As a result, Somalia became the perfect illustration of the state-civil society contradiction and its implosion, precisely because the Cold War had imposed an exceedingly costly military state on a decentralized, relatively democratic civil society, surviving on meager resources.

MISSED OPPORTUNITIES

Could the Somali catastrophe have been anticipated and prevented? What preemptive measures were appropriate to confront the causes? Ambassador Mohamed Sahnoun raised these issues in his USIP publication, *Somalia: The Missed Opportunities*. He concludes, "if the international community had intervened earlier and more effectively in Somalia, much of the catastrophe that has unfolded could have been avoided."[2] The international community could have limited if not prevented the prolonged Somali civil wars, "but its statecraft was flawed, inadequate or even absent."[3] Failures to take timely, appropriate actions in response to early warnings of an emerging crisis constituted "missed opportunities." My arguments for appropriate responses are based on what was known at that time in order to approach the policy maker's point of view. The discussion is limited to three specific and major instances that meet criteria for missed opportunities. In my judgment, this includes the period of the switch from Soviet dependency to American hegemony (1977–1978), the 1988 civil war in northern Somalia, and the scramble on the eve of Siyad's impending fall in 1990–1991.

Following the 1977–1978 so-called Ogaden War, Somalia switched sides from being a close ally of the USSR to voluntarily coming under American hegemony. During this period of transition, high tension, and flux, the US missed the opportunity to impose conditionalities that would have redirected Somalia toward a different political trajectory. The US relied on the IMF and the World Bank to press for market reforms and economic liberalization while remaining silent on political liberalization and issues involving human rights.

Preventive diplomacy requires identification of early warning signs. Such warnings were available in Somalia during this period. Repression was observable in many areas. The Siyad regime had, for some time, been blacklisted by Amnesty International, Africa Watch, and other human-rights organizations. The earliest phase of the Somali civil wars erupted during this early period of American hegemony. After the failed 1978 coup, Colonel Abdullahi Yusuf launched the SSDF from bases in Mengistu's Ethiopia. These visible, violent events should have provided the earliest warning signal to the US and the international community that the Siyad regime was intent on waging war against its own people. The US could have used this warning to tighten the terms of the 1980 military agreement and put necessary pressure on the regime. Perceptions of the costs involved in taking action often dim a policymaker's receptivity to an early warning of an impeding catastrophe. However, in 1977–1980, the warning signals did not call for a unilateral military intervention; US and international actions at that moment could have limited the problems through forceful military and economic sanctions and tough political reforms.

In May–June 1988, the international community received a "loud and crystal clear" warning of the impending Somali tragedy in the form of a large and explosive insurrection in northern Somalia. President Mengistu of Ethiopia and Siyad Barre signed a peace agreement in 1988, intended to prevent armed movements directed against their governments from using each other's country as a base. As a result, Mengistu told the Somali National Movement (SNM)—by this time, the SSDF was a spent force—that they could seek refuge in Ethiopia but they could no longer use Ethiopia as a base for military attacks on Somalia. Consequently, the SNM launched a major return military campaign against Somalia. Siyad's response was vicious, full of savagery. He launched full-scale military and aerial campaigns destroying most of cities, towns, and infrastructures in the area. An estimated 5,000 people belonging to the northern Isaq clanfamily were reported to have been killed in May 1988 alone; overall, 50,000 people lost their lives and many more were injured over the following months as revolt and repression spread throughout the region. Over 500,000 people either crossed the border into the Haud area of Ethiopia or were displaced within northern Somalia. These tragic events were covered by the global media and even in a series of reports by the US government and by human rights organizations. Lyons and Samatar conclude their discussion of these events thus: "This catastrophe should have served as an unmistakable and compelling early warning signal to the international community."[4] An international humanitarian intervention was probably not an option given the costs involved and the norms of territorial sovereignty. At that time, however, the US and other donors could have applied stringent pressure upon Siyad through drastic and coordinated military/economic sanctions coupled with international diplomatic mediations that would have compelled him to resolve problems through negotiations. Unlike the costly intervention undertaken later, these policy tools could have exerted, in my judgment, appropriate pressure without the crushing costs of a huge military involvement. There is some evidence to indicate that the US Congress would have supported a drastic cut in all military and economic aid in order to apply pressure for significant political reforms. Influential members of Congress had a visceral distaste for the US-Somalia aid program because they "personally disliked Barre."[5] In June 1988, US Ambassador Crigler recommended freezing lethal military material to Somalia and the State Department agreed with his position. The Pentagon, however, opposed it and actively lobbied against a change in policy because of the Defense Department's interests in access to Somali military facilities. These internal debates show that a window of opportunity did exist which, had it been taken, the impeding crisis could have been limited, if not prevented.

A third window of opportunity opened up in 1990, on the eve of Siyad's fall from power. This opportunity elicited external responses from Italy and Egypt. Unfortunately, this represents the case of misused opportunity involving Italian and Egyptian responses that were misconceived, harmful, and highly inappropriate given the circumstances. By 1990, armed rebellion had spread like wildfire and the international press referred to Siyad as the "Mayor of Mogadishu." The rapid successes of the armed opposition movements encouraged the latent civilian opposition into action. On 15 May 1990, they launched a protest and issued a "Manifesto." It called for a peaceful end to the civil wars through a national conference that would initiate constitutional changes and guide the nation towards electoral politics and a multiparty system. The regime reacted by jailing forty-five manifesto signatories. Italian and Egyptian protests led to their release. Nevertheless, distorted Italian and Egyptian strategies and tactics led them to misuse this window of opportunity that could have led to political reforms, thereby limiting the catastrophe. On this issue, Italian political scientist Novati is both succinct and blunt:

While Somalia was ravaged by civil war, hastening the downfall of Siyad Barre's regime in a dramatic crescendo of bloodshed and despair, Italy sought once more to manage the crisis by offering her good offices. The aim was to effect an orderly transfer of power to a large coalition of forces, parties and persons in which Siyad Barre would continue to play an important transition role in order to avoid, it was argued, a dangerous power vacuum. A self-fulfilled prophecy, Siyad's enemies firmly refused to join such a deal, pleading that the President should be personally responsible for crimes, malpractice and political chaos. An eleventh hour reconciliation conference, co-chaired by Italy and Egypt, was called in Cairo but it was doomed from the start and at the last minute was canceled. General Aidid wouldn't forget the activism of Boutros Boutros-Ghali, then foreign minister of Egypt, to "save" Siyad. The flight of Siyad Barre from Mogadishu deprived Italy of her best card. The setback was definitive. A regime Italy had tried stubbornly to preserve for over twenty years as a token of stability, was in shambles. The University, the jewel of Italian technical assistance, was destroyed and vandalized.[6]

Soon after the fall of Siyad, Mohamed Sahnoun argued that the Djibouti Conference held in June and July 1991 constituted another missed historical opportunity. Regrettably, the Djibouti effort was bound to fail even before the conference doors opened. There are several reasons: First, Djibouti was the brain child of distorted Italian and Egyptian strategies. The most positive role the Italians and Egyptians could have played at this point would have been to prevent RENAMO-type spoiler wars and a Bosnia-type tragedy in Bay by offering Siyad the incentives to leave Gedo and go into exile. Another strategic mistake they made was to over-invite members of the Manifesto Group and under-invite representatives from the armed opposition movements. This was a blatant attempt to legitimize and substitute the Manifesto Group for the armed movements. "The conference failed to address the real issue and the root cause of the chaos, and endorsed Ali Mahdi Mohamed, who was part of the problem, as interim president for two years ..."[7] It resolved to revive the 1960 Constitution for an interim period even though a majority in former British Somaliland had voted against it in the 1961 referendum. The US ignored Somalia and concentrated its diplomatic efforts towards resolving the Ethiopian crisis and ensuring a peaceful transition from Mengistu Haile Mariam to Meles Zenawi.

THE DECISION TO INTERVENE

After showing much reluctance and discouraging others (e.g., the United Nations) from intervening, the lame-duck Bush administration decided to launch a humanitarian military intervention late in 1992. The United States intervention, some alleged, was motivated by the need to combat the threat of Islamic fundamentalism financed by Sudan and Iran. Since 1991, Somalia and Somaliland have both witnessed pockets of Islamic fundamentalism from the Islamic Unity group. During that period, their strength lay in northeast Somalia where they tried to gain power but were evicted by the SSDF and a coalition of clan-based forces. Since US and UN forces left, their strength lies in the Gedo region in southwest Somalia near the Kenyan and Ethiopian borders. Islamic fundamentalism is not a significant issue in Somalia. This is demonstrated by the fact that US and UN troops have not staged even one raid against the fundamentalists in Gedo; those in the northeast were too far from their area of operations.

Other writers raised the issue of access to Somali military bases as another reason for US intervention. The most attractive Somali military installations consist of the Berbera naval and airport facilities in the self-declared Republic of Somaliland. The elites who control Somaliland would be glad to renew US access to the Berbera base and facilities, in exchange for recognition or, at the very least, for economic assistance. As of March 1995 all US and UN intervening forces had left Somalia without deployment anywhere near the Berbera base. Besides, "even if one accepts the globalist rationales for ensuring U.S. military access to the region, the Somali bases were unnecessary in the light of other, more extensive, facilities readily available in the region."[8] Some have argued that the US simply wishes to deny base access to hostile regional powers including Iran, Sudan, and Iraq. Once again, the evidence is simply not there; intervening forces have come and gone without deploying to protect Somali military bases.

The least satisfactory explanations are those derived mainly from the Cold War context of US strategic interests. Even if one cannot resist the conclusion that American foreign policy has historically been driven by economic and/or strategic determinants rather than by humanitarian considerations, one has to admit that the Somali intervention was a unique phenomenon. Bush administration officials argued that the United States had to intervene because of the "massive proportions" of the tragedy and because the United States had the means to "do something" about it. This global explanation argued that Somalia could enhance both US and UN credibility in the post–Cold War era.[9]

Those who use globalist explanations go on to point to the convergence of vision between Bush's New World Order and the then-United Nations Secretary-General Boutros-Ghali's commitment to assertive multilateralism: "Secretary-General Boutros-Ghali has an ambitious agenda for peace, through which he plans unprecedented UN involvement in peacemaking, peacekeeping, and peace enforcement. He is convinced that the UN now has an opportunity to achieve the great objectives for which it was established . . ."[10] There is no doubt that when Bush finally took the decision to intervene, the Secretary-General and the UN supported its implementation. These attractive, globalist explanations assumed that Somalia would pave the way for a New World Order in which the US would act as a vanguard for UN-approved responses to humanitarian crises in various regions of the Third World. Yet early in 1992, the United States' mission to the UN did its best to keep the Somali case off the UN Security Council agenda. Even when it became clear that the Security Council was willing to send 3,500 peacekeepers to facilitate food distribution, the US tried to water down the resolution by suggesting a 50-man force.[11] The shortcomings of the globalist interpretations have more to do with timing: "Despite the lefty rhetoric, however, this interpretation of events fails to explain why the Bush administration ignored domestic and international appeals to aid Somalia during 1991, as well as the timing and nature of White House responses during 1992. In other words, why did Bush decide to launch Operation Provide Relief during August 1992 as opposed to July 1992 (or earlier), and why did he decide to launch Operation Restore Hope only after (as opposed to prior to) the presidential elections of November 1992?"[12] Obviously, the dynamics of US electoral politics played a critical role.

Another view advanced to explain the decision to intervene is based on the structural dynamics of American politics, reflected by two factions: On one hand, there are those who want to transcend militarism to promote domestic social progress at home under the slogan "the peace dividend." On the other hand, there are those who argue that post–Cold War fragmentation and diffusion of power among multiple actors have made the contemporary situation even more dangerous and volatile: "an even more unstable and dangerous system of anarchy, requiring the United States to remain engaged militarily ... Herein lay the logic of neocontainment-militarism, calling for leaving the military establishment and expenditures intact."[13] In other words, the US military establishment needed the large Somali intervention to rationalize the retention of its size and expenditures.

Globalist and structural militarist explanations were used in retrospect to rationalize the decision to intervene but they did not trigger it. Domestic politics explanations involve the role of the media, nongovernmental organizations (NGOs), and the US Congress. By 1992, the effects of state collapse became manifest in a devastating man-made famine and a brutal multisided civil war that claimed the lives of at least three hundred thousand men, women, and children. At its peak in 1992, the magnitude of human suffering in Somalia was overwhelming: out of a total estimated population of eight million, approximately 4.5 million Somalis required urgent external assistance. Of those, some 1.5 million people were at immediate risk of starvation, including one million children. US television screens carried the humanitarian disaster in Somalia on a saturated basis. The sense of urgency about the Somali crisis filtered from the media to the public and the Congress, significantly raising pressures on the Bush administration.

Visits by a number of prominent individuals, from Irish President Mary Robinson to United Nations' Children's Fund (UNICEF) spokesperson Audrey Hepburn, provided the focal points for media coverage. In Washington, the House Select Committee on Hunger ... drew further attention to the crisis ... Major international nongovernmental organizations, most notably the International Committee of the Red Cross and the US-based CARE, lobbied aggressively for greater international involvement. Boutros-Ghali ... complained publicly that the West was more interested in the "rich" man's war' in Bosnia than in the Somali catastrophe.[14]

The growing media, public, and congressional pressure provided a compelling, if not sufficient explanation for the reversal in US policy. For example, on 3 August 1992, a bipartisan resolution advocating a tangible humanitarian response overwhelmingly passed the Senate; the same bill was adopted by the House of Representatives on August 10. A more sufficient explanation for President Bush's decision to intervene has to do with presidential politics in an election year. It offers the best interpretation for the timing of the decision. Had Bush been motivated mostly by his "New World Order" and neo-containment militarism, he would certainly have acted earlier than he did. Criticisms by Democratic Party rivals as well as some members of his own Republican Party obliged his staff to pay more attention to the growing Somali emergency and they responded by launching Operation Provide Relief in August 1992.

Operation Provide Relief involved an American airlift operation to selected points in southern Somalia and to Somali refugee camps in northern Kenya. It operated out of bases in Mombasa and other parts of Kenya. Although US military aircraft airlifted much needed food, bypassing the warlord dominated Mogadishu harbor, it did not succeed in overcoming fundamental problems of state collapse, chaos, insecurity, and looting. Other militia fought serious battles for food in remote areas. As a result, by August–September 1992, unprecedented numbers of people died of hunger and disease. Large outbreaks of infectious diseases, including measles and dysentery, devastated the population, especially the weakened, malnourished children.

Bush remained satisfied with his Operation Provide Relief as he campaigned for reelection. Somalia became an issue in the presidential campaign as Democratic candidate Bill Clinton criticized President Bush for inaction in dealing with problems such as Somalia and Bosnia and for weak support of the United Nations. Therefore, in his October 1992 address to the United Nations General Assembly, Bush declared that the Pentagon would prepare the US military for a new and more active role in peacekeeping efforts in the "New World Order."[15] It is important to observe that his NSC staff began serious preparations for the Somali intervention only *after* Bush lost his reelection bid. Accordingly, partisan critics argue that he would not have sent US troops to intervene in Somalia's humanitarian crisis had he won a second term in office. "In an effort to leave office on a high note, President Bush finally decided that something had to be done about the humanitarian disaster in Somalia."[16] Schraeder concludes on this point: "The presidential politics approach ... explains Bush's decision to launch Operation Restore Hope after his defeat in the 1992 presidential elections: the understandable desire to ensure that the history books remember him as a 'decisive leader' in the realm of foreign affairs as opposed to a 'vanquished politician' unable to secure a second term in office."[17] President Bush and his Chief of Staff were, of course, aware as they undertook the Somalia mission that it would provide a counterweight to the powerful domestic impetus to focus public investment at home. His harsh critics saw the dispatching of American troops to Somalia as a cynical effort on the President's part to deflect domestic and international criticisms for his abject failure to act in Bosnia. In retrospect, the US-led multinational force was possibly a convergence of interests between Boutros-Ghali and President Bush.

OPERATION RESTORE HOPE (ORH)

Security Council Resolution 794 of 3 December 1992 authorized the United States to lead a Unified Task Force (UNITAF) code-named Operation Restore Hope (ORH) under Chapter VII of the UN Charter. Chapter VII sanctions the use of forceful means to enhance UN objectives; in this case the delivery of relief supplies to starving people in Somalia. The resolution gave UNITAF the right "to use all necessary means to establish as soon as possible a secure environment for humanitarian relief operations."[18] Resolution 794 authorized the deployment of twenty-four thousand American troops to Somalia; the initial cost of the operation to the United States was estimated at $500 million. More in line with his royal exit opportunism than with his "New World Order" vision, President Bush wrote Boutros-Ghali to underline that the mission was "limited and specific: to create security conditions which will permit the feeding of the starving Somali people and allow the transfer of this security function to the UN peacekeeping force."[19] At another point he seemed aware that the situation is much more complicated when he stated, "Our mission is humanitarian, but we will not tolerate armed gangs ripping off their own people, condemning them to death by starvation."[20] He contradicts himself further by declaring that US troops should depart from Somalia by the time of the inauguration in January 1993: a forty-day time span that does not allow for the time it takes to settle them on the ground.

As the US prepared to send forces to Somalia, and within a week of their arrival, differences emerged between the UN Secretary-General on one hand, and President Bush and UNITAF's American commander on the other. One key problem involved time, and on this issue, Boutros-Ghali had a point. President Bush's goal of withdrawing the troops in six weeks contradicted his own statement of the problem. It meant that the US could not undertake any credible steps to promote peace and reconciliation. It meant that the US was thinking about exiting before entering; it sent a wrong signal to the so-called warlords, confirming to them that they could outlive the foreign intervention. The complicated Somali situation called for a strategy that would have needed a longer time frame for implementation. On this issue, Boutros-Ghali refused to be pushed around; he delayed deployment of UN forces to relieve UNITAF forces until 4 May 1993.

The Bush Administration intuitively understood that, even though the Somali state had collapsed, residual forms of sovereignty resided with Somali civil society including clan and religious elders as well as the protopolitical armed groups. It wisely decided to send Ambassador Oakley to conduct consultations with key local leaders including those heading the armed factions to get them to request and welcome the international intervention force; they all agreed to do so. UN Secretary General Boutros-Ghali had a rigid conception of sovereignty (residing only in statehood) and would have preferred overwhelming force to consultations. His dismissal of Ambassador Sahnoun ultimately rested on the fact that Sahnoun rejected Boutros-Ghali's interventionist ambitions by insisting on working out agreements with clan elders and faction leaders. ORH, UNO-SOM I and II (United Nations Operation in Somalia) effectively postponed and ulti-mately buried the Secretary-General's concept of United Nations-trained and led rapid-deployment military forces.

A major bone of contention involved the issue of disarmament. Nowhere in Security Council Resolution 794 do we find a directive to the Unified Task Force to disarm the Somalis. However, Boutros-Ghali later claimed that he had an understanding with the White House that the force would disarm armed Somali bands, groups, factions, includ-ing individuals. UNITAF's American commanders felt that disarming armed Somalis needed more troops than were available. They also believed that such an exercise would be fraught with serious risks and dangers, that nobody knew the scope and size of armaments in Somalia or how the Somalis would react to this form of humiliation. It is a pity that this critical issue led to polarized positions—total disarmament versus no disarmament—when a judicious middle position would have led to the destruction of heavy weapons without humiliating the average Somali who needs a hand weapon to defend himself, his family, and his property.

Perhaps another casualty of the arbitrary six-week timetable President Bush pro-posed was that this required that the US Army remove civil affairs and military police training components from the ORH program. "This was unusual; civil affairs officers are specialists in foreign cultures and are used for liaison with local communities. The U.S. military deployed approximately 1,000 civil affairs officers to Panama in December 1989 and about 300 to northern Iraq after the Gulf War. Under UNITAF, the numbers ranged from 7 to 30."[21] This meant that UNITAF was crippled from the start; it was not able to mount a viable program to demobilize armed youth, train a Somali police force, and revive the legal and court systems. The international intervening force was doomed to fail because it lacked a credible exit strategy. This key lesson the US learned from this failure in Somalia led to a more positive situation in Haiti where, "the United States reverted to the immediate and effective use of civil affairs units. In addition to civil affairs troops, more than eight hundred police advisers were sent to Haiti. Shortly after the initial landing, the United States began a police recruitment and training program."[22] Under ORH, the Australian force had a civil-military affairs unit and was able to achieve tangible success in rebuilding Baidoa's police forces and strengthen its civil society.

At its peak, UNITAF strength reached approximately 37,000 troops, including 8,000 on ships offshore. The United States provided the largest contingent by far, with a peak strength of about 28,000 marines and infantry. About 9,000 troops from over twenty countries joined ORH. For example, France provided 2,500 French Legionnaires from neighboring Djibouti, Australia provided 900 elite soldiers while Pakistan contributed 4,000 soldiers, some of whom became embroiled in conflicts with General Aidid's faction. Estimates of troop figures representing a point in time is as follows.

Table 8.1
International Troop Commitments for Somalia (Estimates)

Country	No. of Troops
Australia	900
Belgium	570
Botswana	300
Canada	900
Egypt	250
France	2,500
India	3,000
Italy	3,800
Kuwait	230
Morocco	1,250
New Zealand	60
Nigeria	550
Norway	80
Pakistan	4,000
Saudi Arabia	700
Sweden	130
Tunisia	130
Turkey	300
UK	90
USA	24,000
Zimbabwe	400

Source: Adapted from *UN Africa Recovery Briefing Paper,* 15 January 1993, p. 3. Reproduced from Samuel M. Makinda, *Seeking Peace from Chaos: Humanitarian Intervention in Somalia* (New York: International Peace Academy Occasional Paper Series, 1993), p. 73.

ORH was implemented in four phases. The first phase involved controlling the port harbor facilities and airfields in Somalia's capital city, Mogadishu. This was accomplished through a Marine landing exercise. Phase two involved securing selected areas inland. The US Army and allied forces joined the Marines to open supply routes and secure other towns and major feeding centers with a clear emphasis on Baidoa, the epicenter of the civil-war-induced famine. The third phase involved extending operations south to the port town of Kismayu. Phase four involved the handoff from UNITAF to UNOSOM II. The troop deployment essentially involved Mogadishu, Merca, Kismayu, Bardera, Baidoa, Oddur, Beled Weyne, Dusa Mareb, Jowhar, Jalalaqsi, Baledogle, and back to Mogadishu: an area journalists termed "the triangle of death." The whole international intervention from 1992 to 1995 was confined to this southern area, between

Somalia's two main rivers (the Shebele and the Juba), a zone that is between a quarter to a third of the whole country. Boutros-Ghali's pleadings that troops be deployed in most parts of the country, including the northeast and the northwest (Somaliland) were ignored by the US and the other members of the Security Council. It is very difficult to understand the logic of deploying troops in areas of the country that were relatively peaceful.

There is no doubt that prior to 1992 ORH and UNOSOM represented the most radical and most ambitious operations that the United Nations had undertaken in a sovereign state. Since Somalia did not present a military threat to surrounding states, this represented the first time ever that the United Nations organization had intervened in purely domestic affairs involving a humanitarian crisis. The United Nations Security Council showed that it was now freed from the paralysis of the Cold War epoch, during which the United States and the Soviet Union often blocked Security Council action. For the first time, the Security Council authorized enforcement action under Chapter VII of the UN Charter, bypassing Article 2, paragraph 7, which prohibits interference in the domestic affairs of a sovereign state. The world confronted a concrete case of the clash between two international principles: the respect for state sovereignty versus the imperative to protect life, to safeguard human rights. The decision goes beyond Somalia; it has potential for wide applications.

It is very misleading to conclude that the US/UN humanitarian intervention was a complete failure. The US—the Clinton Administration—should claim deserved credit for the partial success of the operation. The UNITAF/ORH operation permitted the distribution of relief food to previously famished populations. "More than 250,000 lives are estimated to have been saved during the famine emergency."[23] However, the operation did not achieve its maximum objectives: reconstituting viable political system(s) and facilitating democratization and development. It has achieved as much as could be hoped for under the circumstances—it created an environment that was tangibly better than what would have existed without it, at least in certain aspects.

As soon as ORH was on the ground, throughout central and southern Somalia, looting, extortion, and attacks on relief workers dropped sharply. Food arriving in Mogadishu could be shipped to inland towns in convoys of trucks. The improved security conditions attracted old and new NGOs as well as other (UN) international staff to return to Somalia. UNICEF, WFP (World Food Program), and NGO partners helped feed 200,000 children a day by January 1993. UNICEF expanded its operations during this period. It provided medicines and staff to 16 hospitals, 62 mother-and-child health centers and 156 health posts throughout Somalia. By March 1993, cereal prices had fallen by sixty per cent of their September 1992 level; deaths from starvation and disease fell sharply due to a significantly increased food supply.

Operations began to shift from emergency relief to development programs including the revival of agricultural production, restocking livestock herds, restoring some of the country's shattered services and infrastructure. In March 1993, the United Nations unveiled a comprehensive Relief and Rehabilitation Program for all of 1993, budgeted at $159 million. It included projects ranging from the resettlement of displaced persons and refugees to restoring health, sanitation, water, and administrative services. By 1994, some 130,000 refugees came back to Somalia from camps in Kenya. The exodus of refugees to neighboring countries began to dwindle. Seeds and agricultural tools were distributed by the United Nations agencies and NGOs. Good rainfall fell in 1992–1993. While relief continued to receive top priority, greater emphasis was being placed on rehabilitation and reconstruction. The mechanism to carry out such activities involved the Civilian-Military Operations Center located at UNOSOM headquarters: nearly one hundred participants met daily for briefings, from the UN agencies, ICRC (International Committee of the Red Cross) and NGOs, as well as representatives from UNITAF headquarters and the military commands.

It is on the political front that the international humanitarian intervention met with insurmountable challenges. In Somalia, the United States had no evident reason to favor any one of the several armed factions. Most Somalis continue to believe this in spite of the conflict that ensued. There are particular errors that occur in the conduct of such operations, including those that belong to the inherent structure of the situations in which the intervening (international) forces found themselves. Normally, the intervention freezes the military situation, and thus prevents factions from pressing their military advantage. The intervention therefore favors and aids the faction with the weakest military position that manipulates the intervening force against its rivals. General Aidid had succeeded in defeating former President Siyad and his remaining forces, chasing them from Somalia into Kenya in May 1992. Siyad's son-in-law, General Morgan, and loyalist troops, began to steal towards the Somali border in November-December 1992, timing his armed faction's movements with the arrival of UNITAF-ORH.

Ambassador Oakley, Bush's and Clinton's representative to Somalia during ORH reports that "Morgan's forces had been moving toward Kismayu when UNITAF landed in December. They moved back to near the Kenyan border, but after the Addis Ababa cease-fire agreement they began to move south."[24] Following discussions with UNITAF officers, Morgan "sounded reasonable and compliant, seemingly reconciled to keeping his forces outside the city."[25] In Kismayu, Morgan's SNF faction was confronting Omar Jess' SPM faction allied to General Aidid and his USC-SNA:

In February 1993 . . . an anti-Aidid faction managed to seize part of Kismayu by a *coup de main*, catching UNITAF peace keepers by surprise. When Aidid's ally, Omar Jess, tried a similar trick a few days later, peace keepers were on their guard and managed to foil it. From Aidid's point of view, it was hard to avoid the conclusion that UNITAF had sided with his opponents, but if this particular event had not occurred to create that impression, another incident would have had the same effect.[26]

General Aidid and his allies believed that there was outright UNITAF-Morgan collusion against Jess. Even though at that point, UNITAF troops in Kismayu were mostly from Belgium, Aidid and his irate supporters mounted angry demonstrations outside the US embassy compound in Mogadishu. He was also angry at the Nigerian government for having granted asylum to ex-dictator Siyad Barre. He followed the protest demonstrations with an attack on Nigerian UNITAF forces. "The subsequent UNITAF arrest of Colonel Jess as he tried to drive from Mogadishu to Kismayu, heavily armed and without permission," [27] rubbed salt to the wound. More protests and demonstrations followed. Though anti-UNITAF actions by the USC-SNA stopped for a while as cooperation resumed, the Kismayu events marked the beginning of bad blood between General Aidid and UNITAF; it had all the ingredients for "clanizing" the United States and the United Nations, from the perspective of many Somalis.

THE WAR WITH GENERAL AIDID

Early in 1992, the UN Security Council sanctioned a feeble presence in Somalia under the United Nations Operation in Somalia (UNOSOM I) headed by Special Representative Mohamed Sahnoun. Towards the end of 1992, the UN sanctioned the United States-led multinational force, UNITAF, with its Operation Restore Hope. Later, in May 1993, the United Nations itself took command of the mission, UNOSOM II, whose mandate explicitly included enforcement powers. UN Secretary General Boutros-Ghali appointed American Admiral Jonathan Howe as his new Special Representative. International intervention confronted two broad strategies: A) working with the existing forces—mostly factional leaders and warlords—as a critical source of legitimate authority whose cooperation must be sought; and B) encouraging new institutions and leaders by promoting Somali civil society.[28] Mohamed Sahnoun felt that this complicated situation did not call for an either/or policy and he tried his best to pursue a two-track strategy. Ambassador Oakley, representing President Clinton under ORH, leaned heavily for strategy A and got on very well with all the so-called warlords, especially General Aidid, in spite of the suspicions that had begun to emerge. Admiral Howe did not seem to have a strategy. Instead, he developed an obsession with military action that he shared with Boutros-Ghali. As John Drysdale[29] and others have argued, Ghali and Howe became convinced that peace and a government could only come to Somalia once Aidid was removed from the political scene. Two cardinal aspects of leadership for such unprecedented operations is the ability to think and act strategically, and the personal aptitude to absorb relevant aspects of indigenous history and culture rapidly as well as the diplomatic skills to work effectively with all other actors involved in the peace building effort. It does not appear that Admiral Howe and his team possessed such qualities.

Once the attitude of confrontation with Aidid (probably mutual at this point) had set in, the issue became how to find an incident that would provoke him. If the June 5 incident had not occurred, hindsight tells us that other incidents would have followed. That morning, Pakistan UNOSOM soldiers were, at very short notice, sent to inspect Aidid's armaments near his radio station. UNOSOM had already targeted his radio as "hostile" to UNOSOM's mission. An armed confrontation between this UNOSOM unit and Aidid's militia left twenty-four Pakistani soldiers dead. Did General Aidid give the order to kill UNOSOM soldiers or was this a spontaneous act undertaken by his militia in the heat of suspicions and high tensions? There is no clear answer to this question. Under Howe's leadership, UNOSOM took precipitate military action in response to this attack. A far better response would have been to call for an impartial investigation by an esteemed group leading to a judicial decision arrived at in a fair and transparent manner. Before any such assessment was undertaken, UNOSOM had fixed blame on Aidid and launched an operation to either capture or kill him. Wanted posters with Aidid's picture were displayed all over south Mogadishu, and a price of $25,000 was placed on his head. A clandestine American military operation was launched against him. The Italians recommended isolating Aidid but recognizing and dealing with other leaders of his clan and its protopolitical organization—the Somali National Alliance (SNA). Boutros Ghali and Howe rejected their suggestions, rebuked them for their initiatives, and deployed them out of Mogadishu.

Elders and other prominent personalities from Aidid's Habar Gedir clan met on 23 July 1993 to assess their situation and explore various options. US/UNOSOM helicopters bombed the building on the grounds that Aidid could be attending the meeting. As it turned out, Aidid did not attend and at least fifty-four Habar Gedir clan members, mainly civilians, were killed without provocation. Such activities led to the perception that UNOSOM was behaving simply like another "rival clan." Aidid's hand was in fact strengthened among his clan members who perceived UNOSOM's activities as an attack against their entire clan. As long as this new external threat persisted, Habar Gedir clan members decided to rally behind Aidid. The clan took heavy casualties while inflicting serious damages and paralyzing the whole UNOSOM mission and operations. From June to October 1993, the hunt for Aidid suspended most of UNOSOM's work at reconciliation and reconstruction. In October 1993, Aidid's faction shot down at least two US helicopters and, in the ensuing combat, eighteen American soldiers were killed, one was captured, and over seventy-five were wounded. This event prompted President Bill Clinton to shift both American and UN policy back to politics and diplomacy, as he ordered an end to the manhunt. Even though the hunt for Aidid was aborted in October 1993, UNOSOM II had been so discredited that it was subsequently unable to play an effective role as interlocutor in the Somali civil wars. This result emerged from a culture of arrogance within UNOSOM II.

LESSONS LEARNED AND LEGACY

One can draw preliminary lessons from these experiences. While assisting a country devastated by ethnic/clan conflicts, it is important for international intervention forces to avoid overt political activities that favor one side as opposed to another. This is not a question of simple neutrality; it is the effort to achieve impartiality to the best extent possible. The Somali case invariably draws our attention to the importance of the role of leadership in fomenting and sustaining civil wars and also in nurturing peace. Political leaders have the choice of attenuating or exploiting ethnic/clan cleavages. A number of the so-called warlords promoted actions and decisions that perpetuated Somali civil wars. Even though environmental and structural factors played critical roles, what political leaders do decide to do or not to do ultimately matters. Sahnoun and Oakley had diplomatic instincts that allowed them to be flexible and judicious; Howe was rigid, stubborn, and mediocre. A mix of factors led to incorrect UNOSOM decisions: incompetence, personal vanity and ambition, a short-term orientation, and bureaucratic infighting. The leadership of such large operations must be carefully chosen. There is the need for an overall strategy for peace building. With sophisticated, sensitive, pragmatic, and nuanced leadership, strategy A and B could have been synchronized and pursued with the long-run aim of "civilianizing" most of the leaders and demobilizing the clan militia. The design and implementation of a peace building strategy should have been guided by considered, professional decisions that were responsive to local cultural and political conditions.

The issue of disarmament showed that UNOSOM lacked insight into the general situation. To have succeeded, UNITAF/UNOSOM disarmament strategy would have needed a comprehensive, multidimensional approach: a demobilization program to provide job-training for the youthful militias; a serious program to train and equip local police forces; and a program to equip and restore the courts and the legal justice system. The funds the Security Council allocated for UNOSOM troops could not be used to support such developmental efforts. The handful of justice and police systems UNOSOM was able to establish have declined or disappeared after UNOSOM II's financial support evaporated. On its own initiative, the northern Somaliland Republic has carried out a successful demobilization and disarmament program. Northeast Somalia, or Puntland, has achieved similar success including the establishment of a police training school. UNOSOM promoted elite level reconciliation conferences in Addis Ababa and Nairobi. The Addis Ababa Conference of 15–27 March resisted UNOSOM pressure to form a centralized state and adopted a regional-autonomy approach. UNOSOM finally backed this plan and attempted the establishment of regional and district councils as an exit strategy. As of 1994, UNOSOM had assisted in the formation of fifty-three district councils out of eighty-one (excluding Somaliland), and eight out of thirteen regional councils (again, excluding Somaliland). The legacy of these institution-building efforts is also mixed. Those that survive are in the process of being incorporated into wide clan-based authorities. Others have been subsumed by indigenous alternative institutions that have emerged without donor support. The UNOSOM method of establishing District and Regional Councils was based on a top-down approach, rather than being locally generated. UNOSOM eagerly announced the number of District Councils formed, a reflection of its "product" rather than "process" orientation. Facilitating qualitative rather than quantitative processes that would have eventually led to authentic local governance would have been a more sound policy to pursue.

Paradoxically, even though UNOSOM moved to support decentralization in Somalia, UNOSOM itself was highly centralized in Mogadishu. UNOSOM should have been decentralized with strengthened offices in the various zones and a small mobile headquarters in Mogadishu. Somali civil wars and territorial fragmentation had, de facto, diminished Mogadishu's previous hegemony. UNOSOM could have avoided becoming hostage to events in a particular part of the country, as it became in Mogadishu. UNO-SOM had to learn to overcome serious coordination problems. In military affairs, certain units, the Italians for example, continued to seek directives from their own national capitals rather than from UNOSOM headquarters. UNOSOM tried to create entirely new divisions to carry out its development-oriented mandate, rather than seeking to incorporate the efforts and harness the expertise of UN agencies, particularly UNDP (United Nations Development Program), to assist in institution building and economic reconstruction. There were ups and downs in coordination with humanitarian agencies and the press; this function was later routinized in the form of daily UNOSOM-NGO-Press briefings and information exchanges. UNOSOM invested tremendous political capital on the reconciliation process involving the factional leaders. Highlighted conferences involving these elements took place in Addis Ababa and in Nairobi. The UN placed a great deal of pressure on the faction leaders to reach agreements quickly, since its own mandate was of limited duration. All such factional elite conferences pre- and post-UNOSOM II have failed. Unfortunately, UNOSOM ignored the need to support, simultaneously, grass-roots peace and reconciliation conferences like the one that was held in Borama, Somaliland. In such conferences, more indigenous methods of reconciliation were applied, and sufficient time was allowed for agreements to be reached. One of the negative legacies of UNOSOM is that it did not give much attention and resources to support areas that were more stable and peaceful such as Somaliland and Puntland.

The lack of a comprehensive and consistent strategy meant that the UNOSOM mission faced serious difficulties in pursuing an appropriate sequence of actions: should, for instance, reconciliation and institution-building precede, or follow, disarmament? Should reestablishment of law and order (e.g., police) precede establishment of local or national authority, or follow it? There was no reason not to pursue a two-track reconciliation process: bottom-up and top-down. However, for a bottom-up approach to succeed, demobilization and disarmament would have to be pursued consistently and energetically. This would have provided the necessary political space for civil society. Unfortunately, UNOSOM did not have either a clear strategy or resources. Continuity in both policy and personnel which is essential for the success of a peace operation was lacking. Investments in indirect peace building, such as the promotion of business, professional, and communal associations, is a critical element in building a web of bridges across conflict lines, and should be a major component of future peace operations, with appropriate budget and expertise. UNOSOM had distorting impacts on both Somali political and economic life. UNOSOM's massive presence, especially in Mogadishu, caused indigenous and sustainable Somali employment to decline while an artificial service sector mushroomed. At the same time, UNOSOM preferred to import many items that were in fact available in local markets.

The international community's preference for local NGOs rather than local business led to a mushrooming of unauthentic Somali "NGOs." All this led to opportunists with resource-driven mentalities and a revival of the "culture of dependency" of the Siyad era. Had UNOSOM been in the business of promoting sustainability, their approach would have resulted in a series of initiatives, beginning with institution-building assistance to Somaliland, which had formed its own civilian government, followed by efforts in the Puntland areas and other relatively stable clan-controlled zones. That strategy would have involved building on the stable and authentic cases and then expanding to surround and eventually include more and more of the war-torn areas.

UNOSOM's war with Aidid left a significant and broader legacy on international affairs: it dimmed or perhaps extinguished ambitious dreams for a New World Order.[30] The plan called for the creation of a separate UN standing military rapid-response mechanism. These proposals were put on hold. The United States promptly drew the wrong conclusions from the Somali experience and delayed the Haiti mission to restore elected President Aristide. The US went so far as to prevent or delay humanitarian action elsewhere. Obviously Rwanda became the greatest tragedy that resulted from a wrong reading of the Somali lessons. Thomas Weiss observes,

Somalia cast an ominous shadow on Washington, where the Clinton team and the commander in chief in May 1994 issued Presidential Decision Directive 25 (PDD25). Supposedly the remaining superpower had "wisely retreated from the overly sanguine expectations held by the administration when it began its term." The first real test of the policy was Rwanda. As one senior State Department official close to human rights policy quipped during an off-the-record discussion, "It was almost as if the Hutus had read it." The new restrictive guidelines made it possible for the United States not only to remain on the sidelines but also to prevent others from getting involved while genocide proceeded apace.[31]

The Somali experience has also thrown a new light on debates about Africa's "juridical" versus "empirical" sovereignty and rhetoric about recolonization and trusteeship: "As anachronistic as it may seem, we need to consider ways to recommit countries (like Somalia) to the good offices of the UN Trusteeship Council."[32] The war with Aidid's faction (actually only one clan out of a potential hundred) shows that recolonization advocates must be willing to pay a heavy price in casualties and must possess unlimited resources. There is, after all, a residual empirical sovereignty in African civil society even after the collapse of the state. Should the society choose to reject foreign intervention, recolonization, or absorption into another state, this residual sovereignty is manifested in the resistance movements.

THE POST-SIYAD ENVIRONMENT

Let us recall that the most positive legacy of the US and UN involvement in Somalia was their success in defeating a man-made (civil war-induced) famine. UNOSOM learned that the roots of the Somali crisis were much deeper than originally believed. The international community and the UN lacked adequate knowledge of the inner workings of Somalia. The collapsed state in Somalia has produced unique formations as well as survival and coping strategies. Powerful new forces make it virtually impossible for foreigners and Somalis to revive the old collapsed state. So great was Siyad's malevolence and abuse of power that virtually all Somalis now hold a deep-seated fear and distrust of any centralized authority. Any notion of a central army is met with bitter hostility. An Islamic revival draws its inspiration from the need to resist Siyad's anti-Islamic measures. Donor-driven attempts to bring quick-fix unitary governance actually prolonged the civil wars and facilitated fragmentation. Future prospects could involve a federal or confederal states or even two states.

The immediate impact of UNOSOM II's departure did not result in the violence that many had predicted. During the post-UNOSOM period, donors have become more pragmatic and flexible. They have come to provide rehabilitation assistance in a more decentralized manner—to units of variable size, as long as they provide security and effective local counterparts. With the collapse of UNOSOM-sponsored institutions, more authentic entities, including authoritative local leaders, have emerged. With the distorting effect of UNOSOM no longer present, the process of both political and economic transformation has been facilitated. In certain places, including northern Mogadishu, alternative institutions have emerged without any external support. One such significant institution has been the sharia court movement.

Given Somalia's clan-divided and clan-driven society, it is natural that proposals and events are viewed and assessed through clanist perspectives. Clans that perceived themselves as having lost the civil war advocated and campaigned for the insertion of international forces into Somalia. Initially, they hoped for the immediate arrest of Aidid and the other victorious warlords. They were greatly disappointed when this did not happen. The UNOSOM II war with their arch-villain Aidid raised their hopes again. They were once again bitterly disappointed by the turn of events. One of them told me: "We tried to use foreigners to fight our own Somali battles and it turned out that we were chasing a *mirage!*"[33]

RECOMMENDATIONS

Enabling conditions upon which sound governance for Somalia could be built include the following:

Autonomy: A spirit of regional authority pervades Somali society and ought to be enhanced and formalized. In Somaliland, this spirit of autonomy has been pushed by specific circumstances, to attain the extreme form of a de facto independence.

Power sharing: People seek broad-based power sharing both as an echo of the pastoral past and as a key to a more participatory future. This aspiration should be reinforced and information be provided about various power-sharing models.

Decentralization: People favor decentralization and devolution of power. The UN and even the faction leaders were obliged to pay lip service to this preference at the March 1993 Addis Ababa conference.

Role of Women: Women are playing an increasingly prominent and constructive role in Somali society—both at home and in the diaspora. They have been building bridges between hostile clan groups. Supporting their efforts enhances reconciliation and lasting peace.

Islamic revival: There are pockets of Islamic fundamentalists on the margins of Somali society (the Gedo region bordering Ethiopia and Kenya). For most Somalis however, a spirit of revivalism reflects core values, based on Somali Sunni tradition avoiding radical politicized Islam. Somalia's Islamic revival promises to strengthen civic values and institutions of civil society and should be reinforced. Unlike the centrifugal politics of clan division, Islamic beliefs and behavior manifest a latent centripetal political tendency of integration.

Market economy: With the demise of Siyad's controlled economy with its numerous parastatals, the post-Siyad period has witnessed a vibrant, free, and unregulated economy. Its growth should be encouraged and facilitated. However, there is also need to encourage necessary and select regulations to protect the environment and to protect resources for future generations.

Local adaptation: The civil wars and the lack of goods and services that used to be imported has fostered a spirit of innovation and self-reliance. This creativity needs to be encouraged and expanded.

Traditional institutions: The new environment has also obliged Somalis to resort to their rich cultural traditions and institutions to handle grazing and agricultural systems, conflict mediation, legal adjudication, and a number of other related functions. Somaliland has provided an example of innovative governance by establishing a National Assembly with two houses—one of these, the *Guurti* or House of Elders, comprises traditional clan and religious elders. Traditional law—the *xeer*—is now widely practiced in both rural and urban areas. Traditional law and practices are part of the support system needed to make new settlements effective and sustainable.

Free Press: The pre-Siyad Somali Republic was well known for having a tradition of an irreverent free press. The tradition has returned. Mogadishu has fourteen private newspapers while Hargeisa in Somaliland has about four. They present various perspectives on the current situation in the Somali language. A number of them are often critical of the political elements. They often use cartoons to drive home their critical point. All of them would be more effective with training and technical assistance. Free speech and open debate have to be encouraged to promote lasting peace, accountability, and the gradual civilizing of the political elite.

Regional links: Independent Somalia, with its policy of irredentism, confronted hostile relations with Ethiopia and Kenya. All that has changed; relations with neighboring states have improved greatly. There is, however, a minor danger signal posed by Ethiopia's forays into parts of Gedo to combat pockets of Islamic fundamentalists. There is also the greater danger posed by the Ethiopia-Eritrea War.

Somalia is gradually healing, but is a fragmented society. The northern zone, ex-British Somaliland has proclaimed itself into a de facto independent Republic of Somaliland. The northeast zone is now Puntland seeking only internal autonomy in a future Federal Republic of Somalia. After the departure of UNOSOM II the Rahanweyn and related clans of Bay, Bakool, and parts of Gedo and Lower Shabelle regions formed a Governing Council for the Digil Mirifle. This is another example of civilianization and autonomy process. Unfortunately, this process in Bay was interrupted by Aidid's invasion of the area in September 1995. The Rahanweyn have continued to organize against Aidid with the formation of a Rahanweyn Resistance Army (RRA) and the struggles continued until they were able to liberate their territory from Aidid forces in 1999. As Somaliland, Puntland, and, hopefully, Bay zones seek power-sharing mechanisms of governance, strongman (warlord) solutions continue to prevail in Mogadishu with Hussein Aidid, Ali Mahdi, Musa Sudi, and Osman Ato; and the Kismayu and Lower Juba areas with Siyad's son-in-law General Hersi Morgan, General Gabio, and Ahmed Omas Jess. Morgan has since been driven from Kismayu by forces allied to Aidid. Post–UNOSOM factional leader conferences have been held in Addis Ababa (Sodere), Nairobi, Sana (Yemen), and Cairo—they have all failed to achieve reconciliation and coordination. Somaliland (and to some extent, Puntland) has managed to create a de facto state that insures sovereign control over territory through the loyalty of the clans legitimizing the Somaliland state. The House of Elders *(Guurti)* has increased the emerging state's capacity for governance and the maintenance of law and order. Lacking recognition from large donors such as the World Bank, it does not possess the capacity to build and maintain adequate national infrastructures. The capacity to render basic services such as education and health care, unlike in the past, is assumed more and more by the private sector and the NGO sector. Somaliland has a long way to go to assure effective and rational revenue extraction from people, goods, and services. It has relied on taxing livestock exports to Saudi Arabia and the Gulf. Such exports bring in about $400 million a year. The Somaliland state also received remittances from Somaliland populations in the diaspora, estimated at $500 million a year.

Apart from the lessons of the international intervention, does Somalia have lessons on state-society to offer Africa in the twenty-first century? The Somali experience is full of tantalizing paradoxes. Does Somali anarchy represent national nihilism or a misfortune brought about by a brutal and cynical form of bad governance? Has Somali irredentism disappeared into the dustbin of history or is the current obsession with separate development temporary? Are the aspects of indigenous governance we witness a new constitutionalism or a pragmatic expediency? Rudimentary local banks, Western Union–type due to diaspora linkages, now dominate the financial sector with women dominating the petty-trade and money-changing services. Private phone systems in several of Somalia and Somaliland's larger towns and cities may be more efficient and cheaper than most phone systems in Africa. There are more Somali-owned airlines flying in and out of more towns and cities than at any time in the past. Does Somalia and Somaliland present the World Bank's dream of structural adjustment carried to its logical conclusion? The arms trade continues to flourish in Somalia (not in Somaliland): will the country continue to be a nightmare for armaments and smuggling in the Horn of Africa? Will it also turn out to be an environmental nightmare? Will the Somali experience and Somali sacrifices yield positive lessons for the rest of Africa or are the Somalis the last of the Mohicans, the last of the great outlaw nations?

NOTES

This is a modified version of the original prepared as Chapter Nine of my book-length manuscript *Somalia: From Tyranny to Anarchy* (Washington, DC: United States Institute of Peace, forthcoming).

1. Ali Mazrui, "Crisis in Somalia: From Tyranny to Anarchy," in *Mending Rips in the Sky: Options for Somali Communities in the 21st Century, ed.* Hussein Adam and Richard Ford (Lawrenceville, New Jersey: The Red Sea Press, 1997), pp. 9–10.

2. Mohamed Sahnoun, *Somalia: The Missed Opportunities* (Washington, DC: United States Institute of Peace, 1994), p. xiii.

3. Bruce W. Jentleson, "Preventive Diplomacy in the Post–Cold War World: Opportunities Missed, Opportunities Seized and Lessons to be Learned," a mimeographed paper (Washington, DC: Carnegie Commission, 1996), p. 20.

4. Terrence Lyons and Ahmed I. Samatar, *Somalia: State Collapse, Multilateral Intervention and Strategies for Political Reconstruction (*Washington, DC: The Brookings Institution, 1995), p. 27.

5. Jeffrey Lefebvre, *Arms for the Horn: US Security Policy in Ethiopia and Somalia, 1953–1991* (Pittsburgh, PA: University of Pittsburgh Press, 1991), pp. 260–262.

6. Giampaolo Calchi Novati, "Italy and Somalia: Unbearable Lightness of an Influence," in *Mending Rips in the Sky,* ed. Adam and Ford, p. 567.

7. Abdisalam Issa-Salwe, *The Collapse of the Somali State* (London: Haan Associates, 1994), p. 86.

8. Peter Schraeder, "The Horn of Africa: U.S. Foreign Policy in an Altered Cold War Environment," *Middle East Journal* 46, no. 4 (Autumn, 1992), p. 17.

9. Lyons and Samatar, *Somalia,* pp. 33–34.

10. Samuel M. Makinda, *Seeking Peace From Chaos: Humanitarian Intervention in Somalia* (New York: International Peace Academy Occasional Paper Series, September 1993), pp. 59–60.

11. Clark 1992–1993: 109–123.

12. Schraeder, "The Horn of Africa," p. 18.

13. Johannes 1997:252.

14. Lyons and Samatar, *Somalia,* pp. 31–32.

15. Robert Oakley and John Hirsch, *Somalia and Operation Restore Hope: Reflections on Peacekeeping and Peacemaking* (Washington, DC: United States Institute of Peace, 1995), p. 40.

16. Walter Clarke and Jeffrey Herbst, eds., *Learning From Somalia: the Lessons of Armed Humanitarian Intervention* (Boulder, Colo.: Westview Press, 1997), pp. 8–9.

17. Schraeder, "The Horn of Africa," p. 21.

18. United Nations, *The United Nations and Somalia: 1992–1996* (New York: The United Nations Department of Public Information, 1996), p. 214.

19. Cited in Boulton 1994:60.

20. Cited in Lyons and Samatar, *Somalia,* p. 34.

21. Clarke and Herbst, *Learning From Somalia,* p. 9.

22. Clarke and Herbst, *Learning From Somalia,* p. 35.

23. United Nations, *The United Nations and Somalia: 1992–1996,* p. 5.

24. Oakley and Hirsch, *Somalia and Operation Restore Hope,* p. 76.

25. Oakley and Hirsch, *Somalia and Operation Restore Hope,* p. 77.

26. Clapham in Cilliers and Mills, editors, 1995:146.

27. Oakley and Hirsch, *Somalia and Operation Restore Hope,* p. 78.

28. See Lyons and Samatar, *Somalia,* pp. 70–73.

29. John Drysdale, *Whatever Happened to Somalia? A Tale of Tragic Blunders* (London: Haan Associates 1994), p. 4.

30. Boutros Boutros-Ghali, *An Agenda for Peace: Preventive Diplomacy, Peacemaking and Peacekeeping* (New York: United Nations, 1992).

31. Clarke and Herbst, *Learning From Somalia,* p. 207–208.

32. Robert Rotberg in Clarke and Herbst, *Learning From Somalia,p.* 233.

33. Ahmed Ali Omar from Gedo, personal communications in Nairobi, Kenya, 26 May, 1997.

9

Mozambique

What Nexus among Peacemaking, Peacekeeping, and Development?

João Honwana

The cycle of violence that engulfed Mozambique for nearly thirty years[1] has ended and, since October 1992, the country has been grappling with the challenges of the journey from war to peace, and from socialism to parliamentary democracy and economic liberalism.

The journey certainly entails very complex challenges and there are no guarantees of the ultimate success of long-term peacebuilding in Mozambique. However, a more modest success can be claimed with regard to both the peace negotiation process, which produced the General Peace Agreement of Mozambique (GPA), and the short-term implementation of the accord, facilitated by the United Nations Mission in Mozambique (ONUMOZ). How do we define success in both instances? What specific factors and actors made such positive outcomes possible? What impact do these earlier successes have on the long-term peace building and development in Mozambique? In the search for explanations, this paper begins with a brief discussion of the origins and consequences of the war in Mozambique, followed by an examination of the negotiation process, the peace accord, and ONUMOZ. Finally, the paper assesses the obstacles to postwar peace building and the overall impact of the international community's assistance to reconstruction and development in Mozambique.

The paper argues that the civil war in Mozambique was externally instigated and supported and, when the foreign sources of support disappeared, the disputant parties were forced to seek mutual accommodation to survive as viable political entities.

It maintains that the peace negotiations were successful because they resulted in an agreement that the parties found acceptable and, thus far, have adhered to. The paper highlights the mediators' critical role in the successful outcome to the negotiations. The paper argues further that, in spite of some severe weaknesses, ONUMOZ generally succeeded in fulfilling its mandate, thereby contributing to a self-enforcing conclusion of the war and the establishment of the institutional foundations for the peaceful resolution of political conflict in Mozambique. Finally, the paper warns that the postwar reconstruction strategies advanced by the international community may have the unintended and paradoxical consequence of jeopardizing Mozambique's yet fragile peace.

THE CONFLICT: A "WAR BY PROXY," AN EXTERNAL AGGRESSION, OR A CIVIL WAR?

The origins, characteristics, and impact of the war in Mozambique have been well documented.[2] Centrally characterized by a complex interaction of domestic, regional, and global variables, the conflict in Mozambique defies simple categorizations. It was a civil war in the sense that Mozambicans fought it. But it was also a war between states as it originated from irreconcilable political differences among neighboring countries within the framework of a bipolar international system. In this regard, it should be noted that peace was established in Mozambique only after the end of the Cold War and the radical transformation of the nature of the state both in Mozambique and in South Africa. In other words, the Cold War dynamics and the regional struggle against white minority regimes were central factors in both the onset and termination of the Mozambican civil war.

In hindsight, it is reasonable to say that the Mozambican government would have been stronger to face its external foes if it had adequately addressed the internal factors of conflict. This could have been achieved through the adoption of political inclusiveness in governance, a greater sensitivity to issues of identity and culture, particularly in the rural areas, and wiser economic policies. However, to suggest that FRELIMO's[3] policies were solely responsible for Mozambique's socioeconomic collapse, ignoring that its external enemies intended precisely to undermine those policies, would be to blame the victim. This is not to deny that RENAMO[4] developed a distinct Mozambican identity as the war progressed, but simply to locate the emergence and evolution of the rebel movement within the broader context of southern African political and security dynamics.

THE ROAD TO PEACE

Initial Contacts

The difficulties created by RENAMO's actions—economic devastation and social chaos in the rural areas, the collapse of the state and the confinement of the government to towns and garrisons—were compounded by the constraints imposed by foreign assistance.[5] Moreover, the implosion of the Soviet Union and the collapse of the socialist system in Eastern Europe in 1989–91 left FRELIMO without the sources of critical military support required to continue the war effort. At the same time, a rapidly changing South Africa abandoned the strategy of regional destabilization and severed supply lines to the rebels. The Cold War was over and the danger of "communist expansion" had been reversed. Even for the most radical anti-Communist international forces, the maintenance of RENAMO as a military operation was no longer necessary. The time had come to end peripheral proxy wars and make peace.

In early 1988, President Chissano understood that the war had reached a stalemate and preparations were necessary for peace negotiations. He encouraged leaders of the Mozambican Catholic Church as well as the governments of Kenya and Zimbabwe to initiate exploratory contacts with RENAMO, aimed at convincing the rebels to renounce violence as a means to promote political change, and bringing them into direct talks with the government.[6] At its fifth congress in July 1989, FRELIMO embarked on a process of internal reform and approved the principle of peace negotiations with the rebels. The adherence to Marxism-Leninism was replaced with a return to the posture of a broad nationalist front, and the intransigence towards RENAMO was replaced with a discourse on peace and national reconciliation.[7] At the same time, the rebels declared a unilateral cease-fire in Nampula as a gesture of good will towards the government and a means of improving their domestic and international image.

In July 1989 the government circulated a twelve-point "non-paper" which set the basis for dialogue. In essence, the document demanded that RENAMO abandon terrorism and violence in all forms, offering the rebels amnesty and the promise of reintegration into society as part of a plan of "normalization of the life of all Mozambicans." In response, RENAMO issued a sixteen-point document in August rejecting FRELIMO's demands and indicating that it would renounce violence under certain conditions. The government had to formally acknowledge the rebel movement as a political force and accept the drafting up of a new constitution jointly with RENAMO. The document also called for the withdrawal of all foreign troops from the country. The document further stated RENAMO's commitment to genuine reconciliation and a new Mozambique, without victors or vanquished.

Thus both parties indicated their readiness to start some form of dialogue. Both parties expressed a commitment to a peaceful settlement, democracy, national reconciliation, and unity. However, despite their success in establishing an atmosphere conducive to dialogue, the Mozambican religious leaders and the Kenyan and Zimbabwean officials failed to bring the government and RENAMO to direct talks. This was due primarily to an intense mutual mistrust between the parties, reflected in their opposing views on the negotiation process and different choice of mediators. While the government called for a discrete and direct dialogue with minimum outside involvement, RENAMO preferred a high-profile process of mediated negotiations, with a strong international presence.

The Rome Negotiations[8]

The government and RENAMO eventually began talks in Rome on 8–10 July, facilitated by representatives of the Italian government (the Sant'Egidio Community and the Mozambican Catholic Church) who were accorded a "process observer" status. The Community of Sant'Egidio had connections in Mozambique since the mid-70s, mainly through Don Jaime Gonçalves, the archbishop of Beira, who had studied in Rome and established friendly relations with Sant'Egidio's members. In the early 1980s, the Community developed efforts to improve the relationship between the government and the Mozambican Catholic Church. In the same period, they negotiated the release of nuns and priests being held hostage by RENAMO and facilitated discrete and informal contacts between FRELIMO leaders and the Holy See. Moreover, Sant'Egidio launched a series of humanitarian initiatives in support of Mozambican victims of the war. Thus, they built a relationship based on trust and respect with both the government and RENAMO.[9]

At the end of first round of talks, the parties produced a joint communiqué expressing their satisfaction that negotiations had begun, and that the dialogue, which had been frank and constructive, was inspired by the shared commitment to peace and reconciliation. Most importantly, the parties expressed mutual acknowledgement as members of the "great Mozambican family," recognizing superior national interest as more valuable than the issues that divided them. Therefore, they chose dialogue as the method to resolve the conflict. Following an unproductive second round of talks, on 11–14 August, the parties agreed to accord a mediator status to the process observers.

After three weeks of negotiations during the third round of talks, the mediators presented the parties with a written proposal on the issue of the Zimbabwean troops present in the country and worked out an agreement in separate meetings with each delegation. This "Agreement on a Partial Cease-Fire" regulated the presence and role of the Zimbabwean troops in the period before the general cease-fire. The agreement, valid for a period of six months and renewable by mutual consent, determined that the Zimbabwean troops would be restricted to a strip of three kilometers outside the furthest edge of each corridor and would not engage in offensive military operations. RENAMO, in turn, would refrain from attacking the corridors. A Joint Verification Commission was set up including representatives from Kenya, the United States, Portugal, Zambia, Zimbabwe, Congo, France, the Soviet Union, and the United Kingdom that would monitor the implementation of the agreement.

The mediators thus achieved the first major breakthrough in the negotiation process, whereby each disputant party accepted a fundamental principle of political compromise: lose something and gain something. The government lost the possibility of employing the very effective Zimbabwean contingent in offensive operations, but gained the guarantee that the corridors would remain open and threat free, generating much-needed income, and providing an essential service to Zimbabwe. RENAMO lost an important instrument to pressure the government, but gained a critical image boost and the added security that came with the confinement of Zimbabwean troops.

Throughout the remainder of the negotiation process, the mediators' skills, commitment, and patience would be severely tested. Each disputant party tried to reach a settlement that advanced its own interests. The government wanted to maintain control of the decision-making process and the allocation of state resources. RENAMO was interested in domestic and international recognition and guaranteed access to political power and material wealth. The major obstacles to a swift settlement were the high level of mistrust between the parties, the preemptive political and economic reforms conducted by the government which pulled the rug from under RENAMO's feet, and RENAMO's lack of experience in complex negotiations.

The spiraling economic and social crisis, exacerbated by a situation of drought and famine of unprecedented proportions, made the human cost of the war increasingly unbearable to the domestic supporters of either side. By late 1991, negotiations gathered some momentum, due to a large extent to the further aggravation of the situation in Mozambique, which put the opponents under great pressure. The speeding up of the process caused some dissension amongst RENAMO's negotiators. Some of them wanted to reach a settlement conducive to elections and the transformation of RENAMO into a political force; others wanted a trade-off between a cease-fire and the granting of security and material conditions as they believed that RENAMO would not be able to become a significant political force. This quest for material (particularly financial) security by RENAMO remained a major issue throughout the entire peace process.

Throughout these negotiations, the mediators played an extremely constructive role. By approaching their task with great sensitivity to the concerns of the disputant parties, the mediators helped the parties to gain confidence in the negotiation process itself, to trust the mediators as honest brokers and, more importantly, to build sufficient mutual trust. The government and RENAMO negotiators did not become allies as a result of the negotiation process. But they moved from mutual perceptions of enmity and existential threat to mutual acknowledgement and respect as political adversaries and inevitable partners in the search for peace, thus building the political will reflected in the Mozambique General Peace Agreement of 4 October 1992.

The General Peace Accord

Mozambique's transition to peace began with the signing of a General Peace Accord (GPA) between the government and RENAMO in Rome on 4 October 1992, and culminated in the general elections of 27–29 October 1994. The Accord consisted of seven Protocols and a number of joint declarations and communiqués dating from 18 October 1991, when the first round of talks ended, to 4 October 1994, when the negotiation process formally ended.[10]

The GPA determined the procedures, organization, and timetable for the concentration, disarmament, and demobilization of armed forces; the selection, training, and establishment of a unified defense force, the *Forças Armadas de Defesa de Moçambique* (FADM); the organization and conduct of presidential and legislative elections; and the provision of humanitarian assistance to the distressed population. The GPA also made provisions for the United Nations to monitor the implementation of the Accord. All these actions were to take place within a period of twelve months. The Protocols addressed themes such as the basic principles for the negotiation process, the establishment of political parties, the principles of the Electoral Act, military issues, the timetable for the conduct of the electoral process, and the cease-fire.

In summary, the Peace Accord illustrates how the mediators assisted the parties to understand and accept the principle of political compromise, with both sides exchanging concessions. It established a functional partnership between the government and RENAMO in the peace process, and gave the United Nations a central political role in the conduct of that process. The Accord was at once fairly comprehensive and sufficiently vague to allow for a degree of flexibility of interpretation. An example of that flexibility was the establishment of the Trust Fund to assist RENAMO's transformation into a political party. This initiative raises ethical questions that I will discuss later. Thus far, they do not seem to be an issue in Mozambique; however, their long-term implications remain to be seen. Another important feature of the Peace Accord was that it created a powerful political structure to supervise its implementation. In effect the Supervision and Monitoring Commission (CSC) and its subsidiary commissions were the ultimate decision-making bodies in all matters pertaining to the implementation of the peace agreement. The fact that all decisions were made by consensus of the two major Mozambican parties in these commissions created a valuable space for confidence building.

THE UNITED NATIONS OPERATION IN MOZAMBIQUE (ONUMOZ)

The Mandate

Besides cease-fire and election monitoring, the mandate of ONUMOZ included important elements of peacebuilding such as the demobilization and social reintegration of former combatants, the clearance of land mines, and the collection and destruction of weapons. Moreover, ONUMOZ was responsible for providing humanitarian assistance to millions of Mozambicans in critical need: returning refugees, internally displaced people, and the victims of drought and famine in vast areas of the countryside. The operation's structure comprised a multinational military contingent, police monitors, and international civilian staff.

Seven multilateral commissions were established to implement the GPA, comprising representatives of the government, RENAMO, and the international community. These were the Supervisory and Monitoring Commission (CSC), an overarching political body responsible for the management of the entire peace process; the Joint Commission for the Formation of the Armed Forces (CCFADM); the Cease-Fire Commission (CSF); the Commission for the Reintegration of the Demobilized Combatants (CORE); the Police Commission (COMPOL); the Intelligence Commission (COMINFO); and the Joint Commission for Territorial Administration (CCAT). At the formal request of the Mozambican government following the signing of the Peace Accord, the UN Security Council established ONUMOZ in December 1992, with the general purpose of facilitating the implementation of the Accord and monitoring the country's first democratic elections.

In the political sphere, ONUMOZ was responsible for the impartial supervision of the implementation of the Peace Accord. To this end, it assumed the chair of three Commissions: the Supervisory and Monitoring Commission (CSC), the Commission for the

Reintegration of Demobilized Combatants (CORE), and the Cease-Fire Commission (CCF). The National Electoral Commission (CNE), which was established to manage the organization and conduct of the elections, also benefited from ONUMOZ logistic support and technical assistance from the United Nations Development Program (UNDP).

In the military field, ONUMOZ was mandated to monitor and verify the cease-fire; the concentration and demobilization of armed forces; the collection, storage and destruction of weapons; the disbanding of irregular and private armed groups; and the complete withdrawal of foreign troops. It was responsible for providing security to UN personnel and installations, as well as other international agencies involved in supporting the peace process. ONUMOZ was also to provide security in vital transport corridors in order to guarantee the free circulation of people and humanitarian assistance.

Initially, according to the Peace Agreement, there were no provisions for ONUMOZ's involvement in the creation of the new national defense force. This task was to be undertaken by the government and RENAMO, assisted by representatives of the countries that they had previously selected, i.e., France, Portugal, and the United Kingdom. However, at the request of the two parties and the supporting countries, ONUMOZ was integrated into the Joint Commission for the Formation of the Armed Forces (CCFADM) and assumed its Chair at a later stage. This was done in order to help overcome the differences between the government and RENAMO and speed up the process. The UN Security Council authorized ONUMOZ to assume an exclusively facilitating role "on the strict understanding that this would not entail any obligation on the part of the United Nations for training or establishing the new armed forces."[11]

The humanitarian mandate of ONUMOZ included the coordination of humanitarian assistance operations. This was put under the responsibility of the United Nations Office for Humanitarian Assistance coordination (UNOHAC) in Mozambique.

To undertake this set of complex tasks, ONUMOZ at its peak comprised 5,914 military personnel including military observers, staff officers, and formed units, and 1,068 civilian police.[12] The general elections were monitored by approximately 2,300 UN observers provided by UN Member States, a range of UN offices, ONUMOZ, the European Union, the diplomatic community in Maputo, non-governmental organizations working in Mozambique, the Organization of African Unity, and the Association of European Parliamentarians for Southern Africa.[13] The cost of the operation in 1994 was estimated at US $294.8 million, with outstanding contributions as of 15 November 1994 amounting to US $105.9 million.[14]

Challenges to Implementation[15]

ONUMOZ initiated its activities on 15 October 1992, when Aldo Ajello, Interim Special Representative of the UN secretary-general (ISRSG) arrived in Maputo leading a team of 25 UN observers. From the outset, the leadership of ONUMOZ was confronted with the fact that the timetable for the implementation of the General Peace Accord (GPA) was highly unrealistic. It did not take into account three critical factors. First, the recently established major UN peacekeeping operations in the former Yugoslavia (UNPROFOR), Cambodia (UNTAC), and Somalia (UNOSOM I) in March and April 1992 required a total of 70,000 UN peacekeepers just before the establishment of ONUMOZ. These demands would result in a delay between the decision to establish ONUMOZ and the actual deployment on the ground of its civilian and military personnel. Second, the political and logistical impact of ONUMOZ's presence in Mozambique. Third, the high level of mistrust between the government and RENAMO. For its role in considerably slowing down the pace of implementation, this last factor is briefly examined below.

Mistrust between the Government and RENAMO

As described earlier, the lengthy peace negotiations revealed that neither party had much confidence in the other's good faith. In spite of all the good work by the team of mediators, which eventually resulted in the signing of the Peace Accord, this deep mistrust between the parties remained a central feature of the transition period. It slowed down the whole process considerably, particularly the assembly, disarmament, and demobilization of troops, as well as the extension of state administration to RENAMO-controlled areas.

By early June 1993, when the full UN contingent was finally in place and ONUMOZ was ready start the implementation of the Rome Accord, the Mozambican parties were unwilling to cooperate. RENAMO presented a variety of reasons for not concentrating its forces in the designated assembly areas: the unacceptable logistical conditions in most of these areas, the lack of guarantees for the personal safety of RENAMO's leaders, and the lack of funds necessary to transform itself into a political party. Dlakhama, who had refused to move to Maputo on security grounds and remained at RENAMO's stronghold in Maringue, was clearly using his military power as a bargaining tool to force the government and the international community into concessions. To overcome this impasse, the Special Representative of the Secretary General (SRSG) employed a "carrot and stick" strategy. The carrot was the promise to make available to RENAMO the necessary funds for its transformation into a political party; and the stick was the threat that the UN would terminate its mission in Mozambique even before the elections, if RENAMO did not move speedily into the assembly areas.

Apparently, Ajello succeeded in convincing Dlakhama of three things. First, that RENAMO stood a better chance of surviving as a political party in a peaceful Mozambique, rather than as a military organization. Second, that the international community was prepared and willing to assist RENAMO's transformation if the movement gave a clear indication of its commitment to the peace process and the elections. And third, that the presence of the United Nations was a critical guarantee of free and fair elections. Thus, in early June 1993 RENAMO resumed its participation in the peace accord commissions. However, by September 1993 the implementation of the accord showed little progress. At the political level, there was no agreement on the draft Electoral Law and the composition of the National Electoral Commission. And in the military sphere, troops from both sides were not moving to the assembly areas and, consequently, the processes of demobilization and collection and destruction of weapons could not start. At this stage, RENAMO issued a declaration reaffirming its commitment to the peace process and raising the possibility of holding elections in October 1994 even if demobilization were not completed. The UN could not accept the risks involved in this option:

With the situation in Angola offering clear evidence of the dangers of this approach, my Special Representative reasserted ONUMOZ's determination to hold elections only after full demobilization had taken place. He publicly warned RENAMO that it could no longer try to preserve both a political and a military option.[16]

In view of this lack of progress, the UN Secretary General visited Maputo in October 1993. His main concern was to make it clear to President Chissano and Mr. Dlakhama that unless they both showed real political will and took urgent steps to overcome the impasse, the international community would consider withdrawing ONUMOZ. Addressing the Mozambican people on national television, Boutros Boutros-Ghali warned,

Time is short. Solutions must now be found. While the international community continues to show a willingness to assist in the process of building peace, peace cannot be imposed from the outside, nor can it be built where there is not sufficient political will to make peace.[17]

The Mozambican leaders seemed to have understood what was at stake. Within three days of Boutros-Ghali's visit, compromise was reached on the issues that had prevented progress. Thus, the government and RENAMO accepted new principles for the deliberations of the Cease-fire Commission. They agreed that the National Electoral Commission would include ten members appointed by the government, seven by RENAMO and three from other political parties. It was also agreed that the parties would hold technical meetings to discuss the draft electoral law that would then be submitted to the national parliament *(Assembléia da Republica)* by the end of November 1993. It was also decided that Chissano would appoint the chairperson of the National Police Affairs Commission, while Dlakhama would select the chairperson of the Commission for Information. And the National Commission for Administration would operate under two rotating chairpersons, one selected by the government and the other selected by RENAMO. Moreover, the parties undertook to start moving their troops to the assembly areas in November 1993 in order to guarantee that demobilization would be completed between January and May 1994. On his departure from Maputo, the UN Secretary General expressed optimism with regard to the peace process.[18]

Demobilization and Disarmament

Contrary to earlier promises, the troops from both sides only began arriving at the assembly areas in late January 1994. This delay was due to disagreements on the final list of assembly areas and the poor logistical conditions in many of them. More importantly, both sides were reluctant to dispose of their best operational units and senior officers, and were unable or unwilling to give reliable numbers of troops to be demobilized. Thus, it was only by late February that all assembly areas were operational. By mid-April around 49,000 soldiers were concentrated in these areas, of which 14,000 were from RENAMO and 34,000 from the government.[19]

The process of demobilization comprised four distinct phases: the identification and opening of assembly areas; cantonment, registration, disarmament, and selection for the new armed forces; demobilization; and return home. A Demobilization Technical Unit (DTU), comprising civilian experts from the United Nations Volunteers and a number of bilateral and multilateral agencies, was created in the office of the Special Representative of the Secretary General to coordinate and supervise the entire process.

Demobilization started in early March and was concluded in late August 1994. The International Organization for Migration provided transportation for the demobilized soldiers and their dependents. The first serious problem in this process involved the selection and approval of the assembly areas. From the outset it was agreed that 49 sites (29 for government troops and 20 for RENAMO's) should be set up to accommodate a total of 82,000 soldiers (61,000 from the government and 21,000 from RENAMO), plus their close relatives (another 38,000 people). Since neither party wanted to give the other a strategic advantage, assembly areas were often chosen in places with inadequate living conditions and difficult access, creating serious logistical problems.

Disarmament was approached as a mere component of the process of demobilization, rather than a specific aim of ONUMOZ. As a result of this linkage between demobilization and disarmament, the peacekeepers were restricted to disarming demobilized soldiers within the assembly areas. Under the rules approved by the Cease-Fire Commission, the peacekeepers were prevented from searching and disabling surplus weapons both in the arsenals and caches of either party and in the hands of the civilian population at large. Furthermore, most demobilized soldiers kept possession of their weapons in good condition, surrendering only those of poor quality.[20]

The uncertainty about the quantity of weapons present in Mozambique only compounded the problem facing ONUMOZ. Estimates vary from 1.5 million to 6 million AK-47s and there is no reliable documentation available to check either of these figures, just as there is no information about the quantities of other types of light weapons, ammunition, hand grenades, mines, etc.[21] In short, ONUMOZ failed to accomplish an effective disarmament for a number of reasons. First, both the government and RENAMO were intent on frustrating disarmament and retaining as many functioning weapons as the process would allow them, in anticipation of a reversal of the peace process. This enabled individual soldiers to keep their weapons for personal gain. Second, ONUMOZ failed to establish the conceptual distinction between demobilization and disarmament, had a restrictive mandate with respect to disarmament, and did not have sufficient resources to undertake even that limited mandate. This resulted in confusion amongst the implementers, and the destruction of very few weapons. Third, no measures were taken to ensure the continuity of the disarmament process after the departure of the peacekeepers. As a consequence, Mozambique is awash with uncontrolled weapons that have been used to fuel criminal activities both domestically and in neighboring countries.

Be that as it may, on 15 August all assembly areas were formally closed. Demobilization of non-assembled troops continued for some time and by late November 57,540 government and 20,538 RENAMO soldiers had been demobilized from a total of 91,691 registered troops.[22] ONUMOZ had collected a total of 189,827 weapons from the military and paramilitary forces, having disabled a small number of arms, ammunition, and explosives, and transferred the remainder to the FADM.

Social Reintegration of Ex-Combatants

UNOHAC was also responsible for planning, organizing, and supervising the process of reintegrating demobilized soldiers. To do so, its representative assumed the chairmanship of the Commission for Reintegration (CORE) and guaranteed a permanent dialogue and consultation between the government and RENAMO on matters pertaining to this critical aspect of the peace process. The local Office of the United Nations Development Program, in turn, implemented a Reintegration Support Scheme (RSS) for demobilized soldiers.[23] This was a Trust Fund to provide the demobilized soldiers with eighteen months' salary, in addition to the six months severance pay from the government.

The demobilized troops were also eligible to benefit from training through an occupational skills development program and had access to a fund to support small-scale business ventures. Additionally, UNOHAC set up a countrywide Information and Referral Service. This was a central element of the CORE/UNOHAC program and sought to provide institutional support to revive the Mozambican Ministry of Labor's vocational training and employment network. UNOHAC considered it unrealistic to believe that former combatants would quickly stop feeling like soldiers. For that reason, UNOHAC felt it was important to create a government mechanism that would continue to implement the donors' programs once they had stopped assisting the process of reintegration.

In the donors' opinion, however, UNOHAC should have limited its activities to the short term, i.e., the implementation of the Peace Accord, and left the long-term programs to be covered by the permanent agencies of the UN system. While reporting to the SRSG in Mozambique, UNOHAC was also answerable to the UN Department of Humanitarian Affairs in New York. In the view of some members of the diplomatic community in Maputo, this led to excessive bureaucracy, slow decision making, and duplication of efforts.[24] With regard to mine clearance and demobilization, these sources argue, UNOHAC was mistaken in trying to promote a long-term developmental approach aimed at empowering the Mozambican government of the day. This would have required much more time than was available, thus endangering the successful completion of ONUMOZ within the agreed schedule.

Humanitarian Assistance

Despite the tension between the government and RENAMO, the cease-fire held throughout the transition period. This, coupled with a good rainy season, allowed subsistence farmers to resume production and achieve fairly good harvests in many areas. It also led government and nongovernment organizations to undertake the reconstruction of rural hospitals and schools, while the humanitarian assistance agencies were able to initiate their activities, now that the main transport corridors were under UN military protection. This general improvement in the security situation, in turn, encouraged refugees and displaced people to begin the long-awaited journey home.

The United Nations Office for Humanitarian Assistance Coordination (UNOHAC) was responsible for coordinating the humanitarian mandate of ONUMOZ. This entailed the resettlement of refugees, displaced people, and demobilized soldiers with their dependents; mine-clearance activities; rehabilitation of roads, schools, and rural hospitals; distribution of seeds and agricultural tools; improvement of access to safe water; and social reintegration of ex-combatants. To perform its coordinating role, UNOHAC established provincial and local humanitarian assistance committees in which both the government and RENAMO had representatives. These were units that planned food distribution and the construction and improvement of basic social services. More importantly, through these committees UNOHAC promoted a degree of dialogue and confidence building between the government and RENAMO at provincial and local levels.[25]

The Office of the United Nations High Commissioner for Refugees (UNHCR) undertook the resettlement of "vulnerable groups" (refugees, displaced people, and ex-combatants with their dependents) with the assistance of the government's relief agency and various NGOs. Although it formally operated under UNOHAC coordination, UNHCR was in fact locally subordinated to the head of UNOMOZ. It is estimated that UNHCR supported the resettlement of approximately 1.6 million refugees and 200,000 demobilized soldiers and their dependents between October 1992 and December 1994. Most observers agree that UNHCR action contributed to averting a major humanitarian tragedy in Mozambique.[26]

The humanitarian operation raised some controversy when local RENAMO officials began to circulate the idea that food, clothing, health care, and education services were being provided by RENAMO and not the government. The government insisted that ONUMOZ should force RENAMO to open such areas to free circulation, in compliance with the Peace Accord; however, as in other instances when RENAMO dragged its feet, the ONUMOZ leadership adopted a strategy of patient negotiation. In the government's perception, this approach allowed RENAMO to perpetuate a dual territorial administration and use humanitarian assistance as a propaganda tool. ONUMOZ, which had no enforcement powers, requested the UN Secretary General to raise the issue with the Security Council which addressed it in its resolutions. In addition, Ajello made it clear that RENAMO's interpretation of the Peace Agreement was wrong, both publicly in his weekly press briefing and privately in numerous meetings with RENAMO's leader

Dlakhama. As a result of this pressure, RENAMO abandoned the "dual administration" approach and gradually opened the areas it controlled.

The Electoral Process

The organization and conduct of the electoral process was regulated by an Electoral Act and managed by a National Electoral Commission (CNA). Preparations for the elections were undertaken in three phases: voter registration, voter education and electoral campaigning. Since multiparty democracy and elections were new to most Mozambicans, voter education covered both electoral education (how to vote) and education for democracy (why vote). Whereas for the majority of the population the election of a leader did not raise doubts, the role of political parties and parliament was not fully understood by the electorate. The relationship between voting for a party and electing representatives for parliament was not clear in the minds of many voters.

The high rate of illiteracy amongst Mozambicans and the lack of good communications networks (both in terms of access roads and mass media) hampered substantially the effectiveness of voter education campaigns. Innovative methods such as dance and theatre were often employed with good results. However, voter education received a higher profile in the urban areas where voters were more exposed to all sorts of information. The rural areas were much less targeted by voter education campaigns.

A major issue in the electoral campaign was the funding of the so-called "non-armed" opposition. These parties claimed that they needed support from both the government and the international community in order to compete with FRELIMO and RENAMO, both of which had access to considerable funding and resources. Eventually the non-armed political parties received approximately US $15,000 from the government and an additional US $100,000 from the international community.

Freedom of political activity was another problem. In RENAMO-controlled areas, such activity by parties other than RENAMO was not allowed until the end of the concentration of troops in the Assembly Areas, which happened very late in the peace process. Some opposition parties also accused the government of harassment in the areas it controlled. All in all, the electoral campaign was generally free but seldom fair, particularly for the non-armed parties. Their lack of strong party machinery and the fact that they were "new faces in the game" without a convincing program undermined their campaigns.

The opposition parties based their campaign on the mistakes made by FRELIMO during its nineteen years in power and on the need for a more even distribution of power and resources to the central and northern regions of the country. FRELIMO emphasized continuity and its experience in governance. Backed by the international community, most of the opposition parties, including RENAMO, called for the establishment of a government of national unity after the elections. FRELIMO refused to discuss this option, arguing that the election results should determine the composition of the new government. Among the opposition parties, there was no consensus on the criteria for the formation of a government of national unity. In the end, the issue was dropped, though not before an intense and virulent exchange of views in the media. This affected certain foreign embassies that were perceived as favoring power sharing and therefore "interfering in the internal affairs of Mozambique."

Elections took place on 27–29 October 1994, with twelve parties and two coalitions running for parliament, and twelve presidential candidates. Elections were held in a peaceful and orderly manner and the only serious hiccup occurred when RENAMO threatened to withdraw from the voting on the eve of the elections, alleging preparations for widespread fraud on the part of the government. The crisis was solved after negotiations between RENAMO's leader Afonso Dlakhama and the representatives of the international community. The incident did not affect the casting of votes or the course of events: voter turnout was very high, with around 87.4% of voters participating and 91.4% of the ballots cast counted as valid.

FRELIMO (44.33%) and its president Chissano (53.3%) won the elections and RENAMO (37.78%) and Dlakhama (33.73%) came second. Only a third political force, the União Democratica coalition, managed to pass the 5% threshold and elect members to parliament. Interestingly, Chissano proved more popular than his party, whereas RENAMO appeared stronger than its leader. FRELIMO and RENAMO showed that they were the only parties with national appeal, although both feature regional strongholds: FRELIMO in the south and far north, and RENAMO in the center and center/north.

Having resisted pressure from ONUMOZ and some Western diplomats for a pre-election deal on power sharing in a government of national unity to guarantee a place in the Executive for RENAMO, FRELIMO adopted a winner-take-all position. FRELIMO claimed that the electoral results had given it the right to govern alone and that one of the central tenets of democracy was precisely the existence of a viable opposition. It would therefore be nondemocratic, the argument went, to absorb the opposition into the government. In any event, RENAMO has accepted FRELIMO's choice and is playing the role of the main opposition party. This may be based on the conviction that during its five-year mandate, FRELIMO will fail to meet the popular expectations and lose credibility, while with the passage of time the memories of RENAMO's cruelty during the war fade away.

Assessing ONUMOZ

Measured against the operation's mandate and schedule, ONUMOZ was successful in that it contributed to a reasonably stable and quick transition from war to peace, and to the organization and conduct of peaceful, free, and fair elections that marked the symbolic birth of Mozambique as a liberal democracy. However, a more rigorous analytical perspective is taken here in assessing the operation. Assuming that the ultimate purpose of peacekeeping is to create the conditions for a *positive peace*,[27] thus avoiding the recurrence of violent conflict, an analysis follows of the strengths and weaknesses of ONUMOZ. Nevertheless, it is worth mentioning two critical contextual factors that contributed significantly to ONUMOZ's relative success. First, the overwhelming will for peace on the part of the Mozambican people exerted decisive pressure on the signatories of the Rome Accord. This, coupled with the country's material and psychological exhaustion and the absence of foreign sources of support for war, made peace the only viable option for both the government and RENAMO. In my view, this was the real source of the much-acclaimed political will for peace displayed by both parties.

Strengths

The leadership of ONUMOZ seized and never surrendered the initiative in the management of the peace process. This was possible largely because the SRSG was effectively the representative of the entire international community. To achieve that, the SRSG performed his function in a proactive and imaginative way. Ajello managed the peace process in a fairly transparent fashion, holding weekly press briefings, showing a strict adherence to the principle of decisions by consensus, and, most importantly, ensuring the active involvement of the local representatives of the international community in the peace process. Thus Ajello built a broad consensus within the representatives of the international community (European Union and United States, OAU, SADC members, UN agencies) around all issues relevant to the implementation of the Peace Accord. Ajello also regularly briefed other international representatives who were not part of any of these groups. As a result of the common understanding and unity of purpose that were developed through this process of consultation, the SRSG enjoyed the unequivocal support of the international community. This enhanced his influence and negotiating power vis-à-vis the Mozambican parties.

Another contributing factor to the success of ONUMOZ was that the United Nations proved to be more flexible a bureaucracy than it is is normally credited for. Confronted with the proactive and at times unorthodox approach of Aldo Ajello, the UN headquarters were able to accommodate his initiatives in the field, despite their technical nonconformity with UN rules and procedures.

Weaknesses

On a par with the positive features above, ONUMOZ revealed some severe shortcomings. The first such problem was the long time that elapsed between the formal establishment of ONUMOZ and the full deployment of the peacekeepers in the mission area. This led to a high level of uncertainty in Mozambique and fears that hostilities might start again. This motivated the desirability for the UN to be able to deploy peacekeepers immediately at the beginning of a peace process.

The second problem was a perennial one: the lack of enforcement powers, (which would have required a different mandate), that determined that ONUMOZ strictly observe the principle of decision making by consensus. This had both a positive and negative impact on the peace process. Decision by consensus by the government and RENAMO was useful in the sense that it enabled a degree of ownership of the process and the attendant accountability for its outcome. It formally respected and enhanced the will of the signatories of the Rome Agreement. However, it was also a weakness because it gave the Mozambican parties enough latitude to maneuver to seek tactical advantages at every step of the peace process. Moreover, it led to significant delays with the cantonment and demobilization of troops, and the establishment of an effective state administration and freedom of movement throughout the country. It also led to the UN's failure to accomplish the effective disarmament of former combatants and the destruction of surplus weapons.

The vastly different levels of professionalism displayed by the different national contingents of peacekeepers and police observers was another element of concern that suggests the need for clearly defined training requirements, as well as tighter selection criteria for peacekeepers. While the Botswana contingent was generally held in high esteem as a result of their professionalism and respectful and sensitive treatment of the Mozambican population and authorities, there were allegations of grave misbehavior leveled against the Italian contingent. For example the Mozambique representatives of Save the Children Fund (USA, UK, and Norway) have insistently accused the Italian Battalion Albatross, tasked with the protection of the Beira Corridor, of repeatedly abusing young girls for sexual purposes.[28]

Another important weakness revealed by ONUMOZ was the difficulty experienced in overcoming the divergent institutional cultures of peacekeepers, on the one hand, and the international humanitarian agencies, on the other. The United Nations should develop a new conceptual framework for peace operations that takes into account this tension between the demands of maximum results in minimum time and the long-term development requirements, a inherent feature in contemporary peacekeeping.

OBSTACLES TO POSTWAR RECONSTRUCTION AND PEACEBUILDING

Context

By way of conclusion, an exploration follows of the obstacles to postwar reconstruction and peacebuilding, and the potential support that the International Community can offer to Mozambique in addressing those challenges.

In the immediate aftermath of the October 1994 elections, most observers argued that the peace process was based on very shaky foundations. Their pessimism was based partly on ethical considerations around the political compromise between FRELIMO and RENAMO, partly on concerns regarding FRELIMO's "winner takes all" approach, and partly on the enormity of the legacy of the war. The transformation of the rebel movement into a political party was a critical precondition to ensure that RENAMO had a stake in the peace process. Accordingly, at the request of the Mozambican government, the international community established a trust fund in May 1993 to receive and channel voluntary contributions to RENAMO. The Fund was administered by ONUMOZ according to UN standard rules and procedures. ONUMOZ adopted this approach emphasizing the fact that the UN was providing a technical instrument to implement peace building upon a request made by the international community and with the full consent of the Mozambican government.[29]

A more cynical view is that the international community, with the UN's nod and the support of the Mozambican government, bought RENAMO out of a military option. Whether or not RENAMO would have resumed fighting if it were not paid off remains an open question. It is clear, however, that not only was RENAMO not held accountable for its massive violations of human rights during the war, it was also rewarded with international community funds.[30] In this way, the war crimes allegedly committed by either side are not likely to be investigated or punished. It can be argued, therefore, that justice is the price to pay for peace. This raises a critical question: in the long run, can there be peace without justice?

Since the war ended without a clear winner, the only losers were the "anonymous" people of the land. Their quest for justice failed to stimulate the attention of the international media. Under these circumstances, the human rights abuses committed during the war were ignored for the sake of national reconciliation. "National reconciliation" in this sense reflected the political compromise between government and RENAMO, rather than the establishment of harmony and justice among all Mozambicans. How durable and sustainable such reconciliation can be remains to be seen.

Having won by a narrow margin—44.3% against RENAMO's 37.7% and the Democratic Union's (UD) 5.1%—FRELIMO rejected suggestions to include opposition members in a government of national unity. This, it was argued, would sooner or later lead RENAMO to return to violence as a means of imposing a power-sharing outcome to the war.

So far, these gloomy predictions have been proven wrong. Even though Mozambique is obviously far from being a stable democracy, it enjoys a general atmosphere of peace and relative economic recovery. Despite the absence of a government of national unity, the former rebels seem to have accepted electoral defeat with grace and are now trying to re-invent themselves as a political party. No longer branded as "armed bandits," "terrorists," or "agents of an external aggression," these self-proclaimed "fathers of the Mozambican democracy" now enjoy the respectability, social status, and material privileges previously reserved to the FRELIMO elite. To put it crudely: a slight reconfiguration of the political and social elite has taken place whereby FRELIMO retains political power while sharing with RENAMO whatever material benefits the state can provide. To date, the broader Mozambican society seems to have accepted this state of affairs as an imperative for breaking the cycle of violence that wracked the country since the early 1960s.

Nevertheless, underdevelopment, the profound psychological trauma of the war, a weak state in terms of both material and human resources, a fragile civil society, and an incipient democratic political culture still remain causes for concern. Coupled with the severe impact of the economic Structural Adjustment Program (SAP) and the complex issue of defense and security restructuring, these factors pose serious challenges to long-term peace and stability in Mozambique.

Political and Socioeconomic Issues

Mozambique's Constitution—one of the most liberal on the continent—is firmly based on sound democratic values and principles. It entrenches fundamental individual rights and freedoms, a clear separation between the Executive, Judiciary, and Legislative powers of the state, as well as the broadest freedom of the press. However, these noble values and principles alone do not ensure effective and democratic governance and have little positive impact on the life of ordinary citizens. A critical condition for political stability and peacebuilding, democratic governance demands the adherence to democratic values and principles, as much as it requires that the state have the ability to deliver basic services and manage society in a fair and harmonious fashion. Furthermore, political parties have subjected Mozambique's citizens to intense and frequent calls to their ethnic, religious, and regional loyalties. In the absence of a strong sense of nationhood and internal cohesion, such manipulation of primary identities is potentially very divisive.

Failure to address this problem may inhibit the democratic transformation of the Mozambican polity because a weak state is less effective and more likely to feel threatened by, and react negatively to, civil society demands of more transparency and accountability in the conduct of public affairs. Equally, a weak civil society is unable to make substantial inputs in policymaking and keep the state and its agencies in check. This means that those in power are more at liberty to formulate and implement unpopular policies, or even worse, to use their positions to promote their narrow self-interests against the public interest.

FRELIMO and RENAMO are likely to remain the dominant political parties in Mozambique in the foreseeable future. The way in which they manage their differences is, therefore, of critical importance to political stability in the country. As stated earlier, through the distribution of financial benefits, FRELIMO has skillfully given the RENAMO leadership a stake in the maintenance of peace. Arguably this is the single most important reason why RENAMO leaders seem to have abandoned the military option. The weakness of this approach, however, is quite obvious: it is an arrangement that can only serve the immediate material concerns of a small group of people. It does not provide a safety net for the thousands of demobilized RENAMO soldiers who expected some form of compensation for their participation in the war. Similarly, former government soldiers who have been demobilized have received very little, if any, support for their return to civilian life. Former combatants from both sides have created the *Associação Moçambicana dos Desmobilizados de Guerra* (AMODEG), a war veterans association that has been trying to raise the profile of the issue of reintegration in the government's agenda.

So far, the government has refused to accord special treatment to former combatants, arguing that war veterans are part of the wider community of "vulnerable groups" that includes orphans, infant soldiers, refugees, and internally displaced persons. As such, the argument goes, former combatants should not try and maintain a specific military identity and can only receive as much or as little support as any other vulnerable group. The danger of this approach stems from the fact that the war veterans have the motivation, the institutional instruments, and the ability to mobilize forces and seriously challenge their former leaders, to the extent of resorting to large-scale armed violence. Recent developments in Zimbabwe provide Mozambican authorities with ample early warning with regard to the ability of war veterans to destabilize an apparently strong government.

In turn, the economic liberalization program agreed with the International Monetary Fund and the World Bank has had mixed results. On the positive side, the government achieved impressive results in terms of macroeconomic performance: in 1994, inflation was at 77%; in 1995, 55%; in 1996, 17%; and 1997, 4.3%. The currency exchange rate has stabilized at around 12,000.00 Meticais to the US Dollar. It is well known that such results bring important benefits to Mozambique, both with regard to the long-term health of its economy and in terms of the immediate boost in investors' confidence. On the negative side, however, the search for monetary stability and the holding back of public expenditure exacerbates the country's social crisis. First, unemployment has risen as a result of privatizations, rationalizations, and bankruptcies. Second, salaries both in the public and private sectors have been kept at very low levels, against the ever-increasing cost of living. Third, the sharp containment of credit and monetary circulation resulted in a dramatic reduction in internal investment that, in turn, negatively affected economic growth. The growth in GDP over the last few years is due fundamentally to foreign investment and, to a lesser extent, to investment by the very few Mozambicans who have accumulated enough to invest without the need to resort to bank credit. Paradoxically, these people were the main beneficiaries of bank credit since they were the only internal economic operators able to offer sufficient guarantees of credit worthiness. Moreover, neither foreign nor domestic investments have thus far created enough jobs to impact on unemployment in any significant way.

Since the end of the war, most major investments have been concentrated in the southern provinces of Mozambique. Such is the case of initiatives like the Maputo Corridor, Mozal, the exploitation of the Panda natural gas reserves, and Blanchard's tourist development project. It is true that the government is promoting a few agricultural and mining projects elsewhere. Investors, however, seem to prefer to invest in the south where the infrastructure is better and there are better prospects for return on investment. This has the unintended consequence of reinforcing the widely held perception that the Southerner-dominated FRELIMO government gives preferential treatment to the south.

A related issue is the question of regionalism. In its most benign form, regionalism is manifest in the debates in Parliament. Often, parliamentarians from northern provinces representing different parties will have a common position on a given agenda item, independently of instructions given them by their respective party leaders. This suggests a deep sense of primary loyalty to the region of origin, rather than to party. The ability of regional MPs to transcend party political lines may facilitate investment outside of the south. Equally, investment that is directed to those regions outside the south may help to redress the imbalance that currently exists. A less positive manifestation of regionalism is the proliferation of regional civic groups. Invariably, their aim is to affirm aggressively a distinct identity, on the basis of the language and place of origin of its members.

In stable, democratic states, this is a normal phenomenon that does not threaten the sense of national identity. In the case of Mozambique, I would argue, the concept of nation has little substance. This, coupled with perceptions of unfair treatment from the central government and unequal access to resources, may promote and reinforce separatist tendencies. In Mozambique regionalist tendencies are particularly dangerous because they can easily be manipulated to undo the fragile political balance.

Such structural weaknesses of the Mozambican society and its body polity determine that the process of political democratization occurs without the mutually enriching interaction of a strong state with a strong civil society. More importantly, they may seriously hinder the consolidation of peace and stability and dramatically increase the country's propensity to be drawn into violent conflict. This is not to deny the fundamental importance of political and economic reform, but simply to highlight the tension between *process* and *product*. In the haste to establish the formal symbols of a liberal democracy, the need for Mozambique to develop a correspondent political culture and economic base may be neglected. In this case, democracy stands little chance to succeed if it is rushed in from the outside. A democratic state will only emerge when the Mozambican society has taken possession of the concepts and values that underpin democracy, anchoring them in its own specific cultural, political, and social universe, and developed the institutions and mechanisms to deliver effective democratic governance.

Defense and Security Issues

The on-going process of establishing armed services consistent with the new democracy in Mozambique is one of the central challenges of postconflict peace building. When RENAMO challenged the legitimacy of the state, the FRELIMO government employed the armed services to ensure the maintenance of the status quo and guarantee its own political survival. In this process the distinction between the various branches of the coercive agencies of the state became blurred. The armed forces were deployed internally to deal with domestic threats to the state, rather than used to face a clear external aggression, just as the police and intelligence services, in turn, became highly militarized and were frequently employed interchangeably with the military in counterinsurgency operations. This is at variance with the practice in stable Western democracies where civil-military relations are based on the principle of subordination of the armed services to civilian political control and a clear distinction between the role and functions of the military, the police, and the intelligence agencies.

For this reason, although occasionally the military are specifically mentioned in this section, the analysis is generally valid for the armed services as a whole, i.e., the military, the police, and the intelligence agencies. The creation of a defense force consistent with a democratic system is faced with complex obstacles that demand action beyond the initial training provided by a body of instructors from well-established democracies.

First, in many countries in Africa, Asia, and Latin America, despite the fact that their officers were trained in mature democracies, armed forces have interfered in the political affairs of the state to the extent of staging coups and establishing military regimes. Second, the officers and soldiers selected to integrate the new defense force, the *Forças Armadas de Defesa de Moçambique* (FADM), originate from armed forces which were neither designed nor oriented to serve a democracy, and were central actors in a particularly vicious and cruel conflict. Therefore, they need to be educated in the patterns of legitimate interaction with society in a peaceful and democratic environment. Third, despite the introduction of a new constitution in 1990 that formally defines Mozambique as a liberal democracy, it will certainly take more than a constitutional change to transform the political culture of Mozambican society.

The challenge facing the Mozambican armed services is to combine the qualities of professional competence and political legitimacy needed to serve in a democratic order. How will they acquire a democratic culture, accept the principles of civilian control, accountability, transparency, and public scrutiny, in a society with no liberal democratic traditions?

While the armed services should be nonpartisan with regard to party politics, they *need to be politically oriented in democratic values.* The purpose, cohesion, and sense of loyalty of the new armed services should be built around the ideals and values of democracy, in order to enable its interaction with the state and society to be framed by the respect for the principles upon which peace is being built in Mozambique. Specifically, its members should undergo a program of education covering matters such as the constitutional provisions on basic rights and defense, the principles and mechanisms of democratic civil-military relations, international law on armed conflict, human rights, and the ethical dimensions of military professionalism. This will contribute to ensuring that military power is legitimately used to serve society as a whole, rather than misused to promote ethnic, regional, or partisan ambitions, or indeed the corporate self-interest of the military itself.

Moreover, for the mechanisms of civilian control over the military to be effective, a number of additional measures are required. First, general public debate of defense and security matters needs to be promoted to encourage citizens to contribute inputs to defense policymaking. Second, the politicians and senior civil servants of the Ministry of Defense and the members of the parliamentary defense committee need to be trained in areas such defense planning, budgeting, and military procurement, to be able of performing their task effectively. This last aspect is particularly relevant because, as in other emerging democracies, Mozambican politicians and civil servants typically lack the experience and skills to manage defense policy implementation. As a result, their relationship with the military leadership is characterized by a considerable degree of tension and frustration. Moreover, civilian inexperience may open the doors for military involvement in politics.[31] Stable civil-military relations will also depend on the government's willingness and ability to fulfill its responsibilities with regard to the FADM. In this connection, a conscious effort by civilian and military leaders to build trust and mutual respect is crucial.

Just as the military should avoid taking actions that may undermine the position of democratically elected politicians, politicians and bureaucrats should respect the military chain of command and not interfere in the tactical and operational aspects of defense. Besides demanding that the military observe legality, the government itself should operate within the law, refrain from using the armed forces for partisan purposes, and respect their professional input and corporate interest in defense policymaking. In particular, the government should provide the necessary material and financial conditions to guarantee the effectiveness of the armed forces.[32]

In other words, the development of stable civil-military relations in Mozambique demands more than the uncritical application of the principle of civilian political control. It requires that military and civilian leaders consider themselves as partners, even if with unequal powers and responsibilities, cooperating towards the broader process of national reconciliation which is a central feature of Mozambique's transition to democratic rule. Nathan has described civil-military relations as "the distribution of power and influence between the armed services and the civilian authority."[33] In this sense, the nature of civil military relations, that is, *how* power and influence are distributed between the military and the civilian authorities, both reflects and shapes the political system. In the case of Mozambique, this means that *just as democratic civil-military relations are essential for democracy to succeed, so the democratization of the state and society are critical to the establishment of a democratic civil-military interaction.*

A particularly difficult question in this regard is the issue of legitimacy of the new defense force. The resolution of this question is largely dependent on the attitude of both the state and society in general towards those officers and soldiers who allegedly committed acts of terrorism and human rights abuses during the war. Three broad options can be identified to approach this issue, none of which is totally free from undesirable political and ethical consequences. As a first option, the state could decide that it is in the interest of national reconciliation and internal cohesion of the FADM to ignore past human rights abuses. This seems to be the prevailing view. However, it will lead to war criminals being treated with impunity in the emerging democracy, and more importantly, being entrusted with the very means of organized violence they so gravely abused in the past. As a result, the credibility of the FADM could be seriously undermined from the outset, and the expectations of justice of vast sections of the Mozambican society would be frustrated. Moreover, the healing of the wounds of war demands that such wounds be acknowledged unambiguously in the first place. Only after the crimes have been exposed and the perpetrators identified can amnesty and forgiveness be considered.

A second option, therefore, would be to tackle the issue uncompromisingly in the interest of justice and transparency by investigating thoroughly all allegations of atrocities, excluding from the new military those involved, and bringing them to justice. This would give the FADM a high moral and ethical standing but it would entail considerable political and practical difficulties. First, the investigation would necessarily have a negative impact on the internal cohesion of FADM. Second, it would probably lead to the exclusion of most of RENAMO's military leaders and soldiers, since they perpetrated acts of terrorism against the population as a matter of policy. Third, taken to its extreme conclusion, it would raise questions about the ultimate political responsibility for the behavior of the men on the ground, with the inevitable destabilizing effect on peace building.

Nathan suggests a third option which is a compromise between "total amnesia" and the quest for "total justice" concerning war crimes.[34] This would entail either the exclusion from the new military of just a group of "notorious individuals and units," rather than a complete purge, or the creation of a Truth Commission to investigate alleged violations of human rights, without the imposition of sanctions upon those found guilty. In the particular circumstances of Mozambique, the establishment of a Truth Commission would arguably satisfy the citizens' sense of justice and contribute to enhancing the moral standing of the FADM and the state.

The three options briefly outlined above do not exhaust the range of possible approaches to the question of legitimacy. They simply illustrate the point that democratization has profound implications regarding how the state and society in Mozambique face their recent past and how the history of the war is written. The discussion also raises difficult questions: is it really necessary to tackle the issue of legitimacy? Does Mozambique have the material resources and emotional energy to revisit the most brutal and inhuman aspects of its own history? In the short term, it seems more comfortable to simply ignore it. But, in the long run, is it wise? Can this problem just be wished away? Or are we exacerbating the problem by just mentioning it? How do we accommodate the imperative of justice and the need to maintain peace? Does the Mozambican society as a whole understand and accept that justice be the price to pay for peace?

Whatever answers Mozambicans find, whatever options they chose, this extremely complex and sensitive issue is likely to be one of the most challenging tasks in creating a legitimate FADM, trusted and respected by the citizens it is meant to serve.

The Role of the International Community

From the previous discussion an image emerges of Mozambique, that of a country which is still grappling with the material and psychological legacy of the war. Mozambique remains one of the poorest countries in the world and faces a host of complex political, social, and economic challenges for which there are no easy solutions. These range from a weak state and body polity, to an alarming growth of the crime rate, to conflicts around identity and fair and equitable access to resources, to real or perceived political exclusion of significant sectors of the population, to unstable civil-military relations. The international community can play a critical role in assisting Mozambique to address these concerns, given the country's dramatic lack of financial and skilled human resources.

It should be acknowledged that in the last twenty years, the international community has contributed significantly to Mozambique's survival and development efforts by participating in various economic and social development programs. Moreover, foreign aid also helped the country face the disruption caused by the war and natural disasters, mainly through the provision of emergency assistance. In 1994, for example, it was estimated that the international community contributed more than 50% of the Mozambican State budget.

Yet, aid and development assistance are also sources of concern, partly because foreign aid further aggravates the country's foreign debt position, and partly because the interests of the donors, rather than the recipients, usually drive the design of development projects. This situation has certainly prevailed in Mozambique and contributed to the country's dependency on aid. As a result of complex designs and unrealistic time frames beyond local capacity, burdensome technical assistance budgets are in place to hire foreign consultants and experts to actually implement the projects, instead of building a domestic capacity for self-sustained development. Commenting on the role of the international community in supporting the process of democratization and the reconstruction of Mozambique, Willet argued,

The test for the international community is whether they can transcend the limitations of the old political and economic paradigms which have been imbued with short-termism and an orthodoxy which blinds the faithful to the realities of their policy prescriptions. Only if they have the willingness to support the "ripening" of the democratic process by helping to eradicate the underlying structural problem of human insecurity will peace and democracy flourish in Mozambique.[35]

Unless widespread poverty and the attendant moral degradation are radically challenged, the situation may develop into social and political chaos, thereby undermining the prevailing climate of peace. Moreover, democratization will only succeed if the efficiency of the state is dramatically improved and the weaknesses of civil society are addressed. In order to undertake its responsibilities regarding national reconstruction, the state needs to be enabled to attract and maintain an effective public administration, as well as improve its capacity to invest in infrastructure and deliver basic services. The emerging institutions of civil society, in turn, need to develop the capacity to interact critically with the state, thus promoting the specific interests of their particular constituencies. A shift in approach as proposed by Willet could substantially enhance the international community's effectiveness in supporting Mozambique to address these challenges. By being recipient-driven, the International Community could achieve the following broad objectives: poverty alleviation, reduction of economic dependence and creation of an environment conducive to sustainable growth, promotion of democratic consolidation, enhancement of regional integration, and improvement of aid effectiveness.

Of course no amount of foreign assistance, no matter how well intentioned, organized, and generous, will excuse the Mozambicans from their responsibilities. No amount of foreign assistance will ever be sufficient or even worthwhile without the commitment of the Mozambicans to build their own future. The international community can, at best, be supportive and avoid taking action that may undermine the domestic effort. In particular, it is the place of the Mozambican political elite to rise above sectarian interests and show the courage, the vision, and the qualities of leadership required to build the nation; to rise to the challenge and sow, today, the seeds of peace, democracy, and development.

NOTES

This paper is based on my monograph "The United Nations and Mozambique: A sustainable peace?" *Cadernos Lumiar* 7, Instituto de Estudos Estratégicos e Internacionais (IEEI) Lisbon, December 1996.

1. I refer to the national liberation war, from 1962 to 1974, the war with Rhodesia, from 1976 to 1979, and the South African campaign of destabilization, from 1980 to 1990.

2. See for example A. Vines, *Renamo: Terrorism in Mozambique* (London: James Currey, 1991); B. Cole, *The Elite: The Story of the Rhodesian Special Air Service* (Transkei: Three Knights Publishing, 1987); C. Geffray, *La cause des armes au Mozambique: Anthropologie d'une guerre civile* (Paris: Karthala, 1990); R. Gersony, "The Gersony Report: Summary of Mozambican Refugee Accounts of Principally Conflict-Related Experience in Mozambique" (Washington, DC: US Department of State, 1988); M. Hall, "The Mozambican National Resistance Movement and the Reestablishment of Peace in Mozambique," paper presented at the Centre for African Studies, School of Oriental and African Studies, London, 1991; D. Martin and P. Johnson, eds., "Destructive Engagement" (Harare: Zimbabwe Publishing House, 1986); and W. Minter, *Apartheid's Contras: An Inquiry into the Roots of War in Angola and Mozambique* (Johannesburg: Witwatersrand University Press, and London: Zed Books, 1994).

3. FRELIMO—the Front for the Liberation of Mozambique—was created in 1962 and led Mozambique's national liberation struggle against Portuguese colonialism. At independence in 1975, FRELIMO established a one-party state and adopted a radical socialist agenda to promote social and economic development. At its Third Congress, in 1977, FRELIMO became a Marxist-Leninist Party.

4. Originally known as MNR (Mozambique National Resistance), RENAMO (Portuguese acronym) was established in 1976 by the Rhodesian intelligence services. At its inception, RENAMO assisted the Rhodesian security forces in their operations against the Zimbabwean nationalists inside Mozambique, mainly through intelligence gathering. After the independence of Zimbabwe in April 1980, RENAMO was absorbed by the South African security services and employed as the main instrument in apartheid South Africa's campaign to destabilize Mozambique.

5. W. Minter, *Apartheid's Contras: An Inquiry into the Roots of War in Angola and Mozam-*

bique, pp. 272–76.

6. For a detailed description of these prenegotiation contacts see R. M. della Rocca, *Moçambique da Guerra à Paz: historia de uma mediação insolita* (Maputo: Livraria Universitaria–Universidade Eduardo Mondlane, 1998).

7. FRELIMO's decisions at the congress resulted in the adoption of the 1990 Constitution, which initiated a process of democratization of the Mozambican state, and set up the legal framework for the peace process. By creating the institutional space for a legal opposition, the 1990 Constitution addressed in a fundamental way one of the most critical internal factors of conflict.

8. For a detailed analysis of the Rome negotiations see C. Hume, *Ending Mozambique's War—The Role of Mediation and Good Offices* (Washington, DC: United States Institute of Peace Press, 1994), and R. M. della Rocca, *Moçambique da Guerra à Paz: historia de uma mediação insolita.*

9. C. Hume, C. *Ending Mozambique's War,* pp. 15–19.

10. See AWEPPA. *General Peace Agreement of Mozambique.* Amsterdam: African-European Institute, 1992.

11. The United Nations, *The United Nations and Mozambique, 1992–1995* (New York: The United Nations Department of Public Information, 1995), p. 190.

12. Ibid., pp. 296–97.

13. Ibid., p. 60.

14. P. Batchelor, "Disarmament, Small Arms and Internal Conflict: The Case of Southern Africa" (Cape Town: Centre for Conflict Resolution, 1995), p. 20.

15. For a detailed analysis of the implementation of the Rome Peace Accord see issues 1 to 15 of *Mozambique Peace Process Bulletin,* an irregular publication of AWEPAA (European Parliamentarians for Southern Africa), Amsterdam and Maputo. Most of the data for this section of the text draws from this publication edited by Joseph Hanlon.

16. The United Nations, *The United Nations and Mozambique, 1992–1995,* p. 35.

17. Ibid., p. 35.

18. Ibid., p. 203–204.

19. Ibid., pp. 39–40.

20. See Chris Smith and Alex Vines, *Light Weapons Proliferation in Southern Africa,* (London: Brassey's for the Centre for Defense Studies, University of London, 1997), pp. 17–18.

21. Smith and Vines, *Light Weapons Proliferation in Southern Africa,* pp. 18–29.

22. The United Nations, *The United Nations and Mozambique, 1992–1995,* pp. 41–42.

23. This initiative was funded by the international community and implemented by the UNDP in collaboration with the Banco Popular de Desenvolvimento. It lasted until June 1996.

24. See "Lessons Unlearned—Or Why Mozambique's Successful Peacekeeping Operation Won't Be Replicated Elsewhere," a paper circulated by the American Embassy in Maputo in late 1994.

25. The United Nations, *The United Nations and Mozambique, 1992–1995,* pp. 49–50.

26. The United Nations, *The United Nations and Mozambique, 1992–1995,* pp. 47–50.

27. Fetherston defines positive peace as the establishment of "processes within and among societies which facilitate constructive human development and interaction," in A B Fetherston, "Putting the Peace Back into Peacekeeping: Theory Must Inform Practice," *International Peacekeeping* 1, no. 1 (London, Frank Cass, Spring 1994): 4.

28. See for example *Mozambique Peace Process Bulletin,* Issue 8, Amsterdam and Maputo, AWEPAA, February 1994, p. 9.

29. The United Nations, *The United Nations and Mozambique, 1992–1995,* p. 186.

30. For an independent account of RENAMO's violations of human rights during the war see Robert Gersony, "The Gersony Report: Summary of Mozambican Refugee Accounts of Principally Conflict-Related Experience in Mozambique" (Washington, DC: Department of State, 1988).

31. See L. Nathan, (1994), p. 66. Although these remarks were made with reference to Latin American countries undergoing a transition to democracy such as Nicaragua, they are equally applicable to Mozambique.

32. Nathan, pp. 85–86.

33. Nathan, p. 60.

34. Nathan, pp. 92–93.

35. S. Willett, "Ostriches, Wise Old Elephants and Economic Reconstruction in Mozambique," *International Peacekeeping* 2, no. 1 (1995).

10

The Perpetual Civil War in Angola

The Failure of Peacekeeping and Democratization

J. Michael Turner

The analysis that follows is a study of what has become seemingly an intractable conflict in a country where war has been commonplace since 1961. For the people of Angola, achieving political independence in 1975 proved to be a mixed blessing. Long-standing regional rivalries, ethnic differences, and rural/urban disparities were joined to the Cold War's international ideological conflict. Tragically, the conflict initially waged to end Portuguese colonial rule was transformed into fratricidal civil war after independence. Angolan anticolonial movements deftly and routinely sought financial support and armaments from sources as diverse as the People's Republic of China and the United States; the same movements were courted either by Moscow, Havana, and Eastern Europe on the one hand, or Washington and Kinshasa on the other.

The civil war, ushered in by the country's political independence, defied easy or rational solution, dooming to failure all good-faith attempts at conflict resolution, whether coming from Europe, African continental and regional groupings (Organization of African Unity, Southern African Development Community), or the United Nations (UN Angola Verification Missions). Although the international community spent more than a billion dollars through UN operations, the services of national and international Non-Governmental Organizations, and multilateral and bilateral assistance packages, it failed to put an end to Angola's war or to establish a lasting peace. The national death toll eventually surpassed two million people. As the world currently witnesses the ongoing destruction in Angola, the cynicism displayed by both sides in the conflict must call into question our sense of governance and, ultimately, humanity.

ORIGINS OF MODERN ANGOLAN NATIONALISM

The protracted conflict that has come to characterize contemporary Angolan political life began as a series of contradictions and opposing forces that were assembled at the beginning of the anticolonial movement in Angola. Some of these conflicts manifested themselves early in the form of ethnic and geographic anticolonial groups, creating rivalries with other Angolan ethnic groups.

For instance, the now atrophied FNLA *(Frente Nacional de Libertação de Angola)* led by Holden Roberto drew its strength primarily from the Bakongo people in Northern Angola, and from the neighboring Bakongo of the southern Democratic Republic of Congo (former Zaire). Jonas Savimbi's *União Nacional de Indepêndencia Total de Angola* or UNITA garnered its support from the Ovimbundu ethnic group in the country's south and center. Support for the ruling *Movimento Popular de Libertação de Angola* (MPLA) came from the Kimbundu, whites, and mixed-race Angolans.[1]

The rivalries among the competing nationalist movements went beyond ethnicity and geography. Portuguese colonial practices drew marked lines of distinction between those colonial Africans judged to be assimilated *(assimilados)* and the great majority of the colonial African population judged to be indigenous *(indigena/nativo)*. The sharp lines of demarcation in the Portuguese colonies between Africans classified as assimilated or indigenous resulted in hatred and rivalries between the so-called privileged and those compelled to forced labor or *shibaloii*.

The privileged assimilated Lusophone Africans (usually male and often of mixed-race) found themselves often in conflict with less-educated Portuguese rural emigrants, favored by the colonial administration for employment because they were either born in Portugal or descended from Portuguese emigrants. However, those Africans who had had the advantages of a formal Portuguese education and who were not favored by the administration for employment were routinely viewed as untrustworthy by coworkers on work gangs or on Portuguese colonial plantations.[2] The colonial policy of distinguishing between assimilated vs. indigenous became an important point of difference and rivalry in the institutional history of the MPLA with its mixed-race assimilated membership and UNITA's Ovimbundu majority. Portuguese colonial administrators knowingly exploited the differences and hostilities between assimilated and indigenous Africans, distracting them from uniting effectively to combat the colonial regime and all of the negative economic, social, and political consequences of European colonialism.

Individuals' personalities also complicated the major independence movements in Angola. The FNLA's leader Holden Roberto had familial and personal ties to the Congo. Jonas Savimbi linked his well-known intellectual and linguistic abilities to an overwhelming desire to exercise personal power and leadership as the sole ruler of Angola. Initially, these two nationalist leaders clashed with the world view of the late MPLA founder Agostinho Neto and with current MPLA leader and technocrat Eduardo dos Santos. Angola's modern political history unfortunately demonstrates yet another case study of the weakness of civil society that emerged upon independence in contemporary Africa. The collapse of the Portuguese regime brought Angola to the brink of independence in 1974. The implications for Angola of the April 1974 coup became apparent to all three Angolan liberation movements, which had spent thirteen years fighting a colonial and authoritarian regime that stubbornly refused to accept the changes that had already taken place elsewhere on the African continent.[3]

The Portuguese handed power over to one political party, the MPLA. In their haste to transfer power to the MPLA, one casualty of the transfer was a failure to create a legitimate and vibrant civil society. The new Angolan government's bureaucracies were run by individuals without support from civil society. The personalization of the new regime and their political competitors inevitably meant that rather weak and often largely symbolic mass-movement organizations represented women, youth, unions, and rural workers.[4]

After Portugal's disorderly withdrawal from Angola, the conflict became international with the United States supporting Savimbi and UNITA and the Soviet Union and Cuba supporting the MPLA. The transitional coalition government hastily arranged by Portugal at the time of Angolan independence in 1975 soon came apart. With the presence of foreign Cold War patrons supporting major opposing Angolan forces, the positions for the MPLA and UNITA quickly became fixed, almost frozen, in a Cold-War scenario. Little leeway existed for policy decisions that did not originate in Moscow, Washington, or Havana.[5]

As observed by Portuguese diplomat and scholar Fernando Andresen Guimaraes in *The Origins of the Angolan Civil War,* the bitter rivalries among the major anticolonial groups (the FNLA, MPLA, and UNITA) were historic and intractable. While these rivalries predated the independence period, the thrusting of Angola into Cold War geopolitics only provided a new ideological justification for already existing hatreds and resentments.[6] The Angolans' inability to visualize a rational and workable resolution for these conflicts became intensified through the prism of Cold War ideology, rivalry, and political machinations in which one side declared itself a believer and follower of Marxist solutions, while its principal rival, which was supported overtly and covertly by Washington and other western nations, declared itself a staunch believer in western democracy and capitalism. What the labels and ideology failed to mask completely was that access to wealth and political power fueled both the rivalry and the ongoing war in Angola.

Obviously the key to understanding these rivalries and conflicts involved knowledge of the stakes in Angola that created the psychology of a zero-sum game, rendering to the winner all the spoils of victory. Angola's natural resource wealth exacerbated rivalries among competing political groups. Desire for power became more than simply an exercise in prestige; control of the country's vastly rich national resources (i.e., mineral deposits, oil reserves, fertile agricultural areas, and human resources) meant direct access to great wealth.[7] Understanding the importance of political power and potential political dominance in Angola never really encouraged the national leaders of the major independence movements to attempt real power sharing or honest and transparent collaboration. Power in Angola was to be secured for one's group, at any cost. Ironically, the abundance of and geographical locations for national natural resources in Angola contributed to prolonging that country's civil war; each of the belligerents had direct and ample access to a strategic commodity that it could commercialize as a source of income for the purchase of armaments.[8]

GULLIBILITY OF THE INTERNATIONAL COMMUNITY

During the course of the continuing conflict between UNITA and the ruling MPLA government, it has become evident that both sides have manipulated the international community. The willingness of the international community to provide humanitarian assistance to the numerous civilian victims of unceasing power plays in Angola encouraged continuation of the Angolan conflict. While the United Nations-organized and sponsored peacekeeping missions, developed in response to the internal conflicts, filled the justifiable need for such humanitarian operations, it could be argued that the actions of many political leaders in Angola were responsible for putting their own national populations at risk, too often the most vulnerable groups: women, children, and the aged.

This understandable liberal and humane reaction in the face of stark human tragedy now has assumed an almost sinister face and posture. Globally, political leaders and warlords, military heads of juntas, and those supporting or enforcing coups d'état or ethnic cleansing operations around the world now often turn their civilian populations into pawns on battlegrounds and "killing fields." These leaders then await the entry of the international community to provide the necessary social welfare and humanitarian assistance needed to mitigate the consequences of these terrible conflicts.

With its impressive financial resources for humanitarian aid and assistance, the international community seems expected to provide basic care and sustenance to these victims. Too often these victims now are represented by political refugees, stateless persons, the internally displaced, countless thousands of disabled persons, or escaping teen-age army veterans searching for new lives and identities. It can be argued that far too many in this victims' group are hapless subjects of leaders following zero-sum game political scenarios.

Unscrupulous leaders can almost justify their political actions, knowing that as the conflict and carnage worsens, eventually the international community will intervene to rescue the victims. For some leaders, this reckless behavior has become a frequent and well-practiced form of international blackmail. This syndrome or political behavior represents a style of leadership that is all too willing to have its population seen internationally as victims, to be cared for and attended by international humanitarian organizations. This type of local manipulation and international reaction has been cynically categorized as the "Médecins sans Frontières" syndrome; however, our observations do not represent a criticism of those doctors who risk their lives by volunteering for missions in dangerous and difficult situations around the world. While cynical manipulation is not limited to the Angolan situation, this type of government brinkmanship can be seen throughout the world.[9]

THE FLAWED PROCESS OF DISARMAMENT AND DEMOBILIZATION FOR PEACEKEEPING IN ANGOLA

United Nations peacekeeping operations in Angola date back to 1988, when the United Nations Angola Verification Mission (UNAVEM I) was established by the Security Council to verify the withdrawal of Cuban forces under the terms of the Tripartite Agreement.[10] Linking Namibian independence with the withdrawal of South African and Cuban troops from Angola, official verification of the double withdrawal process became the task of UNAVEM I.

By 1991, (a period in which a clear military victory seemed to be elusive for both the MPLA and UNITA), Portugal, with the assistance of the Soviet Union and the United States, invited the belligerents to meet in Bicesse, Portugal, for a new round of negotiations.[11] It is interesting to examine the context and timing of the Bicesse negotiations, which were occurring at the time of the collapse of the Soviet Union. The Soviet Union's collapse diminished the relevance of Cold War ideologies and the Soviet Union's and Washington's support of client states. In the case of Mozambique, this ideological shift pushed reluctant FRELIMO and RENAMO forces into a series of negotiations in Rome, which with the assistance of the good offices of the Sant'Egidio Lay Community, resulted in the 1992 Rome Peace Accords.[12]

Similar conditions prevailed in the Angolan situation at the time of the Bicesse Accords. A relentless and stubborn attitude characterized both sides when discussing the terms for ceding territory. A final agreement was achieved in May 1991 and the Bicesse Accords were signed. The Accords called for a cease-fire and integration of the two armies into a single national army. The Accords also called for general elections to be held between September and November 1992.[13]

In the attempt to guarantee the success of the Bicesse Accords, the United States, Portugal, and the Soviet Union agreed not to supply the two belligerent forces with more weapons. They also agreed to work together to stop arms shipments to the Angolan government and to UNITA from third parties. The Security Council established UNAVEM II in May 1991 to support the new peace process. The Council later expanded UNAVEM II's mandate to include observation of the anticipated general election. The numerically small UN observer force proved unable to discharge its complex tasks of monitoring the demobilization process of UNITA and MPLA military forces.

UNAVEM II consisted of approximately three hundred fifty military observers, ninety police observers, and only seventy-one civilian election observers. After the 1992 elections between UNITA and the Angolan government and its attendant violence, the personnel of UNAVEM II was reduced to some fifty military and police observers.[14] The UN peace monitoring experience in Angola can be contrasted clearly with UN efforts in Mozambique during 1993–1994, which involved a complete demobilization program for combatants and the deployment of a sufficient number of UN monitors and observers to ensure the mission's success.[15]

When contrasted with Mozambique, Angola is a clear example of poorly planned peacekeeping. For instance, reports abounded that when turning in arms, UNITA seemed to be handing in ancient weapons without much military value. A small number of UNAVEM II observers noted this fact, but could do little to alter the situation. It soon became clear that UNITA's willingness even to turn in a few ancient weapons was seen by them as a favor to the UNAVEM II program. UN observers saw that the weapons hand-over program was not functioning. Military demobilization clearly was not taking place. If this was seen by many observers as a disquieting fact, it was also evident that the small UN monitoring staff was clearly not equipped or able to implement a program for effective demobilization of the two belligerent forces. It was on these far-from-ideal conditions that Angola approached the elections scheduled by the Bicesse Accords for October 1992.[16]

THE FAILURE OF 1992 ELECTORAL PROCESS AND THE RESUMPTION OF CONFLICT

The electoral "debacle" of 1992 saw UNITA refusing to accept electoral defeat in the first round of the general elections. Unfortunately (and fatally for the Angolan Peace Process under UNAVEM II), what started as an electoral conflict can be seen in historical context as an almost understandable political reaction to the exceptionally high stakes that always are at risk in Angolan political life. Angola represents a political circumstance in which winning truly becomes everything. Finishing second place is not an acceptable option because national contestants for office refuse to accept power sharing or alternation of power as a viable concept.

The case of the 1992 national elections in Angola is instructive. It is thought that more than ninety percent of the Angolan electorate voted in the first round of the 1992 elections. The results gave President Eduardo dos Santos 49.6 percent of the vote to Savimbi's 40.1 percent. In the parliamentary elections for the National Assembly, the MPLA received 54 percent, while UNITA's tally was only 34 percent.[17]

Under the terms of the Bicesse Accords, President dos Santos' failure to obtain an absolute majority of the vote required a second round of elections. However, opposition by Jonas Savimbi and UNITA to the first round's results prevented the second-round elections' being held. Despite protests by UNAVEM II that the elections had been basically free and fair, UNITA's reaction was to seize a series of towns and small cities across Angola. In a tragic demonstration of the importance of effective demobilization as an integral component of any effective peace process, the Angolan government distributed weapons to MPLA militants in Luanda who promptly attacked hundreds of UNITA militants and supporters who had remained in Luanda following the first round of elections.

The violence directed towards members of UNITA after the October 1992 electoral results fueled the flames of conflict, giving Savimbi justification for renewal of his military campaign against his historic MPLA rival. My discussions with several US and other nationals who worked on the preparations for the 1992 Angolan elections process paint a far more complex picture of the general climate and psychological environment that surrounded Angola's rather troubled 1992 electoral process.[18]

The US government's alleged support to UNITA was said to have totaled several millions of dollars in commodities, vehicles, computers, and office supplies, much of which remained on the Luanda docks at the time of the September 1992 election. This "nonspecified" financial support provided to UNITA came from the rather facetiously nick-named "Black Bag Fund" of the US Government, more formally and innocuously referred to as Economic Support Fund (ESF) donations. The ESF system does not exclude commodity purchases, and receipts were not required from ESF-grantee recipients. In the specific case of the 1992 Angolan elections, much of the ESF support translated into vehicles and other commodities, the purpose being to give UNITA a certain advantage over its rivals, leading to a hoped-for UNITA electoral victory.

These flexible funds, which often have taken on a deservedly negative public image, were provided to reward "friends" of the US government who supported US strategic interests. Interpreting and analyzing official US activities in 1992, this financial support for a UNITA electoral campaign represented an expressed official US desire for a UNITA electoral victory. Having been the recipient of substantial US financial support over decades, Savimbi probably expected that UNITA would win the 1992 elections. Given this expectation, Savimbi's October 1992 first-round loss was probably quite a shock, unacceptable to the party and to the UNITA chief.

Based upon his years of contact with Washington and what Savimbi believed to be the depth of his support among "official" Washington, he believed that victory was certain. His belief no doubt was enhanced by UNITA's support and financing from Western Europe and the apartheid minority-white government in South Africa. The years of unflagging support for UNITA seemed to ensure an electoral victory for Savimbi's political party.[19] Savimbi's lack of psychological preparation for the possibility of an electoral defeat meant also that his diverse international patrons also assumed a UNITA electoral victory. All of these expectations only served to help pave the path for the governance and democratization debacle which followed the September 1992 Angolan primary elections.

WAR FATIGUE, MILITARY STALEMATES, AND THE RESUMPTION OF NEGOTIATIONS

The failure of the 1992 electoral process put UNITA at odds with the international community which had declared the first round of the elections to be generally free and fair, and recognized the initial victor to be the MPLA. Renewed hostilities and the intransigence of Savimbi accompanied a UNITA refusal to negotiate the electoral impasse with either the Angolan government, UN representatives, or other members of the international contact group. The violence directed at UNITA representatives in Luanda served to set off another round of military conflicts between the Government of Angola and UNITA, representing a serious and costly failure in the peacekeeping process. It meant a return to square one, as the flawed Angolan peace process again required a new cease-fire agreement and yet another round of negotiations.[20]

Not stated, but well understood by each side, was the fundamental difference between their public posture and their secret goals and objectives. These would be negotiated in this new process. In the period following the 1992 electoral breakdown, both sides demonstrated the willingness to sacrifice the civilian population to maintain their positions of political power and dominance. The negotiation process after 1992 saw a physical withdrawal of Savimbi from negotiations and an accompanying psychological distance by UNITA in its negotiations with the United Nations and members of the contact group. After 1992, UNITA, at best, had only desultory exchanges with the Angolan government.

The violent denouement of the Angolan electoral process somewhat discredited the institutional reputation of the United Nations, and the Special Representative of the Secretary General for the Operation in Angola, Mrs. Margaret Anstee. For those Angolan and foreign electoral staff who had worked tirelessly in the now discredited peacekeeping and electoral process, the return to violence called into question their commitment and dedication to the electoral process in Angola. The failure of the UN's efforts in Angola served as an alarm for those involved in the Mozambique peacekeeping operation. After the failure in Angola, everyone in Mozambique renewed their efforts and energies, trying to ensure that Mozambique would not repeat the Angolan experience.[21]

The problems of inadequate monitoring capacity and insufficient United Nations human resources, a major source of the ultimate failure of UNAVEM II in Angola, were partly corrected after 1992. In the development and mounting of UNAVEM III, more attention was given to recruiting a far greater number of UN military police to monitor the demilitarization of the UNITA and MPLA armies. Military violations of the Accords by either side were promptly checked and verified by UN military police. At the same time, international pressure again was placed on both sides to embark upon a serious effort to negotiate a new peace treaty. With increased resources, more adequate personnel, and a new Special Representative for the Angolan Peace process (former Malian Foreign Minister Blondine Beye), conditions finally seemed to be in place for the belligerents to arrive at a real and lasting peace in Angola.

Many observers have described the late Maître Alioune Blondine Beye's optimism as key to solutions in the Angolan peace process. His tactics included what has been described as a dogged attempt to bring the belligerents around to his abiding conviction that peace could be achieved in Angola.[22] Beye's personality and his inability to accept defeat or checkmate in the overall process was an important force in keeping that process alive, particularly when faced with so many obstacles. Beye's determination to achieve peace often ran counter to the interests of certain parties who attempted to maintain the country in a state of perpetual conflict. Special Representative Beye's tragic (and never fully explained) demise in the UN plane crash in Abidjan removed from the scene a major force for peace in this long-running African conflict.[23]

Despite Beye's positive role, a recent report issued by Human Rights Watch entitled "Angola Unravels: The Rise and Fall of the Lusaka Peace Process" soberly analyzes a conflict that has had four different phases, and has resulted in the dislocation of more than ten percent of Angola's population. The motives of both belligerents in signing the Lusaka Protocol are studied by the Human Rights Watch report. For UNITA, its weakened military position in 1994 made the terms of the accord an attractive option.[24] The cease-fire provided by the Protocol was accepted at a moment when neither side believed a total military victory would be achieved. Compromise was wrested out of a situation in which each side had few other alternatives. The actual provisions of the Accord and its insistence upon complete demobilization and the integration of UNITA and MPLA military forces into a unified national force were distinct improvements over the conditions under which the country had tried to consolidate peace and prepare for national elections in 1992. The conditions of the Accord also seemed to suggest some of the lessons learned in the Mozambican peace process, in terms of an emphasis on both complete demilitarization before elections and the reintegration of former combatants into the larger society.

Ineffectively administered embargo programs of arms and oil transfers by the government and UNITA, however, undermined the positive features of the Lusaka Protocol. The UN Security Council proved unable or unwilling to monitor and impose binding sanctions on all of the countries selling arms and purchasing oil or diamonds with the two hostile sides. The Human Rights Watch Report reiterates that an embargo against arms sales had been enacted in 1993, but that both sides continued to trade freely in arms and, more importantly, found numerous international arms sellers to re-supply them. The international community engaged in tacit tolerance of the escalating arms traffic in Angola between 1994 and 1998. Commercial motives and political and diplomatic intrigue involving the former Zaire and Congo-Brazzaville and the genocide and massive dislocation of citizens from Rwanda and Burundi all served to create contextual conditions encouraging the arms trade. The fact that the United Nations Peacekeeping mission did not denounce this trade or even make a public appeal to stop it is a serious indictment that history will judge eventually. If the UN Special Representative sincerely believed he was assisting a difficult process by not speaking out about the arms trade and the many violations of human rights that were happening, that decision, in hindsight, may prove to have been a serious error in tactics and judgment.

In fairness, the constraints faced by the UN operation for Angola were many. A full military contingent to monitor the process was assembled only in late 1996.[25] The Human Rights Watch Report claims that in not denouncing human rights violations in Angola, both sides were encouraged to violate systematically the rights of Angolan citizens. The ever-increasing numbers of rural deslocados or dispossessed Angolans streaming into the country's urban areas to escape the fighting, looting, and land mines are the consequence of this policy of neglect by the UN peacekeepers. The ability of small numbers of Angolans to make unimaginable profits from the illegal arms and other trade flourishing in the midst of war has fueled the tragedy. In supporting different failed UN peacekeeping efforts, the cost to the international community to subsidize these operations has surpassed US $1.5 billion dollars.[26] The cost to the people of Angola held hostage by the selfish policies of the Angolan government and of UNITA must be considered to be incalculable.

Another serious indictment of the report by Human Rights Watch concerns the failure of the peacekeepers to monitor and report effectively the human rights violations that regularly occurred after the 1994 Lusaka Protocol. While the human rights safeguards written into the Protocol were given little attention and even less publicity after the 1994 cease-fire became operational, the failure to respond and address adequately these violations undercut the peacekeeping process. The Report posits that had the UN peacekeepers been more vigilant in pointing out human rights abuses, vigilance might have acted as a check on both sides to prevent the routine abuse of Angolan citizens.[27] Because of its failure to enforce human rights protocols, by 1998 there was little public confidence in the UN's ability to administer the peacekeeping effort effectively. Human rights violations and the regular violations of the international embargo on arms sales had drained Angolan confidence in the viability of the Lusaka Protocol and the entire peacekeeping effort.

Government occupation of areas taken from UNITA resulted in human rights violations against UNITA members and supporters. Torture, disappearances, and summary execution of those suspected to be linked to the enemy were commonplace. These human rights violations not unexpectedly discouraged UNITA from trusting or accepting any official government pronouncements. Bolstered by the government's often brutal occupation of former UNITA-held areas, UNITA hardened its official position, making compromise less likely between it and the government. The abduction of people, the arbitrary recruitment of youths for the national army, the harassment of loyal opposition members, and the censorship of the media and the press became characteristic of the government. On the other side, UNITA also engaged in similar activities against those living in UNITA-controlled areas who were suspected either of providing direct support for the MPLA, or were suspected of being opposed to UNITA policies and programs. UNITA engaged in forced recruitment, including the abduction of children to be child soldiers. Arbitrary decisions concerning individuals characterized both government and UNITA violations of human rights, undermining yet again an effective and viable peacekeeping operation for Angola.

UNITA ultimately used time under the Lusaka Accord to re-arm itself to attack the areas being held by the Angolan government. The Lusaka Accord stopped UNITA from losing more territory to the government, which served one of its major strategic objectives. Furthermore, UNITA's pledge under the Protocol to demobilize its armed forces went unfulfilled. Financially desperate and politically unstable countries, including Albania and Bulgaria, continued to supply arms to Angola. Angola's neighbors, including South Africa, Congo, Zambia, the Democratic Republic of Congo (the former Zaire), Togo, and Burkina Faso all assisted in the arms shipments reaching UNITA.[28]

Selling oil illegally for arms, the Angolan government was hardly innocent in breaking the terms of the Lusaka Peace. If UNITA was able to use its captured diamond mines to finance arms sales, the government had the oilfields of Cabinda. While the specific ban on arms shipments had been imposed directly upon UNITA, the government was not living up to the spirit of the Protocol with its vigorous buying spree of destructive weapons. Countries willing to sell weapons and sophisticated warfare technology to the Angolan government included Belarus, Brazil, Bulgaria, China, and South Africa. The report stresses Russia's contradiction as a member of the three governments serving as official mediators/observers (the other two being Portugal and the United States) of the peace process in Angola, while undermining its officially neutral position by selling arms to one of the conflict's major participants.[29]

Cupidity, greed, and quick, short-term financial gain, tragically, have become hallmarks of the ongoing conflict in Angola. They characterize not only the major protagonists (i.e., the government and UNITA), but also soldiers of fortune, private and government arms merchants, and all other willing purchasers of diamonds, precious metals, and petroleum. Because Angola is a resource-wealthy country, it will remain quite attractive for those who seek gems and diverse valuable commodities, and for those who seek to sell arms and armaments.

ANGOLA AND MOZAMBIQUE: SIGNIFICANT DIFFERENCES IN THE PROCESS OF ATTEMPTING TO KEEP PEACE IN AFRICA

Why did Angola, a country with abundant natural resources, and Mozambique, a country with relatively scarce natural resources and limited human resource capacity, take such different paths regarding UN peacekeeping? How does one explain the relative success of UN peacekeeping in Mozambique and its failure in Angola?

Does political will—or the lack thereof—serve as justifiable explanation for such important differences in the peace processes of Angola and Mozambique? Or, are there other important factors that explain the divergence? Is it useful to construct historical psychosocial profiles of Jonas Savimbi, as opposed to RENAMO's Afonso Dhlakama? Does one usefully study the ideology proposed by UNITA and the rather fuzzy mixture of nationalistic capitalism, which was the slogan or mantra taken up by RENAMO in Mozambique—a mantra that supposedly allowed Mozambicans to distinguish RENAMO from the Marxism/state socialism and the modernity/secularism espoused in classic FRELIMO ideology?

Comparing the amount and kind of electoral assistance awarded UNITA in 1992 with the far more modest flexible funds offered the Mozambique government in 1994, we can observe noticeable differences. The US funds to Mozambique were to be used to enable US Special Forces to construct a huge radio transmission tower. The tower was to have been placed in the service of Mozambique's nonpartisan National Electoral Commission (CNE) to broadcast apolitical civic education messages to the countryside and Mozambique's majority rural electorate. The request was politely turned down by the CNE, probably because the idea of US Special Forces constructing a radio tower was seen to have a series of potential political implications for Mozambique, none of which were comfortable for the government nor for most of that country's opposition parties.

One compares this funding environment in Mozambique with that of Angola in 1992 when supposedly millions of dollars were funneled to UNITA for its use in "civic education activities." This US largesse to UNITA resulted in the provision of fleets of vehicles and other commodities, much of which never were received by UNITA partisans in different areas of Angola. UNITA's refusal to accept the election results and its condemnation of the international community's approval and certification of the 1992 Angolan elections escalated into a full-armed conflict throughout Angola by early 1993.

The tragic escalation of conflict and the failures of UN peacekeeping in Angola, however, benefited peace initiatives in Mozambique. Because of the failure in Angola, planning for the United Nations Operation for Mozambique (ONUMOZ) was envisaged to have a full complement of military police and soldiers, eventually six thousand in all, with an additional two thousand technical assistants to monitor implementation of the other components of the ONUMOZ program. After the collapse of the Angola peace process, the UN officials administering the Mozambique program came to insist on the necessity of full demobilization and demilitarization of the RENAMO and FRELIMO armies before holding elections. The assiduous demand from the international community that the demobilization process continue with all reasonable dispatch by both RENAMO and the Mozambican government was, arguably, a key to success of the Mozambican peace initiative.

As discussed by João Honwana in the present volume's chapter on the Mozambique peace process, the 1992 General Peace Accord established a meaningful political structure to supervise its implementation. The Supervision and Monitoring Commission (CSC) and its subsidiary commissions were major factors in promoting the general equanimity of the peace process in Mozambique. These commissions also differed significantly from the faulty monitoring structures created for the Angolan peace process. Equally important for the success of the Mozambican process was the 1992 Rome Accord's demands that all decisions made under the Accord were to be made and implemented by the consensus of the two Mozambican signatories to that Accord.[30] Trust and confidence would have to be created and maintained if the Accord were to be transformed into a lasting peace. That difficult but critical search for consensus would become an integral part of the Mozambican process, and would be pursued by all parties to the peace process from demobilization to elections.

Continuing to utilize the Mozambique-Angola comparative lens, the United States Government apparently did not encourage RENAMO to think they would be victorious in the 1994 general elections. Nevertheless, there were many in the American and international community who hoped for a RENAMO victory or at least significant representation by RENAMO in parliament, if not in the executive branch of government. In a certain manner, that is what happened. RENAMO became the major opposition party within the National Assembly, although RENAMO's candidate for the presidency, Afonso Dhlakama, scored a distant second to Joaquim Chissano's 1994 electoral victory.[31]

THE ELEMENT AND EFFECT OF A UNITED NATIONS "PEACEKEEPING" MENTALITY ON THE PEACEKEEPING PROCESS

Peacekeeping can be considered an income-generating experience for those who are involved in a peacekeeping operation. Salaries and benefits for members of peacekeeping missions are inducements to accept the delays and stop/start points in the negotiations between belligerents. Such delays usually result in longer missions with increased financial benefits to mission members.

A related matter to the extension of peacekeeping missions refers to other elements that benefit from the process. International or third parties can reap significant financial benefits from the confusion and destruction that accompany conflict. Those who violate blockades or who sell their services, (i.e., mercenaries such as those employed by Executive Outcomes or other "private security agencies") received munificent financial benefits and significant commissions. Government oil sales and diamond sales of hundreds of millions of dollars fueled the conflict. Because international diamond purchasers linked to major firms such as DeBeers and the Anglo-American Corporation ignored international sanctions, Savimbi and UNITA used geographical access to diamond supplies in southern Angola to finance their war machine. Because of their access to diamonds and arms, the incentive to prolong fighting becomes clear.

Conversely, the MPLA's access to petroleum in northern Angolan oil fields financed the government's war machine, enabling it to acquire sophisticated weapons for combat. Obvious incentives were in place to prolong the fighting. It was profitable to do so. As has been demonstrated in the case studies of Sierra Leone, Liberia, and Democratic Republic of Congo, the Angolan conflict can be understood as a war for acquisition of wealth and natural resources set in the singular historical realities of that country. Tragically, in the search for wealth, humanity loses.

CONCLUSION

Morality and accountability take on greater significance as one approaches the end of a century. A public discussion of culpability for an ongoing conflict, or responsibility for crimes against a nation, becomes more profound when that nation is approaching a millennial change. Impunity, which characterized the lives of many dictators and tyrants who routinely looted national treasuries or terrorized their own peoples, is now less certain at the end of the century. If Chile's former military dictator General Augusto Pinochet can be detained in London as a consequence of his past actions in Chile, society's perception of accountability has taken on new meaning. The statute of limitations on guilt and culpability are beginning to change in favor of those who traditionally have been the victims. Every attempt by an aggrieved people or nation to track down plundered wealth and stolen assets sends an important message to all leaders who believed their actions were beyond society's judgment, that the will of the people cannot be continually ignored without eventually paying some price.

Every legal challenge by a human rights organization demanding restitution from the estate of a Mobutu Sese Seko or a Ferdinand Marcos constitutes a precedent for dismantling the concept of political impunity for tyrants and dictators. Each international challenge by a peace and reconciliation commission requiring immediate repayment from the private accounts of a deposed Jean Claude Duvalier or a member of the

Somoza family represents another legal challenge to imperious leaders who enriched themselves at the expense of their people. While the legal challenges remain extremely complex, the moral lesson and the potential benefit for civil society appear to be significant. Culpability does exist. Leaders can be held responsible for their actions, which can include their misdeeds against their own citizens.

While this call for conscience and accountability perhaps is still weak when compared to the endless violence symbolizing the Angolan conflict, there are echoes within Angolan civil society. The call for a cessation to the war by diverse civil society organizations within Angola is a plea similar to those demanding financial restitution by Duvalier for the impoverished in Haiti, or justice from Pinochet or General Videla for those disappeared in Chile and Argentina. The calls from civil society organizations in the Philippines, Haiti, and Angola are calls for accountability and justice. They are demands that the crimes committed by their leaders (often with the complicity or through the omission of the international community) cannot remain unpunished. Increasingly, society is beginning to challenge the concept of total impunity for former political leaders.

There is no reason to believe that this civil consciousness will not come to Angola. Accountability and restitution could also become a demand of the victims of Angola's endless war. The countless millions earned by the illegal diamond and oil trade, and the endless profits earned by arms merchants could become a future demand for reparations by Angola's youth of the twenty-first century. The injured and maimed could demand that a substantial portion of what has been looted from their country be returned to Angola to aid them in facing the multiple challenges of the next century. If an international tribunal were to be constituted in Rome to judge war crimes and war criminals, it is not impossible to consider defendants from UNITA, the MPLA, and their international supporters and backers standing trial in the twenty-first century. Three decades of war and devastation have left untold physical and psychological scars upon the Angolan people. The cupidity of national leaders and foreign economic interests not only destroyed the hopes of many at the time of political independence, but they also have gone on to ruin short- or medium-term chances for sustainable development and national well being. If some future international war crimes tribunal were able to award a modicum of social justice by indicting the guilty and provide financial restitution for the Angolan people, their suffering would not have been in vain. Finally, justice would have come to Angola.

NOTES

1. Ethnic origins of the opposing anticolonial Angolan movements of the 1960s are discussed in the text.

2. Jeanne Marie Penvenne, *African Workers and Colonial Racism: Mozambican Strategies and Struggles in Lourenco Marques, 1877–1962* (Portsmouth NH, London, Johannesburg: Heinemann, James Currey, Witwatersrand University Press, 1995), pp. 9, 64–69.

3. Fernando Andresen Guimaraes, *The Origins of the Angolan Civil War: Foreign Intervention and Domestic Political Conflict* (New York: St. Martin's Press, 1998), pp. 85–86.

4. Ibid.

5. Cold War ideology surrounded independence of Lusophone Africa in 1975; see Guimaraes, *The Origins of the Angolan Civil War.*

6. Ibid.

7. Paul Hare, *Angola's Last Best Chance for Peace: An Insider's Account of the Peace Process* (Washington, DC: United States Institute of Peace Press, 1998), pp. 3, 60, 124–126.

8. Ibid., pp. 3, 17, 60, 95, 125; Chester A. Crocker, "Death Is the Winner in Africa's Wars, *The New York Times* Op-Ed, 6 August 1999, A19.

9. *Angola Peace Monitor Angola Emergency Campaign* 3, no. 12 (3 September 1999), discussion of September 1999 humanitarian emergency in Angola and difficulty of raising pledges from the international community to deal with the emergency.

10. Hare, *Angola's Last Best Chance,* p.8; Maj. Gen. Chris A. Garuba, "Elusive Peace: The Experience and Lessons of the United Nations Peacekeeping Mission in Angola" (Bellagio Conference on Peacekeeping, Demilitarization and Development in Africa, June 7–11, 1999), p. 2.

11. Hare, *Angola's Last Best Chance,* p. 31.

12. João Honwana, "Mozambique: What Nexus among Peacemaking, Peacekeeping and Development?" (Bellagio Conference on Peacekeeping, Demilitarization, and Development in Africa, June 7–11, 1999); Cameron Hume, *Ending Mozambique's War: The Role of Mediation and Good Offices* (Washington, DC: United States Institute of Peace, 1994); Richard Synge, *Mozambique: UN Peacekeeping in Action 1992–1994* (Washington, DC: United States Institute of Peace Press, 1997); J. Michael Turner "O papel da capacidade de recursos nacionais e das instituicoes nacionais em relacao a comunidade internacional e as eleicoes," *Mocambique Eleicoes Democracia e Desenvolvimento,* ed. Brazao Mazula (Maputo, Inter-Africa Group, 1995), pp. 643–71.

13. Hare, *Angola's Last Best Chance,* pp. 8–9.

14. Garuba, "Elusive Peace," pp. 4–5.

15. See Richard Synge, *Mozambique: UN Peacekeeping in Action, 1992–1994* (Washington, DC: United States Institute of Peace, 1997), pp. 62, 108–109.

16. Author interview with Ms. Deborah Schein, UNAVEM III Elections Official, Maputo, Mozambique, 15 June 1994, concerning the insignificant number of weapons turned in by UNITA forces in the period before the 1992 general elections supervised by the United Nations in Angola.

17. Hare, *Angola's Last Best Chance,* pp. 57–58, 131.

18. Author discussions with United Nations Development Program Chief Technical Advisor for the Mozambique General Elections of 1994, Eng. Bruno Soares, Maputo, Mozambique, on different occasions between March and September of 1994. Soares had been Chief Technical Advisor for the 1992 Angolan General Elections under UNAVEM III, and assured the author that the 1992 electoral process was reasonably well administered.

19. Author discussions with several members of the UNAVEM electoral team concerning Savimbi's expectation of a 1992 political victory and harsh reaction to defeat at the polls; discussions held in March and April of 1993 in Maputo.

20. Hare, *Angola's Last Best Chance,* pp. 57–58.

21. The Angolan 1992 electoral tragedy had direct impact on election planning for Mozambique's general elections of October 1994.

22. Hare, *Angola's Last Best Chance,* pp. 20–21, 23, 25.

23. Ibid., pp. 145–46. Contrast with Alex Vines' Human Rights Watch Report, 9/26/99, which is extremely critical of Beye's refusal to condemn human rights violations and embargo violations occurring in Angola (http://www.hrw.org/reports/1999/angola).

24. Human Rights Watch, "Angola Unravels: The Rise and Fall of the Lusaka Peace Process", 9 September 1999 (http://www.hrw.org/reports/1999/angola).

25. Ibid., report on full strength of military contingent only in late 1996.

26. Ibid.

27. Ibid.

28. Ibid.

29. Ibid.

30. João Honwana, "Mozambique, What Nexus."

31. J. Michael Turner, Sue Nelson, Kim Mahling-Clark, "Mozambique's Vote for Democratic Governance," *Postconflict Elections, Democratization & International Assistance*, ed. Krishna Kumar (Boulder, Colo. and London: Lynne Rienner Publishers, 1998), chapter 9, pp. 153–175.

III

Political Issues

11

Military Disengagement from Politics and Constitutionalism in Africa

Challenges and Opportunities

Julius O. Ihonvbere

The Minister of Defense shall be a civilian.
> Article 87, The Constitution of the Federal Republic of Ethiopia, 1994.

Every military regime is a fraud. . . . The moment you get in, you suspend the constitution and rule by decrees . . .
> General Ibrahim Babangida (ret.), interview in *Tell* (December 7, 1998).

Political structures and processes remain highly militarized in much of Africa.
> Arnoldo Brenes.[1]

The expectations for democratic renewal in Africa have attracted much euphoria and enthusiasm.[2] The widespread socioeconomic and political contractions and disasters of the 1970s and 1980s had turned Africa into a classic example of failure and spent hopes and expectations.[3] The Economic Commission for Africa (ECA) declared the 1980s as Africa's lost decade.[4] In fact, the former executive secretary of the ECA, Laiyashi Yaker openly lamented that Africa was the only region of the world that came out of the 1980s much worse off than when the decade began.[5] V. S. Naipaul declared that Africa had no future while the late, noted African political economist Claude Ake declared that the choice open to the continent and its peoples was not between socialism and capitalism but between socialism and barbarism![6]

There is still much in the continent to fill the plate of Afro-pessimists and doomsday theorists especially those seeking an excuse to rationalize and justify the increasing marginalization of the continent in the emerging complex global divisions of labor and power. It is true that the contradictions, negative coalitions, and conflicts inherited and accentuated since political independence have hardly abated. In fact, in several instances, these have been magnified and deepened to very dangerous proportions. The character of the state has not changed in any fundamental way. It remains a very violent, privatized, aloof, and insensitive force that the people try to cheat, avoid, or subvert as opportunity permits.[7] The economies are still disarticulated, distorted, and underdeveloped. The industrial base is still weak and dependent. Technology is still very rudimentary and dependent on the outside world.[8] The elites are still very factionalized, fractionalized, weak, corrupt, and incapable of constructing a viable *national* project even in their own narrow interests. Markets are still weak and built around the productive activities and demands of foreign markets. Public policy is still elitist and disorganized, as are public facilities, infrastructure, and institutions. Local cultures, values, world views are still denigrated and seen as indicators of being "unmodernized." Finally, politics in Africa still has very little to do with the people but so much to do to the people who are still seen as objects of manipulation and exploitation rather than objects of participation and mobilization. Taken together these challenges and contradictions have precipitated unprecedented instability, political violence, ethnic and regional suspicions, and the breakdown of law and order. It was hardly amazing when, in country after country, the largely undemocratic neocolonial state and its custodians were unceremoniously swept off the political scene by military interests and institutions constructed and nurtured under colonialism.[9]

THE MILITARIZATION OF AFRICA'S POLITICAL SPACE

In some sense, the continent's political space has been militarized since the advent of Western colonization. The colonial state was an undemocratic and very violent force. In order to keep colonized subjects under control, compel them to grow particular crops, control urban labor, acquire forced labor for special projects, collect legal and illegal taxes, and reproduce its *political* hegemony, the colonial state combined the duties of the executive, judiciary, and legislature. It employed unprecedented violence to impose its will, hardly ever consulted with the people in its administration, and had absolutely no respect for human values. This violent, undemocratic, inaccessible, and essentially abhorrent state was not dismantled at political independence. It was simply "Africanized," modified, and repackaged to serve the interests of the emerging African elite. This is exactly why the nationalist project disappeared with independence as the new elite began to sound and behave like the departed colonial dictators.[10] The struggle for liberation was taken up at this stage by students, workers, peasants, women, professionals, and academics. This struggle suffered a setback as country after country fell under the authority of the military as they intervened to "restore" order rather than to push the popular agenda.[11]

The reasons why the military intervenes in politics have been explored elsewhere.[12] Suffice it to note that the reasons cannot be divorced from the character of the state, the lack of elite hegemony in the society, the weakness and fragmentation of civil society, the fragility and limited legitimacy of public institutions, and the lack of a political and constitutional culture and tradition that subjects the military to civil authority and order. It is these factors that give meaning to issues of ethnicity, religion, region, personality, political corruption, ambition among officers, and the impact of particular policies on the military. It is, however, important to discuss the overall impact of the advent and politics of the military on the character of politics and society. Military rule in Africa has generated a siege or conflict mentality. It has forced progressive initiatives and interests underground. It has encouraged reliance on unorthodox or extra-legal methods of political engagement. Military rule has hardened political positions, encouraged the arrogance of power, and promoted a culture of intolerance and disregard for consultation and dialogue.[13] As Claude Ake has put it,

Because African society is at war the specialists of warfare, the military, have come to dominate it. This is the objective basis of military rule in Africa as well as the enormous influence of the military even in those African states which are not formally under military rule. The ascendancy of the military is one of the great tragedies of Africa, for the military is nothing other than a highly specialized apparatus of violence whose salience begins when sociability has become impossible and civilized values no longer apply, when we must take to the "killing fields." That is why military rule is inherently and inevitably de-civilizing.[14]

The militarization of society and politics actually transcends the illegal seizure of power by sections of, or a clique within, the military. It is important to conceive of militarization as also including indirect governance through pressures, control, threats, manipulation, and the exercise of undue influence on so-called civilian regimes. Militarization equally involves the negative influence that armed gangs, warring factions, and elements in society exercise over the state and public policy. As well, in conditions where the economy has been uncharacteristically militarized, democratic regimes are quite often forced to operate under unfavorable conditions where democratic projects become hostage to direct and indirect military interests. The consequence, even in poverty-stricken and debt-ridden states, is a huge defense and security budget and an oversized army that feeds off the people in a parasitic manner. A careful study of societies that have been ruled by the military would reveal that they are highly violent, intimidated, and generally unstable. Weak state structures and a divided ruling class can further complicate contradictions arising from history and a hostile global environment. Frequently, this would mortgage or subvert the democratic project leading to further instability, waste, and the reproduction of underdevelopment:

In countries where the state is weak or has ceased to exist, the long history of militarization has brought about a gradual diffusion of violence through the splintering of official militaries and the emergence of guerrillas and warlords, swelling the number of informal entrepreneurs of violence. In some cases, coups d'état, internal strife, interstate conflict and even genocide have reversed the course of democratic consolidation.[15]

True, there are a few exceptions. Even such exceptional cases are often temporary reliefs from the immediate impact of military dictatorships. The consequences of military adventurism in African politics have included the following:

1. The abrogation or suspension of constitutions and rule through undemocratic decrees and edicts;

2. The termination of democratic projects and the curtailment of the process of developing and nurturing democratic values;

3. The dismantling of democratic institutions such as parliaments and thus the forced termination of the process of building democratic practices, networks, and relationships;

4. The abrogation of political parties and a ban imposed on political activities thus terminating opportunities for nurturing new leaders, strengthening political organizations, promoting party philosophies, articulating party programs, training new leaders, and presenting these leaders for office by mobilizing public support;

5. The corruption of the entire society through undemocratic, non-transparent, and non-accountable activities and attitudes that rely heavily on commandist approaches to power and politics;

6. The intimidation of civil society through the general harassment of prodemocracy, human rights, environmental, and other community-based leaders and activists;

7. The militarization of popular discourse, values, attitudes, and life styles as public language or discourse in the public sphere takes on the authoritarian, insensitive, and commandist lexicon of the military;

8. The nurturing of a brand of political leaders under military rule who amass wealth, build networks under military tutelage and find themselves unable to perform with the end of military rule and thus become a liability to the democratic project;

9. The construction of a well-armed, arrogant, and corrupt military and security structure with a direct interest in politics and power that continues to pose a threat to postmilitary political arrangements; and

10. The difficulty of eroding the contradictions and negative values cultivated by the military in a democratic era where pressures on the political elite for the democracy dividend easily provides excuses for the return of the military to power.

Taken together therefore, the military has been a disaster to the cultivation of democratic institutions, values, networks, and institutions in Africa. For countries like Nigeria and Ghana, it will take several decades to get on the path for constructing a nonmilitary influenced democratic process. Even then, the challenge of ensuring that the military does not return to power remains ever present. The military, if it must be said, has no business in power. No amount of so-called breakdown of law and order should warrant the unconstitutional takeover of power, the abrogation of political activities, the suspension of the constitution, and the suffocation of civil society. This is a message that is yet to be clearly articulated and made part of the national political discourse in African states. In the African scenario, the very poor record of the military in office damns the intervention in the first place and exposes the arrogance and opportunism of the military officers who have arrogated to themselves the right to serve as the barometer of good governance, good politics, and when and where the military should seize power.

What has become clear however, is that internal divisions, coups and counter-coups, corruption, failed policies, and pressures from civil society for redemocratization have combined to force the military to adopt several democratic transition programs in the continent. The new commitment to redemocratization (or at best liberalization) has not come from the magnanimity of Africa's military leaders. There is not a single instance where this has been the case. Rather, the new acceptance of democracy and multiparty politics has been forced on the military dictators by a combination of international and internal pressures. In particular, the emerging coalition of religious, workers', human rights, prodemocracy, peasant, and women's movements sent the signals to military dictators that used to openly and arrogantly question the necessity for democratic rule. As J. Victor Angelo of the UNDP has rightly noted, African peoples are "reacting to unresponsive governance, exclusionary politics, widespread poverty, the inability of governments to ensure the rule of law and order and the absence of legitimate economic opportunities."[16] In this process, the military has not been an uninterested party. As the case of West Africa shows, retired and active military officers have developed an appetite for political power. They have adopted all forms of legal and extra-legal mechanisms for containing the political faction/fraction of the ruling classes and for advancing their own agendas. Yet, as these struggles for the permanent disengagement of the military from politics continue, it is important that we examine alternative ways for keeping the military out of power and for subjecting it to civil order. There is certainly a need for a continent-wide discussion on civil-military relations with a special focus on how to democratize the military and its institutions and subject it to civil order.

PROCESS-LED CONSTITUTIONAL CONTROL OF THE MILITARY

On the surface, it might sound like a vain and totally unrealistic project to speak of constitutional control of the armed and security forces as a strategy for preventing military coups and subjecting the institutions to civil control, particularly in Africa. In some sense this is tantamount to conceding the democratic political spaces to those who legally monopolize the instruments of coercion even when they clearly utilize such instruments illegally and against popular interests. The fact that military officers suspend the constitution and quite often brag about doing so without repercussion has created an attitude among activists and scholars that the military is beyond control. As well, the enthusiastic reception that many military regimes receive from the public on seizing power has been confused with approval and acceptance of coups. This is very far from the truth. More often, such public displays are reflective of frustrations with displaced regimes and temporary expressions of readiness for change. The fact that pressures are mounted almost immediately on the military to disengage from politics is evidence of the widespread belief that military rule is an abnormality.

A project to democratize the military and subject it to constitutional order requires a lot of work, networking, civic education, education and restructuring of the military, and the conversion of the constitution into a *living* document. In fact, we contend that aside from a visionary, committed, and transparent leadership, the sort of constitution with a capacity to control the military must be *process led.* In other words, a constitution that emerges from widespread consultations and debates, that is deliberately engineered to address the needs and dreams of the majority, and that builds ownership by the people around the constitution can contain the adventurism of some military officers and subject the institution to civil order. If the people are part of the design of the constitution, and if it truly reflects their experiences, desires, and aspirations, they will see it as belonging to them. The people will regard the constitution as the road map for designing and pursuing a better future, and can be counted on to defend it against military coups and other extra-legal attempts at capturing state power.

Africa is changing rapidly. Political discourses are no longer elite driven. The context of politics is changing and so is the content of politics. Power is no longer perceived as an instrument for domination and violence. Rather, it is now seen as a weapon for liberation. In fact, the issues that now constitute the stuff of African politics are those that reflect the interests of the people and reflects their dreams: human rights, gender equality, social justice, good governance, environmental protection, accountability, participation in decision making, basic human needs, and those issues that directly address identity, nationality, and democratization. It is in this context that a new trend in constitution making is beginning to emerge in Africa: the process-led, as against elite organized, manipulated, and imposed constitutions.

This new trend in constitutionalism has been encouraged by several factors:

a) The support for democratization and civil society by subregional, continental, and international organizations such as the Economic Community of West African States (ECOWAS), the Southern Africa Development Community (SADC), the Organization of African Unity (OAU), the Commonwealth, the European Union (EU), and the United Nations. These organizations have demonstrated their opposition to conflicts and dictatorships, and have expressed open support for democratic transitions and constitutionalism. As well, western governments, donors, lenders, international NGOs, especially human rights organizations, have also openly supported opposition movements, prodemocracy and human rights groups, and declared a new commitment to democratic compacts between governments and their peoples.[17]

b) There is new acknowledgement of the salience of pluralism and its centrality to the democratic process. Until very recently, all over Africa, ethnic, religious, and other cultural differences were denied and suppressed by African leaders and governments. The state, in its effort to homogenize society, established a one-party state, and built a personality cult around the "big man," harassed and intimidated the larger society, suffocated communities and initiatives, and imposed all sorts of nebulous ideological ideas on society. Minorities and powerless communities were ignored, exploited, and marginalized in the political and policy process. This is changing and constitutionalism is the critical weapon that is being employed: "... it is increasingly being realized that in order to tackle the root causes of conflicts in Africa and elsewhere, one must help plural societies articulate shared national visions of the future and to develop forms of governance that give all parts of the population a stake in the development of the country. Majorities and minorities must work together and one should consciously engender confidence on the part of minorities that constitutional and legal order will protect them and help them to retain their culture, language and religion."[18]

c) All over Africa, there are new coalitions and networks emerging as platforms for training new leaders, demystifying dictatorships, and articulating alternative agendas for democratization. These new movements involve churches and their leaders, student and trade unions, professional associations, and even some sections of the ruling classes. In Kenya, the 4Cs is a coalition of over forty organizations cutting across religions, regional, and ethnic lines. In Nigeria, the United Action for Democracy (UAD) and the Campaign for Democracy (CD) include representatives of youth, environmental, professional, women, and cultural associations. These organizations are utilizing international declarations and covenants such as the International Declaration of Human Rights, the African Charter for Human and People's Rights, and the Commonwealth Harare Declaration to set the basis for the new struggles for constitutionalism in the continent.

The character of postcolonial politics compelled African leaders to devise ingenious strategies to retain and maintain power. Invariably, this involved the subversion of the democratic process and the construction of authoritarian rule. The ideology of development dictated that the allocation of power and resources was to be used to contain opposition, depoliticize popular communities and groups, and construct networks for the maintenance of so-called law and order. Consequently, the constitutions of most African states were the products of constituent assemblies, parliamentary committees, special task forces or tribunals, or the work of a handful of lawyers and politicians. The hallmark of imposed constitutions was that they were never subjected to popular debates or referenda. If at any point the constitutions were subjected to public debates, these were carefully monitored and manipulated. The documents either in draft or final forms were never made available to the people. If referenda were called, the results were rigged in favor of the state. In some cases, the reports of constitutional commissions were simply ignored after elaborate ceremonies aimed at diverting public attention and convincing donors and the international community that something positive was being done about democracy.

The end product was that the constitutions, riddled with all sorts of contradictions and limitations, failed to serve as compacts for managing a democratic system much less guaranteeing the operations of a democratic order. The documents lacked legitimacy even if they were legal documents. They hampered the workings of the judiciary and failed to guarantee the rights of the poor majority. In some cases, they were simply documents designed to serve the interests of the dictator whose name was written into the constitution as president-for-life as was the case in Banda's Malawi.[19] In all practical senses, these countries had no constitutions because the documents failed in every respect to perform the functions of such a document.

The victory of democratic forces all over Africa, even if partial in some instances, has encouraged a new approach to constitution making. This has emphasized three main important issues:

a) The *process* of constitution making with full emphasis on dialogue, consultation, debates, and open involvement of the people in articulating and presenting their demands;

b) A critical examination of existing constitutions, drawing lessons from other experiences in and outside Africa; and

c) Developing strategies for taking the constitution to the people through the establishment of formal institutions dedicated to translating, abridging, mass producing and distributing the document as well as massive civic education involving government agencies and nongovernmental organizations.

Usually, the draft constitution that results from national debates is subjected to a national referendum in order to gain national legitimacy. As Mpazi Sinjela has noted,

... unlike the constitutional order in the one party state, the emergent new constitutional order includes elaborate human rights provisions and attempts to curb the autocratic power of the executive branch of government. The independence of the judiciary is asserted. Under one party rule, the executive branch wielded wide and all embracing powers. The courts were stripped of any meaningful power to check against abuse of power by the executive branch of government. As a result of this lack of accountability, the principle of good governance was impaired. Corruption was rife and abuse of power could not be questioned. This lack of accountability weakened political institutions.[20]

The new process that draws out political movements and interests invariably has made it possible to pay attention to issues of human rights, the separation of powers, and the clear entrenchment of provisions that guarantee nationality and identity rights among others. Because the military has come to represent such a formidable challenge to the construction of democratic institutions and values, the new genre of constitutions in Africa are paying special attention to strategies for not just controlling the military but also to democratizing it and subjecting it to the constitutional order.

The process of constitution making is critical to the strength, acceptability, and legitimacy of the final product. In fact, by involving the people and their communities, both elites and masses understand the document, its importance, and its relevance to the larger democratic process. A popular constitution improves the quality of political organization and debate and strengthens public confidence in the rule of law. Countries like Eritrea, South Africa, and Ethiopia have shown examples of the value of a process-led constitution-making approach. These countries established independent commissions that utilized a variety of strategies and processes to involve all sectors of society, citizens abroad, and the military in the constitution-making process. This strategy was deliberately designed to build public ownership around the constitution and utilize the document to address directly questions of gender, the rule of law, human and minority rights, language, identity, nationality, and citizenship. But in most African states, an overwhelming majority of the populace never see, much less study and understand, the constitution. This is one of the major challenges of the new constitutionalism in Africa.

Uganda's experience is instructive in this regard. The character and impact of the dictatorships of the past and the cost the country had to pay for the restoration of law and order is well documented. It is instructive that some of the eighteen reasons given by Field Marshall Idi Amin for sacking Milton Obote's government included the "unwarranted detention of people without trial," "prolonged state of emergency, which had been declared in October 1969," "lack of freedom to air political views," and "the failure of political authorities to organize any elections and the proposed three-plus-one electoral method which would only favor the rich." As we now know, Amin's rule did not improve on these conditions. The victory of the Yoweri Museveni-led National Resistance Movement/Army (NRM/A) in January 1986 altered the political direction of Uganda. Legal Notice No. 1 of 1986 suspended parts of the 1967 constitution, and prohibited political parties and activities. The NRM announced a ten-point program of reconstruction that focused on establishment of democracy; restoration of security; consolidation of national unity and elimination of all forms of sectarianism; defense and consolidation of national independence; and building an independent, integrated, and self-sustaining national economy. Other aspects of the program included restoration and improvement of social services and the rehabilitation of war-ravaged areas; elimination of corruption and misuse of power; rectification of errors which had dislocated society; cooperation with other African states in defending human and democratic rights; and the adoption of a mixed economy strategy.

Following the establishment of a fairly broad-based government, the NRM opted for a democratic approach to constitution making. The objective was to set a new path away from the past and to involve all segments of the Ugandan society in the process, and to "enable and empower Ugandans to re-examine the constitutional structures and to make a constitution in line with their aspirations."[21] The grounding of the process in the individual and collective aspirations of the people was well articulated in the view of Stephen B. Akabway, a commissioner for the constituent assembly who noted that the previous constitutions of Uganda "excluded the participation of the ordinary citizenry. This lack of a firm rooting of the constitution in the citizenry has therefore hindered the emergence of a constitutional culture and has equally hampered development of democratic governance."[22] The NRM government established a Ministry for Constitutional Affairs to coordinate the overall process of constitutional engineering and as demonstration of the importance it attached to the issue. An independent twenty-one-member Constitutional Commission under the leadership of Justice Ben J. Odoki was established to undertake the task of mobilizing Ugandans in and outside the country and to collect and collate proposals that would go into a draft constitutional proposal.

Working for four years, the Commission employed every available opportunity to collect views from Ugandans—interviews, public meetings, debates, essay competitions, seminars, and workshops as well as solicited written memoranda—and it "received overwhelming response from the people of all shades of opinion in Uganda and used their views as a basis for formulating its proposals ..."[23] Interest groups, community and professional associations, and academic institutions were all involved in the debates on the draft constitution. It contacted Ugandans living abroad and traveled to several foreign nations to understudy their constitutions and supporting institutions. In the end, it received a total of 25,542 submissions. A twenty-chapter, seven-hundred-fifty-page draft constitution was submitted in December 1992. According to Justice Odoki,

The Draft Constitution was intended to reflect the values, interests and aspirations of the people of Uganda. It was aimed at redressing past injustices. It sought to establish the sovereignty of the people as repository of political power. It recognized the supremacy of the constitution as the fundamental law of Uganda and as the basis for constitutionalism and democracy. It sought to establish democratic institutions and processes that would ensure good governance, transparency, accountability, popular participation, and peaceful change of government. It provided for a form of government in which democratic local self government was guaranteed. It put in place a comprehensive bill of rights that was justiciable by an independent judiciary. It sought to create the necessary environment and conditions for peace, stability, national unity and socio-economic development. It was a home grown, socially relevant document largely influenced by Uganda's historical experience and its vision for the future, but taking into account international developments elsewhere in the world."[24]

This sort of people-centered process can sustain a democratic project and discourage adventurous military officers from seizing state power through coups and counter coups.

The issue of commitment is important to constitutionalism. Unlike Nigeria where the state is distrusted and constitutional initiatives are greeted with cynicism and apathy, in Uganda there was a high degree of trust for the government.[25] The quality and credibility of the Commission's chair and its members and the way it conducted its affairs further won public support for and interest in the process. Thus with a commitment to "break with the past in many respects," the Constitutional Commission's objective was to prepare a draft that would "ensure that the constitution was forward-looking and progressive; that it did not repeat the mistakes of the past; that it provided for a peaceful transition to democratic governance; that it provided measures to prevent the vicious circle of dictatorship, instability and economic decline; that it provided room for constitutional development; and that it ushered in a new democratic culture that would promote sustained development."[26]

Though the NRM, by virtue of Legal Notice No. 1 of 1984 (paragraph 14B) had been empowered to constitute a Constituent Assembly, it gave up that power and opted for a directly elected Constituent Assembly. The government then set up a Commission for Constituent Assembly with the task of conducting the election of delegates to the Assembly. The draft constitution submitted to the government was then subjected to a vigorous debate in an elected constituent assembly. After sixteen months of intensive deliberations, the Assembly completed its work and produced a final document. The

1995 Constitution of the Republic of Uganda is the outcome of this long and expensive democratic process. It is certainly not a perfect document. After all, a constitution is not necessarily the last point in a nation's political life. In fact, given the bitter experiences of the past, the promulgation of a constitution might just be the beginning of the process of political renewal.

ISSUES IN DISENGAGEMENT, DEMILITARIZATION AND DEMOCRATIZATION

In Africa today, even in those countries that have never experienced direct military rule, the triple issues of military disengagement from politics, the demilitarization of the polity, and the democratization of society are all related and ever topical. Interestingly, these issues have become part of the immediate and longer-term agendas of several professional associations like the African Association of Political Science (AAPS), research centers like the Council for the Development of Social and Economic Research in Africa (CODESRIA) and the Center for Advanced Social Science (CASS), as well as international bodies such as the Africa Leadership Forum (ALF) and the UNDP. Many have drawn inspiration from the work of Oscar Arias and the Arias Foundation that have pushed such an agenda for demilitarization in Central America. It must be conceded however that given the huge presence of the military in African politics, the widespread civilianization programs involving several retired and serving military officers, and the growing security problems in the region, issues of demilitarization have not been taken too seriously. It has been stated rather frequently that "During the 1970s and 1980s, Africa was the most militarized continent in the world," and that though "there has been a palpable liberalization of the political space in many countries of the continent, many challenges remain."[27] Yet the dangers that military coups, military misgovernance, and the costs of maintaining largely unproductive armed forces pose to growth and development have never been lost on African peoples. It is the combination of these realizations that has generated new pressures for disengagement, demilitarization, and democratization.

Within African states, there have been efforts at demilitarization. This is evidenced in new commitments to peace and security and a new realization that security is much more than the acquisition of weapons of destruction at the expense of basic human needs, growth, and development. Several countries have designed programs to cut down the size of the military and to provide support that enhance the rehabilitation of demobilized soldiers. There have been programs designed to re-educate serving officers by emphasizing professionalism and awareness of the changing domestic and global political scene that is increasingly in favor of democratic governance. Military academies, universities, institutes, and special colleges have been established for this purpose to complement heavy investment in overseas training. At great political risk, military budgets are being cut by governments, military and civilian alike, to reflect an awareness that the military cannot be an island in an era of stabilization and structural adjustment as demanded by lenders, donors, and investors. Finally, security paradigms are being re-examined in the context of growing civil society initiatives that are demonstrating that security rests not necessarily in the military establishment but in an integrated, educated, enlightened, mobilized, and patriotic populace that has confidence in the state, its custodians, and the national project. Increasingly, senior officers are not just emphasizing professionalism but discipline within the ranks and the need to adjust to the realities and demands of democratic environments.

Clearly, therefore, it is no longer really possible to roll back the democratic wave in Africa. This situation provides several novel opportunities to pursue comprehensive and viable agendas for not just the disengagement of the military from power—as in Benin, Nigeria, Ghana, and the Gambia for example—but also to pursue demilitarization in the shorter and longer terms. Shorter term measures would include reduction in size, budget cuts, re-education, reorientation, rehabilitation and integration of demobilized soldiers, redefining and reassessing the meaning of security, and the conversion of military structures to serve peaceful purposes. Longer-term measures would include the total elimination of standing military forces and the integration of defense into the larger society anchored in the citizenry.[28]

However defined, disengagement and demilitarization agendas must be concretely anchored on democratization projects. By democratization in this study we are speaking of the steady and systematic empowerment of the people, their institutions and communities in a direction that enables them to dictate and determine the content and context of politics with emphasis on pro-people issues: social justice, accountability, transparency, human rights, popular participation, gender equality, environmental protection, and basic human needs. It is only such an agenda of democratization that could make it possible to articulate, present, and adhere to the shorter and longer term measures and implications of disengagement and demilitarization. As it happens, this process is already on in Africa. The new project on constitutionalism is beginning to bring forth new constitutional provisions that are designed to control and contain the African military in rather ingenuous ways.

CONTAINING A DISENGAGED MILITARY: THE NEW CONSTITUTIONAL APPROACHES

There is an urgent need to provide clear constitutional controls on the military. Its composition, training, funding, and role in society need to be clearly defined. To be sure, the constitution is usually the first casualty of military coups. But constitutions, as living documents, can declare that they are not suspendible and provide very stiff penalties in perpetuity for offenders. The constitution has to be clear on treasonable offenses and empower the larger community, through education and mobilization, to be familiar with its provisions and to empower the people to resist, by all means necessary, such violations at all times.

The 1995 Uganda constitution that emerged from a process-led constitution-making approach discussed above includes some rather interesting provisions designed to contain the military. In Chapter One, clause 1, "All power" is vested in the people of Uganda. Clause 2 declares, "Without limiting the effect of clause 1 of this article, all authority in the State emanates from the people of Uganda; and the people shall be governed through their will and consent." A military putsch is clearly a subversion of this provision. Of course, a regime that results from a military coup cannot claim to be based on the "will and consent" of the people. In Clause 3, the constitution declares that "All power and authority of Government and its organs derive from this Constitution, which in turn derives its authority from the people who consent to be governed in accordance with this constitution." Therefore, any undemocratic political arrangement would represent a negation of this provision. Clause 4 is even more direct: "The people shall express their will and consent on who shall govern them and how they should be governed, through regular, free and fair elections of their representatives or through referenda." Those that come to power through military coups can therefore not expect to enjoy the loyalty and support of the people since they have not been elected through free and fair elections and cannot therefore claim to be representatives of the people. Article 3.1 is definitive on violent or undemocratic takeover of power: "It is prohibited for any person or group of persons to take or retain control of the Government of Uganda, except in accordance with the provisions of this constitution." In Clause 2, it declares that "Any person who, singly or in concert with others, by any violent or other unlawful means, suspends, overthrows, abrogates or amends this constitution or any part of it or attempts to do any such act, commits the offense of treason and shall be punished according to law." Of course, military coups go against every portion of this provision. But the Ugandan constitution has attempted to build a perpetual life span for the democratic compact even in the event of such unconstitutional attempt to seize power. In Clause 3 the constitution declares,

This constitution shall not lose its force and effect even where its observance is interrupted by a government established by force of arms; and in any case, as soon as the people recover their liberty, its observance shall be re-established and all persons who have taken part in any rebellion or other activity which resulted in the interruption of the observance, shall be tried in accordance with this constitution and other laws consistent with it (emphasis added).

Clearly, those who seize power and engage in the illegal suspension or amendment of the constitution continue to commit the crime of treason and whenever they leave office voluntarily or by other means would still be tried because the original democratic constitution never lost its "force and effect." This is a very important provision since it preempts any attempt by those that negate the constitution from enacting new laws or drafting new constitutions to protect their illegal actions.

Finally, Clause 4 gives to all citizens of Uganda the "right and duty at all times" a) to "defend the constitution and to resist any person or group of persons seeking to overthrow the established constitutional order;" and b) "to do all in their power to restore this Constitution after it has been suspended, overthrown, abrogated or amended contrary to its provisions." In Clause 5, the Constitution states categorically that any person or persons involved in such a resistance to restore the constitution after it has been illegally amended, abrogated, or suspend or overthrown "commits no offense." Any punishment imposed on such a person or persons as a result of direct and/or indirect involvement in the effort to restore the constitution would be "considered void from the time it was imposed and that person shall be taken to be absolved from all liabilities arising out of the punishment." These provisions represent a major departure from the past and seem to directly address the problem of illegal and violent seizure of state power in Uganda. To be sure, only an educated, enlightened, and mobilized populace can understand and take advantage of these provisions. For Uganda, the process-led approach that went into the production of the constitution did popularize these questions and issues. More importantly, Article 4, a–b clearly requires the state to promote public awareness of the constitution by translating it into all Ugandan languages; disseminating the constitution "as widely as possible"; and "providing for the teaching of the Constitution in all educational institutions and armed forces training institutions and regularly transmitting and publishing programs through the media generally." The fact that this would be taught in schools and that the armed forces were singled out is also evidence of a desire to get the message out that any form of illegal seizure of power would be resisted and those involved would be subject to severe punishment even after they disengage from power for whatever reasons. In Article 51, the Uganda Human Rights Commission is established. Among other functions, Clause e requires the Commission "to create and sustain within society the awareness of the provisions of this Constitution as the fundamental law of the people of Uganda;" and Clause f requires it to "educate and encourage *the public to defend this Constitution at all times against all forms of abuse and violation"* (emphasis added).

Eritrea represents a case that had one of the most consultative process-led approaches to the making of its 1996 constitution. This process involved all the fighters that were on the front line of the liberation struggle. In fact, the Bereket Selassie-led Constitutional Commission of Eritrea (CCE) included some ex-fighters.[29] Reflecting the historical experience and specificities of the country, the Eritrean constitution shows a rather strong role for the state. Article 2.1 declares that the Constitution "is the legal expression of the sovereignty of the Eritrean people" while clause 4 states that "All organs of the State, all public and private associations and institutions and all citizens shall be bound by and remain loyal to the Constitution and shall ensure its observance." Any act, therefore, that goes against the provisions of the constitution which is itself anchored on a democratic process is deemed to be illegal. In Article 12.1 the Eritrean constitution makes it clear that the country's "Defense and security forces . . . shall owe allegiance to and defend the territorial integrity and sovereignty of the country, the Constitution and government established pursuant thereto." The constitution defined the defense and security forces as "an integral part of society" that is expected to be "productive and respectful of the people." It declares that "defense and security are rooted on the people and on their active participation"; and declares that the forces "shall be subject and accountable to the law, shall be competent and pass these requirements for posterity." This sort of socially based articulation of the nature, structure, role, and relationship between the defense and security forces with the larger society is very unusual in Africa. As mentioned earlier, while it reflects the historical experience where every Eritrean was directly and/or indirectly involved in the fight for an independent country, it provides the sort of approach to reforming the military and making it socially and economically relevant to contemporary society. This way, the current culture of a parasitic, violent, corrupted, and privatized military and security arrangement would be gradually negated.

Finally, the Eritrean constitution, in Article 25.5 declares that "All citizens shall have the duty to know, respect and defend the Constitution." For a people that had sacrificed so much for independence, defending all structures and values of that newly won independence should not be that difficult.

The 1994 constitution of Ethiopia is equally innovative in how it tried to subject the military to civil authority. In Article 9.1–3 the constitution is declared to be the supreme law of the land; it calls on all citizens, organs of state, and political organizations to, as a duty, "ensure observance of the Constitution and to obey it"; and declares that "it is prohibited to assume state powers in any manner other than provided under the Constitution." In Article 87, it states that the composition of the armed forces "shall reflect the equitable representation of the Nations, Nationalities and Peoples of Ethiopia." This addresses the problem of lopsidedness in military formations that have led to coups and other forms of violence in several African states. In Nigeria for instance, there is widespread belief that Muslims and northerners dominate the top hierarchy of the military. A rather interesting provision in the constitution is Article 87.2 where it declares that "The Minister of Defense shall be a civilian." This is one direct way of demonstrating the primacy of civil authority and the democratic process. It goes against a common tradition where retired or serving military officers are appointed to this position in democratic contexts. Clause 3 enjoins the armed forces to "protect the sovereignty of the country and carry out any responsibilities as may be assigned to them under any state of emergency proclaimed in accordance with this Constitution." The armed forces, according to Clause 4 "shall at all times obey and respect the Constitution." Of course, a coup that dismantles political parties and parliaments, suspends the constitution, and suffocates civil society hardly demonstrates respect for the constitution. While the Ethiopian constitution has been the most courageous in engaging questions of nationality, identity, gender, language, and regional and subregional autonomy, it has also tried to address the critical issue of the supremacy of the constitution even if not as directly as Eritrea, Uganda, or Ghana (see below).

The 1992 Ghanaian constitution is to date the most radical in terms of clear provisions on the side of civil society against the illegal seizure of power by the military. It has gone beyond vague and general statements that have never frightened or discouraged the military in countries like Nigeria. Of course, military personnel are citizens and do not need to be treated as lepers. As well, their role in society is historically and socially constructed. It is therefore possible to deconstruct it politically. The point is that Africa has matured to a stage where it must directly engage the problems that military coups and other forms of violence pose not just to the well being of citizens but to the construction and nurturing of democratic values and institutions. More than any other group or constituency, the military has posed the most devastating and costly challenge to this process.

The constitution begins in Chapter One section 1.1 by investing sovereignty in the people of Ghana and declares that the "powers of government" are to be exercised for the welfare of the people. Subsection 2 declares the constitution to be the "supreme law of Ghana" and that "any other law found to be inconsistent with any provision of this constitution shall, to the extent of the inconsistency, be void." All citizens are empowered to challenge any law, which contravenes the constitution. In Section 3.1, the constitution declares that "Parliament shall have no power to establish a one-party state." It then makes the categorical declaration that "Any activity of a person or group of persons which suppresses or seek to suppress a lawful political activity of any person or any class of persons, or persons generally is unlawful." Furthermore in subsection 3, the constitution declares that "Any person who a) by himself or in concert with others by any violent or other unlawful means, suspends or overthrows or abrogates this constitution or any part of it, or attempts to do any such act;" or b) "aids and abets in any manner any person referred to in paragraph a) of this clause; commits the offense of high treason and shall upon conviction be sentenced to suffer death."

In order to prevent the usual situation where the army overthrows the government and suspends the constitution to cover its horrible track record, the constitution vests the people of Ghana with the power to resist unconstitutional and illegal military takeovers. In subsection 4.a, it invests "All citizens of Ghana have the duty at all times" a) "to defend this constitution, and in particular, to resist any person or group of persons seeking to commit any of the acts referred to in clause 3 of this article; and b) to do all in their power to restore this constitution after it has been suspended, overthrown or abrogated as referred to in clause 3 of this article." What we have here is quite new in Africa and the 1995 Ugandan constitution drew heavily on the Ghanaian experience. The constitution is directly empowering all citizens to employ all possible means to defend and protect the constitution, in order words, the democratic project.

The constitution goes further to declare that any one who participates in resisting such attempts or acts at suspending or abrogating it commits "no offense." In fact, according to subsection 6, any one who participates in resisting such attacks on the constitution and gets punished in whatever manner in the process, shall, as soon as the situation was restored be "absolved from all liabilities arising out of the punishment." In fact, the constitution in subsection 7 declares that "The Supreme Court shall, on application by or on behalf of a person who has suffered any punishment or loss to which Clause 6 of this article relates, award him adequate compensation which shall be charged on the Consolidated Fund, in respect of any suffering or loss incurred as a result of the punishment."

True, this would not in any way stop ambitious military officers from executing a coup and suspending the constitution. But the fact that this provision is in the 1992 constitution is new and represents a feeling among the people of Ghana that such illegal seizures of power ought to be resisted. The provisions in the paragraph above are the strongest statement against military coups existing anywhere in Africa. It not only absolves those that would try to resist the subversion of the constitution, but it also provides guaranteed financial incentives including if such persons died in the process of resistance! It should also be realized that the 1992 constitution has written into it several commissions including one on Human Rights and Administrative Justice and another on civic education. The mandate of the National Commission for Civic Education (NCCE) must be seen as a deliberate attempt to promote a culture of constitutionalism and education of the public on salient aspects of the constitution.

In Chapter Thirteen of the constitution of Ghana the NCCE is established. Appointed by the president, the commissioners are not to hold office in any political party. Among its functions are creating and sustaining awareness within society on the principles and objectives of the constitution "as the fundamental law of the people of Ghana;" educating and encouraging the "public to defend the Constitution at all times, against all forms of abuse and violation;" formulating programs at all levels of government aimed at "realizing the objectives" of the constitution; formulating, implementing and overseeing "programs intended to inculcate in the citizens of Ghana awareness of their civic responsibilities and an appreciation of their rights and obligations as free people;" and other functions that parliament may prescribe. In Article 234, the constitution stipulates that the Commission "shall not be subject to the direction or control of any person or authority in the performance of its functions." As evidence of how seriously the people of Ghana take the Commission and its work, its chairman enjoys the same terms and conditions of service as a Justice of the Court of Appeal, while the deputy chairman enjoys terms similar to those of the Justice of the High Court. They cannot be removed from office by the president but through the same constitutionally stipulated process for removing a Justice of the Court of Appeal for the Chairman and a Justice of the high court for the deputy. Finally, Parliament, according to Article 237, is required to "provide for the establishment of Regional and District branches of the Commission"; while Article 239 further confirms its autonomy by stipulating that the "administrative expenses of the Commission, including salaries, allowances and pensions payable to, or in respect of, persons serving with the Commission, shall be charged on the Consolidated Fund."

Thus, if the NCCE does its work well, its mandate could sufficiently educate the citizenry as to the illegality of military coups and the constitutionally stipulated responsibility of all citizens to, "at all times" resist anyone that attempts to subvert the constitution. Furthermore, the people could be sufficiently educated to realize that they would be financially compensated directly or their estate could be compensated for performing such a duty as resisting illegal attempts to take over power or subvert the constitution. On the other hand, civic education among the military could send direct messages that the populace has been educated to resist any illegal seizure of power "at all times."

This is a realization that has never existed in the thinking of African soldiers. The autonomy guaranteed in the constitution for the NCCE equally gives it the freedom to carry out its mission and to make significant inroads into influencing discourses, especially in the areas of the constitutionally mandated increase in "awareness," and encouraging the public to "defend this constitution at all times, against all forms of abuse and violation." While the NCCE still has a long way to go, it has translated and abridged the constitution, and has mounted extensive training and civic education programs around the country. On all measures, awareness of the constitution in Ghana today is much higher than it has ever been in the country's history. Some of its most popular documents have included those on human rights as well as those proclaiming that those who resist any attempt to overthrow the constitution commit no crime!

CONCLUSION: BEYOND CONSTITUTIONS

My essential argument in this study has been that the combination of internal and external challenges, pressures, and contradictions has forced a democratization or liberalization agenda on Africa's military dictators. This development provides an opportunity to pursue the triple agendas of disengagement, demilitarization, and democratization. I argue that the emerging trends in constitution making and constitutionalism in Africa point at a special interest or desire to control and contain the military. True, elections are taking place in African societies with experience of military rule. As we have seen in the Gambia, Nigeria, Ghana, and Benin, such elections do not necessarily see the complete ouster of the military from power. They have managed, aided by massive wealth accumulated while in "active service," to hold on to power. In some instances, they have simply manipulated the power of incumbency to retain power. This means that in several ways, we cannot assume that the interests of the military would be eroded because elections have taken place or formal military rule has been terminated. In fact, in several ways the militarization of the society continues with far-reaching implications for the democratic project.

It is true, as I contend, that constitutions are just documents. But they are a special brand of documents, not just like any book or novel. They represent the compact between the governed and the government. The process by which it was drafted and adopted can largely determine its legal and/or political legitimacy. As indicated earlier, where the process was not based on honesty, transparency, national debates, extensive consultations, and dialogues involving every community and constituency, and then subjected to debates in a democratically elected national assembly or adopted through a referendum, such a constitution cannot move the democratic project forward and cannot be the basis for disengagement, much less demilitarization. In fact, when such unpopular constitutions are overthrown, no constituency protests since they hardly claim ownership of the document.

What is missing in the current constitutions is a provision that they are not suspendible, that no matter how long a dictator remains in power, he is still guilty of treason, and that any citizen is empowered to take legal action through the law courts at no cost against such a dictator if and when he leaves power dead or alive. The new constitutions have also not covered the fact that any constitution promulgated by an undemocratic body—such as military "revolutionary," "provisional," "ruling," and whatever council—is illegal and illegitimate. In other words, no constitution can supercede or replace one that was compacted through an open consultative democratic process; that a nonelected and undemocratic body, such as a military junta, cannot promulgate or compact a constitution for a democratic polity. This would significantly enhance the strength of existing constitutions and preempt the political gyrations of military juntas in the name of constitution making. In fact, the new constitutions might develop a national courage and call on civil society to peacefully refuse to cooperate with usurpers and those that illegally seize power and subvert the constitution. Such clear messages, coupled with existing constitutional provisions, would send new and powerful messages to Africa's militaries and significantly alter the context of civil-military relations in favor of democracy and democratization.

It is encouraging to note the on-going discussions within the OAU to the effect that any military force that overthrows a democratically elected government would no longer be welcome at its meetings. What the OAU should do is to make suspension from the OAU automatic in the event of such military interventions. All subregional organizations such as ECOWAS and SADC should, in like manner, provide for automatic exclusion of military dictators. The UN and other western powers should give meaning to this courageous initiative by endorsing an OAU agenda against military subversion of democratic processes. Investors and international NGOs also have a role to play in enhancing constitutional control of the military. They can openly endorse national and continental initiatives or develop their own initiatives to discourage military adventurism.

In countries currently under military rule (and they are the exception rather than the rule today), there is equally the need to work out an arrangement to take care of military officers when they leave power. Without doubt, one of the reasons for not just the struggle for power but also the unwillingness to give it up is because of the absence of an "exit option." By this, I mean what the military leaders would do upon leaving office. Many are young and have limited education or training in other professions. Others have become so used to bossing people and being obeyed that they cannot imagine life as civilians. My view is that such officers, with proper education, exposure, and capacity building can be prepared for life beyond the barracks.[30] The absence of such exit options has also contributed to corruption, factionalization, and violence within the armed forces. This is an issue that has to be clearly articulated in the process of converting the military from a violent, corrupt, divided, and inefficient institution, into a responsible, productive, accountable, and democratic institution.

Finally, the only way to support the disengagement process and promote active demilitarization and democratization is to support the strengthening of civil society. Of course, it is important not to reify civil society or to pose state-civil society relations in a "good guy-bad guy," "we-they" context. Civil society could be the home of a lot of negative and very dangerous tendencies that could hurt the democratization project in Africa. Divided by ethnic, regional, religious, gender, class, and other primordial platforms, it has been easy for the opportunistic military to hijack popular struggles and challenges to the neocolonial state and seize political power. Ironically, the advent of military dictatorships and the merciless suffocation of civil society and political spaces have also increased the number and dynamism of civic organizations and political movements. Thus, one can contend that the strengthening of civil society, the empowerment of the people and their communities, the opening up of political spaces, and the construction of new lines and platforms of dialogue within and between communities is the most viable way to not just prevent coups but also for involving the military and security forces in the construction of democratic values. This, of course, cannot be done under an undemocratic and brutal military junta. It is important to bring back alienated communities, trade unions, students, women, professionals, and others that have been displaced, humiliated, marginalized, and terrorized by the military. Yet, the nurturing and mobilization of popular communities and constituencies, the building of democratic networks, and the articulation of democratic projects designed to promote propeople programs is the only way to redefine sovereignty, community, security, and social justice in Africa. It is now been recognized that

Promoting democracy is one of the key leadership challenges for demilitarization in Africa. Democracy entails much more than just free and fair elections. It also requires a judicial branch that holds corrupt governments and military officials responsible for their actions, an accountable and effective police force, and a political process that is inclusive of all groups, regardless of ethnicity, education, religion, economic status, or gender.[31]

It is hardly encouraging that, at the end of 1997, the report by Demilitarization for Democracy in Washington, DC concluded that only six African states could be regarded as consolidated democracies; seventeen were transitional democracies; twenty-six were under forms of authoritarian rule; and four were "dissolving nations."[32] Strictly speaking, only six African states can be said to face no possibilities of military coups in the future! Civil society would need to retool, reconceptualize, and redefine its strategies to engage emerging issues in Africa's political spaces. If the political terrain is not contested through democratic processes, the military would continue to seize the state, privatize its institutions, suffocate civil society, abridge democratic rights, and contain the democratic enterprise.

NOTES

1. Arnoldo Brenes, ed., *The Leadership Challenges of Demilitarization in Africa: Conference Report* (San Jose: Arias Foundation, 1999), p. 9.

2. John M. Mbaku and Julius O. Ihonvbere, eds., *Multiparty Democracy and Political Change: Constraints to Democratization in Africa* (Aldershot: Ashgate, 1998); Marina Ottaway, *Africa's New Leaders: Democracy or State Reconstruction?* (Washington, DC: Carnegie Endowment for Inter-

national Peace, 1999); Aaron Segal, "Can Democratic Transitions Tame Political Successions?" *Africa Today* 43, no. 4 (1996); and Rene Lemarchand, "African Transitions to Democracy: An Interim (and Mostly Pessimistic) Assessment," *Africa Insight* 22, no. 3 (1992).

3. Adebayo Adedeji, ed., *Africa Within the World: Beyond Dispossession and Dependence* (London: Zed Books 1993); Mulungeta Agonafer, ed., *Africa in the Contemporary International Disorder: Crisis and Possibilities* (Lanham, Maryland: University Press of America, 1996); and Samuel Mutiithi, *African Crisis: Is There Hope?* (Lanham, Maryland: University Press of America, 1996).

4. Julius O. Ihonvbere, "Why African Economies Will Not Recover," *Iranian Journal of International Affairs* (Spring–Summer 1994): 146–73.

5. Laiyashi Yaker, Executive Secretary of the Economic Commission for Africa (ECA), Keynote address at the conference on "Africa in Transition: Challenges and Opportunities," organized by Thunderbird-AGSIM, Glendale, Arizona, February 1993.

6. Claude Ake, *Revolutionary Pressures in Africa* (London: Zed Books, 1978).

7. Claude Ake, *Democracy and Development in Africa* (Washington, DC: The Brookings Institution, 1996) and Leonardo A. Villalon and Philip A. Huxtable, eds., *The African State at a Critical Juncture: Between Disintegration and Reconfiguration* (Boulder, Colo.: Lynne Reinner, 1998).

8. For an interesting discussion, see Julius E. Nyang'oro and Timothy M. Shaw, "The African State in the Global Economic Context," in *The African State...*, ed. L. A. Villalon and P.A. Huxtable. See also Julius O. Ihonvbere, *Africa and the New World Order* (New York: Peter Lang, 1999).

9. Julius O. Ihonvbere, Pita Agbese, George Kieh, and Victor Aikhionbare, *The Military Question in Nigeria* (forthcoming).

10. Julius O. Ihonvbere, "Pan-Africanism: Agenda for African Unity in the 1990s?" in *Issues and Trends in Contemporary African Politics: Stability, Development and Democratization*, ed. George A. Agbango (New York: Peter Lang, 1997).

11. Julius O. Ihonvbere, "Nigeria: Militarization and Perpetual Transition," in *Democratization in Late Twentieth-Century Africa*, ed. Jean-Germain Gros (Westport, Conn.: Greenwood Press, 1998).

12. See Toyin Falola and Julius O. Ihonvbere, *The Rise and Fall of Nigeria's Second Republic, 1979–84* (London: Zed Books, 1985) and Eboe Hutchful and Abdoulaye Bathily, eds., *The Military and Militarism in Africa* (Dakar: CODESRIA, 1998).

13. It is instructive to note that military officers would disagree with this position. They are often quick to regard a critical perspective on the military institution as an attack on ALL military personnel. While they bear collective responsibility for the poor showing of military regimes, I am aware that not all military officers believe in undemocratic values. There is a distinction between the military as an institution and political constituency and construct and military personnel. While there is a so-called *espirit de corps,* the military is ridden with its own contradictions and coalitions and very vulnerable to regional, class, power, gender, ethnic, religious, and ideological factionalization and fractionalization.

14. Claude Ake, "Is Africa Democratising?" in *Crises and Contradictions in Nigeria's Democratisation Programme, 1986–1993,* ed. Nahzeem Oluwafemi Mimiko (Akure, Nigeria: Stebak Publishers, 1995), p. 244.

15. Brenes, *The Leadership Challenges of Militarization in Africa*, p. 9.

16. J. Victor Angelo, Deputy Assistant Administrator of the UNDP in Africa, cited ibid, p. 11. For a very refreshing discussion of the resurgence of "popular power" in Africa, see Alassane D.

Quattara, "Africa: An Agenda for the 21st Century," *Finance and Development* 36, no. 1 (March 1999).

17. Bertrand G. Ramcharan, "The Evolving African Constitutionalism: A Constitutionalism of Liberty and Human Rights," *The Review* 60 (Special Issue, June 1998): 7.

18. Ibid.

19. Julius O. Ihonvbere, "From Despotism to Democracy: The Rise of Multiparty Politics in Malawi," *Third World Quarterly* 18, no. 2 (1997); Melinda Ham and Mike Hall, "Malawi: From Tyranny to Tolerance," *Africa Report* 39, no. 6 (1994); and Andrew Meldrum, "Malawi: New Actors, Same Play," *Africa Report* 39, no. 4 (1994).

20. Mpazi Sinjela, "Constitutionalism in Africa: Emerging Trends," *The Review* 60 (June 1998): 24–25.

21. David Mukholi, *A Complete Guide to Uganda's Fourth Constitution: History, Politics and the Law* (Kampala: Fountain Publishers, 1995), p. 28.

22. Stephen Besweri Akabway, Preface to David Mukholi, *A Complete Guide to Uganda's Fourth Constitution*, p. v.

23. Justice B. J. Odoki, Chair, Uganda Constitution Commission, in Foreword to David Mukholi, *Uganda's Fourth Constitution*, p. iii.

24. Ibid.

25. Though the Museveni government seems to have alienated several communities and interests in the country, its popularity in its first five years in power cannot be questioned. Even today, there is no really strong and organized challenge to its position in the country though this is likely to change once multiparty politics become legal once again.

26. Odoki, Foreword, *A Complete Guide to Uganda's Fourth Constitution*.

27. Brenes, *The Leadership Challenges of Demilitarization in Africa*, p. 9.

28. The debate on demilitarization is far more advanced in Central America than in Africa. In fact, given the fact that the military is a sort of fast track to power and wealth, discussions about demilitarization sound hollow even to a public that has been the primary victim of military misgovernance since political independence in the 1960s.

29. See Bereket Habte Selassie, *The Constitutional Commission of Eritrea (CCE): Information on Strategy, Plans and Activities* (Asmara: CCE, October 1995).

30. This should not be regarded as a form of appeasement for the military. The truth is that it takes a lot of work to turn someone with a military background into a "regular" civilian. The cost of not taking this seriously would always be higher than responding to it in a democratic way.

31. Brenes, *The Leadership Challenges of Demilitarization in Africa*, p. 53.

32. See *Fighting Retreat: Military Political Power and Other Barriers to Africa's Democratic Transition* (Washington, DC: Demilitarization for Democracy, July 1997).

12

Lessons for the Transition to Democracy in Africa

The Experience of the Military in Argentina, Brazil, Chile, Nigeria, and Algeria

Ricardo René Laremont and Habu S. Galadima

The military remains a central actor in politics in Africa and many other parts of the world. Can the military can play prominent and positive roles in the transition to democracy while at the same time preparing a role for their own permanent departure from politics? This paper examines the roles played by the military in the transition to democracy in Argentina, Brazil, and Chile. It then discusses whether aspects of these political processes within Latin America are applicable to transitions to democracies in Africa, specifically Nigeria and Algeria.

Since the 1980s Argentina, Brazil, and Chile have attempted transitions to democracy that have underlined the role of the military establishment itself in both the liberalization and democratization processes. These countries are now more democratic than they were before the 1980s, yet in many ways they are not fully democratic. The military in all these regimes has been placed under partial, rather than full, control of civilian officials. Nevertheless, despite the inchoate nature of the democratization processes in these countries, the military itself has played an important role in the transformation of what were military-authoritarian regimes into fuller democracies. We concede that democracy has not been fully consolidated in Argentina, Brazil, and Chile. Nevertheless, much progress has been made. What is of immediate relevance for those of us who are examining options for democratization in Africa is that many states in Latin America, after experiencing alternating cycles of democratic and military regimes, seem to have broken that cycle in the 1980s. In Africa either military regimes or militarized regimes remain dominant. Can Africa learn from the Latin American models for democratic transition?

In Argentina, Brazil, and Chile, military officers had sound reasons for abandoning politics. After having played prominent roles in the political and economic management of their states for approximately twenty years, military officers themselves decided that it was in the best interests of the military as institution to exit the political arena. Military leaders in Latin America endorsed the democratization process because they believed that their Cold War mission of eliminating leftist subversion and reestablishing order had been accomplished. Having defeated what they believed was the internal threat of communism, the military returned to the barracks. After reestablishing order, they questioned whether they as military officers were the most qualified people for the economic management of their respective states. Further motivation to retire from politics arose from concern that officers' continued involvement in politics would have deleterious effects upon the integrity, professionalism, and command structure of the military. After their intervention in politics, military officers began to understand that there may be real and irreconcilable tensions between the military as institution and the military as government.[1] "Military officers have learned that there are no easy solutions to the intractable economic, social, and political problems confronting their respective countries, and that sustained involvement in politics has disastrous effects on the coherence, efficiency, and discipline of the army."[2]

The experience of the military in Latin America proved that when policy failures occurred, continued military participation in government exposed the military to public criticism and substantial loss of prestige, especially economic policies which failed. When one reviews the process of democratic transition in Brazil and Chile, one begins to understand that it was the risk of continued exposure for policy failure rather than public pressure for political change that finally pushed the military out of politics. The much vaunted "civil society" espoused by political scientists and democracy activists did not by itself drive the military governments from office in Brazil and Chile. Risk of policy failure did. Faced with criticism and diminution of the public's respect for the military, military officers opted to save their institution by quitting politics and transferring responsibility for politics to civilians. By doing so, they insulated the military from further public criticism and helped restore their institution's lost prestige within a new, more democratic political structure. After retreating from daily politics, the military could concentrate on its classic and legitimate role: external security. Three decades of dabbling in government convinced military officers that governance was difficult.

MODALITIES FOR THE DEMOCRATIC TRANSITION: NEGOTIATED TRANSFORMATION OR BREAKDOWN

Beginning in the 1970s, several regimes in Latin America underwent different processes as they tried to become more democratic. In the three Latin American countries discussed in this paper, two different modalities were followed by the military for regime transition. In the cases of Brazil and Chile, the military itself controlled the process of demilitarization and the transition to democracy, by which they largely dictated the terms of their exit from politics. Juan Linz has called this process "negotiated transformation" or *ruptura pactada*.[3] This process has been observed in a number of countries, including Brazil, Chile, Spain, and Hungary. In Brazil, the transition to democracy was actively managed by the military and took eleven years to realize (from the end of the Médici administration in 1973 to the election of President Tancredo Neves in 1985). Throughout this process, the Brazilian military was firmly in control of the democratic transition. Chile's transition process resembles Brazil's. Again, the military establishment essentially controlled the process of transition. Spain, which has served as prototype for transitions from military rule, can be both compared and contrasted with Brazil's and Chile's process of transition. In some ways, Spain's process of change was similar to Brazil's and Chile's because it was led by elites. At the same time, however—and quite importantly—Spain's transition can be distinguished from Brazil's and Chile's because civilians and military officers in Spain formed a civilian-military coalition to democratize the regime, whereas in Brazil and Chile such a coalition was never realized. Spain's democratization process also occurred during a sharply abbreviated time span (three and one-half years).

Argentina provides a different model of transition. In contrast to Brazil and Chile, Argentina's democratic transition was unplanned, having been provoked by defeat in war. Unlike the generals in Brazil and arguably in Chile, the military in Argentina did not anticipate or plan for political change. As a result, the transition process—when it was provoked by the military's defeat in the 1982 Falklands/Malvinas war—was both haphazard and disorderly. Argentina provides a classic case of a breakdown of a military regime that leads to democratization. These three examples will serve as models for the transition to military regimes in Africa.

THE TRANSITION TO DEMOCRACY IN BRAZIL

The example of the transition to democracy in Brazil is valuable for those interested in democratization in Africa because it provides a model for liberalization and democratization led by the military itself. Frances Hagopian has said that the new democratic republic in Brazil had an "authoritarian birth."[4] The democratic transition began in late 1973 when General/President Ernesto Geisel and his chief advisor General Golbery do Couto e Silva decided that Brazil needed to liberalize the polity. When military officers began to liberalize, they decided that 1974 was the optimum time to begin the process; at that time the military had just successfully repressed a leftist insurrection. The economy was also experiencing an upswing. Despite the military's move to liberalize, the military itself was split into two factions with contradictory intentions: one wanted to liberalize the state (the Geisel-Golbery faction); the other wanted to slow liberalization while expanding internal surveillance of Brazilians (the Médici-Frota faction). The Geisel-Golbery faction argued successfully, however, that the military had achieved its objective of restoring civil order and that it was not in the military's long-term interests to extend its control of politics and society further. From the viewpoint of the liberalizing faction, the military needed to reverse Brazil's authoritarian drift if it were to preserve the professionalism of the military and prevent the creation of an authoritarian state resembling Argentina or other notorious Central American governments. From the viewpoint of General/President Geisel, the further extension of military involvement in internal security matters was undermining the military's role as a professional and respectable institution that should be preoccupied with *external* security matters.

The Brazilian democratization experience was notable because it was managed throughout by military elites. Furthermore, it occurred without any substantial pressure for change being exerted from the grass roots. (There were some minor strikes and protests, but none of them posed a real threat to the regime.) The transition process in Brazil was also quite gradual, lasting eleven years. This long, gradual process stands in marked contrast with Chile and Argentina. This transition was, as Alfred Stepan has described it, "a controlled liberation from above, effectively managed by the military."[5]

In 1974 the military began the liberalization process first by approving the election of a military-sponsored president (General Ernesto Geisel) who had been one of the principal proponents of liberalization. This endorsement reflected a policy shift within the military, with Geisel replacing General Emilio Médici who had advocated the continuation of hard-line policies of internal repression. After Geisel's term, Geisel assured that General João Figueiredo, another liberalizer and democratizer, would continue his policies. General/President Figueiredo then oversaw the election of a civilian president (José Sarney) in 1982. From an analytic perspective, Brazil's process of liberalization and democratization was a process of gradual change or *abertura*, not a case of rapid change or *ruptura,* as we shall see was the case of Argentina. The democratization process in Brazil was orderly, taking eleven years, and it provided for the gradual transfer of political authority to civilian officials. In some ways it resembles the failed process of transition (1987 to 1993) undertaken by General/President Ibrahim Babangida in Nigeria.

Viewed comparatively, what was remarkable about the Brazilian transition was that it began without any real pressure from the grass roots. The military itself believed that it was necessary to liberalize the state. Alfred Stepan said that when "[l]iberalization began, there was no significant political opposition, no economic crisis, and no collapse of the coercive apparatus due to defeat in war."[6] In Brazil, the military had the foresight to recognize that its legitimate institutional role was outside daily politics. For the purpose of discussing African military politics and democratic transitions, the most significant aspect of the Brazilian transition was that the terms and the rules of the transition were set by the military itself. The military remained in control and maintained coherence in the transition to democracy while repressing minor public demands to accelerate the process (as when the military suppressed unauthorized automobile workers' strikes in São Paulo between 1978 and 1980). The gradualism, consistency, and length of the process, (beginning in 1974 and concluding with the election of President Tancredo Neves in 1982), enhanced the transition's probability of success.

Testing the Result in Brazil

Despite discussions of processes of liberalization and democratization, eventually transitions must be subjected to some sort of quantitative analysis. We have chosen in all of our cases to examine the effects of democratization, or attempts at democratization, by examining whether defense expenditures or military staffing levels are affected by the democratization process.

The democratization process in Brazil has had some effect on defense expenditures over time. Defense expenditures as a percentage of Gross National Product have dropped marginally without affecting effective staffing levels of the military force.

Table 12.1
Brazil: Military Expenditures as a Percentage of GNP and Staffing Levels

Year	Percentage	Total Forces (in thousands)
1974	1.9	NA
1975	1.1	455
1976	1.2	450
1977	1.0	450
1978	0.8	450
1979	0.7	450
1980	0.7	450
1981	0.7	450
1982	0.9	460
1983	0.9	460
1984	0.8	459
1985	0.8	496
1986	0.9	527
1987	1.0	541
1988	1.4	319
1989	1.5	319
1990	1.7	295
1991	1.3	295
1992	1.2	296
1993	1.4	296
1994	1.2	296
1995	1.7	285

Sources: United States Arms Control and Disarmament Agency, *World Military Expenditures and Arms Transfers, 1968-1977;* United States Arms Control and Disarmament Agency, *World Military Expenditures and Arms Transfers, 1987;* United States Arms Control and Disarmament Agency, *World Military Expenditures and Arms Transfers, 1996* (Washington, DC: US Government Printing Office).

THE TRANSITION TO DEMOCRACY IN CHILE

The transition to democracy in Chile was also managed by the military with General Augusto Pinochet dictating most of the terms of political change throughout the process. Until his defeat in a 1989 plebiscite and his official ouster from political office in 1990, Pinochet ruled Chile essentially as a dictator. His method of governance involved conferring with a few other military officers. He remained in power for seventeen years—from 1973 until his surrender of power to a civilian president in 1990.

The political transfer of power to civilians occurred only after voters rejected Pinochet at the plebiscite. Despite calls from the Catholic Church in 1995 for a "transition to democracy" and demonstrations against Pinochet's rule in 1986 and 1987, Pinochet adhered to his own timetable which called for the holding of a referendum on his rule in 1988.[7] Pinochet expected to win the 1988 plebiscite on his rule; he hoped to continue in office until 1997. In the 1988 plebiscite, Pinochet gambled that the voters would support him. When they did not, (the winner had fifty-four per cent while Pinochet had only forty-three percent of the vote), he negotiated his own "exit" from politics. According to his exit strategy, he promised the Chilean people that he would stop acting as Chief of State. Nevertheless, he demanded his continuation as Chief of the Armed Forces until 1998—surely an odd formula for a democracy.

It was Pinochet's rejection at the 1988 plebiscite that led to the December 1989 elections and the eventual transfer of political power to civilians. The 1989 election results practically replicated the 1988 plebiscite results. Patricio Aylwin, the opposition candidate who became president, garnered fifty-five percent of the vote and his two opponents (Hernán Buchi and Francisco Errázuriz) together won forty-three percent.

Pinochet's process of "reform" or "democratization" can be clearly contrasted with the strategies and tactics of the Brazilian generals: Pinochet had not planned initially to cede his power to civilians. He had not intended either to liberalize or transfer power in 1988. Pinochet tried to use the transition process to ease himself into the Presidential office by constitutional means. Yet even after his electoral defeat he was able to remain as Chief of the Armed Forces and he was able to avoid the imposition of civilian control over that institution. Because of these events, Chile has been less democratized than Brazil where there has been a more substantial transfer of power to civilian officials. In Chile until very recently the military has exercised substantial prerogatives in government.

Furthermore, the regime that was first created by Pinochet and then destroyed by the process of democratization in Chile can be distinguished from the military regimes in Argentina and Brazil because of its highly personal form of leadership. The Chilean regime was, essentially, a personal dictatorship. General Augusto Pinochet essentially functioned independently of both his fellow officers and civilians. Because of this institutional and personalistic difference, the subordination of the military to civilian control in Chile—at least until very recently with the infirmity of Pinochet himself—has been made much more difficult.

Testing the Result in Chile

Using the mode of analysis applied to Brazil, the following figures apply to the transition to democracy in Chile.

Table 12.2
Chile: Military Expenditures as a Percentage of GNP and Staffing Levels

Year	Percentage	Total Forces (in thousands)
1986	3.4	127
1987	4.1	127
1988	3.6	96
1989	3.0	95
1990	3.3	95
1991	3.1	90
1992	2.5	92
1993	3.5	92
1994	3.4	102
1995	3.8	102

Source: United States Arms Control and Disarmament Agency, *World Military Expenditures and Arms Transfers, 1996* (Washington, DC: US Government Printing Office).

In Chile we see a drop in staffing levels while actually observing an increase in military expenditures.

THE TRANSITION TO DEMOCRACY IN ARGENTINA

In clear contrast to Brazil and Chile, the transition to democracy in Argentina was entirely unplanned. The transition process there was one of rather sudden *ruptura* or breakdown rather than *abertura* or negotiated transition. The transition process officially began six months after Argentina's military defeat to Great Britain in the 1982 Falklands/Malvinas war. After defeat, the Argentine public vociferously demanded a change to civilian government.

The transition process in Argentina can be distinguished from the process in Brazil and Chile in at least two ways. First, the process in Argentina was unlike Brazil and Chile because there was substantial grass-roots pressure upon the Argentine military for a return to civilian rule. Second, in clear contrast to either Brazil or Chile, the process of transition was haphazard, improvisational, and beyond the control of the military. In Argentina, the military was simply not in charge of the transition process. The public thrust the transition upon the military. The military's defeat in the Malvinas war and spiraling inflation provoked masses to mobilize for the end of military rule. In this way, Argentina's transition to democracy resembles the replacement of the regime in Greece—which also suffered defeat in war in 1974 and was replaced upon demands from the public.

The Argentine public pushed the military out of politics because it had come to abhor the military for its military loss to Britain, its conduct of the "dirty war" against Argentine civilians, and its mismanagement of the Argentine economy. Unlike the militaries in Brazil and Chile, (which did not encounter massive public resistance), the military establishment in Argentina became fractured after the Malvinas war and could not cohere to resist public mobilization against the regime.

Although public resistance to the military galvanized because of the Malvinas defeat, we can assert that the transition to democracy may have actually preceded the Malvinas war. In May 1981, a multiparty political front of opposition was created to protest the military's mismanagement of the economy. On 30 March 1982 this front organized a large demonstration against the government.[8]

Unlike the generals in Brazil who planned for the political transition and somewhat like General Pinochet in Chile who had not, the military in Argentina had not developed a strategy or tactics for political change. With no plan, the transition process in Argentina was considerably more unstable than the transitions in Brazil and Chile. Massive public protest against the regime and the military's lack of preparedness for political change contributed to this instability. Also, unlike Brazil and Chile, the transition in Argentina took place during an extremely compressed period (between 1981 and 1983). This combination of circumstances inhibited the military from being in a position dictate terms of the transition to the public.

Because of their weakened position, the military conceded to elections that were held on 30 October 1983. Radical party candidate Raúl Alfonsín was elected President and he soon implemented a series of political reforms to bring the military under civilian control. He demanded trials of military officers involved in the deaths and disappearances of Argentines. Second, he imposed civilian control over the administration of the armed forces. Third, he placed civilians in control of the National Defense School. He then asserted civilian control over the military budget, which had previously been determined by the military. Last, he privatized Fabricaciones Militares, a large military-owned enterprise that manufactured armaments and provided profits for the military. By taking these measures, Alfonsín reasserted civilian authority over the military more quickly and more completely than happened in Brazil and Chile.

It is useful for the purposes of comparative analysis to recognize that the transition in Argentina was not a negotiated transition. Therefore, the process of transition in Argentina was entirely unlike the processes in Brazil and Chile. Argentina was a case of *ruptura* or non-negotiated rupture from an *ancien regime* marked by military defeat, mismanagement of the economy, and public disapproval of the "dirty war" campaign. Unlike Brazil and Chile, where the military occupied a strong position and where mass public demonstrations had little effect upon the politics of transition, the outpouring of masses in the streets of Argentina crippled an already weakened military government. Six months after the Malvinas defeat, public demonstrations against General Reynaldo Bignone's regime ended military rule in Argentina. Because the end was brought swiftly and in the midst of massive public demonstrations, the military was clearly in a weakened position and unable to bargain from a position of strength in its exit from politics. When the military in Argentina belatedly offered to negotiate their exit, it was already too late. The public and President Alfonsín were able to reject resoundingly the military's offer of a brokered transition to democracy.

Testing the Result in Argentina

Argentina's defense expenditures and military force staffing levels are provided in the following table.

Table 12.3
Argentina: Military Expenditures as a Percentage of GNP and Staffing Levels

Year	Percentage	Total Forces (in thousands)
1981	3.8	155
1982	6.5	175
1983	4.6	175
1984	3.7	174
1985	3.8	129
1986	3.9	104
1987	2.6	118
1988	2.6	95
1989	2.6	95
1990	1.9	85
1991	1.3	70
1992	1.9	65
1993	1.7	65
1994	1.7	69
1995	1.7	65

Sources: United States Arms Control and Disarmament Agency, *World Military Expenditures and Arms Transfers, 1987;* United States Arms Control and Disarmament Agency, *World Military Expenditures and Arms Transfers, 1996* (Washington, DC: US Government Printing Office).

The democratization process in Argentina reveals real and substantial changes in both military expenditures and total military force staffing. In Argentina, in contrast to Brazil and Chile, we observe a more substantial demilitarization of the polity.

THE TRANSITION TO DEMOCRACY IN NIGERIA

In 1999 Nigeria may have broken free from the grip of military dictatorship. Since 29 May 1999, another transition to democracy has been attempted. Nigerians are expecting that this transition will lead to the consolidation of democracy.

Since independence, Nigeria has attempted to adopt the liberal democratic standards that subordinate the military to civilian authority. Events in the country, however, have set in motion processes of militarism and military rule. In Nigeria's 39 years of independence, the military has ruled the country for about 28 years. During this period, they intervened three times to flush out democratic institutions. They have also organized five separate transitions to civil rule under Gowon (1970–1974), Murtala / Obansanjo (1975–1979), Babangida (1987–1993), Abacha (1995–1998), and Abubakar (1998–1999). Of these five military-organized transitions, only two resulted in the successful transfer of power to civilian rule. These occurred under the Muhammad Murtala/Olusegun Obansajo (1975–1979) and the Abdulsalami Abubakar (1998–1999) regimes.

What were the processes and modalities of attempted transitions from military rule to democracy in Nigeria? In this discussion of transitions, we will focus on the 1970–1979 and 1987–1999 processes.

Processes and Modalities of the 1970–1979 Transition

The military in Nigeria, as in Brazil and Chile, controlled the process of transition to democratic rule. Nigeria's first attempt took place between 1970 and 1974 under the leadership of General Yakubu Gowon. Like the process of transition in Argentina, the transition under Gowon was unplanned as there was no concrete political program for an orderly return to civilian rule. The transition process was provoked by pressures from the civil population that compelled General Gowon to announce on 1 October 1970 a nine-point program for a transition to civilian rule that was to have been completed by 1976.[9]

General Gowon's transition process was, however, illusory rather than real. Gowon was not really interested in transferring power in 1976. On the occasion of the fourteenth anniversary of Nigeria's independence in 1974, General Gowon informed the public that "it would indeed amount to a betrayal of trust to adhere rigidly to that target date."[10] He argued that it was the military's responsibility "to lay the foundation of a self-sustaining political system which can stand the test of time . . . which will ensure a smooth and orderly transition from one government to another."[11] General Gowon then dismissed 1976 as an unrealistic deadline for the return to civilian rule. Many Nigerians, especially political elites and elements of the military, found Gowon's statements unacceptable. On 29 July 1975, these elites overthrew General Yakubu Gowon, replacing him with General Murtala Mohammed who continued the process of transition.

Nigeria's new Head of State did not leave anyone in doubt about his intentions to embark on a transition to civilian rule. On 1 October 1975, General Mohammed announced a five-stage program leading to military hand-over of power to civilians. His target date for democratization was 1 October 1979. The five-stage program involved

a) appointment of a Constitution Drafting Committee in October 1975;

b) creation of new states by April 1979;

c) election of a Constituent Assembly by October 1977;

d) ratification of the Constituent Assembly by October 1978 and lifting of the 1966 ban on political parties; and

e) State and Federal elections by October 1979.

Each element of the transition program of transition was meticulously implemented by the military. On 13 February 1976, during the course of implementation, General Mohammed was assassinated. Upon his death, his deputy, General Olusegun Obasanjo, became Head of State. Obasanjo then continued the transition process, adhering to the wishes of his predecessor. The military set up the Federal Electoral Commission (FEDECO) in 1976 which registered voters, organized the delimitation of the nation into constituencies, and conducted the elections for the State and National Assemblies as well as for Governors and the President. The transition process impressed Shehu Shagari, the president-elect. He observed that "It is rare in the history of developing countries for those in power to organize their own retirement from government, and to welcome, indeed entertain, their successor."[12]

The transition process under the Murtala/Obansanjo military regime ushered in a democratic government in a very organized manner. The military withdrew to their barracks after thirteen years of military rule. The civilian government of Alhaji Shehu Shagari, however, soon encountered political and economic difficulties in this new experiment with democracy. After barely four years, the military once again intervened and overthrew the civilian government and dismantled all democratic structures. General Mohammadu Buhari then took over the mantle of leadership in December, 1983.

Processes and Modalities of the 1987–1999 Transition

Between 1987 and 1999, three transitions were attempted in Nigeria. The first two were unsuccessful and did not lead to a transfer of power to civilians. The three transitions provide us with three models: the Babangida model, the Abacha model, and the Abdulsalami model. Indeed the Babangida and Abacha models are models of failed transitions. Let us examine briefly these three models.

The Babangida Transition (1987–1993)

General Ibrahim Babangida ousted the Buhari government and took over the mantle of leadership on 27 August 1985. Babangida ruled the country for eight years. Like the Brazilian transition, the transition under Babangida started without any real grassroots pressure to hand over power to an elected civilian government. Babangida felt that the military was not to be disgraced by continuing in government but should return to the barracks as one cohesive unit. Babangida had always maintained that the military had no business with politics. He appealed to his colleagues by saying that "the military must not allow itself to fall prey to the divisive antics of our detractors. We must not let the military as an institution be humiliated or be disgraced out of office as was the case in some countries which are now back to square one or even worse."[13]

The military under Babangida tried to execute a transition similar to Brazil's. Like Brazil, the Nigerian military under Babangida appeared to be conscious of its professional role and the need to exit from politics. The entire transition was planned, monitored, and guided by the military.

On 13 January 1986, General Babangida set up a Political Bureau to conduct a nationwide debate on the political future of Nigeria. The Bureau organized debates and collected suggestions from many Nigerians.[14] The report of the Political Bureau, submitted on 27 March 1987, formed the basis of the detailed transition program that was drawn up by the military. The transition to Civil Rule Decree (1987) was promulgated to give the transition legal backing. The year in which the military would transfer power to a democratically elected civilian government was fixed as 1990. During the transition process, the military government banned certain categories of politicians from participating in the transition process in order to make a clean break from the past and create room for the emergence of "new breed" politicians.

During the transition process, a new constituent Assembly was set up to examine the recommendations of the 1979 Constitution Review Committee. The Assembly submitted its report in May 1988. They met for about ten months and considered about 800 amendments proposed by twenty-one of the assembly's twenty-three committees.[15]

From this process a National Electoral Commission was set up and the government permitted the creation of two political parties. The designation of only two parties emerged as a compromise solution to encourage national unity because otherwise numerous associations that did not have national appeal would have tried to form political parties along narrow, ethnically based lines. After the designation of the two parties, the ban on political activities was lifted and elections were conducted for all levels of government except for the Presidency.

The transition process under General Babangida was the longest in the political history of Nigeria since independence. The hand-over date to civilian authority changed four times. The transition program was also the most manipulated: it was altered forty-one times.[16]

The transition to democracy under the administration of General Ibrahim Babangida, despite all the engineering, never succeeded in Nigeria. In its final stage the Military Government of General Babangida had organized a presidential election that was to have been the last stage in the final hand-over of power to civilians. The election was conducted on 12 June 1993. Many Nigerians and members of the international community believed that the election would lead to the restoration of civilian rule. Elements within the military, however, thought otherwise.

General Babangida's military government decided on June 23 to annul the June 12 elections. According to the unsigned press release announcing the annulment, "all acts or omissions done or purported to have been done or to be done by any person, authority, etc., under the above named decrees are hereby invalid."[17] The annulment of the 12 June 1993 elections started a process that caused Nigeria to revert to authoritarianism.

During this process, General Ibrahim Babangida stepped aside and swore in Chief Ernest Shonekan as Head of an Interim National Government. General Sani Abacha at that time was made Shonekan's deputy. The Interim National Government (ING) was then given a mandate to bring about national reconciliation and conclude the democratization of the presidency within six months. This task proved impossible as the ING found itself embedded in the quagmire of social resistance and civil unrest that went beyond the ING's competence to contain. These protests severely weakened the Interim National Government. After eighty-two days in office, the Interim National Government was jettisoned by Shonekan's deputy, General Sani Abacha, who assumed office as Head of State and Commander-in-Chief of the Nigerian Armed Forces. General Abacha abolished all democratic structures in the country and suspended the country's constitution. He then reinstalled a full-fledged military regime in the country.

The Abacha Transition (1995–1998)

The administration of General Sani Abacha was installed at a time when military-authoritarian regimes became less acceptable to the international community. After its installation, General Abacha's military government faced immediate and substantial opposition from social and democratic forces both within and without the country, the degree and intensity of which was unprecedented in the military's political history. Against this background of hostility, General Abacha decided to organize a National Constitutional Conference to chart the political future of Nigeria. That National Conference was inaugurated on 27 June 1994.

The National Constitutional Conference preceded Abacha's own attempted transition program. According to his plans, the transition would have spanned 36 months, culminating in the swearing-in of an elected civilian president on 1 October 1998. Dates for elections, screening of candidates, petitions, and bye-elections were promulgated. Abacha then lifted the ban on political organizing.

What followed the lifting of the ban on politics was a parody of a democratic transition to civilian rule. All opposition voices were drowned in the deep ocean of authoritarianism. Even slight disagreements with Abacha's style of governance were characterized as unacceptable opposition. Opposition groups were muzzled and crushed. Many prominent Nigerians were detained without trial and tortured for several months and years. Many others were sentenced to various jail terms by kangaroo courts without any due process. Even ex post facto laws were promulgated to jail perceived enemies of the regime. These laws had clauses making them applicable outside of the normal jurisdiction of the courts. Nigerians were hanged for expressing their grievances while others were simply assassinated by special military death squads. Many opposition groups went out of circulation and their members escaped into exile. Abacha even purged potential rivals from the military.

Essentially, there are a lot of similarities between Abacha's model and General Augusto Pinochet's. Abacha, like Pinochet, dictated the terms of the transition to such an extent that the entire transition process became Abacha-centered. Abacha, like Pinochet, ruled Nigeria as a ruthless dictator. Abacha, like Pinochet, attempted to use the transition process to ease himself into the presidential office by constitutional means.

Abacha emulated Pinochet's style well. He re-inaugurated the National Electoral Commission and charged it with the responsibility of registering political parties, screening candidates, and conducting elections. Fifteen political associations applied for registration. After a "verification exercise," five of these associations were registered and approved as parties. The party registration exercise turned out to be fraudulent. To many Nigerians, the five registered parties appeared to be influenced and controlled by Abacha. They shunned the entire transition process being sponsored by Abacha, leaving Abacha and his cohorts in charge of the process.

Under this arrangement, "elections" were organized for contestants who were screened by "security agencies" loyal to Abacha. No real opponents to Abacha's rule were permitted to register as candidates. Only pro-Abacha, "worthy candidates" were finally registered.

During this period General Abacha ruled the country with the support of a politicized military that was determined to loot the country. Using instruments of coercion and repression, the government terrorized and intimidated the civilian populace.

Despite his efforts at repression, by mid-1997, an assortment of politicians, military officers, government officials, and businessmen gathered and organized a well-orchestrated and well-financed campaign of pressure on Abacha to have him stand for a presidential election. Members of this group of prominent Nigerians were intimidated from expressing their interest in holding a presidential election. As a result of this pressure, all five "official" political parties quickly organized national conventions to endorse General Abacha as the presidential candidate of all five political parties.

Both local opposition groups and the international community became exhausted by General Abacha's resilience and dogged commitment to actualize his plans. As the local opposition became fatigued, they pleaded with the international community to apply more pressure. The international community responded by simply condemning and threatening Abacha without much effect. Just as Nigerians began despairing that democratic change would not come to Nigeria, General Sani Abacha died suddenly and mysteriously. After his death, General Abdulsalami Abubakar, his Chief of Defense Staff, was sworn in as his replacement.

The Abdulsalami Transition (1998–1999)

The transition process under General Abdulsalami Abubakar was the shortest in the political history of Nigeria, spanning barely one year. General Abubakar freed all political prisoners. Among these prisoners were two who had contested Abacha in the presidential election: General Olusegun Obasanjo and Chief Olu Falae. A general amnesty was granted to all those accused of treason by the previous government. Abubakar pleaded with all opposition groups both within and without the country to participate freely in the transition to democracy.

Table 12.4
Nigeria: Military Expenditures as a Percentage of GNP and Staffing Levels

Year	Percentage	Total Forces (in thousands)
1975	5.5	270
1976	3.9	270
1977	4.0	300
1978	3.6	204
1979	2.8	164
1980	2.7	150
1981	2.7e	144
1982	2.2e	144
1983	2.1e	144
1984	1.6e	144
1985	1.5	134
1986	1.2	138
1987	.8e	138
1988	1.0e	107
1989	N.A.	NA
1990	.9e	94
1991	.8	94
1992	.6	76
1993	.7	76
1994	.8	80
1995	N.A.	89

Note: e= estimate. Data not reliable. N.A.= not available.

Sources: United States Arms Control and Disarmament Agency, *World Military Expenditures and Arms Transfers, 1987;* United States Arms Control and Disarmament Agency, *World Military Expenditures and Arms Transfers, 1996* (Washington, DC: US Government Printing Office).

General Abdulsalami Abubakar unfolded his transition program on 21 July 1998, barely six weeks after he assumed office. This transition program was the fifth in the country's political history. He announced the scrapping of all transitional agencies established under Abacha and he annulled all previous elections because they were declared fraudulent. An Independent National Electoral Commission (INEC) was inaugurated to register new political parties and conduct elections. As a result of the registration process, the All Peoples party (APP), the Peoples Democratic Party (PDP) and the Alliance for Democracy (AD) were registered.

The three political parties competed in the 9 January 1999 State House of Assembly and Gubernatorial elections, the 20 February 1999 Federal House of Representatives and Senatorial elections, and the 27 February 1999 Presidential elections. The AD and APP went into a working alliance and sponsored Chief Olu Falae, a one-time finance minister, as their presidential candidate, while the PDP sponsored General Olusegun Obasanjo, former Head of State and Commander in Chief, as their presidential candidate. In a keenly contested election, the APP lost to the PDP and General Olusegun Obasanjo emerged victorious to become Nigeria's third civilian President. On May 29, the military handed over power to the elected President Obasanjo.

President Obasanjo inherited a military whose professionalism had been lost to such an extent that subjecting it to civilian authority would only become possible with radical reform of the military. Like the military in Latin America, the military in Nigeria had become subject to public criticism for every ill within the society. Its long period of rule enabled it to engage in unbridled opportunism. The military became a symbol of corruption and lack of discipline. Because of its fall from grace, it was in the military's short-term interests to support the transition to civilian rule. The question is whether this trend can be sustained. Much reform and reorganization is needed.

Testing the Result in Nigeria

In Nigeria, both military expenditures and staffing levels have dropped substantially since the 1970s. It is yet to be seen whether the most recent transition to democracy will have an effect on continued demilitarization. See Table 12.4.

THE TRANSITION TO DEMOCRACY IN ALGERIA

Unlike Argentina, Brazil, and Chile, Algeria had not ever had extensive experience with liberal democracy. From 1870 to 1962 the French who ruled Algeria as a colony neither created a democracy nor provided political and civil rights to most Algerians. French Algerians had political rights while Muslim Algerians did not. Upon independence in 1962, Algeria's new leaders created a state that gradually drifted towards authoritarianism.

Pressure for political change in the Algerian regime began substantively in October 1988, when riots against the regime erupted around the country. The participants in these riots were primarily students and unemployed young people who had become discontented with the regime and who felt disconnected from the government's aging leaders and their exclusionary practices in politics. By 1988, approximately seventy per cent of Algeria's population was composed of persons under thirty years of age.[18] These students and unemployed persons demanded change. The country's leaders, many of whom were either former military officers or linked to the military, decided to respond to their demands by feigning towards liberalization. These leaders hoped that minimal liberalization would stave off continuing protests.

As the leaders decided to liberalize, it eventually became clear that they had embarked on a process that was largely improvisational. Chadli Ben Jadid, the president of Algeria and a former general, felt the need to liberalize in an international context in which Poland, the Soviet Union, Czechoslovakia, and other Eastern-bloc countries were doing the same. The government's attempt to liberalize, however, was undertaken in a unilateral fashion. Ben Jadid decided to pursue liberalization without consulting with other members of the political elite. Similarly, he did not discuss his plans for change with either dissidents within the society in favor of change or dissidents within the military opposing change. This second group—the military—eventually undermined the transition to democracy. Quite mistakenly, Ben Jadid attempted to undertake liberalization without having first obtained the full support of Algeria's military officers. This critical fact distinguishes the Algerian transition from the transitions we have discussed in Brazil and Chile, which were directed by the military. Ben Jadid's failure to consult the military made the Algerian case more similar to Argentina where the military had marginal influence at the beginning of the transition to democracy. We should remember, however, that Argentina's military could not play a critical role in the transition process because it had been severely weakened by its defeat to Great Britain in the Falklands/Malvinas war.

In Algeria, unlike Argentina, the military remained integrated as a political and institutional unit that inhibited democratization. Initially, the military was ambivalent about Ben Jadid's initiatives towards both liberalization and democratization. When military officers eventually decided that both liberalization and the democratic transition were not in the military's institutional interests, they aborted the process altogether. It is clear that if a real transition to democracy is ever to succeed in Algeria, the generals there must become convinced—as the generals in Argentina, Brazil, and Chile eventually were—that the military's long-term interests are to be served by exiting from daily politics. Given the Algerian military's continuous role in politics from 1962 to the present, that prospect seems very unlikely.

The key weakness of the Algerian transition to democracy involved a lack of elite consensus regarding the desirability of liberalization and a transition to democracy. First, the military was not fully consulted or enlisted to support the program of political change. Second, even the putative single party of Algeria, the FLN (National Liberation Front) was riven by internal divisions regarding whether or not democratization would provide any advantages either to them or to Algeria. The chief opposition party, the FIS or Islamic Salvation Front, also sent mixed signals about the desirability of democracy. It is no small wonder that such a transition had little probability of success when so many critically important elements of the society—especially the powerful and indispensable military—were in a state of extreme disagreement concerning the desirability of democracy. Ben Jadid's improvised transition to democracy was only a wish, unfulfillable because of lack of concensus among the critical political actors.

Algeria's Defense Expenditures and Staffing Levels

The following data provide information regarding Algeria's military expenditures and armed forces staffing since the aborted transition to democracy.

Table 12.5
Algeria: Military Expenditures as a Percentage of GNP and Staffing Levels

Year	Percentage	Total Forces (in thousands)
1988	3.3	126
1989	3.0	126
1990	2.0	126
1991	1.7	126
1992	1.9e	139
1993	2.8.	139
1994	3.3e	126
1995	3.2e	120

Note: e = estimate. Data not reliable.

Source: United States Arms Control and Disarmament Agency, *World Military Expenditures and Arms Transfers, 1996* (Washington, DC: US Government Printing Office).

DEMOCRATIZATION AND THE NEED FOR CIVILIAN CONTROL

The ideal relationship between civilian leadership and military officers in a democracy is one in which there is a "[m]inimization of military intervention in politics and of political intervention in the military." This bifurcation of military and civilian responsibilities is done to assure that the military has its clear area of authority and expertise (i.e., security) to which it is assigned responsibility and relative autonomy. The idea is that civilian leadership should broadly define the state's security objectives while permitting its military officers to function professionally and autonomously to devise tactical plans for the realization of these objectives.

In important states in Latin America and Africa, this bifurcation of responsibility evaporated during the 1960s. Faced with what they perceived to be internal security threats or incompetence, the military wrested political control from civilian political leaders and assumed responsibility for governance. What is common to all of these military-led regimes is that military leaders and military organizations began performing governmental functions that were distinct and distantly related to traditional military functions.

Nevertheless, military officers in Latin America learned over time that the military's participation in political, economic, and social decision-making eventually and inevitably undermined the military's reputation, coherence, efficiency, and discipline. The historical experience in Latin America—at least from the 1960s to the 1980s—taught military officers that the military as an institution paid a high price—especially in terms of reputation and credibility—for its continued participation in partisan political squabbles.

Having recognized this particular risk to their military forces, military officers in Latin America negotiated their inchoate departure from or the diminution of their role in politics. Despite their diminished role, however, the military in Latin America did not exit entirely from politics. Military officers often still lurk in the background capable of intimidating those who would otherwise exercise power. Nevertheless, most officers no longer believe that it is institutionally appropriate for them to involve themselves in the quotidian affairs of actual governance. Furthermore, it is not in their interests to do so.

The problem that we have faced and will continue to face is how to reform civilian-military relations to democratic norms of behavior in Africa. If we grant that the military should be subordinated to "effective civilian control," how and when is that to be done in emerging democracies that are also dealing with issues of creating bureaucratic competence, reestablishing respectability of legal systems, creating competitive party systems, liberalizing market economies, establishing fiscal responsibility, limiting crime and corruption, and controlling ethnic violence?

How should African military governments proceed towards democracy? What can be learned from Latin America's experiences? As we have seen in Argentina, Brazil, and Chile, the military can recognize that it is in their interests to encourage the transition to democracy. How can systems of incentives be created that convince both military officials and civilians that it is best for the military to restrict themselves to military affairs? These questions must be resolved if Africa is to democratize fully.

AN IMPORTANT NOTE—HUMAN RIGHTS: A POSTTRANSITION ISSUE

While the military did transfer political control to civilians in Argentina, Brazil, and Chile, in all three states the military decided that it was necessary to negotiate with civilian authorities over important issues that the military thought were critical to its survival. First, in all three cases the military demanded that there would be no prosecution, punishment, or other retaliation against military officers for any criminal acts committed (including murder, kidnapping, torture, rape, and imprisonment without trial) while they were in power. The issue of amnesty was particularly problematic in Argentina where over nine thousand Argentines had simply "disappeared." In Chile the numbers were lower with eight hundred killed during the coup and twelve hundred killed in the years thereafter. In both Brazil and Chile the militaries were able to obtain general clemency in 1979 for crimes committed against their citizens. This guarantee of protection from prosecution was a condition demanded in exchange for the military's transfer of control to civilians.

Unlike Brazil and Chile, in Argentina the military did not fully control the transition process and President Raúl Alfonsín's new government reversed the military's self-granted amnesty. Alfonsín eventually brought several high-ranking military officers to trial for their responsibility in the killing or disappearances of approximately 9,000 Argentines. The accused military officers were subjected to military courts-martial and, after the military courts refused to prosecute the officers, they were turned over to civilian courts for prosecution. Alfonsín believed that these trials were necessary to reestablish the rule of law and to impose civilian control again over the military. These trials were met with resistance by the military and when Alfonsín later tried to continue to extend his prosecution of high-level officers, he was threatened with at least three *coups d'état.* Because of these coup threats, Alfonsín eventually halted the prosecution of military officers in December 1986, thereby stabilizing his government. Alfonsín had to bring these trials to an end to survive politically. Eventually, only sixteen Argentine military officers were brought to trial for their crimes. Of this group, only ten were convicted for the disappearance of nine thousand Argentines.

Amnesty for crimes committed by military officers has raised questions as to whether democracy and justice had really been fully realized achieved in Argentina, Brazil, and Chile. It is clearly arguable that the failure to prosecute criminals for crimes committed did not establish a solid basis for the establishment of a judicial system worthy of public respect.

As a substitute for trials and punishment in Brazil and Chile, the governments there opted for published reports accurately describing the crimes and atrocities committed during the period in military rule. Because the numbers that died and disappeared in Brazil were relatively few (eighty-one dead and forty-five disappeared),[19] the issuance of a Truth Report by the Archdiocese of São Paulo functioned as a substitute for trials. In Chile, President Aylwin appointed a Commission for Truth and Reconciliation that reported fully on political killings and disappearances. Eventually in Argentina the Sábato Commission (headed by novelist Ernesto Sábato) issued a 400-page report documenting the crimes that had occurred under the military regime. In the final analysis, like in South Africa, these regimes in transition forewent prosecution of military officers to consolidate their emerging democratic regimes. To have pursued prosecution might have been ethically recommendable but politically untenable.

Besides these human rights issues, governments in Latin America have had varying success in subordinating the military to civilian control. In Chile, the subordination was weakest with General Pinochet's still functioning until very recently as Chief of the Armed Forces while President Aylwin exercised his authority as Chief of State. In Argentina, the subordination of the military is arguably greatest, with civilian control apparently reestablished over the Defense Ministry, military promotions, and the defense budget. In Brazil, the subordination issue lies somewhere in between, with the military still exerting influence while President Cardoso has tried to extend his control.

Second, after these transitions in Latin America, the military tried—especially in Brazil and Chile—to maintain influential roles in government. In the first freely elected government in Brazil in 1982, military officers controlled six cabinet positions. In Chile, Augusto Pinochet, even after his electoral loss, assured that he would continue as Commander-in-Chief. This kind of assertion of military prerogative in government is highly unusual in constitutional government. Yet it reflects the real power that the military can wield in postmilitary regimes.

Third, even after the transition, the military has often tried to maintain certain prerogatives for the military, especially regarding the appointment and promotion of senior officers and control of military budgets. Ordinarily in constitutional democracies civilian authorities should have ultimate control over both the appointment of senior officers and the appropriation of military budgets. Yet in Brazil the military asserted control over promotions in the military. In Chile the military made it clear that the chiefs of the armed forces and the police could not be removed for seven years after the initial transition. In Chile the military also assured that the government could not reduce the overall force size of the military and that it would not have control over the military budget. These compromises, while highly unusual and even unacceptable from a democratic perspective, reflect the realities entailed in transitions from military governments.

POLICY CONCLUSIONS AND RECOMMENDATIONS

Since the 1980s there has been a substantial worldwide movement towards democratization in states that were formerly authoritarian. Substantial progress towards democratic consolidation (at least in its liberal capitalist form) has been observed in southern Europe, Latin America, and eastern Europe. Some western scholars have even posited the proposition that Euro-American style liberal capitalist democracy will be the political prototype for the twenty-first century. However culturally contentious that proposition may be, there is something positive about political movements that evolve from less inclusive, elitist political structures towards a politics that are more inclusive. Since the 1970s in Latin America, and since the 1980s in Russia and the rest of Eastern Europe, we have seen political processes that have opened up and that have become less elitist and more inclusive. For the purpose of this paper, we have specifically examined the reform of military governments in Argentina, Brazil, and Chile. We have then considered whether aspects of these processes of political change are applicable to Africa. We then provided our critique of the processes of change in Algeria and Nigeria so that we could try to understand how military governments have tried to manage political change towards democracy on the African continent. What we will try to do in this last section in to arrive at policy conclusions and recommendations.

What has become clear through our review of the processes of political change in Brazil, Chile, and Argentina is that the military establishments there, because of foresight (Brazil), or electoral defeat (Chile), or military defeat (Argentina), realized that the military was an important institution within any polity and that its professionalism, integrity, esprit de corps, and survival were contingent upon the military's exit from daily politics. Military officers learned that it was best for them to focus upon their primary role: the defense of the nation from external threat, rather than to focus misguidedly either "internal subversion" or economic management. Military officers in Latin America learned that internal security was a police matter rather than a military affair. They have also learned that economic development should be left to elected civilians, economists, and entrepreneurs, rather than military officers. Military officers are charged with the responsibility of the defense of the nation. That is their role. Politics should not be their bailiwick.

After approximately twenty years of meddling in government, military officers in Argentina, Brazil, and Chile and many other states in Latin America finally learned that their continued involvement in politics was not in the interests of the survival and growth of the military. Unfortunately in Algeria, the military has not learned that lesson. We hope that in Nigeria they have.

Specific Policy Recommendations

This article has been written as a form of policy memorandum for both African military officers and other advocates of democratic change in Africa. It suggests the following recommendations for political change that we hope will be discussed in policy circles.

- The first item for discussion is educational. We must first try to convince African military officers through articles, conferences, and personal communications that the continued involvement of the military in government damages the reputation of the military itself. Military officers should be experts in external security and should limit their involvement in politics to that issue. They are not economists or economic managers. History has proven to us that they usually fail miserably in that role.
- Military officers in Africa need to be reminded that the legitimate role for the military focuses on external security. Internal security is a matter to be left to the police.
- Elected civilian leaders are in a better position to withstand criticism from the public for policy failure (e.g., inflation, education deficits, health care management, infrastructure development, et cetera) than unelected military leaders. The electoral process provides a shield for civilian officials who can later be removed from office.
- Civilian leaders need to let the military develop their expertise in external security. Civilian officials also need to provide the military with sufficient resources so they can get the job done.
- In order to assure that the military does not interfere in politics, adequate provision must be made either from national or international sources so that enlisted men and officers are paid adequately and on a timely basis.
- The military must be professional, adequately paid, and cut off from opportunities to engage in commercial enterprises (that could lead to corruption). While serving in the military, military officers cannot serve two masters. They cannot be dedicated to the defense of the nation and also profiteer from either the black market or commercial connections.
- Industries or farming operations that are under military control must be privatized so military officers do not have access to independent sources of funding.
- Significant attention must be given to the curriculum at Africa's professional military academies so the inculcation of professional military values becomes the norm.

Strategies and Styles of Transition

Upon our review of the democratic transitions in Argentina, Brazil, Chile, Algeria, and Nigeria, it is clear to us that the democratic transition undertaken in Brazil probably serves as the best model for military officers in Africa who are intent upon democratization. One significant advantage of the Brazil model was that the generals there had the foresight to recognize that it was in the best interests of the military to democratize gradually, even if that democratization process would eventually take eight years. Also, the generals in Brazil recognized that it was best for the military's institutional survival to control the process of the transition to democracy rather than to hold on to power without a plan for transition (as in Argentina) or to be sufficiently deluded to believe that the masses preferred the continuation of authoritarian rule (as Pinochet did in Chile). The advantage of Brazil's process of transition was its gradualism which prevented instability.

The models that are less preferable for Africa are Argentina and Chile. Argentina's transition process was highly unstable yet eventually successful. It occurred after the military as an institution was severely weakened by its defeat in the Falklands/ Malvinas war, the military resisted public demands for political change, and the first elected civilian government in Argentina had to deal with coup threats constantly. Eventually democracy was reinstated in Argentina but the process was highly unstable and the result was not assured. Chile, while serving a better model for transition, is still not as desirable as the Brazil model because it was a case of successful improvisation, with Pinochet ceding his authority as Chief of State very reluctantly while still maintaining his position as Chief of the Armed Forces. We cannot say that democracy has been fully consolidated when the military has not been fully and objectively submitted to civilian control as in Chile.

One model that has not been discussed in this paper is Spain, which may in fact serve as an ideal prototype for transitions from military rule. In Spain, elite consensus was obtained among significant elements of the military, the center, the right, the left, and even the Communist party to form a coalition to democratize Spain. The process of change was compressed (from 1975 to 1978) and at times unstable (a counter-democratic coup was attempted) but what was remarkable about the Spanish transition was the formation of a cross-ideological coalition dedicated towards a transition to democracy. Because of this cohesion among political elites, the Spanish transition remains a distinctive example of the transition to democracy.

NOTES

1. Scott Mainwaring, "Transitions to Democracy and Democratic Consolidation," in *Issues in Democratic Consolidation: The New South American Democracies in Comparative Perspective*, ed. Scott Mainwaring, Guillermo O'Donnell, and J. Samuel Valenzuela (Notre Dame, Ind.: University of Notre Dame Press, 1992), p. 324.

2. Samuel Huntington, "Reforming Civil-Military Relations," in *Civil-Military Relations and Democracy,* ed. Larry Diamond and Marc F. Plattner (Baltimore, Maryland: Johns Hopkins University Press, 1996), p. 7.

3. Juan Linz, "Crisis, Breakdown, and Reequilibration," in *The Breakdown of Democratic Regimes,* ed. Juan Linz and Alfred Stepan (Baltimore, Maryland: Johns Hopkins University Press, 1978).

4. Frances Hagopian, "The Compromised Consolidation: The Political Class in the Brazilian Transition," in *Issues in Democratic Consolidation,* p.245.

5. Alfred Stepan, "Introduction," in *Democratizing Brazil: Problems of Transition and Consolidation,* ed. Alfred Stepan (Oxford: Oxford University Press, 1989), p. x.

6. Ibid.

7. Simon Collier and William Slater, *A History of Chile, 1808–1994* (Cambridge: Cambridge University Press, 1996), pp. 377–378.

8. Scott Mainwaring and Eduardo J. Viola, "Brazil and Argentina in the 1980s," *Journal of International Affairs* 38, no. 2 (Winter 1985): 206–207.

9. The nine-point program was the reorganization of the Armed Forces; implementation of a National Development Plan and repair of war damages; introduction of a new Revenue Allocation Formula; eradication of bribery and corruption from the national life; settlement of the question of the creation of more states; conducting a population census; preparation and adoption of a new constitution; organization of genuinely national political parties; and organization of elections of popularly elected government in the states and at the federal level at the center. See Gowon, "Broadcast to the Nation, October 1, 1970," in *Stability and Progress: The Challenge of the Second Decade of Nigeria's Independence* (Jos: Benue-Plateau State Government Printer, n.d.), p. 9.

10. *The Nigerian Standard,* 20 October, 1974.

11. Ibid.

12. Alhaji Shehu Shagari, *Collected Speeches of President Shehu Shagari* (Lagos, Nigeria: State House, 1980), pp. 5–6.

13. General Babangida's Address to the Armed Forces Consultative Assembly on June 5, 1989 at Abuja.

14. The Political Bureau received 27,324 contributions made up of 14,961 memoranda, 1,723 recorded audio cassettes and video tapes and 3,933 newspaper articles. See the *March to Democracy, 30th Anniversary* (Lagos, Nigeria: Federal Ministry of Information), p.46.

15. Ibid.

16. See H. S. Galadima, "Militarism and Governance in Nigeria" in *Governance, a Journal of the Institute of Government and Social Research,* (IGSR) 1, no. 1 (April 1998): 115–40.

17. See *Tell Magazine,* (Lagos, Nigeria), 5 July 1993, p. 10.

18. Ricardo René Laremont, *Islam and the Politics of Resistance in Algeria, 1783–1992* (Trenton, New Jersey: Africa World Press, 2000), p. 177.

19. Alfred Stepan, *Rethinking Military Politics: Brazil and the Southern Cone* (Princeton, New Jersey: Princeton University Press, 1988), p. 40.

Bibliography

BOOKS

Adam, Hussein, and Richard Ford, ed. *Mending Rips in the Sky: Options for Somali Communities in the 21st Century.* Lawrenceville, New Jersey: Red Sea Press, 1997.

Adedeji, Adebayo, ed. *Africa within the World: Beyond Dispossession and Dependence.* London: Zed Books, 1993.

Ahmed, Hassan Mekki Mohamed. *Harakat El Ikhwan El Muslimeen Fil-Sudan, 1944–1969.* Khartoum: Khartoum University Press, 1987.

Agonafer, Mulungeta, ed. *Africa in the Contemporary International Disorder: Crisis and Possibilities.* Lanham, Maryland: University Press of America, 1996.

Ake, Claude. *Revolutionary Pressures in Africa.* London: Zed Books, 1978.

Albino, Oliver. *The Sudan: A Southern Viewpoint.* London: Oxford University Press, 1970.

Alexander, H. T. *African Tightrope.* London: Pall Mall Press 1965.

Alier, Abel. *The Southern Sudan: Too many Agreements Dishonoured.* London and Exeter: Ithaca Press, 1990.

Amselle, Jean-Loup, and Elikia M'bokolo, eds. *Au cœur de l'ethnie: ethnie, tribalisme et état en Afrique.* Paris: Éditions de la Découverte, 1985.

Anderson, Benedict. *Imagined Communities: Reflections on the Origins and Spread of Nationalism.* London: Verso, 1983.

Andreopoulos, George J., and Harold E. Selesky, eds. *The Aftermath of Defeat: Societies, Armed Forces, and the Challenge of Recovery.* New Haven, Conn.: Yale University Press, 1994.

An-Na'im, Abdullahi A. *The Second Message.* Syracuse, New York: Syracuse University Press, 1987.

Anstee, Margaret Joan. *Orphan of the Cold War: The Inside Story of the Collapse of the Angolan Peace Process, 1992–93.* New York: St. Martin's Press, 1996.

Assess, H. *Mediation in Civil Wars: Approaches and Strategies—The Sudan Conflict.* Boulder, Colo.: Westview Press, 1987.

Atiyah, Edward. *An Arab Tells his Story: A Study in Loyalties.* London: John Murray, 1946.

Baddour, Abd el-Fatah el-Sayed. *Sudanese Egyptian Relations.* The Hague: M. Nisheff, 1960.

Bender, Gerald, James Coleman, and Richard Sklar, eds. *African Crisis Areas and U.S. Foreign*

    Policy. Berkeley and Los Angeles: University of California Press, 1985.

Bercovitch, Jacob, ed. *Resolving International Conflicts: The Theory and Practice of Mediation.* Boulder, Colo.: Lynne Rienner, 1995.

Beshir, Mohamed Omar. *Revolution and Nationalism in the Sudan.* London: Rex Collins, 1974.

———. *The Southern Sudan: From Conflict to Peace.* London: C. Hurst and Co., 1975.

Braekman, Colette. *Le dinosaure: le Zaïre de Mobutu.* Paris: Fayard, 1992.

Bratton, Michael, and Nicolas van de Walle. *Democratic Experiments in Africa: Regime Transitions in Comparative Perspective.* Cambridge: Cambridge University Press, 1997.

Bull, Hedley. *The Anarchical Society.* New York: Columbia University Press, 1977.

Cartwright, J. *Politics in Sierra Leone, 1947–1967.* Toronto: University of Toronto Press, 1970.

Chipman, John. *French Power in Africa.* Cambridge, Mass.: Basil Blackwell, 1989.

Clarke, Walter, and Jeffrey Herbst. *Learning from Somalia: the Lessons of Armed Humanitarian Intervention.* Boulder, Colo.: Westview Press, 1997.

Claude, Inis. *Swords into Plowshares.* New York: Random House, 1984.

Cole, B. *The Elite: The Story of the Rhodesian Special Air Service.* Transkei: Three Knights Publishing, 1987.

Collier, Simon, and William Slater. *A History of Chile, 1808–1994.* Cambridge: Cambridge University Press, 1996.

Copson, Raymond. *Africa's Wars and Prospects for Peace.* New York: M. E. Sharpe, 1994.

Crocker, Chester A. *High Noon in Southern Africa: Making Peace in a Tough Neighborhood.* New York: W. W. Norton, 1993.

Daniel, D. C. F., and B. Hayes, eds. *Beyond Traditional Peacekeeping.* New York: St. Martin's Press, 1995.

Davidson, Basil. *The Black Man's Burden.* New York: Times Books, 1992.

Decalo, Samuel. *Coups and Army Rule in Africa: Studies in Military Style.* New Haven, Conn.: Yale University Press, 1976.

Deng, Francis. *Dynamics of Identification: A Basis for National Integration in the Sudan.* Khartoum: Khartoum University Press, 1973.

Diehl, Paul. *The Politics of International Organizations: Patterns and Insights.* Chicago: Dorsey Press, 1989.

Drysdale, John. *The Somali Dispute.* New York: Praeger Publishers, 1964.

———. *Whatever Happened to Somalia? A Tale of Tragic Blunders.* London: Haan Associates, 1994.

Durch, William J., ed. *The Evolution of Peacekeeping: Case Studies and Comparative Analysis.* New York: St. Martin's Press, 1993.

El-Affendi, Abdel Wahab. *Turabi's Revolution: Islam and Power in the Sudan.* London: Grey Seal, 1991.

El-Amin, Mohamed Nuri. *The Emergence and Development of the Leftist Movement in the Sudan during the 1930s and 1940s.* Khartoum: Khartoum University Press, 1984.

Englebert, Pierre. *La révolution burkinabe.* Paris: Karthala, 1986.

Enloe, Cynthia H. *Ethnic Soldiers: State Security in Divided Societies.* Athens: University of Georgia Press, 1980.

———. *Ethnic Conflict and Political Development.* New York: University Press of America, 1986.

Eprile, Cecil. *War and Peace in the Sudan 1955–1972.* London: David and Charles, World Realities, 1974.

Fabian Society. *The Sudan: The Road Ahead.* London: Gollanz, 1945.

Falola, Toyin, and Julius O. Ihonvbere. *The Rise and Fall of Nigeria's Second Republic, 1979–84.* London: Zed Books, 1985.

Fanon, Frantz. *The Wretched of the Earth.* New York: Grove Press, 1968.

Foccart, Jacques. *Foccart parle: entretiens avec Philippe Gaillard.* Paris: Fayard and Jeune Afrique, 1995.

Geffray, C. *La cause des armes au Mozambique: anthropologie d'une guerre civile.* Paris: Karthala, 1990.

Gellner, Ernest. *Nations and Nationalism.* Ithaca, New York: Cornell University Press, 1983.

Gifford, Prosser, and Roger Louis, eds. *The Transfer of Power in Africa.* New Haven, Conn.: Yale University Press, 1982.

Gourevitch, Philip. *We Wish to Inform You that Tomorrow We Will be Killed With Our Families: Stories from Rwanda.* New York: Farrar, Straus, and Giroux, 1998.

Gramsci, Antonio. *Selections from Prison Notebooks.* New York: International Publishers, 1971.

Guichaoua, André, ed. *Les crises politiques au Burundi et au Rwanda, 1993–1994.* Lille: Presses de l'Université de Lille 1, 1995.

Guimaraes, Fernando Andersen. *The Origins of the Angolan Civil War: Foreign Intervention and Domestic Political Conflict.* New York: St. Martin's Press, 1998.

Hall, Margaret, and Tom Young. *Confronting Leviathan: Mozambique since Independence.* Athens, Ohio: Ohio University Press, 1997.

Harbeson, John W. and Donald S. Rothchild, eds. *Africa in World Politics: Post–Cold War Challenges.* Boulder, Colo.: Westview Press, 1995.

Harris, John, ed. *The Politics of Humanitarian Intervention.* New York: Pinter, 1995.

Hasan, Yusuf Fadl. *The Arabs and the Sudan.* Edinburgh: Edinburgh University Press, 1967.

Henderson, K. D. D. *Sudan Republic.* London: Ernest Benn Ltd., 1965.

Hill, Stephen M., and Shahin P. Malik. *Peacekeeping and the United Nations.* Aldershot, England and Burlington, Vermont: Ashgate and Dartmouth Publishing Co., 1996.

Hochschild, Adam. *King Leopold's Ghost: A Story of Greed, Terror, and Heroism in Colonial Africa.* Boston: Houghton Mifflin Co., 1998.

Hodgkin, Thomas. *African Political Parties: An Introductory Guide.* Harmondsworth, England: Penguin, 1961.

Hoffman, Stanley. *The Ethics and Politics of Humanitarian Intervention.* Notre Dame, Ind.: University of Notre Dame Press, 1996.

Horowitz, Donald L. *Ethnic Groups in Conflict.* Berkeley and Los Angeles: University of California Press, 1985.

Huntington, Samuel P. *The Third Wave: Democratization in the Late Twentieth Century.* Norman, Okla.: University of Oklahoma Press, 1991.

Ihonvbere, Julius O. *Africa and the New World Order.* New York: Peter Lang, 1999.

Issa-Salwe, Abdisalam. *The Collapse of the Somali State.* London: Haan Associates, 1994.

Jackson, E. *Meeting of Minds.* New York: McGraw-Hill, 1952.

Jackson, Robert, and Carl Rosberg. *Personal Rule in Black Africa.* Berkeley and Los Angeles: University of California Press, 1982.

James, Alan. *Peacekeeping in International Politics.* New York: St. Martin's Press, 1990.

Janowitz, Morris. *The Military in the Political Development of New Nations.* Chicago: University of Chicago Press, 1964.

Johnson, John J., ed. *The Role of the Military in Underdeveloped Countries.* Princeton, New Jersey: Princeton University Press, 1962.

Jørgensen, Jan Jelmert. *Uganda: A Modern History.* New York: St. Martin's Press, 1981.

Joseph, Richard, ed. *State, Conflict, and Democracy in Africa.* Boulder, Colo.: Lynne Rienner, 1999.

Kalb, Madeleine G. *The Congo Cables: The Cold War in Africa from Eisenhower to Kennedy.* New York: Macmillan, 1982.

Kasfir, Nelson. *The Shrinking Political Arena: Participation and Ethnicity in African Politics, with a Case Study of Uganda.* Berkeley and Los Angeles: University of California Press, 1976.

Khalid, Mansour. *The Government They Deserve: The Role of the Elite in Sudan's Political Evolution.* London and New York: Kegan Paul, 1990.

Koroma, A. K. *Sierra Leone: The Agony of a Nation.* London: Andromeda Publications, 1996.

Laitin, David, and Said Samatar. *Somalia: Nation in Search of a State.* Boulder, Colo.: Lynne Rienner, 1987.

Laremont, Ricardo R. *Islam and The Politics of Resistance in Algeria, 1783–1992.* Trenton, New Jersey: Africa World Press, 2000.

Lefebvre, J. *Arms for the Horn: U.S. Security Policy in Ethiopia and Somalia, 1953–1991.* Pittsburgh, Pennsylvania: University of Pittsburgh Press, 1991.

Lemarchand, René. *Rwanda and Burundi.* New York: Praeger, 1970.

Lewis, Sir Arthur. *Politics in West Africa.* London: Allen and Unwin, 1965.

Lewis, I. M. *A Pastoral Democracy.* Oxford: Oxford University Press, 1969.

———. *A Modern History of Somalia.* Boulder, Colo.: Westview Press, 1988.

Lijphart, Arend. *Democracy in Plural Societies: A Comparative Exploration.* New Haven, Conn.: Yale University Press, 1977.

Linz, Juan, and Arturo Valenzuela, eds. *The Failure of Presidential Democracy: Comparative Perspectives.* Vol. 1. Baltimore, Maryland: Johns Hopkins University Press, 1994.

Lyons, Gene M., and Michael Mastanduno, eds. *Beyond Westphalia? State Sovereignty and International Intervention.* Baltimore, Maryland: Johns Hopkins University Press, 1995.

Mahjoub, Mohamed Ahmed. *Democracy on Trial: Reflections on Arab and African Politics.* London: Deutsch, 1974.

Maier, Karl. *Angola: Promises and Lies.* London: Serif, 1996.

Mainwaring, Scott, Guillermo O'Donnell, and Samuel Valenzuela, eds. *Issues in Democratic Consolidation: The New South American Democracies in Comparative Perspective.* Notre Dame, Ind.: University of Notre Dame Press, 1992.

Makannah, T. J., ed. *Handbook of the Population of Sierra Leone.* Freetown: Toma Entreprises Limited, 1996.

Malwal, Bona. *People and Power in the Sudan.* London and Exeter: Ithaca Press, 1981.

Marcum, John. *The Angolan Revolution (Vol. II): Exile Politics and Guerilla Warfare, 1962–1976.* Cambridge, Mass.: MIT Press, 1978.

Maren, Michael. *The Road to Hell: The Ravaging Effects of Foreign Aid and International Charity.* New York: Free Press, 1997.

Martin, D., and P. Johnson, eds. *Destructive Engagement.* Harare: Zimbabwe Publishing House, 1986.

Maxwell, Kenneth. *The Making of Portuguese Democracy.* Cambridge: Cambridge University Press, 1995.

———. *Chocolate, piaratas e outros malandros ensais tropicais.* São Paolo: Paz e Terra, 1999.

Mayall, James. *Africa: The Cold War and After.* London: Elek, 1971.

Mazrui, Ali A. *Soldiers and Kinsmen in Uganda: The Making of a Military Ethnocracy.* Beverly Hills: Sage Publications, 1975.

———. *Africa's International Relations: The Diplomacy of Dependency and Change.* London: Heinemann; Boulder, Colo.: Westview Press, 1977.

Mazrui, Ali A., and Michael Tidy. *Nationalism and New States in Africa from about 1935 to the Present.* Nairobi, Kenya: Heinemann, 1984.

Mbaku, John M., and Julius O. Ihonvbere, eds. *Multiparty Democracy and Political Change: Constraints to Democratization in Africa.* Aldershot, England and Burlington, Vermont: Ashgate, 1998.

Minter, W. *Apartheid's Contras: An Enquiry into the Roots of War in Angola and Mozambique.* Johannesburg: Witwatersrand University Press; and London and New York: Zed Books, 1994.

Morganthau, Ruth Schachter. *Political Parties in French-Speaking West Africa.* Oxford: Clarendon Press, 1964.

Mukholi, David. *A Complete Guide to Uganda's Fourth Constitution: History, Politics, and the Law.* Kampala: Fountain Publishers, 1995.

Murphy, Sean D. *Humanitarian Intervention: The United Nations in an Evolving World Order.* Philadelphia: University of Pennsylvania Press, 1996.

Museveni, Yoweri Kaguta. *Sowing the Mustard Seed: The Struggle for Freedom and Democracy in Uganda.* London: Macmillan, 1997.

Mutiithi, Samuel. *African Crisis: Is There Hope?* Lanham, Maryland: University Press of America, 1996.

Niblock, Tom. *Power and Class in the Sudan: The Dynamics of Sudanese Politics, 1898–1985.* Albany: State University of New York Press, 1987.

Newbury, Catherine. *The Cohesion of Oppression: Clientship and Ethnicity in Rwanda, 1860–1960.* New York: Columbia University Press, 1988.

Nyerere, Julius. *Ujamaa: Essays on Socialism.* London: Oxford University Press, 1968.

O'Brien, Conor Cruise. *To Katanga and Back: A UN Case History.* New York: Grosset and Dunlap, 1966.

Omara-Otunu, Amii. *Politics and the Military in Uganda, 1890–1985.* New York: St. Martin's Press, 1987.

Onwuka, Ralph I., and Ahmadu Sesay, eds. *The Future of Regionalism in Africa.* New York: St. Martin's Press, 1985.

Penvenne, Jeanne Marie. *African Workers and Colonial Racism: Mozambican Strategies and Struggles in Lourenco Marques, 1877–1962.* Portsmouth, New Hampshire: Heinemann; London: James Currey; and Johannesburg: Witwatersrand University Press, 1995.

Peters, Jimi. *The Nigerian Military and the State.* London: Tauris Academic Studies, 1997.

Plischke, Elmer, ed. *Contemporary U.S. Foreign Policy: Documents and Commentary.* Westport, Conn.: Greenwood Press, 1991.

Prunier, Gérard. *The Rwanda Crisis: History of a Genocide.* London: Hurst and Co., 1995.

Ratner, Stephen R. *The New UN Peacekeeping: Building Peace in Lands of Conflict After the Cold War.* New York: St. Martin's Press, 1996.

Reno, William. *Corruption and State Politics in Sierra Leone.* Cambridge: Cambridge University Press, 1995.

———. *Warlord Politics and African States.* Boulder, Colo.: Lynne Rienner, 1998.

Reilly, Ben, and Andrew Reynolds. *Electoral Systems and Conflict in Divided Societies.* Washington, DC: National Academy Press, 1999.

Reyntjens, Filip, and Stefan Marysse, eds. *L'Afrique des grands lacs: annuaire 1997–1998.* Paris: L'Harmattan, 1998.

Richards, P. *Fighting for the Rain Forest: War, Youth, and Resources in Sierra Leone.* London: James Currey, 1996.

Robertson, James W. *Transition in Africa: From Direct Rule to Independence.* London: Hurst, 1974.

Rocca, R. M. della. *Moçambique da guerra à paz: historia de uma mediaçao insolita.* Maputo: Libraría Universitaria-Universidade Eduardo Mondlane, 1998.

Samatar, Ahmed. *Socialist Somalia: Rhetoric and Reality.* London: Zed Books, 1988.

Scott, James C. *Seeing Like A State: How Certain Schemes to Improve the Human Condition Have Failed.* New Haven, Conn.: Yale University Press, 1998.

Scott, James M. *Deciding to Intervene: The Reagan Doctrine and American Foreign Policy.* Durham, North Carolina: Duke University Press, 1996.

Shultz, George Pratt. *Turmoil and Triumph: My Years as Secretary of State.* New York and Toronto: C. Scribner's Sons, 1993.

Somerville, Keith. *Foreign Military Intervention in Africa.* London: Pinter Publishers; and New York: St. Martin's Press, 1990.

Stepan, Alfred. *Rethinking Military Politics: Brazil and the Southern Cone.* Princeton, New Jersey: Princeton University Press, 1988.

Stepan, Alfred, ed. *Democratizing Brazil: Problems of Transition and Consolidation.* Oxford: Oxford University Press, 1989.

Stremlau, John J. *The International Politics of the Nigerian Civil War, 1967–1970.* Princeton, New Jersey: Princeton University Press, 1977.

Teson, Fernando R. *Humanitarian Intervention: An Enquiry into Law and Morality.* Second Edition. Hudson, New York: Transnational Publishers, 1997.

Thakur, Ramesh Chandra, and Carlyle Thayer, eds. *A Crisis of Expectations: UN Peacekeeping in the 1990s.* Boulder, Colo.: Westview Press, 1995.

Toure, Sekou. *Toward Full Reafricanization.* Paris: Présence Africaine, 1959.

Treverton, Gregory F. *Covert Action: The Limits of Intervention in the Postwar World.* New York: Basic Books, 1987.

Tripp, Aili Mari. *Changing the Rules: The Politics of Liberalization and the Urban Informal Economy in Tanzania.* Berkeley and Los Angeles: University of California Press, 1997.

Ulam, Adam Bruno. *Expansion and Coexistence: Soviet Foreign Policy, 1917–73.* Second Edition. New York: Praeger, 1974.

Vail, Leroy, ed. *The Creation of Tribalism in Southern Africa.* Berkeley and Los Angeles: University of California Press, 1989.

Villalon, Leonardo O., and Philip A. Huxtable, eds. *The African State at a Critical Juncture: Between Disintegration and Reconfiguration.* Boulder, Colo.: Lynne Rienner, 1998.

Vines, A. *RENAMO: Terrorism in the Mozambique.* London: James Currey, 1991.

Wai, Dustan M. *The African Arab Conflict in the Sudan.* New York: African Pub. Co., 1981.

Wallerstein, Immanuel Maurice. *Africa, The Politics of Independence: An Interpretation of Modern African History.* New York: Vintage Books, 1961.

Wesley, Michael. *Casualties of the New World Order: The Causes of Failure of UN Missions to Civil Wars.* New York: St. Martin's Press, 1997.

Wheeler, D. L., and R. Pelissier. *Angola.* London: Pall Mall Press, 1971.

Widner, Jennifer A., ed. *Economic Change and Political Liberalization in Sub-Saharan Africa.* Baltimore, Maryland: Johns Hopkins University Press, 1994.

Willame, Jean-Claude. *L'automne d'un despotisme: pouvoir, argent et obéissance dans le Zaïre des années quatre-vingt.* Paris: Karthala, 1992.

Young, Crawford. *The Politics of Cultural Pluralism.* Madison: University of Wisconsin Press, 1976.

————. *The African Colonial State in Comparative Perspective.* New Haven, Conn.: Yale University Press, 1994.

————, ed. *Ethnic Diversity and Public Policy: A Comparative Enquiry.* London: Macmillan, 1998.

Young, Crawford, and Thomas Turner. *The Rise and Decline of the Zairian State.* Madison: University of Wisconsin Press, 1985.

Zack-Williams, A. B. *Tributors, Supporters, and Merchant Capital: Mining and Underdevelopment in Sierra Leone.* London: Avebury, 1995.

Zartman, William I. *Ripe for Resolution: Conflict and Intervention in Africa.* New York: Oxford University Press, 1989.

————, ed. *Collapsed States: The Disintegration and Restoration of Legitimate Authority.* Boulder, Colo.: Lynne Rienner, 1995.

ARTICLES

Abdajo, Adekeye, and Michael O'Hanlon. "Africa: Toward a Rapid-Reaction Force." *SAIS Review* 17, no. 2 (1997).

Abdullah, I. "Bush Path to Destruction: The Origin and Character of the Revolutionary United Front/Sierra Leone." In *Africa Development* 22, no. 3 and no. 4 (1997).

Abdullah, I., and P. K. Muana. "The Revolutionary United Front: A Revolt of the Lumpenproletariat." In *African Guerillas*, edited by C. Clapham. London: James Currey, 1998.

Abd al-Rahim, Muddathir. "Arabism, Africanism, and Self-Identification in the Sudan." In *The Southern Sudan: The Problem of National Integration*, edited by Dustan M. Wai. London: Frank Cass, 1973.

Abraham, A. "War and Transition to Peace: A Study of State Conspiracy in Perpetuating Armed Conflict." *Africa Development* 22, no. 3 and no. 4 (1997).

Adeleke, Ademola. "The Politics and Diplomacy of Peacekeeping in West Africa: The ECOWAS Operations in Liberia." *Journal of Modern African Studies* 33, no. 4 (1995).

Ake, Claude. "Is Africa Democratising?" In *Crises and Contradictions in Nigeria's Democratisation Programme, 1986–1993*, edited by Nahzeem Oluwafemi Mimiko. Akure, Nigeria: Stebak Publishers, 1995.

An-N'aim, Abdullahi A. "The Islamic Law of Apostasy and its Modern Application: A Case from the Sudan." *Religion* 16 (1986).

————. "The National Question of Constitutionalism: Secession and Constitutionalism." In *Constitutionalism and Democracy: Transitions in the Contemporary World*, edited by Douglas Greenberg et al. Oxford: Oxford University Press, 1993.

Armon, Jeremy, and Andy Carl. "The Liberian Peace Process: 1990–1996." *Accord: An International Review of Peace Initiatives*, Issue 1. Conciliations Resources, 1996.

Armon, J., D. Hendrickson, and A. Vines. "The Mozambican Peace Process in Perspective." *Accord: An International Review of Peace Initiatives*, Issue 3. Conciliations Resources, 1998.

Bangura, Y. "Reflections on the Sierra Leone Peace Accord." *Africa Development* 22, no. 3 and no. 4 (1997).

Bazenguissa-Ganga, Remy. "The Spread of Political Violence in Congo-Brazzaville." *African Affairs* 98 (1999).

Behrend, Heike. "Is Alice Lakwena a Witch? The Holy Spirit Movement and Its Fight against Evil in the North." In *Uganda Now: Between Development and Decay,* edited by Holger Bernt Hansen and Michael Twaddle. London: James Currey, 1988.

Carment, David. "The International Dimension of Ethnic Conflict: Concepts, Indicators, and Theory." *Journal of Peace Research* 30, no. 2 (1993).

Diamond, Larry. "Is the Third Wave Over?" *Journal of Democracy* 7, no. 3 (1996).

Doom, Rudy, and Koen Vlassenroot. "Kony's Message: A New Koine? The Lord's Resistance Army in Northern Uganda." *African Affairs* 98 (1999).

Durch, William J. "The U.N. Operation in the Congo." In *The Evolution of Peacekeeping: Case Studies and Comparative Analysis,* edited by William J. Durch. New York: St. Martin's Press, 1993.

Drysdale, John. "Somalia: the Only Way Forward." *Journal of the Anglo-Somali Society* (Winter 1992/93).

Dziedzic, Michael J. "Policing the New World Disorder: Addressing Gaps in Public Security during Peace Operations." In *Toward Responsibility in the New World Disorder*, edited by Max Manwaring and John T. Fishel. London: Frank Cass, 1998.

Ekeh, Peter. "Colonialism and the Two Publics in Africa: A Theoretical Interpretation." *Comparative Studies in Society and History* 17, no. 2 (1975).

El-Affendi, Abdel Wahab. "Discovering the South: Sudanese Dilemmas for Islam in Africa." *African Affairs* 89, no. 358 (July 1990).

Fetherson, A. B. "Putting the Peace back into the Peacekeeping: Theory Must Inform Practice." *International Peacekeeping* 1, no. 1 (1994).

Galadima, H. S. "Militarism and Governance in Nigeria." *Governance: A Journal of the Institute of Government and Social Research (IGSR)* 1, no. 1 (April 1998).

Gberie, L. "The May 25 Coup d'État: A Military Revolt?" *Africa Development* 22, no. 3 and no. 4 (1997).

Gregory, Shaun. "The French Military in Africa: Past and Present." *African Affairs* 99, no. 396 (2000).

Hagopian, Frances. "The Compromise Consolidation: The Political Class in the Brazilian Transition." In *Issues in Democratic Consolidation: The New South American Democracies in Comparative Perspective,* edited by Scott Mainwaring, Guillermo O'Donnell, and J. Samuel Valenzuela. Notre Dame, Ind.: University of Notre Dame Press, 1992.

Ham, Melinda, and Mike Hall. "Malawi: From Tyranny to Tolerance." *Africa Report* 39, no. 6 (1994).

Hamid, Mohamed Beshir. "Confrontation and Reconciliation within an African Context: The Case of Sudan." *Third World Quarterly* 5, no. 2 (April 1983).

Horowitz, Donald. "Ethnic Conflict Management for Policymakers." In *Conflict and Peacemaking in Multiethnic Societies*, edited by Joseph V. Montville. Lexington, Mass., and Toronto: Lexington Books, 1990.

Howe, Herbert. "Lessons of Liberia: ECOMOG and Regional Peacekeeping." *International Security* 21, no. 3 (Winter 1996–97).

Huntington, Samuel. "Reforming Civil-Military Relations." In *Civil-Military Relations and Democracy*, edited by Larry Diamond and Marc F. Plattner. Baltimore, Maryland: Johns Hopkins University Press, 1996.

Ihonvbere, Julius O. "Why African Economies Will Not Recover?" *Iranian Journal of International Affairs* (Spring-Summer 1994).

———. "Pan-Africanism: Agenda for African Unity in the 1990s?" In *Issues and Trends in Contemporary African Politics: Stability, Development, and Democratization*, edited by George A. Agbango. New York: Peter Lang, 1997.

———. "From Despotism to Democracy: The Rise of Multiparty Politics in Malawi." *Third World Quarterly* 18, no. 2 (1997).

———. "Nigeria: Militarization and Perpetual Transition." In *Democratization in Late Twentieth-Century Africa*, edited by Jean-Germain Gros. Westport, Conn.: Greenwood Press, 1998.

Imobighe, Tom. "ECOWAS Defense Pact and Regionalism in Africa." In *The Future of Regionalism in Africa*, edited by Ralph I. Onwuka and Ahmadu Sesay. New York: St. Martin's Press, 1985.

Jackson, Robert, and Carl Rosberg. "The Marginality of the African State." In *African Independence: The First Twenty-Five Years*, edited by Gwendolyn M. Carter and Patrick O'Meara. Bloomington: Indiana University Press, 1986.

———. "Why Africa's Weak States Persist: The Empirical and the Juridical in Statehood." In *The State and Development in the Third World*, edited by Atul Kohli. Princeton, New Jersey: Princeton University Press, 1986.

Kandeh, J. "Politicisation of Ethnic Identities in Sierra Leone." *African Studies Review* 35 (1992).

———. "What Does the Militariat Do When It Rules? Military Regimes in the Gambia, Sierra Leone, and Liberia." *Review of African Political Economy* 69 (September 1996).

———. "Transition without Rupture: Sierra Leone's Transfer Elections of 1996." *African Studies Review* 41/2 (1998).

Kennes, Erik. "La guerre au Congo." In *L'Afrique des grands lacs: annuaire 1997–1998*, edited by Filip Reyntjens and Stefan Marysse. Paris: L'Harmattan, 1998.

Kriesberg, Louis. "Varieties of Mediating Activities and Mediators in International Relations." In *Resolving International Conflicts: The Theory and Practice of Mediation*, edited by Jacob Bercovitch. Boulder, Colo.: Lynne Rienner, 1995.

Lambert, Michael. "Casamance: Ethnicity or Nationalism?" *Africa* 68, no. 4 (1998).

Laitin, David. "A Constitutional Democracy for Somalia." *Horn of Africa* 13, no. 1 and no. 2 (January–March and April–June 1990).

Lemarchand, René. "African Transitions to Democracy: An Interim (and Mostly Pessimistic) Assessment." *Africa Insight* 22, no. 3 (1992).

Lewis, I. M. "The Ogaden and the Fragility of Somali Segmentary Nationalism." *Horn of Africa* 13, no. 1 and no. 2 (January-March and April-June 1990).

Linz, Juan. "Crisis, Breakdown, and Reequilibration." In *The Breakdown of Democratic Regimes*, edited by Juan Linz and Alfred Stepan. Baltimore, Maryland: Johns Hopkins University

Press, 1978.

Lipjhart, A. "Consociation and Federation: Conceptual and Empirical Links." In *Canadian Journal of Political Science* 22, no. 3 (September 1979).

——. "The Power-Sharing Approach." In *Conflict and Peacemaking in Multiethnic Societies*, edited by Joseph V. Montville. Lexington, Mass., and Toronto: Lexington Books, 1990.

Mainwaring, Scott. "Transitions to Democracy and Democratic Consolidation." In *Issues in Democratic Consolidation: The New South American Democracies in Comparative Perspective*, edited by Scott Mainwaring, Guillermo O'Donnell, and J. Samuel Valenzuela. Notre Dame, Ind.: University of Notre Dame Press, 1992.

Mainwaring, Scott, and Eduardo J. Viola. "Brazil and Argentina in the 1980s." *Journal of International Affairs* 38, no. 2 (Winter 1985).

Mazrui, Ali A. "The Multiple Marginality of the Sudan." In *Sudan in Africa*, edited by Yusuf Fadl Hasan. Khartoum: Khartoum University Press, 1971.

——. "Crisis in Somalia: From Tyranny to Anarchy." In *Mending Rips in the Sky: Options for Somali Communities in the 21st Century*, edited by Hussein Adam and Richard Ford. Lawrenceville, New Jersey: Red Sea Press, 1997.

Mbanza, Jacques. "La guerre comme un jeu d'enfants." *Rupture* 10, no. 2 (1997).

McHenry, Donald F. "The United Nations: Its Role in Decolonization." In *African Independence: The First Twenty-Five Years*, edited by Gwendolen Margaret Carter and Patrick O'Meara. Bloomington: Indiana University Press, 1985.

Meldrum, Andrew. "Malawi: New Actors, Same Play." *Africa Report* 39, no. 4 (1994).

Michaels, Marguerite. "Retreat From Africa." *Foreign Affairs* 72, no. 1 (1992).

Miller, Laura, and Charles Moskos. "Humanitarians or Warriors? Race, Gender, and Combat Status in Operation Restore Hope." *Armed Forces and Society* 21, no. 4 (1995).

Muana, P. K. "The Kamajoi Militia: Violence, Internal Displacement, and the Politics of Counter-Insurgency." *Africa Development* 22, no. 3 and no. 4 (1997).

Mugisho, Emmanuel Lubala. "La situation politique au Kivu: vers une dualisation de la société." In *L'Afrique des grands lacs: annuaire 1997–1998*, edited by Filip Reyntjens and Stefan Marysse. Paris: L'Harmattan, 1998.

Munya, P. Mweti. "The Organization of African Unity and Its Role in Regional Conflict Resolution and Dispute Settlement: A Critical Evaluation." *Boston College Third World Law Journal* 19 (Spring 1999).

Novai, Giampaolo Calchi. "Italy and Somalia: Unbearable Lightness of an Influence." In *Mending Rips in the Sky: Options for Somali Communities in the 21st Century*, edited by Hussein Adam and Richard Ford. Lawrenceville, New Jersey: Red Sea Press, 1997.

Nzongola-Ntalaja, Georges. "The Continuing Struggle for National Liberation in Zaire." *Journal of Modern African Studies* 17, no. 4 (December 1979).

——. "The Second Independence Movement in Congo-Kinshasa." In *Popular Struggles for Democracy in Africa*, edited by Peter Anyang' Nyong'o. London: Zed Books, 1987.

Ofuatey-Kodjoe, W. "Regional Organization and the Resolution of Internal Conflict: The ECOWAS Intervention in Liberia." *International Peacekeeping* 1, no. 3 (Autumn 1993).

Olonisakin, Funmi. "African 'Homemade' Peacekeeping Initiatives." *Armed Forces and Society* 23, no. 3 (1997).

Omach, Paul. "The African Crisis Response Initiative: Domestic Politics and Convergence of National Interests." *African Affairs* 99, no. 394 (2000).

Onyango-Obbo, Charles. "So Who Really Did Overthrow Mobutu?" *The East African* (July 1997).

Peters, Krijn, and Paul Richards. "Youth in Sierra Leone: 'Why We Fight?'" *Africa* 68, no. 2 (1998).

Peterson, Donald K. "Somalia and the United States, 1997–1983: The New Relationship." In *African Crisis Areas and U.S. Foreign Policy*, edited by Gerald Bender, James Coleman, and Richard Sklar. Berkeley and Los Angeles: University of California Press, 1985.

Prunier, Gérard. "Forces et faiblesses du modèle ougandais." *Le Monde Diplomatique* (February 1998).

Przeworski, Adam, and Fernando Limongi. "Modernization: Theories and Facts." *World Politics* 49, no. 2 (January 1997).

Quattara, Alassane D. "Africa: An Agenda for the 21st Century." *Finance and Development* 36, no. 1 (March 1999).

Ramcharan, Bertrand G. "The Evolving African Constitutionalism: A Constitutionalism of Liberty and Human Rights." *The Review* 60, Special Issue (June 1998).

Rashid, I. "Subaltern Reactions: Lumpens, Students, and the Left." *Africa Development* 22, no. 3 and no. 4 (1997).

Reno, William. "African Weak States and Commercial Alliances." *African Affairs* 96, no. 383 (April 1997).

Rivlin, Benjamin. "Prospects for a Division of Labor Between the UN and Regional Bodies in Peacekeeping: A Long Term Challenge." In *Agenda for Change*, edited by Klaus Hufner. Oplander: Lesko and Budrich, 1995.

Salih, Kamal Osman. "The Sudan, 1985–1989: The Fading Democracy." *The Journal of Modern African Studies* 28, no. 2 (1990).

Schraeder, Peter J. "The Horn of Africa: U.S. Foreign Policy in an Altered Cold War Environment." *Middle East Journal* 46, no. 4 (Autumn 1992).

———. "U.S. Intervention in the Horn of Africa amidst the End of the Cold War." *Africa Today* 40, no. 2 (1993).

Segal, Aaron. "Can Democratic Transitions Tame Political Successions?" *Africa Today* 43, no. 4 (1996).

Simpson, Mark. "Foreign and Domestic Factors in the Transformation of the FRELIMO." *The Journal of Modern African Studies* 31, no. 2 (1993).

Sinjela, Mpazi. "Constitutionalism in Africa: Emerging Trends." *The Review* 60, Special Issue (June 1998).

Spencer, Dayle E., and William J. Spencer. "Third Party Mediation and Conflict Transformation: Experiences of Ethiopia, Sudan, and Liberia." In *Conflict Transformation*, edited by Kumar Rupesinghe. New York: St. Martin's Press, 1988.

Stepan, A., and C. Skatch. "Presidentialism and Parliamentarism in Comparative Perspective." In *The Failure of Presidential Democracy: Comparative Perspectives*, Vol. 1, edited by Juan Linz and Arturo Valenzuela. Baltimore, Maryland: Johns Hopkins University Press, 1994.

Touval, Saadia. "The Organization of African Unity and African Borders." *International Organization* 21, no. 1 (1967).

Turner, J. Michael. "O papel da capacidade de recursos nacionais e das instituicoes nacionais em relacao a communidad internacional e as eleicoes." In *Moçambique Eleicoes Democracia e Desenvolvimento*, edited by Brazao Mazulo. Maputo: Inter-Africa Group, 1995.

Turner, J. Michael, Sue Nelson, and Kim Mahling-Clark. "Mozambique's Vote for Democratic Governance." In *Postconflict Elections, Democratization, and International Assistance*, edited by Krishna Kumar. Boulder, Colo.: Lynne Rienner, 1998.

Venter, Al. "Arms Pour into Africa." *New African* 370 (January 1999).

Voll, John Obert. "Northern Muslim Perspective." In *Conflict and Peacemaking in Multiethnic Societies,* edited by Joseph V. Montville. Lexington, Mass., and Toronto: Lexington Books, 1990.

Warburg, Gabriel R. "National Identity in the Sudan: Fact, Fiction, and Prejudice." *Asian and African Studies* 24 (1990).

Ware, Glenn T. "Just Cause for Intervention." *United States Naval Institute Proceedings* 123, no. 12 (December 1997).

Widner, Jennifer A. "States and Statelessness in Late Twentieth Century Africa." *Daedalus* 124, no. 3 (1995).

Willett, S. "Ostriches, Wise Old Elephants, and Economic Reconstruction in Mozambique." *International Peacekeeping* 2, no. 1 (1995).

Young, Crawford. "Nationalism, Ethnicity, and Class in Africa: A Retrospective." *Cahiers d'Études Africaines* 26, no. 3 (1986).

————. "Self-Determination and the African State System." In *Conflict Resolution in Africa,* edited by Francis Deng and William I. Zartman. Washington, DC: Brookings Institution, 1991.

————. "Zaire: The Shattered Illusion of the Integral State." *Journal of Modern African Studies* 32, no. 2 (1994).

————. "The Heritage of Colonialism." In *Africa in World Politics: Post–Cold War Challenges,* edited by John W. Harbeson and Donald S. Rothchild. Boulder, Colo.: Westview Press, 1995.

————. "Zaire: The Anatomy of a Failed State." In *History of Central Africa: The Contemporary Years since 1960,* edited by David Birmingham and Phyllis M. Martin. London: Longman, 1998.

Zack-Williams, A. B. "Sierra Leone: The Political Economy of Civil War, 1991–98." *Third World Quarterly* 20, no. 1 (1999).

Zakaria, Fareed. "The Rise of Illiberal Democracy." *Foreign Affairs* 76, no. 6 (1997).

Zunes, Stephen. "The Role of Non-Violent Action in the Downfall of Apartheid." *Journal of Modern African Studies* 37, no. 1 (1999).

MONOGRAPHS, REPORTS, LECTURES, AND OTHER DOCUMENTS

Adekanye, J. B. *Power-Sharing and Public Sector Reform: New Approaches to the Distribution and Management of Governmental Power.* Geneva: United Nations Research Institute for Social Development, 1999.

Africa Watch. *Human Rights Abuses and Civil War in the North: A Report from the U.S. General Accounting Office.* New York: 1989.

Ake, Claude. *Democracy and Development in Africa.* Washington, DC: The Brookings Institution, 1996.

Amnesty International. *Somalia: Imprisonment of Members of the Isaq Clan Since Mid-1988.* New York: 1988.

————. *Somalia: A Long Term Human Rights Crisis.* New York: 1988.

————. *Somalia: An Update on Human Rights Developments Since Mid-July.* New York: 1989.

———. *Somalia: A Government at War with Its Own People: Testimonies about the Killings and the Conflict in the North.* New York: 1990.

———. *Somalia: Report on an Amnesty International Visit and Current Human Rights Concerns.* London: 1990.

———. *Democratic Republic of Congo: A Long-Standing Crisis Spinning Out of Control.* AFR62/033/1998.

AWEPAA. *General Peace Agreement of Mozambique.* Amsterdam: African-European Institute, 1992.

Batchelor, P. *Disarmament, Small Arms, and Internal Conflict: The Case of Southern Africa.* Cape Town: Center for Conflict Resolution, 1995.

Binagi, Lloyd. *The Genesis of the Modern Sudan : An Interpretative Study of the Rise of Afro-Arab Hegemony in the Nile Valley A.D. 1260–1826.* Temple University, Ph.D. Dissertation, 1981.

Boutros-Ghali, Boutros. *An Agenda for Peace: Preventive Diplomacy, Peacemaking and Peace-keeping.* New York: United Nations, 1992.

Brenes, Arnoldo, ed. *The Leadership Challenges of Demilitarization in Africa: Conference Report.* San José: Arias Foundation, 1999.

Charter of the Organization of African Unity. Adopted at Addis Ababa, Ethiopia, on May 25, 1963.

Damrosch, Lori Fisler, ed. *Enforcing Restraint: Collective Intervention in Internal Conflicts.* New York: Council on Foreign Relations, 1993.

Deng, Francis M. *War of Visions: Conflict of Identities in the Sudan.* Washington, DC: Brookings Institution, 1995.

Deng, Francis M., and William I. Zartman, eds. *Conflict Resolution in Africa.* Washington, DC: Brookings Institution, 1991.

Foray, C. P. "The Road to the One Party State: The Sierra Leone Experience." Africanus Horton Memorial Lecture, November 9th, 1998. Center of African Studies, University of Birmingham.

Gersony, Robert. *The Gersony Report: Summary of Mozambican Refugee Accounts of Principally Conflict-Related Experience in Mozambique.* Washington, DC: US Department of State, 1988.

———. *Why Somalis Flee: Synthesis of the Accounts of Conflict Experience in Northern Somalia by Somalia Refugees, Displaced Persons, and Others.* Washington, DC: Bureau of Displaced Persons, U.S. Department of State, 1989.

———. *The Agony of Northern Uganda: Results of a Field-Based Assessment of the Civil Conflicts in Northern Uganda.* Kampala: USAID, 1997.

Government of Nigeria. *The March to Democracy, 30th Anniversary.* Lagos, Nigeria: Federal Ministry of Information, 1990.

Government of Sudan. Report of the Commission Enquiry. *Southern Sudan Disturbances, August 1955.* Sudan: McCorquedale, 1956.

Gowon, Yakubu (General). "Broadcast to the Nation, Cotober 1, 1970." In *Stability and Progress: The Challenge of the Second Decade of Nigeria's Independence.* Jos: Benue-Plateau State Government, n.d.

Hall, Margaret. *The Mozambican National Resistance Movement and the Reestablishment of Peace in Mozambique.* Paper presented at the Centre for African Studies, School of Oriental and African Studies, London, 1991.

Hare, Paul. *Angola's Last Best Chance for Peace: An Insider's Account of the Peace Process.* Washington, DC: United States Institute of Peace, 1998.

Harris, Peter, and Ben Reilly, eds. *Democracy and Deep-Rooted Conflict: Options for Negotiators.* International Institute for Democracy and Electoral Assistance Handbook Series. Stockholm: International Institute for Democracy and Electoral Assistance (IDEA), 1998.

Hume, Cameron. *Ending Mozambique's War: The Role of Mediation and Good Offices.* Washington, DC: United States Institute of Peace, 1994.

Hutchful, Eboe, and Abdoulaye Bathily, eds. *The Military and Militarism in Africa.* Dakar: CODESRIA, 1998.

Jaster, R. S. *South Africa and Its Neighbours: the Dynamics of Regional Conflict.* IISS, Adelphi Papers no. 209, 1986.

Jentleson, Bruce W. *Preventive Diplomacy in the Post–Cold War World: Opportunities Missed, Opportunities Seized, and Lessons to be Learned.* Washington, DC: Carnegie Commission for Preventing Deadly Conflict, 1996.

Karefa-Smart, J. *UNPP Statement.* May 7, 1999.

Lewis I. M. *A Modern History of Somalia.* Washington, DC: GPO for Foreign Area Studies, American University, 1982.

Lund, Michael. *Preventive Diplomacy.* Washington, DC: United States Institute of Peace, 1994.

Lyons, Terrence, and Ahmed I. Samatar. *Somalia: State Collapse, Multilateral Intervention and Strategies for Political Reconstruction.* Washington, DC: The Brookings Institution, 1995.

Makinda, Samuel M. *Seeking Peace From Chaos: Humanitarian Intervention in Somalia.* New York: International Peace Academy, 1993.

Malan, Mark, ed. *Resolute Partners: Building Peacekeeping Capacity in Southern Africa.* Institute for Strategic Studies (ISS) Monograph Series, no. 21. Halfway House, South Africa: Institute for Strategic Studies, 1998.

Nelson, Harold D. *Area Handbook for Somalia.* Washington, DC: GPO for Foreign Area Studies, American University, 1982.

Nzongola-Ntalaja, Georges. *Le mouvement démocratique au Zaïre, 1956–1996.* Contemporary World Monographs, Center for Interdisciplinary Research in Sciences and Humanities. Mexico City: National Autonomous University of Mexico, 1997.

Oakley, Robert B., and John L. Hirsch. *Somalia and Operation Restore Hope: Reflections on Peacekeeping and Peacemaking.* Washington, DC: United States Institute of Peace, 1995.

Ottaway, Marina. *Africa's New Leaders: Democracy or State Reconstruction?* Washington, DC: Carnegie Endowment for International Peace, 1999.

Prendergast, John. *The Gun Talks Louder Than the Voice: Somlia's Continuing Cycles of Violence.* Washington, DC: Center of Concern, 1994.

Sahnoun, Mohamed. *Somalia: The Missed Opportunities.* Washington, DC: United States Institute of Peace, 1994.

Selassie, Bereket Habte. *The Constitutional Commission of Eritrea (CCE): Information on Strategy, Plans, and Activities.* Asmara: CCE, 1995.

Shagari, Alhaji Shehu. *Collected Speeches of President Shehu Shagari.* Lagos, Nigeria: State House, 1980.

Sisk, Timothy D. *Power Sharing and International Mediation in Ethnic Conflicts.* Washington, DC: United States Institute of Peace, 1996.

Smith, Chris, and Alex Vines. *Light Weapons Proliferation in Southern Africa.* London: Brassey's for the Center for Defense Studies, University of London, 1997.

Smock, David, ed. *Making War and Waging Peace: Foreign Intervention in Africa.* Washington, DC: United States Institute of Peace, 1993.

Smock, David R., and Chester A. Crocker, eds. *African Conflict Resolution: The U.S. Role in Peace-keeping.* Washington, DC: United States Institute of Peace, 1995.

Synge, Richard. *Mozambique: UN Peacekeeping in Action, 1992-1994.* Washington, DC: United States Institute of Peace, 1997.

Tejan-Kabbah, A. "Letter to SLPP Members: The Role of Government in a Democratic Sierra Leone." August 31, 1998.

United National Peoples Party (UNPP). "Comments on the Presidential Run-Off Elections." Freetown, March 15, 1996.

United Nations. *The United Nations and Mozambique: 1992–1995.* New York: The United Nations Department of Public Information, 1995.

———. *The United Nations and Somalia: 1992–1996.* New York: The United Nations Department of Public Information, 1996.

United Nations Commission on Human Rights. *Report on the Question of the Use of Mercenaries as Means of Violating Human Rights and Impeding the Exercise of the Right of Peoples to Self-Determination.* Fifty-Fifth session, 1999. Submitted by Enrique Bernales Ballesteros, Special Rapporteur, pursuant to the Commission Resolution 1998/6, 13 January 1999. E/CN.4/1999/11.

United Nations Department of Peacekeeping Operations. Lessons Learned Unit. *Multidisciplinary Peacekeeping: Lessons from Recent Experience.* New York: United Nations, 1996.

———. Lessons Learned Unit. *Comprehensive Report on Lessons Learned from United Nations Assistance Missions to Civil Wars.* New York: St. Martin's Press, 1997.

United Nations Development Program. *Human Development Report.* Oxford and New York: Oxford University Press, 1994.

United States Department of State. *Country Reports and Human Rights Practices: 1990.* February 1991.

United States General Accounting Office. *Somalia: Observations Regarding the Northern Conflict and Resulting Condition.* Washington, DC: U.S. General Accounting Office, 1989.

World Bank. *World Development Report.* Oxford and New York: Oxford University Press, 1997.

———. *The World Bank Group in Africa.* Washington, DC: World Bank, 1998

Zartman, William I. *Elusive Peace: Negotiating an End to Civil War.* Washington, DC: Brookings Institution, 1995.

NEWSPAPERS AND MAGAZINES

Agence France Presse.
Concord Times (Sierra Leone).
Democrat (Sierra Leone).
Facts on File.
Focus on Africa.
Jeune Afrique Economie (Paris).
Le Monde Diplomatique (Paris).
Le Soir.

New Vision (Uganda).
Reuters News Agency.
Standard Times (Sierra Leone).
Tell Magazine (Nigeria).
The Guardian (Nigeria).
The Mail and Guardian.
The Monitor. (Uganda)
The New Yorker.
The New York Times.
The Nigerian Standard.
The Times (London).
The Washington Post.
The Wall Street Journal.
Time Magazine.
West Africa.

WEB SITES AND WEB PAGES

BBC Africa Web Page.
Human Rights Watch Report. *Angola Unravels: The Rise and Fall of the Lusaka Peace Process.*
     http://www.hrw.org/reports/1999/angola
NCN Special Report. *An Interim Report on the Case of Moving Tantalum and Niobium Minerals
     from Congo to Rwanda.* http://www.marekinc.com/NCNSpecialTantalum3.html
United Nations Department of Public Information. *Completed Peacekeeping Operations.*
     http://www.un.org/Depts/DPKO/Missions/onuc.html

Index

About the Contributors

HUSSEIN ADAM is Associate Professor of Political Science at the College of the Holy Cross in Worcester, Massachusetts. He has edited two volumes on Somalia, including *Mending Rips in the Sky: Options for Somali Communities in the 21st Century*. He has also written numerous articles on African and development studies.

YUSUF BANGURA is Project Coordinator at the United Nations Research Institute for Social Development for projects on Public Sector Reform and Crisis States and for Technocratic Policy Making and Democratization. Before joining UNRISD, he was Lecturer in political science at Ahmadu Bello University, Nigeria. He has published widely on the politics of the African crisis, structural adjustment and livelihood strategies, democratization, and ethnic conflicts.

FRANCIS M. DENG is Distinguished Professor of Political Science at the Graduate Center, City University of New York. Formerly he was Senior Fellow of the Foreign Policy Studies Program at the Brookings Institution. He has been a guest scholar at the Woodrow Wilson International Center for Scholars, a Rockefeller Brothers Fund Distinguished Fellow, and a Jennings Randolph Fellow of the United States Institute of Peace. He has authored or edited over a dozen books in the fields of law, anthropology, history, politics, and folklore. His more recent publications include *African Reckoning: A Quest for Good Governance* (with Terrence Lyons), *War of Visions: Conflicting Identities in the Sudan,* and *Conflict Resolution in Africa* (with I. William Zartman).

HABU S. GALADIMA is a Lecturer at the University of Jos, Nigeria, and a research consultant to the Institute of Governance and Social Research at Jos. He has published widely on militarism, federalism, communal conflicts, and foreign policy.

JOÃO HONWANA is the Chief, Conventional Arms Branch, United Nations Department for Disarmament Affairs. A retired colonel, he was the commander of the Mozambican Air Force and Air Defense from 1987 to 1993. Before joining the United Nations, he was a senior researcher on defense and security issues at the Centre for Conflict Resolution, University of Cape Town, South Africa.

JULIUS O. IHONVBERE is Program Officer for Governance and Civil Society at the Ford Foundation. He is also a Professor of Government at the University of Texas at Austin. Professor Ihonvbere has written extensively on democratic transitions, political economy, and civil-military relations in Africa. His more recent publications include *Labor, State, and Capital in Nigeria's Oil Industry, Illusions of Power: Nigeria in Transition* (with Timothy Shaw); *Economic Crisis, Civil Society, and Democratization: The Case of Zambia;* and *Nigeria: The Politics of Adjustment and Democracy.* He is also the first winner of the Mario Zamora Award of the Association of Third World Studies.

RICARDO RENÉ LAREMONT's recent work focuses on the comparative politics of Africa, Latin America, and Europe. His publications include *Islam and the Politics of Resistance in Algeria, 1783–1992* and a forthcoming book, *Borders, Battles, and Blood: Colonial Boundaries, Warfare, and the New Nationalisms in Africa* (with William G. Martin). He is the Associate Director of the Institute of Global Cultural Studies and has joint faculty appointments in the Sociology, Political Science, and Africana Studies Departments at the State University of New York at Binghamton.

ALI A. MAZRUI is Director of the Institute of Global Cultural Studies and the Albert Schweitzer Professor in the Humanities at SUNY-Binghamton. He is also past president of the African Studies Association. He has authored over twenty books, including *The African Condition, Nationalism and New States in Africa* (with Michael Tidy); and more recently, *The Power of Babel: Language and Governance in the African Experience* (with Alamin M. Mazrui). He is also the creator and author of the critically acclaimed PBS/BBC television series, *The Africans: A Triple Heritage* and its companion book.

GEORGES NZONGOLA-NTALAJA is Professor Emeritus of African Studies at Howard University in Washington, DC. He served as president of the Sub-Commission on Political Files at the Congo's Sovereign National Conference in 1992 and as the deputy president of the National Electoral Commission in 1996.

W. OFUATEY-KODJOE is Professor of Political Science at both Queens College and the Graduate Center of the City University of New York. He also serves as director of the fellowship program at the Ralph Bunche Institute of the United Nations. A visiting professor at the University of Lagos, Dr. Ofuatey-Kodjoe's recent publications include "The United Nations and the Protection of Individual and Group Rights," *International Social Science Journal,* and "Regional Organizations and the Resolution of International Conflict: The ECOWAS Intervention in Liberia," in *International Peacekeeping.*

ROBERT L. OSTERGARD, JR., is Research Fellow at the Institute of Global Cultural Studies and the Center on Democratic Performance, and Visiting Assistant Professor in the Department of Political Science at Binghamton University, State University of New York. He has conducted research on international and African political economy, focusing on intellectual property rights and their impact on developing countries. His current research is on the impact of intellectual property rights protection in Africa's AIDS pandemic.

J. MICHAEL TURNER is Associate Professor of African History and Latin American History at Hunter College–City University of New York and Director of the College's Latin American and Caribbean Studies Program. A specialist in African–Latin American relations, he has worked in economic and social development, and managed programs in democratization and governance for the Ford Foundation, the United States Agency for International Development, and the World Bank. He has consulted for the United Nations, the Secretariat for Women and Children of the Global Board of the Methodist Church, and United Support of Artists for Africa.

CRAWFORD YOUNG is Professor Emeritus of Political Science at the University of Wisconsin, Madison. He has written extensively on African politics, cultural pluralism, comparative politics, and the state. He has many publications, including The *African Colonial State in Comparative Perspective, The Rise and Decline of the Zairian State, Ideology and Development in Africa,* and *The Politics of Cultural Pluralism.*